AMERICAN
LEARNED
SOCIETIES

American
Learned
Societies

By JOSEPH C. KIGER

Public Affairs Press, Washington, D. C.

061.3
K55a
72759
January, 1971

FOREWORD

As national director of the Historical Records Survey, as executive officer of the Library of Congress, as Director General of UNESCO, and to some extent in other activities, it has been my good fortune to cooperate with many of the organizations referred to in this important book.

I think few of us realize how much our lives are controlled by the work of men of the intellect, both in their individual and in their group activities. Certainly, as Professor Kiger's book makes clear, there has not been an adequate recognition of this influence by the public in general. That progress is being made to achieve this recognition is to be welcomed.

I commend *American Learned Societies* as a serious, outstanding and exciting contribution to the all-too-meager literature on a subject which is critical to the advance of mankind's capacity to live in the complex world of today.

LUTHER H. EVANS

CONTENTS

Introduction   1

Acknowledgements   5

I
Early Learned Societies   6

II
Modern Learned Societies   14

III
Councils and Societal Institutes   120

IV
Relationship to Philanthropic Foundations   147

V
Relationship to Government, Industry and Universities   169

VI
International Relations   190

VII
Retrospect and Prospect   207

References   218

Bibliography   246

Appendices   262

Index   268

INTRODUCTION

Although two American learned societies, the American Philosophical Society and the American Academy of Arts and Sciences, were created in the eighteenth century, our national learned societies, and the councils and institutes connected with them, remain phenomena of the intellectual history of the nineteenth and early twentieth century America when the remainder of them were founded. This study of these organizations was written to provide scholars and the public with a conspectual history of each one of them together with a description of their relationships to each other and to other segments of our society, *viz.* philanthropic foundations, government, industry, and colleges and universities. Finally, the role of these organizations on the international scene is chronicled, and an attempt is made to assay future trends among them.

That such a study is needed has been remarked by a number of historians and political scientists. In 1932 the then Secretary of the American Historical Association, Dr. J. Franklin Jameson, wrote that prior to 1884 most American historians and academicians in general did not know one another and that their horizons were thereby limited. "Now," he concluded, "nearly all professors have a two fold loyalty, to the college in which they teach and to the profession to which they consciously belong. It is, of course, not in history alone that this beneficent expansion of mind has taken place. The organization of the American Historical Association in 1884 was but one of a dozen or more instances in which, between 1869 and 1894, the votaries of this or that academic subject, scientific or humanistic, drew together by the formation of national societies. It was an important general movement, the value of which to the intellectual life of America has perhaps not yet been duly estimated."[1]

The late distinguished intellectual historian, Dr. Robert C. Binkley, in commenting upon organizations devoted to learning at the international level, said:

"The world of power—the political world—has been studied as a whole. Its processes have been examined; its history and its physiology are analyzed in whole libraries of books, descriptive and analytical. The same can be said of the economic world. However, most of our descriptive and analytical study of the intellectual world has been devoted to the product rather than the process. Our scholarly literature, critical and historical, is in the main a travel literature . . .

"We have at hand the cumulated results of the thinking of many generations in analyzing the economic and political worlds. We know something of the quantities that are involved; we can estimate resources and arma-

1

ments; we have statistics on credits and business activity. We do not all agree in the analysis of the dynamics of these worlds, but at least we are accustomed to looking at them as wholes. But we have no corresponding vision of the world of intellectual cooperation.

"Yet intellectual cooperation is the house in which we live. We have lived in it so long that we think we can take it for granted. We have looked from its windows and described the other houses; we know that some alterations have recently been made. But we lack even a floor plan of the building as a whole."[2]

In a more recent (1951) publication, Lyman C. White states: "Perhaps no aspect of international relations has received less attention, even from students of international organization itself, than the part which non-governmental organizations have played in world affairs." He observes that these organizations were very influential and would probably become more so but for the fact that "the study of their function has been almost completely ignored in textbooks, in university courses, and in the training of those who represent governments in international negotiations."

White attributes this situation to the preoccupation of historians and political scientists with the rivalry between states and illustrates it by the political scientists' almost exclusive concern, several decades ago, with the formal organs of government to the exclusion of the role played by trade unions, churches, etc.[3]

Definition of what constitutes a learned society varies historically and is subject to exception. The same is, of course, true in defining similar organizations, councils, institutes, universities, philanthropic foundations, etc. In twentieth century United States, a learned society may be generally defined as an organization composed of individuals devoted to a particular learned discipline or branch or group of disciplines in the humanities, social sciences, or natural sciences and primarily committed to the study and acquisition of knowledge in such discipline. Such a definition excludes professional societies in medicine, law, engineering, etc., where the *raison d'etre* and primary emphasis is upon the application of knowledge for professional and/or pecuniary purposes,[4] and societies whose primary purpose has been the giving of recognition to individuals for achievements in the sciences or humanities.[5]

Several other characteristics of an American learned society can be noted. It usually carries on no teaching function, except incidentally through studies, publications, etc. Its membership may be open or closed but, normally, would include a significant portion of the outstanding persons engaged or interested in the particular discipline or disciplines. Its main source of revenue is usually from membership fees rather than from endowments, bequests, or grants. Finally, although they perform other functions, the learned societies' foremost ones are the holding of periodic meetings wherein papers are presented and where members become personally acquainted and mutually stimulated in their scholarly endeavors, and the provision of a medium or mediums for publications, usually described as learned journals.

Such societies may be national, regional, or local in scope. The category into which they fall turns on several factors: the stated purpose of the society, the size and composition of its membership, and its activities. In this last connection, national learned societies are usually co-members with other societies in groupings called councils or institutes and their major activities, in addition to those enumerated above, are with these groupings and the philanthropic foundations and the universities. In the last few decades a considerable number of the societies, and most of the councils and institutes, have had relations with the federal government and industrial concerns.

Although many regional and local learned societies have performed and are performing a valuable service to the nation, only the 60 foremost learned societies which are national in scope and which clearly meet the other requirements outlined above are included in this study. Their number includes 30 societies which are members of the American Council of Learned Societies, 7 associated members of the Social Science Research Council, 32 cooperating member societies of the National Academy of Sciences-National Research Council, and 5 societies which are associate members of the American Council on Education. The total number of societies studied, 60, is different from the total provided in the figures above because several societies are members of two or more councils.

These 60 learned societies fall into three broad categories: 29 humanistic-social science societies, 29 natural science societies, and two societies which span all three areas of knowledge. The study which follows is based on these three divisions.[6]

Also included in the study are the four councils mentioned above and five institutes. The councils are the four national associations of organizations concerned respectively with the humanities, social sciences, natural sciences, and education. There is, of course, some degree of overlapping in their respective areas of interest.

The five institutes—the American Association for the Advancement of Science, the Federation of American Societies for Experimental Biology, the American Institute of Physics, the American Institute of Biological Sciences, and the American Geological Institute—are the national associations of organizations, some also including individuals as members, concerned with particular disciplines within the natural sciences. The American Association for the Advancement of Science is a variant in this group in that its interests take in all of the natural sciences as well as the social sciences and education.

Each of these councils and institutes include at least several of the learned societies in their membership and have had continuous relationships with them. In some cases various learned societies or officials of societies created a council or institute, and in others a council or institute was responsible for the creation of a learned society.[7]

This study, in essence, is an attempt to set forth and interpret the historical development of these organizations,[8] provide a compendium on them, and to shed light on their operations and relationships to each other and to other domestic and international organizations concerned with scientific and cultural advancement.[9]

JOSEPH C. KIGER

ACKNOWLEDGMENTS

Although their number prohibits naming them, the writer is indebted to the officers and staff personnel of the 60 societies, four councils, and five institutes under study. Without their cooperation this work would not have been possible. Prior to publication, officers of each of these organizations were provided with a copy of those sections of the history which dealt with their organization and many provided helpful information and suggestions.

Various foundation, government, educational, and industrial officials have been most helpful in reviewing pertinent portions of the study and providing access to vital source material.

Portions of the study were read by F. Emerson Andrews, Wallace W. Atwood Jr., Raymond F. Howes, Milton O. Lee, Henry A. Barton, Robert C. Stephenson, James C. Charlesworth, Vernon C. Porter, Pendleton Herring, Frederick Burkhardt, Dael Wolfle, and Hiden T. Cox.

Special mention must be made of Dean Emeritus A. B. Moore of the University of Alabama, Dean Don K. Price of the Graduate School of Public Administration of Harvard University, Dr. M. H. Trytten, Director, Office of Scientific Personnel, National Academy of Sciences—National Research Council, Mrs. Harriet C. Owsley, Senior Archivist, Tennessee State Department of Archives and History, and Mr. Harold M. Keele, Attorney, Chicago, Illinois. The writer wishes to thank each of them for their critical review of all portions of the study.

The writer is particularly indebted to his wife, Jean M. Kiger, who has rendered aid in all phases of the work from its inception.

The writer is grateful to officials of the University of Alabama for approving a request for a leave of absence in 1960 from that institution. He is grateful to fellow staff members and colleagues at the University of Mississippi for their cooperation while this study was being completed.

Several libraries, including the Library of Congress, the New York Public Library, the National Academy of Sciences—National Research Council Library, the Foundation Library Center, and the United Nations Library, were most helpful in the course of this study. The libraries of the University of Alabama and the University of Mississippi were unstinting in their efforts to procure material and to render other aid.

Finally, a fellowship from the John Simon Guggenheim Memorial Foundation for 1960-61, a Rockefeller Foundation grant, and several grants from the Research Committee of the University of Alabama provided the financial means for travel and research which brought this history to completion.

JOSEPH C. KIGER

5

CHAPTER I

EARLY LEARNED SOCIETIES

We of the Western World and the present are prone to think of our colleges and universities as pioneering organizations composed of leaders working on the frontiers of knowledge. While, idealistically, this is true today, in the past it has not always been so.

The world of today is as it is, to a preeminent degree, because of the changes which took place in the sixteenth and seventeenth centuries in the way Western European man looked at himself, at his neighbor and, particularly, at this material universe. The universities of that place and period were not in the forefront in advancing this changed way of thought but, on the contrary, they actively opposed it. All organized centers of learning in the Western World, from the fifth to the sixteenth century A. D.— roughly that period in history known as the medieval—were controlled by the Church. The universities which arose during this period, were no exception to this rule. The Church was committed to Scholasticism, a form of learning which was confined to studying what previous learned men, particularly Aristotle and the Church fathers, had said. In order to study the works of these ancients a knowledge of Greek and Latin was an absolute necessity. Acquisition and mastery of such knowledge required years of study and, once this tool was acquired, learning consisted in comparing and harmonizing the viewpoints of the ancients. Everything else, if not deemed outright heresy thus subjecting the dissenter to various moral and physical reprisals, at the very least was dubbed questionable and of no value. The classic example of this viewpoint was, of course, the persecution by the church and university officials of Galileo for his contra-Aristotelian views that the sun rather than the earth was the center of the universe. Indeed, until the nineteenth century universities in the United States and abroad taught the heliocentric and terrocentric theories side by side, or that the heliocentric concept of our universe was but one theory among other theories about it. It was not until 1822 that the Roman Catholic Church's College of Cardinals declared that it was permissible to teach the heliocentric theory in Catholic countries as anything more than a mathematical device.[1]

This situation made for what amounted to a learned oligarchy which was closed to those not capable or willing to assume the mental blinders for which it called. Thus, the intellectual system was primarily a non-innovative and non-productive one which did not advance but merely transmitted learning from one generation to the next, and is the primary explanation for the static life and culture which prevailed in Western Europe from the fifth to the sixteenth century. This is not to say that the period *en toto* can be characterized as the "Dark Ages." Many a modern man yearns for the attitude toward the cosmos described by Henry Adams in *Mont St. Michel and Chartres*. Significantly, this work, which Adams was reluctant to publish for an unsympathetic nineteenth century and which he had privately printed for limited distribution, is now being sold in paper back edition at drug stores and lunch counters.[2] Yet, the Church and its hand-maiden the university were opposed to a form of learning which we have come to call the experimental; and it is this experimental form of learning which is the basis of modern science which, in turn, has shaped our modern world.

The experimental method is the intellectual process by which man observes and experiments with his own brain and hand the physical world of which he is a part, and draws conclusions therefrom. This is in direct contrast to the scholastic process. This experimental method required no long period of tutelage; anyone with a keen and inquiring mind could engage in it. It was not restrictive and all those accepting it could under-stand or at least share in its method. Why did it develop in the sixteenth and seventeenth centuries? It is impossible to answer this question com-pletely because the development is part of a complex of other changes which transformed western Europe. It can be stated, however, that the develop-ment was spurred by and resulted in large part from the emergence of societies in the sixteenth and seventeenth and early eighteenth centuries whose members adopted and practiced a different outlook from the prevailing *genre* of the Church and the universities.[3]

Although learned societies and academies devoted to the advancement of learning and science extend far back into history, witness Plato's Academy and the Alexandrine Museum, the learned academies and societies of the modern world originated in Italy in the late sixteenth and early seventeenth centuries and thence spread throughout Europe. The Academia Secretorum Naturae was established in Naples in 1560; the Academia dei Lincei at Rome in 1603; the Academia Naturae Curiosum at Leipzig in 1651; the Royal Society of London in 1660; and the Academie des Sciences at Paris in 1666. In the course of the seventeenth and on into the eighteenth centuries, similar academies and societies were founded at Florence, Berlin, Edinburgh, Dublin, Brussels, Lisbon, Prague, Danzig, St. Petersburg and in a great many other European cities.

Although not the first to be established, the Royal Society is the oldest learned society which has enjoyed a continuous existence and it is probably the best known and most influential of the group because of its connection with such great figures of seventeenth and eighteenth century science as Newton, Hooke, Wren, and Boyle. The reason and method of its origin are similar in many ways to those of the other seventeenth and eighteenth century societies. The Royal Society originated as the result of the intermittent meetings of a dozen or so men connected with Oxford University and an institution, established in London in 1589 by a bequest of Sir Thomas Gresham, known as Gresham's College. The members of this group, particularly those at Gresham's College, were as a body pragmatic men more interested in practical problems than theological or philosophical discussion, and it was at a November 28, 1660 meeting in a room at Gresham's College that the previous intermittent meetings of this group were regularized in the form of weekly discussions. In 1661 a petition to Charles II, newly restored to the throne, for the incorporation of a Royal Society was submitted. A charter was granted on the fifteenth of July, 1662 and, in a subsequent one of 1663, Charles declared himself founder and patron of the Society. The Royal Society went into a temporary eclipse in the nineteenth century because it had been gradually changed into a gentlemen's social club. In the seventeenth and eighteenth centuries, and now again in the twentieth century it has become the home of the leading British scientists and has been a tremendous influence in the advancement of scientific knowledge.[4]

The complete story of the widespread importance of the Society is outside the purview of this volume. Its influence, however, in the English colonies of North America, where distinguished men from various sections were elected to membership, is noteworthy. Governor John Winthrop of Connecticut, for instance, was elected a Fellow of the Society in 1663. He was named its representative in the Western World and corresponded with the Society on scientific matters throughout the remainder of his life. Benjamin Franklin, who was elected to Fellowship in 1756, had in the meantime taken the lead in establishing at Philadelphia the American Philosophical Society, and it is certain that the American society was to a large degree inspired by and patterned after the Royal Society.

AMERICAN PHILOSOPHICAL SOCIETY

The American Philosophical Society is the oldest existing learned society in the United States. Although its founding date is debatable,[5] its beginnings actually go back to 1727, when Benjamin Franklin organized a club in Philadelphia whose members read essays and discussed scientific questions of mutual interest. Of this group, called the Junto, little is known. In 1758 another group, either an outgrowth of the original Junto or separately organized but similar to it, was formed and in 1766 took the name of the American Society for Promoting and Propagating Useful Knowledge. In the meantime, in 1743, Franklin, seeing the need for a society of wider scope, had proposed and carried out the creation of a national society entitled the American Philosophical Society. Rivalry in activity and membership eventually led, in 1769, to a union of the two groups under the title, "The American Philosophical Society held at Philadelphia for Promoting Useful Knowledge," usually shortened to the American Philosophical Society. Benjamin Franklin became the first President of the Society and was annually re-elected to that office until his death in 1790.

An initial scientific research project conducted under the auspices of the Society was the observation of a transit of Venus in 1769. Acclaimed internationally, this enterprise also marked, in the British Colonies in America, the first scientific effort conducted on something more than a local basis.

Thomas Jefferson during the period that he was President of the United States (1801-1809) was also President of the American Philosophical Society (1797-1814). Following an earlier attempt by Jefferson to have the region west of the Mississippi explored under the auspices of the Society, he arranged to have the manuscript records of the government sponsored Lewis and Clark expedition deposited with the Society. The records of several other Western exploratory groups and a great deal of the Indian language material, which forms the basis for the Society's present day program in Indian ethnohistory and linguistics, were also collected during Jefferson's Presidency. In 1840 members of the Fox family presented the Society with much of the papers and correspondence of Benjamin Franklin. Since these original ventures, the Society has continued to add to its literary holdings, concentrating on the early history of science and learning in America. To house its collection, in excess of 112,000 books and 45,000 pamphlets and 500,000 manuscripts, the Society in 1959 erected a new library opposite its headquarters in historic Philosophical Hall.

From 1769 until 1911 the Society held fortnightly meetings, except for a three year period during the American Revolution. After the latter date, monthly meetings were instituted. Previously, in 1902, an annual general meeting in the spring was inaugurated and in 1936 an autumn meeting was begun. Subsequent to the latter date, the monthly meetings were discontinued and only the annual meetings and special, called ones have been convened. These meetings are characterized by the presentation of scholarly papers and symposia spanning all areas of knowledge.

The Society began publishing at the time of its first meetings. The first volume of the *Transactions* was completed in 1771 and was followed by others in 1786, 1793, 1799, 1802 and 1809. The year 1818 saw the beginning of the New Series of the *Transactions* and 50 volumes have been published since that date. The *Transactions,* which originally contained works of a varied nature, is now primarily employed for the printing of monographs, particularly those of a specialized nature. The *Proceedings* was established in 1838. This journal is now issued bimonthly and contains many of the papers read before the meetings. Prior to the establishment of the *Year Book* in 1937, the *Proceedings* also contained the minutes of the meetings, lists of members, and other news of the Society which now appears in the former volume. The *Memoirs,* inaugurated in 1935, rounds out the publication media of the Society, and includes scholarly books in all disciplines.

An important activity of the Society, since its receipt of various bequests in the past three decades, has been a program of grants-in-aid for research in a variety of areas. The more important of these bequests are: the Penrose Research Fund, the Johnson Research Fund, and the Doland Fund. The income from such funds provides the Society with approximately $275,000 annually for grants-in-aid. In addition, the Society awards prizes, such as the Henry M. Phillips Prize and the John M. Lewis Prize for outstanding essays and papers on various subjects.

Membership in the American Philosophical Society has always been an honorary distinction and election thereto has been restricted. Prior to 1902, by common agreement the number of domestic and foreign persons annually elected to membership was small, averaging about 20 new members per year. Since that time progressive restrictions have been placed on membership and it is now limited to 500 residents of the United States and 75 foreigners. Since these limits were reached in the late 1940's, persons are now elected to membership only to fill vacancies caused by death. Women have on rare occasions been elected to membership in the Society, but through the years it has been almost wholly male. Initially the members of the Society were drawn preponderantly from the Philadelphia area. Today the geographical distribution of members is much more widespread with only about ten percent residing in this area.[7] The offices of the Society are located at 105 South Fifth Street, Philadelphia, Pennsylvania.

AMERICAN ACADEMY OF ARTS AND SCIENCES

The moving spirit behind the creation of the second learned society in the United States, the American Academy of Arts and Sciences, was another American statesman, John Adams of Massachusetts. Conversations with academicians in France and concern for Boston's reputation for learning in the light of Philadelphia's American Philosophical Society led to the incorporation of the Academy in 1780. Governor James Bowdoin of Massachusetts was its first president. He was succeeded in 1791 by John Adams. In the 1820's John Quincy Adams was simultaneously president of the United States and the American Academy, and members of the Adams family have continued since to be intimately connected with the Academy. Other early members included such notables as George Washington, Benjamin Franklin, Thomas Jefferson, Alexander Hamilton, and James Madison. One of the first research activities of the Academy, undertaken in conjunction with Harvard College, was to dispatch a committee to Maine to observe the solar eclipse of October 27, 1780. Undertaken with special permission from blockading British naval forces, the expedition was hampered by bad weather and ultimately missed observing the total eclipse because of miscalculations in latitude. The mistake did result, however, in the discovery of the solar astronomical phenomenon now known as "Bailey's Beads."

Originally members of the Academy met quadri-annually in October, January, March and May. Beginning in 1846, monthly meetings have been held during the period October through May. Of these, the meeting in May is an "annual" meeting devoted to the transaction of much of the business of the Academy and attracting the largest attendance. In the early days meetings were apparently convened at the residences of members, Harvard College or other public buildings. Sentiment for a permanent meeting building of its own was often expressed by members, but it was not until 1904 that a building was purchased at No. 28 Newbury Street, Boston. In 1911 additional space, No. 26 Newbury Street, was provided by the generosity of Alexander Agassiz, President of the Academy from 1894 to 1903, and in addition to providing administrative and meeting rooms, was used to house the library of the Academy which included a special collection of the serial records of other learned societies.[8] Finally, in 1957, the Academy moved to its present House at Faulkner Farm in Brookline, Massachusetts.

Beginning with the establishment in 1796 of the Rumford Fund by Benjamin Thompson, Count Rumford, the income from a number of such bequests, including the Cyrus M. Warren Fund, the Francis Amory Fund, and a Permanent Science Fund and Publication Fund, have made it possible for the Academy to support research and publication in a number of scientific and cultural fields. Such funds presently total about $600,000.

Prior to the middle of the nineteenth century there were no regular publications of the Academy, except intermittent *Memoirs* and pamphlets. Between 1846 and 1873 eight volumes of *Proceedings* appeared, containing condensed accounts of the meetings during that period. Beginning in 1873, records of meetings, reports of officers, biographical notices of deceased members, and research works have been published annually. In addition to the *Proceedings,* intermittent sets of *Memoirs* have been published. During the early years the *Memoirs* usually contained short communications to the secretary describing the results of scientific experiments. Since

1833 the communications have taken monographic form and usually treat some limited phase of scientific activity.

In 1955 the Academy superseded Volume 86 of the *Proceedings* with a new publication called *Daedalus*. The reason for this change was that the Academy "recognized that the professional specialized journals are now the preferred publishing outlets for articles of the kind formerly published in the *Proceedings* when that journal was one of the few such in existence in America. On the other hand, a new need, a new challenge, exists precisely because of the fragmentation and specialization of modern knowledge."[9]

The original act of incorporation designated 62 residents of Boston as Fellows and charter members of the Academy. Early limitations on membership in terms of number and residence were gradually changed so as to make it a national organization. By 1911 the limitation on resident members, those within a 50 mile radius of Boston, had been raised to 400 and that on non-resident members to 200. Since that time membership regulations have been amended so that today there is no limitation and the Academy has a membership of about 1500 Fellows, less than half of whom are residents of the Boston area.

Maria Mitchell, the astronomer, who was elected a Fellow in 1848, was the first woman member. By 1960 a total of 39 women had been elected to membership.

Election to membership in the Academy, as in the American Philosophical Society, has always remained honorific with a rigorous nominating and electing procedure.[10] The address of the Academy is 280 Newton Street, Brookline, Massachusetts.

These two societies, the American Philosophical Society and the American Academy of Arts and Sciences, were the only permanent national learned societies created during the eighteenth century in what was to become the United States of America.[11] They were and are very similar to European societies established in the seventeenth and eighteenth centuries, particularly the Royal Society and the French Academy. A desire to have American counterparts of these European societies provided a major impetus for their organization and, as was the case with the European societies, the Americans who were the prime movers in their organization were pre-eminently non-academicians, men of affairs.

Originally the members of the two societies were almost wholly elected from and concerned with what we term today the natural sciences. In the nineteenth century, however, both organizations broadened their basis of membership to include all segments or divisions of knowledge. Today, both are divided into four analogous divisions. The Society includes: I Mathematical and Physical Sciences, II Geological and Biological Sciences, III Social Sciences, and IV Humanities; while the Academy lists the following divisions: I The Mathematical and Physical Sciences, II The Biological Sciences, III The Social Arts and Sciences, IV The Humanities. In the case of each the number of members in any one division may not exceed a certain proportional number and the same restriction is applied to elected foreign members. This proportional sectioning was opposed in the past by some members because, it was maintained, it would have a tendency to fragmentize the societies and science in general. There appears today, however, to be a conviction of the need for such a device so that the societies may include leaders in all intellectual fields.

The history of the Royal Society has been quite different. Because of the "palace revolt" of a group of British scientists about 1847 which gradually ended the naming of the well-to-do and socially prominent to fellowship, the practice of electing, with a very few exceptions, only distinguished natural scientists followed and has been continued to the present day. In 1901, the creation of the British Academy, restricted to those distinguished in the humanities and social sciences, served to buttress this practice of the Royal Society. A somewhat similar development can be noted in France, Germany and other European countries with the creation of various other academies in addition to those devoted to the natural sciences.

In conclusion, several similarities of the first two American societies with the older European societies may be noted. Membership has always been by invitation and, in practice, is limited to the men of eminence in the sciences and arts or who are distinguished in some other capacities. Still another similarity is that these two American societies, although the overwhelming majority of their members have close ties with or are actually faculty members of academic institutions, are not officially connected with any college or university. They are not financially or otherwise dependent upon such institutions for support; they occupy and have headquarters in buildings of their own; possess an independent fulltime staff; and maintain their own libraries and publications.

CHAPTER II

MODERN LEARNED SOCIETIES

Of the 58 national learned societies founded in the nineteenth and twentieth centuries, 29 may be placed in the humanistic-social science, and 29 in the natural science category. In terms of the time, place, and purpose for which they were organized, the humanistic-social science ones fall into three general groups.

The first group contains the following seven societies: the American Antiquarian Society (founded in 1812), the American Statistical Association (1839), the American Oriental Society (1842), the American Numismatic Society (1858), the American Philological Association (1869), the Archaeological Institute of America (1879), and the Society of Biblical Literature and Exegesis (1880). Four of them were founded in or near Boston and the remaining three in or near New York City at intervals of from one to 27 years. With the exception of the American Statistical Association, all are associated or concerned with the humanities. They are all different from the two older American societies because their founding purpose and continuing interest has been with one particular aspect of the humanities or the social sciences.

Two members of this group—the American Antiquarian Society and the American Numismatic Society—have several points of similarity, however, to the two ancients of the breed. They were founded independently of a college or university and are located in buildings of their own with magnificent collections of objects and literature in their particular fields of interest. Their members, designated Fellows, are elected and such membership is honorific and restricted. The five remaining societies are quite similar to those that followed in the late nineteenth and early twentieth centuries, with membership in one form or another being open to all interested persons. The membership of the five, however, does not begin to compare with the numbers enrolled in the later societies. The societies in this first group can be considered, therefore, as transitional between the two older societies and the second group. The latter emerged within a twenty year period at the close of the nineteenth and opening of the twentieth century.

The 11 societies comprising the second group are undoubtedly among the best known to the average American . They are: the Modern Language Association of America (founded in 1883), the American Historical Association (1884), the American Economic Association (1885), the American Folklore Society (1888), the American Psychological Association (1892), the American Philosophical Association (1901), the American Anthropological Association (1902), the American Political Science Association (1903), the Bibliographical Society of America (1904), the Association of American Geographers (1904), the American Sociological Society (1905).

With the exception of the American Folklore Society and the Bibliographical Society of America, each represents a particular discipline in the humanities or social sciences. Four were founded in New York, two each in Massachusetts, two in Philadelphia, and one each in New Orleans, St. Louis, and Baltimore. They all reflect the burgeoning academic interest in the formation of learned societies since the vast majority of the founding fathers of all of them were instructors in American colleges and universities who felt the need of a professional organization to help them in their academic work. A characteristic of the group is a chain type reaction, the organization of one society spurring the creation of another. This is particularly noticeable in the case of the American Historical Association. The American Economic Association grew directly out of it, to be followed in turn by the American Political Science Association and the American Sociological Society.

Three divergent types can be noted in the third group of societies, those 11 formed from about the time of World War I down to the present. On the one hand the College Art Association of America (1912) and the American Musicological Society (1934), were organized along the same lines and for the same reasons as those falling in the second group, *viz.* professional need. A second, and by far larger type, however, appears to be the speciality society in a particular subject-matter or region. Interest in a particular period or aspect of history, for instance, has resulted in the creation of the History of Science Society (1924), the Mediaeval Academy of America (1925), the Society of Architectural Historians (1940), and the Renaissance Society of America (1954). Such societies as the Linguistic Society of America (1924) and the Association for Asian Studies (1941) also appear to fall into this category. Recently, a third type has developed, which includes the American Society for Aesthetics (1942), the Metaphysical Society of America (1950), and the American Studies Association (1950). It appears quite certain that all three were organized for the same basic reason, i.e., dissatisfaction with what they maintained was rampant over-specialization resulting in the fragmentation of knowledge thereby rendered virtually unattainable. Consequently, the latter three societies in this third group were organized with the stated purpose of providing a cohesive force in their field of interest.

In the natural sciences, learned societies devoted entirely to specific disciplines were not established until 1876 when the American Chemical

Society was founded. From 1876 to 1931 the Chemical Society and 24 other natural science societies founded during that period fall into two broad, equally divided groupings, the chemical-mathematical-physical grouping and the biological-medical. Other than these groupings, no discernible pattern emerges; now a society in one group was formed, now one in the other. Some opened their membership to all interested persons while others restricted it, those biological societies which were medically oriented tending to be the most restrictive. Turning to founding locations, the first ten societies established were in New York City or in New England; from 1900 on they were founded in all sections of the country.

With the founding of the Econometric Society in 1930, a development occurs which is analogous to that which took place in the humanities and social sciences a decade or two later. This development is an attempt to re-unify scholars in what had become separate disciplines. In other words, with the establishment of the Econometric Society, followed by the establishment in 1935 of the Institute of Mathematical Statistics and the Association for Symbolic Logic, and, in 1955, the Geochemical Society, there appears a movement among scholars in the chemical-mathematical-physical grouping away from the specialization which one observer has described as "now approaching the *reductio ad absurdum.*" Furthermore, the members of these societies have not only been attempting to bridge the gap between the various natural science disciplines, they have also, albeit to a lesser extent, been trying to bridge the veritable chasm between them and the social sciences and humanities. A similar movement did not occur in the biological-medical group. It appears that this lack can be explained by the development of societal institutes such as the Federation of American Societies for Experimental Biology, and the American Institute of Biological Sciences, which were specifically created to bring together the biological-medical societies encompassed in their membership.

Several general and common characteristics in the development of both the humanistic-social science societies and the natural science societies can be noted. First, all of them established prior to the twentieth century were founded in the Middle Atlantic or New England States. Since that time many of them have been founded in other parts of our country. Second, in the last few decades, a number of societies have been established that attempt to develop a union of two or more disciplines in various intellectual areas.

Turning now to the general administration and operation of the learned societies, almost all of them have been incorporated by a state or national charter, in order that they may receive bequests, and for other legal purposs. All have adopted constitutions and by-laws which provide for the election of a governing body, usually called a council, board of trustees or directors, or, in a few cases, an executive committee. Although most of their constitutions provide for the election of a president and a vice president, the chief administrative officer in practically all cases is the secretary or, as he is variously called, the executive officer, executive secretary, or permanent secretary.

The urban to campus location of the administrative offices of the societies is in approximately the same ratio for the humanities-social sciences and the natural sciences, i. e., about two thirds of each group are located on university campuses (three of these being colleges) and the remaining one third were located in city offices. A characteristic of those located on campus is that the administrative officer's principal duties are those of a teacher in his university and his societal duties are of a secondary or peripheral nature; he is almost invariably designated "secretary"; he is elected for a definite period of time, normally one to four years; and he does not usually receive compensation other than expenses and a modest honorarium for his services. Those societies with offices located in the cities usually employ a full-time administrative officer with the title of executive director or executive secretary; his term of office is normally for an indefinite period; and he receives full compensation. Naturally the societies with larger memberships fall into the latter category, those with smaller into the former.

The duties of all of these secretaries are many and varied. They usually arrange for the annual and other meetings; have custody and charge of the records and files of the society; handle its membership rolls and carry on its routine correspondence; many act as treasurer; and about 50 per cent also serve as editor or chairman of a board of editors for their society's publications. This last duty is one of if not the most important in a learned society for, despite the fact that most societies have a committee which usually invites and reviews articles, monographs, book reviews, etc., for publication, the editor naturally exerts a powerful influence on such committees. If he is, in addition, the chief administrative officer of the society it is apparent that he carries considerable weight in deciding what is published. Since the reputation, certainly the national one, of any scholar is considerably enhanced by publication in his appropriate learned journal, the editors of such journals have a tremendous responsibility in selecting papers for publication. Also, the tenor and quality of publications in specific disciplines is often determined in large measure by the erudition and discretion of the editor.

Brief histories of these 58 learned societies follow the tables of statistical information set forth on pages 18-22.

TABLE 1

BASIC INFORMATION REGARDING LEADING HUMANISTIC AND SOCIAL SCIENCE SOCIETIES

Society	Place of Origin[a]	Date of Origin[a]	Principal Office[a]	Number of Members[a]	Total Assets[b]	Total Income[b]	Total Expenditures[b]
American Anthropological Association	Pittsburgh, Pa.	1902	Washington, D. C.	4,200	$ 9,000	$ 109,000	$ 100,000
American Antiquarian Society	Worcester, Mass.	1812	Worcester, Mass.	200	1,663,000	123,000	107,000
American Economic Association	Saratoga, N. Y.	1885	Northwestern University—Evanston, Ill.	14,018	285,000	81,000	55,000
American Folklore Society, Inc.	Cambridge, Mass.	1888	University of Pennsylvania—Philadelphia, Pa.	1,240	4,000	13,000	13,000
American Historical Association	Saratoga, N. Y.	1884	Washington, D. C.	8,400	873,000	198,000	119,000
American Musicological Society	New York, N. Y.	1934	University of Michigan—Ann Arbor, Mich.	1,264	30,000	26,000	27,000
American Numismatic Society	New York, N. Y.	1858	New York, N. Y.	991	177,000	260,000	245,000
American Oriental Society	Boston, Mass.	1842	Yale University—New Haven, Conn.	1,022	160,000	68,000	31,000
American Philological Association	Poughkeepsie, N. Y.	1869	Hunter College—New York, N. Y.	1,400	55,000	18,000	18,000
American Philosophical Association	New York, N. Y.	1901	Washington University—St. Louis, Mo.	1,718	30,000	4,000	4,000
American Political Science Association	New Orleans, La.	1903	Washington, D. C.	7,000	72,000	120,000	105,000
American Psychological Association	Worcester, Mass.	1892	Washington, D. C.	18,215	63,000	904,000	841,000
American Society for Aesthetics	Washington, D. C.	1942	Cleveland, Ohio	685	1,000	13,000	11,000
American Sociological Association	Baltimore, Md.	1905	New York University—New York, N. Y.	6,638	5,000	160,000	155,000
American Statistical Association	Boston, Mass.	1839	Washington, D. C.	7,200	285,000	81,000	55,000
American Studies Association	Washington, D. C.	1950	University of Pennsylvania—Philadelphia, Pa.	1,380	10,000	19,000	15,000

TABLE 1 (CONTINUATION)

BASIC INFORMATION REGARDING LEADING HUMANISTIC AND SOCIAL SCIENCE SOCIETIES

Society	Location	Year	Address	Members			
Archaeological Institute of America	Boston, Mass.	1879	New York University—New York, N. Y.	2,500	350,000	90,000	90,000
Association for Asian Studies, Inc.	New York, N. Y.	1941	University of Michigan—Ann Arbor, Mich.	1,124	70,000	43,000	38,000
Association of American Geographers	Philadelphia, Pa.	1904	Washington, D. C.	1,985	50,000	37,000	28,000
Bibliographical Society of America	St. Louis, Mo.	1904	New York, N. Y.	1,037	322,000	20,000	12,000
College Art Association of America	Cincinnati, Ohio	1902	New York, N. Y.	2,905	53,000	95,000	68,000
History of Science Society	Washington, D. C.	1924	University of California—Los Angeles, Calif.	1,200	1,000	18,000	17,000
Linguistic Society of America	New York, N. Y.	1924	University of Texas—Austin, Texas	2,474	64,000	20,000	20,000
Mediaeval Academy of America	Boston, Mass.	1925	Cambridge, Mass.	1,547	251,000	81,000	75,000
Metaphysical Society of America	New Haven, Conn.	1950	Haverford College—Haverford, Pa.	450	1,000	1,000	1,000
Modern Language Association of America	New York, N. Y.	1883	New York University—New York, N. Y.	11,000	444,000	162,000	159,000
Renaissance Society of America	New York, N. Y.	1954	Columbia University—New York, N. Y.	1,952	12,000	10,000	9,000
Society of Architectural Historians	Cambridge, Mass.	1940	University of Pittsburgh—Pittsburgh, Pa.	1,370	12,000	23,000	20,000
Society of Biblical Literature and Exegesis	New York, N. Y.	1880	Northwestern University—Evanston, Ill.	2,158	9,000	30,000	21,000

a These items are based in part on *ACLS Newsletter*, Vol. XI, No. 3, Directory Issue. March, 1960, pp. 7-32 and *Scientific and Technical Societies of the United States and Canada.* Seventh Edition. Publication 900. Compiled by John H. Gribbin and others. National Academy of Sciences—National Research Council, Washington, D. C., 1961.

The principal offices are those of record 1962. The number of members listed are those of record of 1960.

b The financial figures presented herein were derived by the author from financial reports of the societies and other data and information made available to him. They are for a twelve month period ending at some time in 1960, depending upon the accounting procedures used, and have been rounded off to the nearest thousand.

19

TABLE 2

BASIC INFORMATION REGARDING LEADING HUMANISTIC AND SOCIAL SCIENCE SOCIETIES

Society	Place of Origin[a]	Date of Origin[a]	Principal Office[a]	Number of Members[a]	Total Assets[b]	Total Income[b]	Total Expenditures[b]
American Association of Anatomists	Washington, D. C.	1888	University of Pennsylvania—Philadelphia, Pa.	1,300	$ 35,000	$ 6,000	$ 6,000
American Association of Immunologists	Minneapolis, Minn.	1913	New York, N. Y.	574	21,000	15,000	15,000
American Association of Pathologists and Bacteriologists	New York, N. Y.	1901	University of Kansas Medical School—Kansas City, Kans.	980	42,000	25,000	24,000
American Astronomical Society	Boston, Mass.	1897 1876	University of Illinois—Washington, D. C.	1,273	20,000*	7,000*	7,000*
American Chemical Society	New York, N. Y.		Urbana, Illinois	97,515	19,809,000	8,628,000	8,222,000
American Geophysical Union	Washington, D. C.	1919	Washington, D. C.	6,300	34,000	80,000	45,000
American Institute of Nutrition	Rochester, N. Y.	1928	Bethesda, Md.	749	1,000	20,000	18,000
American Mathematical Society	New York, N. Y.	1888	Providence, R. I.	7,166	845,000	421,000	352,000
American Meteorological Society	St. Louis, Mo.	1919	Boston, Mass.	7,726	426,000	191,000	191,000
American Physical Society	New York, N. Y.	1899	Columbia University—New York, N. Y.	17,700	550,000	780,000	716,000
American Physiological Society	New York, N. Y.	1887	Washington, D. C.	2,009	600,000	350,000	350,000
American Society for Experimental Pathology	Washington, D. C.	1913	University of North Carolina—Chapel Hill, N. C.	679	4,000	4,000	4,000
American Society for Microbiology	New Haven, Conn.	1899	Detroit, Mich.	6,255	40,000*	136,000*	123,000*
American Society for Pharmacology and Experimental Therapeutics, Inc.	Baltimore, Md.	1908	Washington, D. C.	981	100,000	75,000	42,000
American Society of Biological Chemists, Inc.	New York, N. Y.	1906	University of Florida—Gainesville, Fla.	1,666	20,000	17,000	13,000

Table 2 (Continuation)

BASIC INFORMATION REGARDING LEADING HUMANISTIC AND SOCIAL SCIENCE SOCIETIES

Society	Location	Year		Principal office			
American Society of Parasitologists	Washington, D. C.	1924	1,102	University of Illinois—Urbana, Ill.	7,000*	20,000*	20,000*
American Society of Zoologists	Boston, Mass.	1890	1,920	Goucher College—Baltimore, Md.	10,000	40,000	22,000
Association for Symbolic Logic	New York, N. Y.	1935	625	Providence, R. I.	15,000	12,000	12,000
Botanical Society of America, Inc.	Brooklyn, N. Y.	1894	2,400	University of Texas—Austin, Texas	25,000	50,000	50,000
Ecological Society of America	Columbus, Ohio	1915	2,200	Michigan State University—East Lansing, Mich.	36,000	17,000	17,000
Econometric Society	Cleveland, Ohio	1930	1,600	Yale University—New Haven, Conn.	11,000	41,000	39,000
Electrochemical Society, Inc.	Philadelphia, Pa.	1902	3,182	New York, N. Y.	315,000	126,000	126,000
Entomological Society of America, Inc.	New York, N. Y.	1906	4,300	College Park, Md.	25,000	224,000	227,000
Genetics Society of America	New Orleans, La.	1931	1,217	Oak Ridge, Tenn.	16,000	12,000	9,000
Geochemical Society	New Orleans, La.	1955	2,400	Washington, D. C.	5,000	5,000	4,000
Geological Society of America, Inc.	New York, N. Y.	1888	5,341	New York, N. Y.	7,368,000	463,000	370,000
Institute of Mathematical Statistics	Ann Arbor, Mich.	1935	2,300	University of North Carolina—Chapel Hill, N. C.	129,000	43,000	51,000
Mathematical Association of America	Columbus, Ohio	1915	9,113	University of California—Davis, Calif.	597,000	617,000	497,000
Paleontological Society	Baltimore, Md.	1908	861	Harvard University—Cambridge, Mass.	7,000	13,000	13,000

a These items are based in part on *Scientific and Technical Societies of the United States and Canada.* Seventh Edition. Publication 900. Compiled by John H. Gribbin and others. National Academy of Sciences—National Research Council, Washington, D. C., 1961. The principal offices listed are those of record 1960. The number of members listed are those of record 1962.

b The financial figures presented herein were derived by the author from financial reports of the societies and other data and information made available to him. They are for a twelve month period ending at some time in 1960, depending upon the accounting procedures used, and have been rounded off to the nearest thousand.

* Figures marked with asterisks are estimates made by the author from information available to him. The figures for the American Astronomical Society are probably much lower than is actually the case.

TABLE 3

TOTAL MEMBERSHIP, ASSETS, INCOME, AND EXPENDITURES OF 58 LEARNED SOCIETIES, 1960[a]

Based on Statistical Information in Tables 1 and 2 above

	Total Membership	Total Assets[b]	Total Income[b]	Total Expenditures[b]
29 Natural Science Societies	191,434	$31,113,000	$12,438,000	$11,585,000
29 Humanistic and Social Science Societies	107,273	5,361,000	2,827,000	2,459,000
Totals of 58 Societies	298,707	36,474,000	15,265,000	14,044,000

[a] Note should be made that the figures for the Natural Science Societies are in imbalance relative to those in the Humanistic and Social Science Societies due primarily to the inclusion in the former of the American Chemical Society's 97,515 members and approximately $20,000,000 in assets, annual income of $8,600,000 and annual expenditures of $8,200,000.

[b] The financial figures presented herein have been rounded off to the nearest thousand.

PART ONE

HUMANISTIC AND SOCIAL SCIENCE SOCIETIES

AMERICAN ANTIQUARIAN SOCIETY

The American Antiquarian Society, the first of the learned societies created in the nineteenth century, is different from the American Philosophical Society and the American Academy of Arts and Sciences in that its activity has been confined to one particular aspect of the humanities. It is similar to the two eighteenth century societies in that its membership is restricted.

The American Antiquarian Society traces its origin to a Massachusetts printer, Isaiah Thomas. Born in poverty and deprived of formal schooling, Thomas became a successful businessman, and during the War of Independence published one of the leading Revolutionary newspapers in the colonies. He continued to accumulate wealth after the war and turned his attention to the acquisition of documents and other materials relating to the early history of the American colonies. The culmination of these endeavors was the incorporation, in 1812, of the American Antiquarian Society which was empowered to collect and preserve the materials for a study of American history and antiquities. Thomas was elected the first President of the Society. Since that time many distinguished Americans have been members or served as officers of the Society, including 12 Presidents of the United States.

Membership in the Society has always been honorary and is conferred by election at any meeting upon any person eminent in the field of the Society's activities. Rules adopted in 1831 limited the number of members at 140, which has since been raised to 200. During the nineteenth century various fees were charged members but, in 1925, all fees and dues were abolished. Although the founder often expressed the wish that the Society "comport with the name it bears" by embracing all of the Americas within its membership, for practical reasons approximately half has been chosen from New England. The names of many of the leading historians of the past and present century have appeared on the Society's rolls, though a substantial portion of the membership has always been composed of persons whose interests in historical studies were those of writers and collectors rather than teachers.

In the early days of the Society's existence it devoted attention to the encouragement of historical study and the collection of objects of American antiquarian interest for its museum, but its chief interest lay in the books and manuscripts from which its library gradually came into being. The founder, author of a *History of Printing in America,* had a considerable collection of American printed matter which he proposed to turn over to the Society as soon as it had a safe and convenient repository. By the time that the condition was fulfilled in 1820 this nucleus of a library had expanded, largely through the generosity of Mr. Thomas, to nearly 6,000 volumes. By its continued increase, the library soon overshadowed the museum, and the other objects the Society had been collecting were placed with other organizations. Since then the library has been the sole object of the Society's efforts.

The Society's library of Americana is a broad one chronologically and otherwise. By 1854 its 6,000 volumes had increased to 23,000. In the next three decades it more than tripled to 80,000. Twenty-five years later it passed the 100,000 mark; by 1927 it had nearly 500,000 titles, and now its approximately 800,000 entries form one of the most imposing collections in the country, ranking with the Lenox Library, the John Carter Brown Library, and the Library of Congress. It has attempted to "collect everything printed in this country before 1820," including books, manuscripts, and newspapers. So well has it succeeded that three-fourths of the titles that come under this description are found on its shelves.

The library is particularly strong in its collection of early American schoolbooks, local histories and genealogies, biographies, Spanish-Americana, bibliographies, American religious works, and pamphlets and broadsides. These are all surpassed in completeness and value, however, by the Society's collection of American newspapers. This collection was built upon the acquisitions of its founder, Isaiah Thomas, in the preparation of his work on printing in America. According to its librarian: "The first function of the American Antiquarian Society is the collection and preservation of such source material. Its next function is to make that material available for study, not primarily in its reading room, but by the construction of bibliographic tools."[1]

Since the main activities of the Society center around the library, the meetings are relatively simple, bi-annual affairs. At the April meeting, regularly held in Boston, the Society hears the report of its governing council, usually a lengthy discussion of some phase of the Society's activities rather than a mere report, elects new members, listens to two or three papers, and adjourns for luncheon. The program of the annual meeting in October is similar save that the treasurer and the librarian also submit reports and new officers are elected. In recent years approximately 50 members have been present at the various meetings.

Two series of publications carry the seal of the Society, the *Transactions* and the *Proceedings*. The former, published from 1820 to 1911, was given over to manuscript and documentary materials for American history. Since the latter date this material has been incorporated in the *Proceedings* of the Society which have appeared since the beginning of the Society and contain reports, by-laws, obituary notices, papers read at meetings, and lists of officers. From time to time have appeared incidental publications, handbooks of information, and catalogues of the library. Currently the Society is engaged in reprinting in microprint form everything, except magazines, printed in the several states from 1640 to 1800; the project has been nearly completed. Headquarters of the Society are at Salisbury Street and Park Avenue, Worcester, Massachusetts.[2]

AMERICAN STATISTICAL ASSOCIATION

The dean of practically all social science organizations in this country, the American Statistical Association, was founded in 1839. It resulted from a general interest in the establishment of statistical societies evident between the years 1830 and 1840 in France, Germany, Italy, and the United States, but more than anywhere else in England, there being no less than six such societies founded in Great Britain within the decade. The first to be established in America was the New York Statistical Society, incorporated in 1836, but like several of those abroad it had an ephemeral existence. The American Statistical Society, founded in Boston in 1839, was doubtless inspired largely by the London (now Royal) Statistical Society, founded in 1834, as it followed the latter in its form of organization. A statement of the field and aim of the American Association, published in 1840, shows a familiarity with German statistics, and indicates that the statistics which the society intended to cultivate were of the type developed in the German universities, rather than the earlier English studies of political arithmetic.

At the organizational meeting of the American Statistical Society, held in Boston on November 27, 1839, it was announced that the object of the new society would be "to collect, preserve, and diffuse statistical information in the different departments of human knowledge" and indicated that it construed "statistics" in the sense of including all information relative to the structure of society and not merely that susceptible of mathematical interpretation. It adopted its first constitution on December 11, 1839, changed its name to the American Statistical Association on February 5, 1840, and was incorporated in Massachusetts in the following year. From the first the Association sought to avoid the danger of becoming a merely local organization. Its by-laws provided that "the operations of this Association shall primarily be directed to the statistics of the United States; and they shall be as general and as extensive as possible and not confined to any particular part of the country." Of the 54 active members of the Association in its first year of existence all but two lived in New England, but contact with a wider field was at once sought through corresponding and foreign members in the United States and abroad.

Of the small group who founded the Association, the name of Lemuel Shattuck, its first secretary, is a memorable one in the history of statistics in this country. The first adequate and scientific city census, that of Boston in 1845, was taken under his direction. It was primarily at his suggestion that the U. S. Congress created the census board for planning the census of 1850 and five of the six schedules used in that census were designed by him.

The nature of the Association's interests has brought it into close contact with local, state, and federal government. It has constantly urged on state legislatures the creation of sanitary commissions, state boards of health, and similar bodies; the extension of registration areas; and the collection and compilation of statistical information. On the Federal Census, in particular, the Association has left its mark. The census of 1850 determined the direction of subsequent ones and the Association, as the result of incessant urgings, was largely instrumental in the establishment of the Bureau of the Census as a permanent institution. Its members have been directors of the census and members of the Bureau. In 1933 it was instrumental in the establishment of the Federal Central Statistical Board, now the Office of Statistical Standards of the Bureau of the Budget. The latter is the central statistical office which plans and coordinates the Federal statistical system.

Some 40 chapters of the Association have been established in New York, Philadelphia, and most of the other principal cities from coast to coast.

They are semi-autonomous organizations and meet irregularly for dinner and discussion. Members now belong to one or more of five national sections: Business and Economics, Physical and Engineering, Social, Training, and Biometric Statistics. These five sections are responsible for the 60 odd program sessions of the annual meetings.

The Association has had at least one meeting in every year since 1839. Throughout a large part of the period, it has met quarterly except during the summer, the principal meeting being the one that was held in December of each year. So long as all meetings were in Boston and the membership was primarily local, quarterly meetings were practicable, but with an expansion and broadening of membership annual meetings became inevitable. At the present time these annual meetings are often held in conjunction with such organizations as the American Economic Association, the Institute of Mathematical Statistics and the Biometric Society, usually in early September or December. The place of the quarterly meetings has been taken by regional meetings of the local chapters of one or more of the Association's five sections.

One of the first acts of the Association was the appointment of a Publishing Committee, which brought out in 1843 Part 1 of Volume I of the *Collections of the American Statistical Association*. Parts 2 and 3 followed in 1845 and 1847; all three parts were bound into one volume. For 20 years thereafter only desultory papers appeared. It was not until 1888 that the Association undertook the regular production of a quarterly journal. In that year appeared number one of Volume I of the *Publications of the American Statistical Association,* which has appeared ever since. In 1915 its title was changed to *Quarterly Publication of the A. S. A.* and in 1922 to the *Journal of the A. S. A.* It is devoted to articles, short notes, reviews, classified lists of recent literature, and a short digest of the proceedings of the annual meetings. The Association also publishes, five times yearly, the *American Statistician,* which includes articles of general interest, news items and announcements of interest to statisticians as well as discussions of professional problems, and *Technometrics,* a quarterly recently initiated jointly with the American Society for Quality Control.

The earliest members of the Association were denominated Fellows: Ordinary, Honorary, Corresponding, and Foreign. Throughout the nineteenth century this nomenclature obtained, except that for a considerable period the terms Fellow and Member were used interchangeably. In the first decade of the twentieth century the title Member was adopted as applying to all the groups named above, and that of Fellow became a new and distinct classification. Since that time, the only qualification for membership is that the candidate be "interested in statistics." Fellows must be elected by a Committee on Fellows and not more than 30 may be elected in any one year.

For the first 50 years of its existence, the Association's membership rarely exceeded 100, confined almost entirely to New England residents. In the 1880's and '90's, a large addition of college and university teachers ensued, a class that had previously shown little interest in the Association, so that by 1897 the Association numbered 500. At present the Association has over 7,200 members, resident in most foreign countries and all parts of the United States.

Today, while most of the members have had formal university training in statistics, those engaged in teaching number only about 25 per cent of the membership. The remainder are what might be termed "practical" statisticians in government bureaus, business and other organizations. The offices of the Association are at 810 Eighteenth Street, N.W., Washington 6, D.C.[3]

AMERICAN ORIENTAL SOCIETY

The American Oriental Society was founded in 1842, only 30 years after the American Antiquarian Society. Its founder and first president was John Pickering, a cultured Boston businessman. The purposes of the Society according to its original constitution were: "1. The cultivation of learning in the Asiatic, African and Polynesian languages. 2. The publication of Memoirs, Translations, Vocabularies and other works relating to Asiatic, African, and Polynesian languages. 3. The collection of a library."[4]

In pursuing these objectives the members of the Society have concentrated on three major fields of interest: the Near East, South and South-East Asia, and the Far East. In 1925 the Secretary estimated that the percentage of the Society interested in these areas was, respectively, 70 per cent, 20 per cent, and 10 per cent. Today the percentages would be about evenly divided. The early weighting was undoubtedly due to the greater interest in that day and time in Biblical studies.

Although the American Oriental Society does not officially carry on research, it has been a means of encouragement for members pursuing philological studies in the ancient and modern worlds of the East through its publications.

The Journal of the American Oriental Society, published since 1849, now appears four times a year and through articles and other literature there presented helps to keep members abreast of advances in the field. In 1924 the Society began publication of an American Oriental Series which provides a medium of publication for book length works.

Originally there were two classes of membership in the Oriental Society:

corporate and honorary. The corporate members were the active members of the society who carried on its work and activities. Candidates for such membership were proposed by the Directors and had to receive a three-fourths vote of members present at a meeting. Foreigners were eligible for honorary membership under the same conditions. Corresponding members, in the persons of attachés and others located abroad, were admitted in the 1850's and 1860's but discontinued in 1876 because improved means of communication precluded the benefits that had been derived from the maintenance of this type of membership. In the 1920's the laws were revised so that candidates for corporate membership could be proposed by any member and an honorary associate membership (now discontinued) was added for persons of distinction in the United States who were not actively interested in the work of the Society. Today, corporate membership is open to any person in sympathy with the purposes of the Society and recommended by a member of the Society, and life memberships have been added. The total membership of the Society is now approximately 1,000.

Annual meetings of the Society are held during the Easter week, generally in cities along the northern Atlantic seaboard. The program is prepared by a special committee, reports of officers and committees are presented, and papers by members are read. Some of these papers and the business matters connected with the meeting are published in the *Journal of the American Oriental Society*.

Provision was made in 1917 for the creation of branches of the Society to provide for meetings for groups of members living at too great a distance to attend its annual meetings.[5] A Middle West Branch and a Western Branch have been organized under this proviso and annual meetings, occurring at approximately the same time as the major meetings on the East Coast, have been held by these branches.[6] The offices of the Society are presently at 329 Sterling Memorial Library, Yale University, New Haven, Conneticut.

AMERICAN NUMISMATIC SOCIETY

The American Numismatic Society was organized in New York City on April 16, 1858 by 12 New Yorkers with the object of "the collection and preservation of coins and medals, with an investigation into their history, and other subjects connected therewith." In 1865 the Society was incorporated in New York under the corporate name of The American Numismatic and Archaeological Society. In 1907, however, the Society's name was changed back to the original American Numismatic Society.

Coins and medals and books about them were collected from the first days of the Society. For 50 years the Society was forced to rent rooms to house its collection and hold meetings. Finally, in 1910, the Society erected its own Museum and headquarters in upper Manhattan in New York City. The Museum is unique in that it is the only museum in the world devoted exclusively to numismatics. Elsewhere coin and metal collections form a department or section of national libraries and similar institutions. Also, unlike national collections abròad, such as the Department of Coins and Medals of the British Museum or the *Cabinet des Medailles* in Paris, it is not supported by our government, relying entirely on membership fees and endowments.

The collections of coins and the related library in the Museum are the core and *raison d'etre* of the Society. These collections are among the most important in the world, comprising about 500,000 coins. All ages and areas are represented; the ancient Greek and Roman, Mohammedan, and Far Eastern collections are exceptional. The library consists of over 75,000 books, periodicals, and pamphlets covering all facets of numismatics, together with a file of mounted illustrations of ancient coins, 75,000 in number, and a collection of plaster casts of coins not possessed by the Museum. Every effort is made by the Society to make these collections available to archaeologists, historians, and other scholars of numismatic problems. Since 1952, a summer seminar for a limited number of graduate students has become a successful feature of the Society's program.

The Society founded the *American Journal of Numismatics* in 1866 and published articles and reports therein until 1923 when it was suspended. The *Proceedings,* containing the officers' and committee reports, has been published from 1874 to date. The present major publishing activities of the Society are *Numismatic Notes and Monographs* and *Numismatic Literature.* Published in intermittent series since 1920, the former publication consists of some 140 numbers dealing with extensive study of some numismatic area. *Numismatic Literature* is the only periodical published by the Society today, and it contains book reviews, resumes of articles, lists of coin dealer catalogues, and similar literature.

There are three regular annual meetings of the Society plus special ones from time to time. The annual meeting in January is devoted to the reports of officers and committees; lecture meetings are held in the spring and fall.

There are four classes of members within the Society: Fellows, Honorary Fellows, associate members, and corresponding members. Fellows are limited to 150; Honorary Fellows, those who have rendered special service to the Society, are limited to 50. Only the Fellows are eligible to vote and hold office in the Society. Associate membership is open to all residents with an interest in numismatics. Persons or organizations abroad may be elected corresponding members. Total membership in the Society is approximately 1,000. Headquarters are located at Audubon Terrace, Broadway and 155th Street, New York 32, N. Y.[7]

Founded in 1869, the American Philological Association may reasonably be designated as an off-shoot of the American Oriental Society, which since 1848 had maintained a Classical Section. Some 20 members of this Section constituted the nucleus of the new Association and furnished its first officers. Another organization which doubtless contributed to the founding of the Philological Association was the Greek Club of New York, a group of scholars who cherished the classical tradition and who met periodically for reading in the original from their favorite authors.

The time was ripe for the organization of a philological association. In Europe philology had become a dominating scholarly interest, and in the United States many European trained philologists were at the peak of their intellectual vigor. Such, then, was the situation when Professor George F. Comfort, of Allegheny College, engaged in correspondence with a considerable number of scholars, educators and others to secure their cooperation in the organization of a national society devoted to philological studies. Professor Comfort, was, indeed, the active agent in bringing the Association into existence; encouraged by the response to his overtures he called a conference in New York, on November 13, 1868. To some 50 assembled scholars at this conference, he proposed the organization of an association modeled on the *Sammlung der Deutschen Philologen und Schulmänner,* founded at Göttingen in 1837. The scope of the associations' activities should, he held, embrace the entire field of philological investigation and instruction. Those in attendance concurred in his proposal and a representative conference was scheduled for the following summer. Accordingly, a convention, attended by some 40 scholars from a score of states, met in Poughkeepsie in July of 1869 and proceeded to organize the Association.

Until 1905 the annual meetings of the Association were scheduled in July. At that time, as the result of the insistence of many members, particularly those from the Mid-West, who pointed out that most of the other learned societies held their meetings in December and that the July meetings conflicted with summer university sessions and travel plans, the time of the annual meeting was changed permanently to the Christmas-New Year's period. The first winter meeting of 1905 was held jointly with the Archaeological Institute of America, and all of the subsequent meetings, except that of 1913, have been also. Occasionally other societies, such as the Modern Language Association of America, the American Historical Association, and the Linguistic Society of America have joined this combination.

The various annual meetings have been held in all sections of the country, although the majority have been in the East. An affiliated Pacific Coast Branch of the Association was constituted in 1900; this was followed, in 1918, with an arrangement whereby a double affiliation was established by the Branch between the American Philological Association and the Modern Language Association of America.

The organ of the Association and its regular publication is the annual volume which, until 1896, bore the title *Transactions* and since then of *Transactions and Proceedings.* Each annual volume is divided into two parts: the *Transactions,* which contain papers read at the annual meetings and selected for publication and the *Proceedings,* which contain minutes of the meetings, other administrative matters, and the record of the meeting of the Philological Association of the Pacific Coast, as the former Branch is now called.

From its organization, membership in the American Philological Association has been open to "any lover of philological studies," upon election by the Directors, such election being a matter of form, although furnishing a potential safeguard against the admission of undesirable persons. The Association presently numbers about 1,400 members. They are served from an office at Hunter College, Bedford Park Boulevard, West, New York 68, N. Y.[8]

ARCHAEOLOGICAL INSTITUTE OF AMERICA

Among Charles Eliot Norton's contributions to American classical scholarship was the role he played in the founding of the Archaeological Institute of America. The Institute was begun at Boston in 1879 as a result of his catalytic effort with a small group of scholars. The *Regulations,* drawn up by a committee appointed at the organization meeting, stated that the Institute would further archaeological research by "sending out expeditions for special investigation, by aiding the efforts of independent explorers, by publication of archaeological papers and of reports of the results of the expeditions which the Institute may undertake or promote, and by any other means which may from time to time appear desirable."

At first an integral organization, it began to take on the aspect of a group of affiliated societies in 1884. In that year local organizations were formed in New York and Baltimore. Since that time 48 affiliated societies, extending from coast to coast, have been established. These local societies have a large measure of autonomy, but their principal source of revenue is a portion of the dues which are returned to them from the general fund of the Institute. They cannot publish under the aegis of the Institute without its consent. At the same time representatives of the affiliated societies form part of the Council, the governing board of the Institute.

Early in its career the Institute subsidized individual explorers and organized extensive archaeological expeditions, such as the investigation of Assos, a Greek city in Asia Minor. Toward the end of the 1880's, however, this system of investigation was suspended for the one now in use. Under it, the actual work of research is done by schools founded by and affiliated, to a greater or lesser extent, with the Institute. The first of these was the American School of Classical Studies in Athens, founded in 1881. A similar school appeared at Rome in 1895. In 1900 the work spread to Jerusalem, with the organization of the School of Oriental Research in that place. The number of schools was augmented by the School of American Research at Santa Fe, New Mexico, in 1907; the American School of Prehistoric Research in 1921; and the American Research Center in Egypt in 1948. Each school conducts its own excavations; results are published by the schools or appear in one of the Institute's journals.

Regular general annual meetings, the principal activity of many learned societies, were begun by the Institute only in 1899 and have been held during the last week in December since that date. The meetings, conducted in various cities, are devoted to routine business matters and to the reading of papers. The latter are often read in joint sessions with other societies, particularly the American Philological Association.

Three regular publications appear under the auspices of the Institute, the annual *Bulletin,* a scientific quarterly *American Journal of Archaeology,* and the popular quarterly *Archaeology.* The *Bulletin* contains the reports of officers, committees, and the affiliated schools and societies; it superseded the *Annual Reports* published from 1879 to 1908. The *American Journal of Archaeology and of the History of Fine Arts* was founded as a semi-independent publication of the Institute in 1885. Through the years its relationship to the Institute grew closer and in 1896-97 the Institute took complete charge of the *Journal* and at that time brought out Vol. 1 of the *American Journal of Archaeology.* In 1914 *Art and Archaeology* was established to appeal to laymen. It was published until the depression of the 1930's caused its cessation. Revived in 1948 as *Archaeology,* this illustrated quarterly for non-professionals has since been a source of revenue for the Institute.

Because of its affiliated societies and the large group of non-professionals interested in its work, the Institute has a wider variety of membership than most learned organizations. At one time there were eleven different categories of members which presently number eight. Membership in one or another category is open to all interested persons and presently totals about 2,500 persons. Women play an important part in the activities of the affiliated societies, but they are less active in the Institute's general affairs. Headquarters of the Institute are at 5 Washington Square North, New York 3, N. Y.[9]

SOCIETY OF BIBLICAL LITERATURE AND EXEGESIS

Frederic Gardiner, a noted Biblical scholar, and a group of about 35 compatriots from the New England, New Jersey, New York and Pennsylvania areas were instrumental in the formation in 1880 of the Society of Biblical Literature and Exegesis to "stimulate the critical study of the Scriptures by presenting, discussing, and publishing original papers on Biblical subjects." Although the last word in its title, meaning interpretation, has become semi-archaic, the Society continues to retain its original name.

In carrying out its stated purpose the Society has not taken a doctrinal position and, consequently, its publications and meetings have provided a forum for Jewish, Roman Catholic, and Protestant scholars. The *Journal of Biblical Literature,* published by the Society for over 80 years, carries articles by members of all faiths and is one of the chief mediums for American Biblical scholarship. Annual meetings of the Society, devoted primarily to the reading and discussion of scholarly papers, and similar ones sponsored by Sections of the Society in various parts of this country and Canada also provide a sounding-board for differing interpretations. These Sections include: Mid-West (established 1936), Canadian (1939), Pacific Coast (1941), Southern (1948), New England (1950), and Southwestern (1957).

Activities of the Society include the encouragement its members have given to cooperative and special projects in the area of Biblical study. Various revisions of the Bible, such as the *American Standard Version* of 1901 and the recently completed *Revised Standard Version,* such large scale publications as the twelve-volume *The Interpreter's Bible* and the several volumes of *The Beginnings of Christianity,* and the International Greek New Testament Project, have all involved active participation by members of the Society. While the center of interest of the Society is thus the study and interpretation of the Bible, philology and archaeology, where pertinent, have received considerable attention from Societal members. A case in point was the furor over the Dead Sea scrolls which were found by members of the American School for Oriental Research in Jerusalem. This school has long been affiliated with the Society.

Although the original founders of the Society were Protestant, there

have long been many Roman Catholic and Jewish scholars actively participating in its affairs, and its present-day active membership of about
2,200 includes rabbis, priests, and ministers as well as teachers, students
and other persons interested in Biblical scholarship. In addition, there are
at present 19 honorary members, limited to distinguished foreign scholars
residing outside the United States. Headquarters of the Society are at
the Garrett Biblical Institute, Northwestern University, Evanston,
Illinois.[10]

MODERN LANGUAGE ASSOCIATION OF AMERICA

The first meeting of the Modern Language Association of America, or
the MLA as it is popularly known, was held in New York City at
Columbia College on December 27 and 28, 1883. Some 40 instructors
from 20 institutions of learning were present.

In discussing the founding of the new organization, a former Secretary
and Past-President of the MLA stated, "Our parent was the American
Philological Association, with which we still have some overlapping membership. Our grandparent was the American Oriental Society."[11] Other
Secretaries have challenged this idea pointing out that almost three-fourths
of the founding members were not members of the classics-oriented
American Philological Association and that, although these founding
members were not opposed to the teaching, research, etc., in the classics,
they were primarily interested in elevating the study and teaching of the
modern foreign languages to the status held by the classics. The same
Secretaries maintain that the primary factor leading to the formation of
the Association was the influence of the German universities. At these
universities the study of modern foreign languages was regarded as of
equal importance with the classics and the formation there of associations
for such study provided a stimulus to American scholars, who more often
than not were trained in the German institutions, to organize an American
association for the purpose of elevating their subject by mutual research,
discussion and publication.

Prior to the turn of the nineteenth century, members of the Association
devoted considerable attention to pedagogical problems and in 1899 the
Association, in cooperation with the National Education Association, prepared a report on foreign language teaching and study. From this time
on, however, there was a shift of emphasis to research coupled with an
interest in the production of well-qualified graduate students. By the
1920's Association interest in the actual teaching of modern languages
and particularly foreign languages in secondary schools had declined to
the point of abandonment. Concern with pedagogy, particularly as it

related to the primary and secondary schools, became the province of a host of new and disconnected organizations. Coincidentally, interest in and study of foreign languages declined at a rapid rate in these same schools.

Various Association officials and members called attention to this situation and maintained that, although the study of English as a subject was ever-increasing, the decline in interest in the problems connected with the teaching of modern languages and concurrent decrease in enrollment in modern foreign languages, particularly at the secondary level, boded ill for the MLA, scholars in the modern language field, and the American people as a whole. Officially, however, the Association stood aloof. In 1923, for instance, although three past-presidents played an important role in a five year study of the problem, the Association did not participate. In the 1930's the tide turned and in 1939 a Commission on Trends in Education was established. This Commission, and a succeeding Committee dealing exclusively with modern foreign languages, emphasized the responsibilities of the MLA in these areas. In 1950 the Committee declared that the MLA could not exist by itself; it must rest upon the work carried on in the schools and colleges of the country. The promotion and support of the study of English and of foreign languages at all scholastic levels must, therefore, be a matter of concern to the Association. Today, one of the chief activities of the Association is the fostering of interest in and better methods of teaching of foreign languages at all levels of instruction.

Through the years the Association has endeavored to provide information and data of particular interest to its members. Recent efforts in this area include a list of "Research in Progress" in the modern language field; an annual "International Bibliography" published in the May issue of *Publications of the Modern Language Association of America (PMLA)*; and the *MLA Style Sheet*, widely used as a standard in the publication of articles, monographs, and books. Several prize contests with the purpose of spurring better scholarly writing have been established under MLA auspices.

Since 1883 annual meetings of the MLA have been held in all sections of the country. Prior to World War II colleges and universities generally acted as hosts. The pressure of increased membership since that time forced a virtual cessation of this custom and has restricted the meetings to large cities. Traditionally the annual meetings have been held during the Christmas week although occasionally they have been held in Mid-September prior to the opening of colleges and universities. Because of the large membership and the range of interests represented, recent MLA programs present a bewildering variety of subjects. The 1955 meeting, for instance, included 11 addresses, 30 section papers, 186 group papers, 17 conferences, and many special reports, committee meetings, and discussions.[12] More often than not the annual meetings have been scheduled to coincide with those of such organizations as the American Folklore Society and the Linguistic Society of America.

Some of the papers presented at the annual meetings are published in *Publications of the Modern Language Association of America (PMLA)*, now issued six times a year and published since 1884. Notes, Documents, an Annual List of Members, Proceedings of the Business Meetings, including the reports of officers and committees, are also presented in its pages. From time to time the MLA has sponsored or published books on literary or linguistic scholarship and is currently producing a series of Teachers Guides dealing with the teaching of modern foreign languages in the elementary schools. Its textbook *Modern Spanish* (Harcourt-Brace, 1960) is considered by many scholars to be an important innovation in textbooks for a beginning foreign language course in college.

Membership in the Association has been opened to all interested persons upon recommendation and approval of an officer. Beginning with about 400 members in its first ten years of existence, the MLA membership more than tripled by the time of World War I, jumped to over 4,000 in 1932, 7,000 in 1953, and now stands at approximately 11,000.

In ascertaining the cause of this remarkable growth, the frank analysis of a former Secretary is pertinent: "What is the fundamental character of this Association? I have known it under forty-four presidents and six secretaries, under three constitutions and through two major wars. Its personnel and organization vary. . . . Fundamentally the Association is a body of scholars drawn together for intellectual and social companionship. The fascination of these deepens with the years. Despite all our interesting papers half the attendance is always engaged in extracurricular friendly reunion."[13]

The vast majority of the present MLA constituency are members of college and university faculties or graduate students at such institutions.

In the past there were regional branches, including the Mid-West and New England. Today the MLA has close relations with five regional bodies: the Philological Association of the Pacific Coast; the Rocky Mountain MLA; the South Atlantic MLA; the Mid-West MLA; and the South Central MLA. They are autonomous societies, holding their own meetings and electing their own officers, but membership is often overlapping. Coordination with these regional bodies and the other activities of the Association are carried on from the office of the Executive Secretary located at 6 Washington Square, North, New York 3, N. Y.[14]

AMERICAN HISTORICAL ASSOCIATION

The American Historical Association was an off-shoot of the American Social Science Association,[15] and came into being under its auspices at the 1884 annual meeting of the American Social Science Association at Saratoga, New York. During the meeting John Eaton, President of the Association, opposed the creation of a separate historical organization. Those opposed to Eaton's viewpoint stated that the Social Science Association had tended to over-specialize in prison reform, charity, etc., and that the overwhelming sentiment among historians was in favor of a separate organization which would serve to set high, professional standards for historical training and research. The latter view carried the day and the American Historical Association was organized.

The main influencers in the formation of the new organization were Professor Herbert B. Adams of Johns Hopkins University, who became Secretary of the Association and remained so until his death in 1900, and Professors Charles Kendall Adams of the University of Michigan and Moses Coit Tyler of Cornell University.

The new Association grew rapidly. From an initial 41, the membership had risen to 287 by the time of the second meeting in 1885 and by 1890 there were 620 members.

In 1889 the Association, by an Act of Congress, was incorporated in the District of Columbia "for the promotion of historical studies, the collection and preservation of historical manuscripts, and for kindred purposes in the interest of American history and of history in America."

The 1889 Act also provided that the Association should have its offices in Washington, D. C., that it should make reports to the Secretary of the Smithsonian Institution regarding historical matters, and that this official should transmit to Congress such reports as he should see fit. Some members did not like this government connection, alleging the possibility of "censorship" by the Secretary of the Smithsonian Institution. Events have shown that this fear was chimerical and the connection has developed, in actuality, as a mutual and voluntary interchange of services, and the earlier aversion has almost completely disappeared. One of the lasting benefits to the Association of the governmental connection was the arrangement whereby the *Annual Reports* come to be printed at government expense. From the government viewpoint, the advantage of having a trained group to look to for advice in connection with manuscripts, archives, etc., has been inestimable.

The work of the Association is done chiefly by the Association's headquarters staff, headed by the Executive Secretary who acts for the elected governing Council, and through the numerous committees, either permanent or *ad hoc*. These committees utilize the services, freely offered, of some 300 members of the Association. The most important standing committees at the present time, in addition to the administrative ones, are the Historian and the Federal Government, International Historical Activities, Study of War Documents, and a Committee on Teaching. The Association's Service Center for Teachers of History provides help for teachers and school administrators concerned with history through pamphlets summarizing the latest historical research and through a consultant service. It also operates a reference service for college and university instructors.

The Association has frequently been called upon to act in an advisory capacity to the government and has appointed special committees for that purpose, such as the Committee on Governmental Historical Documentary Publications, the Committee on a National Archives Buildings, and others. Due to the efforts of the last-mentioned committee and J. Franklin Jameson, managing editor of the *American Historical Review* during the early 1900's, the National Archives was established.

Seven prizes are currently offered by the Association to encourage historical research and writing. These prizes are offered in European, Asiatic, and American history and range from $100 to $1,500 and publication of the manuscript.

The Association holds a general meeting every year which lasts for three days during the week between Christmas and New Year's. Seven of the first eleven meetings of the Association were held in Washington, D. C., and there was some sentiment, primarily because of the government connection, to continue that city as a permanent meeting place. In 1896, however, opponents forced a move to New York. Since that time an informal practice has been adopted whereby the Association meets one year in an Eastern city, the next in a Western, and the third in Washington. Until World War II these meetings were often held in conjunction with the meetings of other organizations such as the American Economic Association and the American Political Science Association; since that time each of these societies has become too large for such joint meetings. Many sessions at these annual meetings, however, are joint ones with historical groups of a regional or special nature such as the Southern Historical Association and the Agricultural History Society.

The Association has two official publications. The *Annual Report* is published by authority of Congress as a public document, at the Government Printing Office, and is on sale by the Superintendent of Public Documents. It is distributed to the members of the Association, members of Congress, American libraries recognized as depositories of public documents, and to a considerable number of foreign libraries. It is usually in two volumes and contains the *Proceedings* of the Association, reports of its committees, the annual bibliography known as the "Writings on American History," and until curtailed funds prevented it, the publication of collections of documents, articles, and other material. The other publication of the Association is its quarterly, *The American Historical Review*. The *Review* was founded in 1895, and its Editor is also Executive Secretary of the Association. It contains authoritative articles, edited documents, and general historical news and critical reviews of historical publications.[16]

Membership in the Association has always included those professionally engaged in historical work and those with a general interest in history. It is open to any reputable person, upon election by the Executive Council, which is ordinarily a matter of form. Its membership presently totals approximately 8,500 persons, which places it numerically about mid-way between its closely related organizations, the American Economic Association and the American Political Science Association.

A Pacific Coast Branch of the Association was organized in 1904 in order that members living in the Far West might hold meetings and conduct activities of their own while still retaining membership in the parent organization. A few early attempts to work out a similar arrangement with other sections of the country have not materialized and this has undoubtedly been a factor in the organization of a number of separate regional and state historical associations.[17] National headquarters are at 400 A Street, S.E., Washington 3, D. C.

AMERICAN ECONOMIC ASSOCIATION

The American Social Science Association and the American Historical Association were involved in the creation of the American Economic Association. At the second meeting of the American Historical Association, again in Saratoga, New York, held with the American Social Science Association, a group of young historians and allied specialists proceeded to organize the American Economic Association.

The purpose of the Association, according to the Charter of Incorporation, is:

"1. The encouragement of economic research, especially the historical study of the actual conditions of industrial life;

"2. The issue of publications on economic subjects;

"3. The encouragement of perfect freedom of economic discussion. The Association as such will take no partisan attitude, nor will it commit its members to any position on practical economic questions."[18]

Through the years the Association has adhered to this policy statement, particularly in regard to paragraph 3. It has opened its meetings and publications to the adherents of all schools of economics and has endorsed none. These meetings, held annually during the Christmas holidays, are usually planned to cover a broad range of topics of interest to the members. Occasionally a meeting is devoted to the ramifications of a single subject or theme. The Association often meets concurrently with allied associations. For the past few years an employment registry has been conducted at the meetings in an endeavor to provide institutional placement for instructors.

During the first 25 years of its history, 1885 to 1910, the Association published the papers and reports of its annual meetings in connection with the publication of monographs on specialized economic topics. After the latter date, papers and reports of the meetings have been published in the *Papers and Proceedings.* At approximately the same time that this change took place, 1911, the quarterly *American Economic Review* was established. The *Review* contains articles, book reviews, and other note-worthy economic news.

The *Handbook* and *Directory,* containing biographical and statistical material about the Association and its members, is published intermittently. Occasional monographs and the translation of significant foreign economic works are also issued.

Membership in the Association is open to any person interested in economics and endorsed by a member. Prior to World War I, the vast majority of the members were in the academic profession. Increased interest in economics after that time on the part of businessmen, government officials, and professional men saw a large increase in membership among these classes. Professional, and particularly teaching, economists still constitute the largest single element in its membership. There are six categories of membership, the largest being the usual regular membership, which presently numbers over 14,000 members. Headquarters are at Northwestern University, 629 Noyes Street, Evanston, Illinois.[19]

AMERICAN FOLKLORE SOCIETY

This organization traces its ancestry across the Atlantic to Great Britain where in the 1840's an Englishman, William John Thoms, coined a new word, "folklore." According to Thoms and his compatriots it was just as necessary to preserve the folklore, i.e., stories, songs, superstitions, etc., of remote or changing modern civilizations as the material remains of older civilizations. Interest in such ideas gradually developed in Western

Europe and in the United States and, as a result, the American Folklore Society, for the study of folklore in general and in particular the collection and publication of American folklore, was organized at Cambridge, Massachusetts, January 4, 1888.

The main activity of the Society has always been the collection, publication, and preservation of original unpublished folklore material. This is principally accomplished by the production of its quarterly, *Journal of American Folklore,* which has appeared since 1888. Its pages contain articles on such varied subjects as voodoo worship, ballads, child sacrifices, and the literature and songs of the Negroes and the Indians. Included as Supplements to the *Journal* are the annual reports of the officers and committees of the Society. In 1894, after a decision to publish monographic material not suitable for the *Journal* was reached, the first volume of the *Memoirs* appeared. Since then they have appeared at irregular intervals and now number 51. Most of them deal with folklore outside of America in which it is hoped to find evidence as to the provenience of American folklore. The Society has also published 13 volumes in the *Bibliographical and Special Series.*

The Society has sponsored, wholly or partially, a number of interesting research projects. One, for example, shows the value of folklore research to the social sciences, particularly anthropology. This project was headed by Dr. Aurelio M. Espinosa and concerns the origins of the Br'er Rabbit-Tar-Baby story. By applying an analytic method to some 152 versions of the tale, made famous in the Uncle Remus tales of Joel Chandler Harris, Espinosa showed that it had made its way originally from India, to Spain and Portugal and thence to West Africa where a Spanish-African form evolved that was carried into our Southern states by slaves. Thus, the tale was not indigenous to the American Negroes, nor was it originally an African tale.

The first regular annual meeting of the Society was in Philadelphia in November of 1889. Since then two or three day meetings have been held toward the end of every year, usually in conjunction with other societies, such as the Modern Language Association of America or the American Anthropological Association, whose interests lie in the same general field. The meetings follow the normal pattern of official reports and the reading and discussion of papers dealing with various aspects of folklore.

Any person who is interested in the subject of folklore is eligible for regular membership. The Society also provides six other categories of membership: joint husband-wife, student, sustaining, institutional, life, and honorary. The latter includes distinguished foreign scholars. In addition, since World War II, the constitution has provided for the election of Fellows within the Society who have distinguished themselves by their work in the field of folklore.

During its earlier years the Society's membership was made up of professional and amateur elements. After the turn of the century, there was increasing professionalization in its ranks and officials estimate that nine-tenths of its membership now fall in the professional category.

As early as 1889 the Society was encouraging the establishment of local branches throughout the country, partly in order to stimulate the interest of members who lived in distant places, and partly for facilitating the study of the diverse folklore elements of the various regions. While the number of branches established and maintained has waxed and waned, including such diverse states as Massachusetts, North and South Carolina, Missouri, North Dakota, California, Canada, and Mexico, the total membership of the Society, from an original 250, has grown steadily to about 1,200 persons.[20] The office of the Society is at 110 Bennett Hall, University of Pennsylvania, Philadelphia 4, Pennsylvania.

AMERICAN PSYCHOLOGICAL ASSOCIATION

The organization of the American Psychological Association was to a large extent inspired by the activity of German scholars in the field. Although there is some doubt that a meeting actually took place, the official record shows that the date and founding place of the Association was Clark University, Worcester, Massachusetts, July 8, 1892.[21] In any event, G. Stanley Hall of that University is universally credited with being the midwife of the Association, and it was he who issued the invitation to six other men for the July 8th meeting. This group, composed primarily of experimental psychologists, constituted itself a governing council to be renewed by elections and decided to hold its first annual meeting at the University of Pennsylvania on December 27, 1892.

For the first 25 years of its existence the Association was plagued with the problem of what approach it should take to professional psychology. Attempts were made to control and standardize material and personnel in the field. Although some success, such as the creation of various standardized tests, was achieved in the former area, the latter was characterized by complete failure. Most conspicuous was the attempted certification by the Association of Consulting Psychologists. It appears that the group which could qualify under the standards set by the Association did not need or want such certification, whereas attempts to include those at a lower level, the so-called "psychotechnicians", was rejected by the Association. Although the matter was then dropped, it was to a large extent responsible for the emergence of various new and professionally oriented psychological organizations such as the American Association for Applied Psychology and the Society for the Psychological Study of Social Issues. These groups felt that the APA was neglecting the professional side of psychology, and it was not until the reorganization of 1946, led by Dr. Robert M. Yerkes, that they were merged as divisions into a new and united American Psychological Association. Significantly, the new Constitution added to the old statement, "The object of the APA shall be to advance psychology as a science," the new phrases, "as a profession, and as a means for promoting human welfare." The matter of licensing was subsequently considered by the new Association, and it was agreed that a separate, non-profit corporation be established for that purpose.

The divisions which were established by the 1946 reorganization play an important role in the APA. They are flexible in number and can be established or abolished as interest or lack of it develops. They have a large degree of autonomy within their own range of interest. They provide the most numerous representation on the Council of Representatives, chief governing body of the Association. Their most important function, however, is to hold the Association together in the face of its centrifugal tendencies. The merit of this plan is attested by the fact that the APA has continued to attract and hold a wide variety of psychological subgroups within its membership.

Annual meetings have always played an important role in Association activities. During its early years all papers presented to it were accepted and read at the meetings. In time, the increasing number of papers resulted in a shift from a two day meeting to ones lasting two or three times that long, and the institution of symposia and other devices to handle the increased load. Despite such changes, a culling of papers was forced and now only selected ones are presented.

The Association's interest in publication goes back to 1909. An unsuccessful attempt was made at that time to provide Association aid towards the publication of a privately owned journal. The following year a committee to consider the relationship of the Association to journals and publication was established. This committee included the editors of the privately owned psychological journals. After two decades and various changes in nomenclature and personnel, this committee made a report in 1922 which resulted in the acquisition by the Association of five journals including the *Psychological Review,* the *Psychological Bulletin,* the *Journal of Experimental Psychology,* the *Psychological Monographs,* and the *Psychological Index.* In 1926 the *Journal of Abnormal and Social*

Psychology was acquired through the gift of Morton Prince and in 1927, aided by a subvention from the Laura Spelman Rockefeller Memorial, *Psychological Abstracts* was established by the Association. Since that time the Association has sponsored several other journals: the *Journal of Consulting Psychology,* the *Journal of Comparative and Physiological Psychology, the Journal of Applied Psychology, Applied Psychology Monographs,* and the *American Psychologist.* The latter is a monthly providing general information about psychologists and psychological affairs. It came into being as a result of the reorganization of 1946 and is edited by an executive secretary whose full-time office was set up also at that time. This official, in addition to his editorial responsibilities, handles the administrative, financial, public relations, and similar matters for the Association.

Criteria for membership in the Association during its early years were not clearly defined. From an original 31 in 1892, however, the number being elected to membership had increased in 1906 to the point that the Association adopted certain research and occupational qualifications for membership. In 1925 an associate grade of membership, as distinguished from Fellows, was created. Fellows, henceforth, were required to have the doctoral degree and to have published or to have had extensive experience in the psychological field. Associate membership was extended to those with graduate training or experience in the field and devoting full time to professional or graduate work in psychology. Also, a category of life membership was set up.

These three categories of membership were unchanged by the 1946 reorganization, but a new group of affiliates, without membership privileges, was created and the divisions were given the right to set up additional classes of membership within their respective divisions. In 1958 a category of Members was established for those who had the doctors degree in psychology but were not fully qualified to be Fellows. Since 1946, when membership in the APA consisted of 1,083 Fellows and Life Members and 3,344 Associates, there has been an increase to about 2,300 Fellows and Life Members, 2,000 Associates and 14,600 Members.[22] National headquarters are at 1333 Sixteenth Street, N.W., Washington 6, D. C.

AMERICAN PHILOSOPHICAL ASSOCIATION

In the early years following the organization of the American Psychological Association (1892) a considerable divergence of interests between psychologists and philosophers asserted itself. If the subject matter of papers read at the annual meetings is to be taken as a criterion, quite as lively a curiosity existed in purely philosophical as in psychological questions.

Separate sessions for the philosophers was resorted to in 1898 but in 1901 a group of philosophers at Cornell issued a call for an independent organization and in November of that year, in New York, the American Philosophical Association was formed with 98 charter members. Another organization of philosophers, the Western Philosophical Association, had already been in existence since January 1, 1900, and somewhat later, still another, the Southern Philosophical Association, came into being. Shortly after their founding attempts were made to amalgamate the three, and after 1924, to include the newly organized Society for Philosophy on the Pacific Coast, into a truly American Philosophical Association. A complete union has never taken place, but in 1927 the original American, the Western, and the Pacific associations adopted a joint Constitution forming themselves into the American Philosophical Association, but retaining their individual entities as the Eastern, Western, and Pacific Divisions.

While each division controls all questions pertaining to membership, a certain uniformity prevails in that the regular members are almost entirely professors of philosophy in universities and colleges and the associate members are primarily graduate students in philosophy. The total membership is approximately 1,800 and most of the States of the Union are represented in it.

Through the years, the Association has had committees at work in such areas as International Cultural Cooperation, Bibliography of Philosophy, Philosophy in Education, and Advancing Original Work in Philosophy, and has made small awards and grants; its primary activity, however, has been the holding of meetings. Since 1902 the organization now known as the Eastern Division, but then calling itself the American Philosophical Association, has met annually during the last days of December, usually at the principal university cities in the East. Throughout the same period the Western Association has held similar meetings during the spring in the Middle West. Since 1924 the Pacific Division has met annually, usually during the Christmas holidays. Although in recent years there has been some talk of a meeting of the Association as a whole, nothing has come of this and the three divisions have continued to meet separately and at different times. A check of programs in recent years indicates, however, that many individuals attend the meetings of other divisions in addition to that of their home one. Occasionally the divisions meet jointly with other organizations, but the consensus appears to be that the most successful meetings are those attended by the philosophers alone.

None of the three divisions publishes a journal. The papers presented at meetings have been printed by private philosophical periodicals which are largely dependent upon the support and the contributions of the members of the Association. During the early years such papers of the Eastern and the Pacific divisions appeared annually in the *Philosophical Review*, published bi-monthly by a group of philosophers at Cornell University. The Western Division, during the first four years of its career as the Western Philosophical Association, also published papers and reports of its meetings in the *Review*, but since 1905 has utilized for this purpose the *Journal of Philosophy, Psychology, and Scientific Methods* (in 1921 re-named the *Journal of Philosophy*), a private fortnightly publication appearing in New York City.

Since the creation in 1927 of the covering American Philosophical Association a new plan has been followed. Under it, the Association publishes an annual volume, *Proceedings and Addresses,* containing the proceedings of the three divisions, the presidential addresses at their annual meetings, the annual report of the Board of Officers, various committee reports, and a combined list of members. Of this, the first volume appeared in 1928. Since the *Proceedings and Addresses* do not include other papers presented at the meetings, these are usually submitted by their authors to various philosophical journals, including the two mentioned above. The offices of the Secretary of the Association are presently situated at Washington University, St. Louis 5, Missouri.[23]

AMERICAN ANTHROPOLOGICAL ASSOCIATION

Prior to 1902 American anthropologists had no separate national organization. Contact among them was maintained by Section H (Anthropology) of the American Association for the Advancement of Science, by the publication of an independent quarterly journal known as the *American Anthropologist,* and by the existence of local bodies such as the Anthropological Society of Washington. At the turn of the century the advance in the extent and importance of the science and the inadequacy of the existing organizations for promoting and unifying it began to demonstrate the need for a separate national anthropological association. In 1901 and 1902, certain members of the American Ethnological Society of New York, the Anthropological Society of Washington, and Section H (Anthropology) of the American Association for the Advancement of Science, led by W. J. McGee and Franz Boas, met for the purpose of creating such an association, and in May of 1902 the American Anthropological Association was incorporated.[24]

The objects of the organization as defined in the Constitution are "to advance the science of anthropology in all its branches and to further the professional interest of American anthropologists."[25]

We have seen that the national Association was a partial outgrowth of the American Ethnological Society of New York and the Anthropological Society of Washington. After the formation of the national body these two local organizations and the Philadelphia Anthropological Society still retained their separate indentities and are active to this day. More in the nature of a branch of the parent society is the Central States Branch of the Association organized in 1923. The members of these local societies and the branch pay separate dues to their respective organizations.

The Association has appointed committees to investigate the teaching of anthropology in the United States; the status of anthropology in the Government institutions; prevention of vandalism in the ruins of the Southwest. It has gone on record regarding such diverse legislation as treatment of the American Indian, and in support of evolution.

The regular annual meetings of the Association are presently held one week before Thanksgiving. Previously they were often convened in conjunction with those of Section H of the American Association for the Advancement of Science. For the past several decades, however, they have been held from time to time with such societies as the American Folklore Society and the Linguistic Society of America. These meetings have been located in cities in all sections of the United States and the present policy is to have them held in the West one year out of three. The annual meetings follow the usual pattern of reports and papers with a symposium at the end.

There are six classes of membership in the Association. Members, open to any applicant; Fellows, possessing the requisite professional qualifications and approved by the Executive Board; foreign fellows, professional anthropologists in other countries; liaison fellows, persons active in other fields but interested in anthropology; associate fellows,[26] advanced students in anthropology; and institutional subscribers, such as libraries. The growth in membership of the Association has been a steady one. From the original 175 members in 1903, the number had climbed to approximately 1,000 in 1929. Today it is about 4,200.

The official organ of the American Anthropological Association is the *American Anthropologist*. First published in 1888 by the Anthropological Society of Washington, it was reorganized in 1898 and 1899 and in 1900 W. J. McGee and Franz Boas became its co-owners. Following the founding of the Association in 1902 the *American Anthropologist* became its official publication and it is presently published bimonthly. It contains articles on anthropology and allied subjects, reports of field work, book reviews, and discussion. From 1905 to the present the Association has intermittently published the *Memoirs* which included essays of the same type to be found in the *Anthropologist* but too long for inclusion there. The *News Bulletin* of the Association was established in 1947 and, following a change in title to *Bulletin* in 1953, was succeeded in 1960 by the *Fellow Newsletter*. The latter prints information of general interest to the profession, but not scholarly or research reports.[27]

The staff of the Association, headed by an Executive Secretary, carries on its work from offices located at 1530 P Street, N. W., Washington 5, D. C.

AMERICAN POLITICAL SCIENCE ASSOCIATION

This organization was the outgrowth of a 1902 movement for a national society to deal with comparative legislation. In 1903 at New Orleans, where members of the American Historical Association and the American Economic Association had gathered for a joint meeting, developing sentiment for a new organization with a much wider range of interest in political science resulted in the formation of the American Political Science Association. The original members of the new organization were largely members of one or both of the older Associations. A past-president of the Association said that, "In a way, therefore, the American Political Science Association is the god-child of the American Historical and the American Economic Association."[28] The three Associations have always had close and friendly relations and, early in the 1900's, a possible federation of the three was discussed but it did not materialize.

From its beginning the Association, through committee action, has made scientific studies and conducted other projects. Sometimes an effort is made to promote research in political science or to make the material for its study more available; sometimes a report on a matter of current interest is made; investigations of the teaching of political science in the secondary schools and colleges have been conducted; recently, a Congressional fellowship program, wherein those selected work directly with Congressmen or Congressional committees, was inaugurated. All of these projects are carried out under the aegis of Article Two of the Constitution which states that "it shall be the purpose of this Association to encourage the study of Political Science," but adds, as the concluding paragraph: "The Association as such will not assume a partisan position upon any question of practical politics, nor commit its members to any position thereupon."[29]

Annual meetings of the Association are held in the principal cities of the country. Prior to the 1940's these meetings were scheduled in December, often in conjunction with the American Historical or Economic Association; since that time they have been held during the first week in September. At the meetings, some half dozen sessions are devoted to a single subject, with discussion from the floor at the close of the session. It has been the policy of the Association to consider important political questions of current interest.

The *American Political Science Review* has appeared as a quarterly publication of the Association since November, 1906. The *Proceedings* were published separately until 1910, and as a supplement to the *Review* until 1917. They were discontinued at that time and the reports and business matters reported therein were incorporated as part of the information provided in the *Review*. From time to time, by ways of awards and prizes, the Association has sponsored the publication of books dealing with various aspects of political science.

Membership in the Association is open to all persons interested in the scientific study and discussion of government and international affairs. There are four classes of membership: Annual, Life, Family, and Student. The Association numbers about 7,000 persons.[30]

The organization's activities are carried out with the aid of a staff, supervised by an Executive Director, from a headquarters building at 1726 Massachusetts Avenue, N. W., Washington 6, D. C.

BIBLIOGRAPHICAL SOCIETY OF AMERICA

An outgrowth of the Bibliographical Society of Chicago, the Bibliographical Society of America was organized in 1904 in St. Louis. Its object is "to promote bibliographical research and to issue bibliographical publications."[31] At the time of organization most of its officers and members were librarians and members of the American Library Association. There has always been a close bond between the two organizations and a gradual understanding developed whereby the Society came to take over much of the bibliographical and research work of the Library Association.

In addition to providing a forum for the testing of newer bibliographical techniques, putting inquirers into touch with people who can answer their bibliographical questions, the Society has sponsored many outstanding bibliographical indices. It published the 28 volume *Bibliotheca Americana, A Dictionary of Books Relating to America,* and the second and third editions of *Incunabula in American Libraries.* At the present time it is supervising the publication of a ten-volume *Bibliography of American Literature* of which three have already been published. It also plans to publish, in the near future, a supplement to the *Census of Medieval and Renaissance Manuscripts* which will list the thousands of manuscripts which have been brought into the United States since 1940. The major continuous publication endeavor of the Society is the *Papers,* a quarterly journal which has appeared for over 50 years. These contain the papers read at the meetings and occasional longer works of especial interest to the members.

The Society holds two meetings a year, one in January and one in May or June. The former, during the last 20 years has usually been held in New York and the latter in other cities, principally along the Atlantic seaboard. The Constitution provides for and the Society is attempting to form branch or regional societies in other parts of the Union for members and other interested persons who find it difficult to attend these meetings.

Membership in the Society is open to all who are interested in bibliography and bibliographical research and, at the present time, numbers about 1,000 persons. The Society's offices are located at 47 East 60th Street, New York 22, N. Y.[32]

ASSOCIATION OF AMERICAN GEOGRAPHERS

The Association of American Geographers was preceded by two geographical societies that were and are very important in the field. They are the American Geographical Society of New York and the National Geographic Society.[33]

Many professional geographers felt, however, that these two societies did not supply the proper milieu as to membership, meetings, etc., for their profession. This feeling found expression in a paper presented by Professor William M. Davis at the 1903 St. Louis Meeting of the American Association for the Advancement of Science. Professor Davis was Chairman of Section E (Geology and Geography) at that meeting and, attributing much of the high educational esteem in which geology was held to the geologists' establishment of a learned society for their discipline, he urged the creation of a similar learned society for geographers. Subsequent events resulted in the formation of the Association of American Geographers in Philadelphia in 1904.

The Association of American Geographers was formed, therefore, to provide a national organization that would bring its members, particularly those in academic circles, into closer association and provide a forum for the exchange of views on geographical problems. Membership was limited by election to those persons who had done original work in some branch of geography and, consequently, the Association grew slowly from 48 in 1904 to about 275 in 1948. In the meantime, the American Society for Professional Geographers (ASPG), which had been established in Washington in 1943 during World War II, grew rapidly and by 1948 its membership totalled more than 1,000. Since the interests of the two organizations were similar and many prominent geographers were members of both organizations, it was natural that, in 1948, the two were merged into one, retaining the title of the older organization. Since the merger the Association has had a rapid growth in membership and today numbers about

2,000 persons. More than one-half of these members are college and university instructors or teachers in geography.

Prior to 1911, members published papers in various journals, especially the *Bulletin* of the American Geographical Society. At that time the Association's *Annals* was established but the American Geographical Society paid for its publication. In 1922 the Association became able to assume this financial obligation and at that time the *Annals* was changed to a quarterly. In addition to articles, this journal includes abstracts of papers and, since 1956, a special reviews section. In 1943 *The Professional Geographer* was established as the official publication of the ASPG. Upon the merger in 1948 it was continued as a publication of the Association to contain news of interest to members, short reviews, schedules of meetings, reports of committees, etc. In 1956 a *Monograph Series* was instituted, the first volume in the series being published in 1959.

Annual meetings of the Association have been held since 1904, usually in the Eastern section of the country but with occasional ones in the Far West, the South and Canada. They presently extend over a five-day period and, in addition to the reports of officers and committees, feature the presentation of technical papers by members.

In recent years the Association has placed less emphasis upon pedagogical problems and devoted more attention to geographical research. This trend has been accelerated by the creation of various research funds and prizes, such as the Wallace W. Atwood Research Fund. A small administrative staff, to assist in this and other activities, has offices at 1785 Massachusetts Avenue, N. W., Washington 6, D. C.[34]

AMERICAN SOCIOLOGICAL ASSOCIATION
(Formerly American Sociological Society)

The American Sociological Society was formed at the December, 1905 joint meetings of the American Historical, Economic and Political Science Associations which were being held in Baltimore, Maryland. Some 40 members of the three older organizations, led by Professor C. W. A. Veditz and including such prominent social scientists as Lester H. Ward, Charles A. Ellwood, William G. Sumner, Edward A. Ross, Walter F. Willcox, Albion W. Small, Charles H. Cooley and Franklin H. Giddings, created the American Sociological Society, and at that time, defined its aims as the encouragement of sociological research and discussion, and the promotion of intercourse between persons engaged in the scientific study of society.

While the Society has always considered publication and the holding of meetings and conferences its most important scientific activity, it influences sociological study through the medium of its standing committees. Through them it stimulates and coordinates teaching and research in various sociological areas, keeps up an abstract and bibliographical service in sociological literature, maintains professional standards, and cooperates with social scientists abroad.

Up until the 1940's the annual meetings of the Society were held during the last week in December, often in conjunction with the American Economic Association; since that time they have been set for the last week in August. The place of meeting has varied from cities of the East Coast to those of the Middle and Far West. During the first three decades of its lifetime, all of the activities of the meeting, save the reports of committees and the business session, were grouped around one central topic in sociology, such as "The Trend of Our Civilization," "The City," "The Problem of Democracy," etc. This topic was chosen in advance by the president and all papers and discussions conformed to it. Since this early period the programs at the meetings have been arranged by a program committee and the papers and discussions cover a wide variety of topics.

Up until 1936 the principal papers submitted at the meetings were published either in full or in abstract, along with business matters and the reports of committees, in the annual *Publication and Proceedings of the American Sociological Society*. The Society played an important part in the production of the bi-monthly *American Journal of Sociology,* published by the University of Chicago, under the guidance of an Advisory Council composed of the officers of the Society.

In 1936 the Society established an official bi-monthly, the *American Sociological Review,* which published material similar to that found in each of the older publications. In addition, in March, 1956 the quarterly *Sociometry* began publication under the Society's auspices.

Membership in the Society is divided into four broad categories: Fellows, Active, Associate, and Student Members. Fellows and Active membership is restricted to those persons who have a demonstrated professional interest in sociology and Associate membership is open to sociology students who are sponsored by a member. From the original membership of 40 in 1905 the Society grew to approximately 1,300 members in 1926 and now numbers about 6,600 members. Its administrative offices serve these members from a headquarters at New York University, New York 3, N. Y.[35]

COLLEGE ART ASSOCIATION OF AMERICA

The College Art Association of America was an outgrowth of various meetings in the early 1900's of the Western Drawing and Manual Training

Association, the Eastern Art Teacher's Association and the Eastern Manual Training Association. At these meetings college art instructors who were members of the three associations formed a committee which, in 1910, reported that art education at the college and university level was still in an experimental stage and that it had a dubious place in the college and university curriculum. The committee recommended "consideration of the question of the formation of a permanent organization of college art-workers."[36]

In May of 1912 the Western Association held its annual meeting in Cincinnati, and it was there, at the Cincinnati Art Museum in Eden Park, that the College Art Association of America was founded. The first annual meeting was held in Pittsburgh during the Christmas holidays the same year.

The stated purpose of the new organization was "the furtherance and promotion of the study and appreciation of art." Such study and promotion includes all types of art, in the past and present, and in all parts of the world. In furtherance of this objective, it has held annual meetings in all parts of the United States at which papers are read and discussed, information exchanged, and business conducted.

Since 1917, the Association has published annually the *Art Bulletin,* which contains authoritative articles about art and, since 1941, the *College Art Journal,* (as of January, 1961 the name was changed to *The Art Journal)* designed specifically for the collegiate art world. In the past decade the Association, in cooperation with the Archaeological Institute of America, has published a series of monographs in book form.

An early activity of the Association was its cooperation with the study conducted by Hiss and Fansler to determine the exact status of education in the fine arts in American colleges and universities.

One of its major recent accomplishments has been the assembling, for exhibit in Europe, South America, and the Near and Far East, of art treasures held by American colleges and universities, and of works of art produced by students in these institutions. These collections and tours were arranged as the result of a request from the United States Information Agency.

Membership in the Association, in one category or another, is open to all persons interested in art. Institutional membership is also extended. Total membership is approximately 3,000. A business office is located at 432 Park Avenue, South, New York 16, N. Y.[37]

HISTORY OF SCIENCE SOCIETY

Founded in 1924, the History of Science Society traces its origin to a general increase in interest in the historical aspects of science during World

War I and the troubled years following. Two of the foremost figures of
an interested group centering in the American Association for the Advancement of Science and the American Historical Association were Professor
Lynn Thorndike and Professor George Sarton, a Belgian scholar who had
devoted years of study to the relationship of history to science prior to
coming to this country and had founded the quarterly magazine *Isis* in
1913. Shortly after the founding of the new Society, *Isis* became its official
publishing medium.

The primary purpose of the Society is to promote the study of the
history of science. To this end it published the periodical *Isis,* which
contains articles, book reviews, and news of interest to its members and
an exhaustive annual bibliography of books and articles on the history of
science. The Society also holds annual meetings, usually in conjunction
with those of the American Historical Association or the American Association for the Advancement of Science.

The Society brings together in its membership persons of the widest
professional and business background, historians, government officials,
physicists, etc. Membership is open to all persons interested in the history
of science, and to libraries, museums, etc. At the present time there are
approximately 1,200, of which one third are institutions. The Secretary
of the Society is presently located at the University of California, Los
Angeles, California.[38]

LINGUISTIC SOCIETY OF AMERICA

This organization was founded in 1924. One of its founding fathers,
Leonard Bloomfield, in an article entitled, "Why a Linguistic Society,"
stated: "Students of Language do not need to ask *Why a linguistic society?*
but many laymen have asked this question. The answer, to be sure, lies
really in our work and in its results; but, for this very reason, it is desirable
that our motives be understood. The immediate answer is simple; of
course, we seek the possibility of meeting and knowing each other."
Emphasizing that "science of language does exist," Bloomfield declared
that "students of language feel as much need for a professional society as
do adherents of any other science."[39]

Linguistic specialists helped the United States to carry out the various
government language training programs that were so vital in World War
II. In the post-war years, with global industrial activity, the skills developed by members of this society have become of increasing importance
to industry as well as government. At the same time, with an ever in-

creasing school population, new techniques in English language instruction have been developed.

The Society has met annually since its beginnings, during the week between Christmas and New Year's. On occasion these meetings have beeen convened in conjunction with the annual meeting of the Modern Language Association of America. In addition, summer meetings are held in conjunction with the Linguistic Institute. The latter is a separate organization sponsored each summer by the Society and a host University for the study and teaching of linguistics by assembled scholars and students. The University of Michigan has often been host to the Linguistic Institute and in past years Indiana University, the University of North Carolina, the University of Texas, and other institutions have also acted as sponsors.

Another contribution of the Society in the field of linguistics, is its quarterly publication, *Language.* This journal has appeared since 1925 and various supplements to it have also been issued.

Membership in the Society is open to all persons interested in language and linguistics and to libraries, museums, etc. Total membership at the present time is approximately 2,500, of which about 800 are institutions. The Secretary's address is Box 7790, University Station, Austin 12, Texas.[40]

MEDIAEVAL ACADEMY OF AMERICA

This organization received its initial impulse as the result of the presidential address of Professor John M. Manly to the 1920 meeting of the Modern Language Association of America. Manly called for greater organization for research with more specialization regarding subject matter. One of the research groups resulting from these suggestions was one dealing with 'Mediaeval Latin Studies' and it was out of this group that the Mediaeval Academy, with a much broader purpose, evolved. This purpose, according to the by-laws, is "To conduct, encourage, promote and support research, publication and instruction in mediaeval records, literature, languages, arts, archaeology, history, philosophy, science, life and all other aspects of mediaeval civilization, by publications, by research and by such other means as may be desirable, and to hold property for such purpose."[41]

The Academy's primary contribution to scholarship has been its sponsorship of various publications. *Speculum,* a learned journal published since 1926, provides articles and book reviews of interest to members and others interested in the mediaeval period. The Academy has published some 70 volumes dealing with all facets of the Middle Ages. At present some of its major projects in this area include a new and enlarged edition of Charles Gross's *Sources and Literature of English History from the Earliest Times to About 1845,* a revision of Paetow's classic *Guide to the Study of Medieval History,* and an edition of the *Commentaries of Averroes on the Works of Aristotle,* of which seven volumes have been published so far.

The Haskins Medal, a gold medal award established in 1939 by the Academy, is awarded annually for an outstanding book in the mediaeval field. It is an award that is highly prized and has been a definite stimulus for research in the mediaeval areas of study.

Although the Academy holds an annual meeting in the spring, the attendance has always been relatively small (125-150). The meetings have been held in various sections of the United States and in Canada, but the greater number have been called in the Eastern section of the United States.

Membership in the Academy is a combination of closed and open membership. The Fellows and Corresponding Fellows, distinguished resident and foreign mediaevalists respectively, are limited to 50 in each category and are elected by the existing Fellows. The other categories of membership are open to all persons interested in mediaeval studies. At the present time there are about 1,600 members in all categories. The Executive Secretary's offices are at 1430 Massachusetts Avenue, Cambridge 38, Massachusetts.[42]

AMERICAN MUSICOLOGICAL SOCIETY

At the 1929 annual meeting of the American Council of Learned Societies, its Executive Committee, in response to the stated view that "the history and science of music constitutes an important branch of learning," was empowered "to appoint a standing committee on musicology and to take such other measures as may be calculated to promote research and education in that field." This standing committee was appointed and its members were very active in the musicological field. Later, several members of this committee advanced the view that a separate organization was needed. The American Musicological Society was subsequently founded in 1934.[43]

The stated purpose of the American Musicological Society is "the advancement of research in the various fields of music as a branch of learning and scholarship." It is the only organization in the United States with a continuing interest in music as a branch of knowledge or as a field for scholarly research as differentiated from the composition or performance of music.

One of the Society's outstanding activities has been its encouragement of and assistance in the publication of works which were not commercially feasible for publication. Volumes of music by the fifteenth century composers Ockeghem and Dufay are examples of the results of this endeavor. Another aspect of the Society's activities is its periodical publication. From 1936 to 1941 it published annually *Papers of the American Musicological Society,* and from 1936 to 1948, *Bulletin of the American Musicological Society.* Since 1948 it has published regularly three issues each year of the *Journal of the American Musicological Society.*

Since the establishment of the Society, musicology in the United States has grown in strength and maturity. Courses and departments of instruction in musicology have increased in number and in quality. American trained scholars and teachers have come to predominate in a field formerly staffed largely by the European trained. Intellectual stimulation of this corps of American musicologists has been advanced through the Society's chapter and national meetings. At the present time 13 chapters of the Society are located all over the country. Each of these holds periodic meetings for discussion and the reading of papers. Annual meetings for the entire membership have been held in various cities from coast to coast.

Membership is open to all who are interested in the purposes for which the Society was founded and who have been nominated by another member. At the present time membership totals approximately 1,200. This figure includes regular members, student members, and institutional subscribers to the *Journal.*[44] The Secretary of the Society is presently located at the University of Michigan, Ann Arbor, Michigan.

SOCIETY OF ARCHITECTURAL HISTORIANS

Founded at Harvard University, this organization has been in existence since 1940.

For several years in the late 1930's a group of teachers, primarily of architectural history from schools of architecture, were attracted to the summer sessions of Harvard University by the classes conducted by Professor Kenneth John Conant. This was the only center in the country at that time where such instruction could be obtained on a schedule available to active teachers. The outstanding quality of Dr. Conant's lectures encouraged the coalescing of a close-knit group which gradually developed the opinion that a more formal organization should be established to promote the study of architectural history in a systematic manner.

Previous to this time formal affiliation for those concerned with architectural history had been confined, on the one hand, to the American Institute of Architects or, on the other hand, to the College Art Association. The first was rightly dominated by the practicing architects. The second was controlled by art historians and artists who tolerated architecture only as a peripheral field. Also, the professional journals of architecture were reluctant to accept historical articles and *The Art Bulletin,* published by the College Art Association, rarely accepted such articles. Thus, the need for a society devoted to architectural history became increasingly apparent. This situation, moreover, coincided with an expansion of interest in the field, marked and stimulated by an increase in course offerings in the subject and the gradual recognition that the field formed a unique area of intellectual and cultural import.

During the summers of 1939 and 1940 at Harvard many of Dr. Conant's students met informally and discussed the situation. In August, 1940, the group decided to organize as a formal organization, the American Society of Architectural Historians. The name was subsequently changed to its present one, the Society of Architectural Historians, in 1945. In January, 1941, the first issue of the tri-annual mimeographed *Journal of the Society of Architectural Historians* appeared and was distributed gratis to approximately 125 prospective members. In 1947 the *Journal* attained its quarterly schedule and its printed format in 1950. The 20 volumes which have appeared contain articles and other features which have won wide recognition for their interest and value.

Since 1949, the Society has made an annual award for the most distinguished work of scholarship in the history of architecture published by an American scholar during the preceding year and, since 1956, this award has included the presentation of the Alice Davis Hitchcock Medal.

Since 1950 the Society has organized summer field trips to regions containing significant architectural monuments. These tours have become increasingly popular and are usually sold out long in advance. In 1959, a special field trip to Dublin, Ireland, was very successful, and a similar 1960 trip to see Palladio's work in and around Vicenza, Italy, was completely filled eight months in advance.

Because of the stimulus of association with fellow scholars, members have played an important role in studying and publishing topics drawn from their own regions and communities. These studies have served as an important means of bringing many little-known, but significant works to the attention of a large body of scholars and recognition of these works by a widespread group emphasizes their importance to the local audience. Many members have been active in projects to preserve significant local, regional and national monuments.

From the first the Society has welcomed as members, not only architects and professional scholars, but also laymen interested in the field. While the majority are professionals, it has long been evident that many of the amateurs grow to serious status. Thus, the missionary role of the Society fulfills an important function in the promotion of architectural history. In addition to the normal active and student categories of membership, the Society also includes life, patron, contributing, institutional, sustaining institutional, and corporate memberships with proportionately larger dues. At the present time there are some 1,400 members.[45] The offices of the Secretary of the Society are presently located at the University of Pittsburgh, Pittsburgh, Pennsylvania.

ASSOCIATION FOR ASIAN STUDIES

The Far Eastern Association, the predecessor organization of the Association for Asian Studies, Inc., was organized on June 9, 1941, for the primary purpose of publishing *The Far Eastern Quarterly*. It was the result of the interest and drive of a small group of scholars concerned with the Far East, particularly Japan and China, who felt that the existing means of publication were not sufficient for their area of interest. The first issue of the *Quarterly* appeared in November, 1941, on the eve of World War II.

The Association was active in aiding the war effort and maintained publication of *The Far Eastern Quarterly* throughout the war. For several years after the war, leaders in the Association, the American Council of Learned Societies, and other interested persons, discussed the possibility of changing the Association to a learned society with expanded membership, which could sponsor and engage in other activities of interest. At this point, the Committee on Far Eastern Studies of the American Council of Learned Societies, as the result of a conference for all interested parties on January 3, 1948, proposed that the possibility be implemented; thereupon, a small committee was appointed to arrange for an organizational meeting. On April 2, 1948, at a meeting at Columbia University attended by about 200 persons, the Constitution was revised so as to provide for officers, membership, publications, meetings, i. e., the usual organizational structure of a learned society. The original name, Far Eastern Association, was retained and the Association continued to operate under this Constitution until 1956.

By the latter date, although the majority of the members of the Association continued to be mainly interested in Japan, China, and Southeast Asia, there was a surge of interest within and without the Association in the history and culture of South Asia. Also, there was talk of the need for a separate society to concern itself with that area. A meeting of these persons with the governing body of the Association resulted, however, in a decision that it would be for the best interest of all concerned if the

Association were to simply extend its range of interest to include South Asia. In 1956 and 1957 the necessary constitutional revisions were made to reflect this broadening of scope, including, significantly, the changing of the name of the Association to its present Association for Asian Studies, Inc.; the *Quarterly,* correspondingly, being changed to the *Journal of Asian Studies.*

Since its founding the overall achievement of the Association has been its relatively successful attempt to make Americans realize the importance to us of the Far East in the context of our present world position. It rendered material aid in the provision of language and area specialists during the initial stages of combat in World War II and also in the Korean emergency.

Some nine committees have been established by the Association to carry out its objective of promoting interest in and scholarly study of Asia. Among them, the Committee on Chinese Thought and the South Asia Committee have been particularly active. Libraries in the United States have been helped by the establishment of the Committees on American Library Resources on the Far East and Southern Asia. The Association has also administered a series of lectures on Burmese culture, known as the U Nu Lectures.

In addition to the *Journal of Asian Studies,* the Association in 1949 established a monograph series which has presented ten scholarly studies by members of the Association. In 1955 a *Newsletter* was founded and in 1955 an annual *Bibliography* was initiated. It is interesting to note, regarding publications, that non-member subscriptions—particularly foreign subscribers—bulk larger in the Association's subscription list than is ordinarily the case among learned journals, ranging in recent years from 40 to 49 per cent of the total.

The total membership in the Association, of which about 50 per cent has always been academicians, has climbed from an initial 600 in 1948 to approximately 1,200; 1,050 domestic and 150 foreign. Out of the domestic membership over 50 per cent has always been located in the region in and around Boston, New York and Washington, D. C. with the Chicago and Pacific Coast area accounting for the overwhelming majority of the remainder. The Southern and Rocky Mountain areas have few members. Reflecting this loci of membership, the annual meetings of the Association, held since 1948, have usually been convened in the major cities of the Northeast.

In addition to regular membership, which also included students, the Association offers membership in the following categories: patron, life, supporting, associate, and honorary, over ninety percent of the total membership falling in the regular category.[46] The Secretary's office is presently located on the campus of the University of Michigan, Ann Arbor, Michigan.

AMERICAN SOCIETY FOR AESTHETICS

Aesthetics, both as a research branch of philosophy and as a related field of study for various arts, was a recognized field of study in pre-World I Europe. A society and *Journal of Aesthetics* in Germany had been active since 1906 under the leadership of the late Max Dessoir. Despite excellent books on the subject by George Santayana, John Dewey and others in the United States, aesthetics did not achieve much stature in this country until the organization of the American Society for Aesthetics on April 25, 1942.

The Society came into being at the Catholic University of America in Washington, D. C., largely at the instigation of Dr. Felix M. Gatz, head of the Department of Art and Music at the University of Scranton. The stated purpose of the Society was "to promote study, research, discussion, and publication in aesthetics. The term 'aesthetics' shall in this connection be understood to include all studies of art and related types of experience from a philosophical, psychological, scientific, historical, critical, or educational point of view. The term 'art' shall be understood to include all the arts."

One of the most important achievements of the Society has been the bringing together of several previously scattered groups of persons interested in the philosophical approach to the arts. For example, the American Psychological Association, the College Art Association, and the Modern Language Association of America had all held sectional meetings on aesthetics from time to time. Persons attending such meetings, however, lacked, to a considerable degree, the mutual contact which was needed in the broad approach that is deemed imperative for the solution of aesthetic problems. Such contact was facilitated by the organization of the Society and the regional and annual meetings which it has sponsored in all sections of the United States.

Publications sponsored by the Society have also been a boon to those in the field of aesthetics. A *Journal of Aesthetics* had been published at irregular intervals from 1941 to 1945. On the latter date, the official quarterly *Journal of Aesthetics and Art Criticism* was established on a sound basis and has provided a publication medium for research which previously had an extremely limited outlet, i. e., the philosophical periodicals were loath to publish articles with much specific reference to art while the art periodicals avoided articles of a philosophical or theoretical nature. In addition to periodical publication, the Society has aided in the compilation of bibliographies and the translation into English of important German works in the field of aesthetics.

Membership in the Society is open to all persons interested in furthering the study, discussion and publication of aesthetics. Within the general membership there are various regional groups which are remitted a certain percentage of the annual dues paid by the members of such groups. At the present time the Society's membership totals approximately 700.[47] Its Secretary's office is presently housed at the Cleveland Museum of Art, Cleveland 6, Ohio.

METAPHYSICAL SOCIETY OF AMERICA

The Metaphysical Society of America was founded by a Professor of Philosophy, Paul Weiss, at Yale University in March, 1950, at New Haven, Connecticut. Professor Weiss had been disturbed by "the growing neglect of important problems, the proliferation of small groups occupying themselves solely with limited, special issues, and the tendency of philosophers to split themselves up into associations on the basis of religion, doctrine or region." He called for "the formation of a society whose membership would be nationwide, which transcended religious and racial boundaries, and which ignored professional distinctions, in order to devote itself to the intensive pursuit of those questions which underly all others, and which have perplexed mankind from the beginning of its career of reflective thinking and intelligent action."

A few years before he founded the Society, Professor Weiss established the *Review of Metaphysics,* a quarterly journal which has "close, historical, but informal ties" with the Society and provides a medium of publication for its members and prints the yearly presidential address.

The Society has held annual meetings since its beginnings, usually in an Eastern or Midwestern university. Membership has grown in ten years from an initial 60 to approximately 500 persons. Its Secretary is presently located at Haverford College, Haverford, Pennsylvania.[48]

AMERICAN STUDIES ASSOCIATION

Founded in 1950, the American Studies Association was chartered in 1951 to provide an organization whereby American culture and civilization could be studied as an entity rather than from the viewpoint of a single discipline. Membership is open to all who are interested in this approach and it numbers approximately 1,400 persons.

The Association maintains a national office to serve 18 regional chapters all over the United States. All of the members are automatically enrolled in them. These chapters are autonomous units which have their own officers, hold meetings and discussions, and conduct other functions.

The Association holds joint meetings with many other organizations such as the Modern Language Association of America and the American Historical Association, and it sponsors occasional national conferences on the various aspects of American civilization. The international aspects of the study of American civilization are of increasing concern to the Association. It has arranged for meetings and conferences of American Studies scholars from the United States and abroad and has established and maintains contact with such organizations abroad as the European Association for American Studies, the British Association for American Studies, the German Society for American Studies, and the Japanese Society for American Studies.

Other of its activities include studies of American civilization courses in our colleges and universities and the publication of the *American Quarterly,* presenting articles and book reviews on American culture, and *American Studies,* a newsletter reporting on chapter activities and news items of interest to the members.[49] Headquarters of the Association are located at College Hall, University of Pennsylvania, Philadelphia 4, Pennsylvania.

RENAISSANCE SOCIETY OF AMERICA

American interest in the Renaissance period flourished increasingly after World War I as study materials on this span of history flowed into our libraries. It was not until the 1930's, however, that the "need for a synthesis of departmental researches," which the mediaevalists felt ten or twenty years earlier, developed. As the result of discussion as to the need for increased and broader studies of the Renaissance at meetings of other learned societies, particularly the Modern Language Association of America, a conference of interested scholars from varied disciplines was sponsored and financed by the American Council of Learned Societies. Members of this conference submitted a report to the ACLS which recommended the creation, within the ACLS, of a Committee on Renaissance Studies. Such a Committee was subsequently organized in 1938. Although this Committee engaged in various studies and surveys of research in the Renaissance period, its most noteworthy accomplishment was the establishment of various regional conferences which have been active to the present day.

Following a brief lapse during World War II, the ACLS Committee resumed its activities and, in 1948, it was instrumental in establishing the *Renaissance News.* As a result of a change in ACLS policy, however, this Committee was terminated in 1952. Prior to its demise, the Committee voted to organize a new, unaffiliated American Committee on Renaissance Studies (ACRS) to consider the future.

On January 30, 1954, as the result of previous meetings and conferences called by the ACRS, a Renaissance Society of America was organized at Columbia University for the purpose of "the advancement of learning in the field of Renaissance studies, and especially the promotion of interchanges among the various fields of specialization, such as art, architecture, bibliography and the book arts, the classical and modern literature, history, music, medicine, law, philosophy, religion and theology, the sciences and any other field of learning which can deepen or broaden understanding of the Renaissance period."

In the furtherance of this stated purpose special attention is called in the constitution to the establishment of local and regional groups and to cooperation and affiliation with foreign and international bodies with mutual interests.[50] In addition to adopting the constitution and electing officers, the new Society voted to assume publication of *Renaissance News,* a quarterly that has provided a medium for publication of short articles, book reviews and notices, news and reports of the annual meetings of the Advisory Council and the meetings of the Regional Conferences. Longer articles are published by the Society in its *Studies in the Renaissance.*

The Society does not hold general meetings for its members. It is believed that the regional conferences, convened annually in all sections of the country, are of more value and that a general meeting of all members would make inroads on the attendance at such conferences. An Advisory Committee, numbering approximately 45, composed of the executive officers, representatives from the regional groups, and other representatives from various disciplines elected from among the members by mail, does meet annually to elect officers and advise on policy.

Membership in the Renaissance Society of America is open to all who are interested in Renaissance study. There are four categories of membership, including institutional, and the total membership is approximately 2,000.[51] The secretary's office is presently located at Columbia University, New York, New York.

PART TWO

NATURAL SCIENCE SOCIETIES

AMERICAN CHEMICAL SOCIETY

This organization was founded in 1876. Prior to that time and coincidentally with a similar development abroad, various local chemical societies had been formed in New York and other cities during the late eighteenth and early nineteenth centuries.

Some discussion as to the desirability of forming a truly national chemical society took place at the Priestley Centennial Celebration at Northumberland, Pennsylvania in 1874. Action was postponed, however, because of establishment in the preceding year of a sub-section, devoted solely to chemistry, within the framework of the American Association for the Advancement of Science.[52] By 1881 the membership of this sub-section had grown to such dimensions that it was made a full section, one of three in existence at that time.

In the meantime, the American Chemical Society had been established in New York City in 1876. Although the Society had been founded as a national one and although it did have members outside the New York area, it was primarily local in character and outlook. Some of the leaders were aware of this fact and began to remedy it by holding annual meetings outside New York City. Local sections of the Society began to be formed where these meetings were held and finally, at a meeting in Washington, D. C. in 1891, delegates of these sections and officers of the parent organization decided that a reorganization, wherein all should unite as local sections of a national society, should be effected. After several meetings this plan was adopted. The reorganized Society thus began operations in 1892 with sections in New York, Rhode Island, Cincinnati and in 1893, Washington, D. C.

The name and New York charter of the American Chemical Society were retained until 1937 when the U. S. 75th Congress gave it a national charter.

Since the Society was independent of and could not consolidate or merge with Section C of the American Association for the Advancement of Science, it was arranged that the two groups would hold joint annual meetings at the time the Association met. This arrangement proved satisfactory until 1912 when the difficulty of finding suitable accommodations for the members of the two groups and dissatisfaction on the part of members of the Society with the time of meeting of the Association caused a discontinuance of the arrangement.

Since its founding the American Chemical Society has stimulated interest in the field of chemistry by the creation or administration of 25 awards and medals in various areas of chemistry. Several awards and annual lectures in chemistry have been established by sections and divisions of the Society. Prize essay contests in chemistry have been held under its auspices and chemistry books of interest to the general reader have been bought and distributed by the Society to various libraries. World Wars I and II saw the

Society offering its services to the government in various consultative capacities. It was due in large part to the activities of the Society that the Chemical Warfare Service was established, as a unit of the Army, and in recognition the Service adopted the Society's colors, cobalt blue and gold, as its own.

General meetings of the Society, held semi-annually since 1890, usually take place in the spring and fall. They have been convened in various parts of the United States. Society business is transacted, members form contacts with one another, and scientific papers and demonstrations are presented at the meetings. Attendance has increased year by year and registrations of 10,000 persons or more are now common.

Publication by the American Chemical Society has been a primary accomplishment. The foundation of its present day huge publishing program was the *Journal of the American Chemical Society*. Under its present name and ownership this publication dates from 1879, when it succeeded the *Proceedings of the American Chemical Society* which for a time had appeared as a section of a privately owned publication that failed in 1877. In the reorganization of 1891-92, Dr. Edward Hart merged his own *Journal of Analytical and Applied Chemistry,* with the *Journal of the American Chemical Society,* and assumed the editorship of the merged *Journal,* a post he held until 1901. The 1893 volume was the first of the merged *Journal* and it has been published continually since that date. Since this original venture the Society has issued 14 other journals in various specialized areas of chemistry; a weekly magazine *Chemical and Engineering News; Chemical Abstracts;* and a large number of monographs.

Membership in the Society has expanded to nearly 100,000 persons, making it the largest U. S. learned society. Membership, either Senior or Junior Grade, is open to all persons with an adequate background of education and experience in chemistry, chemical engineering, or a closely related field.

Two of the principal reasons for the growth in membership of the American Chemical Society appear to be that the national organization has been able to provide its 163 local sections, scattered all over the United States and its dependencies, with a feeling of oneness and solidarity. Of equal importance, the Society has successfully bridged the chasm that traditionally divides the pure and applied chemical scientists in other countries. The latter accomplishment has been attributed "to the wise foresight of President Bogert, who in 1909, clearly foresaw that the Society was likely to disintegrate unless some method was devised by which specialists in various branches of chemistry might gather together in essentially autonomous meetings. Accordingly, he inaugurated the divisional system, establishing first the Division of Industrial and Engineering Chemistry, followed gradually by others. . . . The divisions are professional groups organized from members of the Society and authorized by the Council to stimulate and develop the growth of the special activity assigned to them. They elect their own officers; they have the right to make by-laws for their own government . . . they may collect funds to be expended for their own purposes, and have the entire control and management of such funds. Their chairmen are Vice-Presidents of the Society and ex-officio members of the Council."[53]

In President Bogert's day there were 17 divisions within the American Chemical Society; today there are 23.[54]

Since 1912 the Society has maintained an office in Washington, D. C. Its central office is now situated there in a recently completed eight story, three million dollar building at 1155 Sixteenth Street, N.W.

AMERICAN PHYSIOLOGICAL SOCIETY

The American Physiological Society is the oldest of the biological-medical societies and the one from which a number of other societies (including the American Society of Biological Chemists, and the Society for Pharmacology and Experimental Therapeutics) were formed.

The study of physiology as a distinct discipline similar to chemistry or physics did not occur in the United States until the latter part of the 1870's. This development at that time was due to the influence of scholars returning from European study who located at various medical centers in the United States. Foremost among this group, and taking the lead in the organization of the American Physiological Society, were Drs. S. Weir Mitchell of the Jefferson Medical College, Philadelphia; Henry P. Bowditch of the Harvard Medical School, and Henry N. Martin of Johns Hopkins University. Acting as a committee, these three sent out the invitations calling for a meeting, on December 30, 1887, of persons interested in the formation of a physiological society. The meeting was held at the Physiological Laboratory of the College of Physicians and Surgeons in New York City and resulted in the formation of the Society.

The idea for the founding of the Society appears to have originated with Mitchell, but there is no doubt that he discussed the plan with Bowditch, Martin and other interested scientists. Twenty-eight persons constituted the original membership and it included some of the most distinguished names in American biological and medical science. Dr. Bowditch was elected the first President of the Society; he served six annual terms in that office. The practice of retaining officers for relatively long periods was continued by the Society until shortly after the turn of the century when an enlarged and diffused membership brought about a change in policy whereby officers were continued in office for one or two years.

Since its founding one of the major scientific achievements of the Society has been the raising of standards of teaching and research in physiology. It has established and administered prizes and fellowships for work in physiology and, from time to time, has appropriated sums towards the defraying of the costs of national and international meetings and towards the erection of memorials to prominent scientists. The Society in 1913 was the prime mover in the establishment of the Federation of American Societies for Experimental Biology, and the Society's administrative offices are now housed in the Federation's building in Washington, D. C.[55]

One of the purposes in the founding of the Society was the encouragement and facilitation of professional intercourse among its members. Annual meetings, which have been held continuously since its founding, have helped to served this purpose. They have usually been scheduled for the larger cities of the Eastern United States with a university playing host. Prior to 1925 the meetings were convened during the last week in December and lasted from one to three days. Since that time they have normally been held in the spring and take up an entire week. The reason for this change in the time and length of the annual meetings has been the desire to hold meetings in conjunction with member societies of the Federation and the great increase in the number and variety of papers to be presented on the programs. In 1955 three-day fall meetings of the Society were inaugurated and have been held annually at various universities.

The Society, during the first 50 years of its existence, restricted the program to expositions of research on specific topics. Since that time a limited number of round-table and conference type sessions have been used. Attendance at the meetings is usually about 40 per cent of the total membership and always includes a sizeable number of non-members as well.

The Society's need for a learned journal was recognized early in its history. A Committee to consider the establishment of such a publication was established in 1894. The *American Journal of Physiology,* first issued in January, 1898, was primarily the result of the efforts of one member of the Committee, Dr. W. T. Porter of the Harvard Medical School. He agreed to assume the financial and editorial obligations of the *Journal* if it were issued under the Society's auspices. The *Journal* was published under his supervision until 1914 when other duties made it too much of a burden for him. He informed the Society of his decision to relinquish responsibilities in connection with the *Journal* and offered to present the Society with his copyright. This generous offer was accepted and the Society at that time assumed control of the publication. The *Journal* was established with the intention that it be a monthly publication and it has been except for the very early years and a short while during both world wars when there were not enough acceptable articles to warrant publication.

In 1921 the publication of *Physiological Reviews* was inaugurated as a quarterly review of progress in physiological subjects. In 1939 the *Annual Review of Physiology* was established. Both of these journals are published today, as well as the bimonthly *Journal of Applied Physiology*, launched in 1948 and the *Physiologist,* established in 1957. The latter is a medium for general information about physiology and physiologists as well as news about the Society.

Active membership in the American Physiological Society is contingent upon proposal by two members and nomination by the governing Council. Candidates are balloted for at the last session of the annual business meeting. Since membership has always been honorific, the growth in members has been slow but steady, and today there are about 2,000 members, 161 of whom are women. Honorary membership, for foreign physiologists, has been afforded relatively few. During the first 25 years of its existence 10 such members were elected; today they number 16. In 1958 the Society established an associate membership for advanced graduate students and others not meeting the qualifications for active membership.[56] Administrative offices are located at 9650 Wisconsin Avenue, N.W., Washington 14, D. C.

AMERICAN ASSOCIATION OF ANATOMISTS

Research in anatomy, as in the other medical sciences, was not well developed in the United States during the first part of the nineteenth century. Although the older universities always had a few competent anatomists, the spread of proprietary medical schools discouraged the growth of research laboratories and left the teaching of anatomy largely to practical surgeons. About 1870, however, a reform of medical education began, which was speeded up around the turn of the century by the American Medical Association and in 1910 by the celebrated report of Abraham Flexner on the state of the medical schools of the United States. In this reform, the American Association of Anatomists played an important part by centralizing and building up research and teaching in the anatomical sciences.

The Association, until 1908 called Association of American Anatomists, was organized by a group of anatomists attending a Congress of American Physicians and Surgeons which was being held on September 17, 1888 at Georgetown University, Washington, D. C. Until 1906 the Association and the Congress were affiliated.

The original organizers were mostly surgeons and practical teachers without great experience in research, but interested in improving teaching as part of the reform movement. Before long, however, the Association was strengthened by a number of young men trained in Europe, who brought the spirit of research into the American school and aimed to make anatomy a scientific discipline as well as an aid to medical and surgical practice.

One of the achievements of the Association in carrying out its stated purpose was to broaden the scope of anatomy by encouraging its members to conduct research in cytology, genetics, hematology and numerous other fields having a morphological basis. Many of the leaders in this development have occupied prominent positions in the Association. Joseph Leidy, one of the outstanding scientists of his day and Professor of Anatomy at the University of Pennsylvania, was the first President of the Association. Franklin P. Mall of Johns Hopkins University, who replaced long lectures and demonstrations on anatomy with guided dissections, Charles S. Minot of Harvard University, renowned for his work in embryology, and many others of equal stature have served as presidents of the Association.

These leaders took an active part in organizing the Wistar Institute of Anatomy and Biology in Philadelphia, which during the first half of the twentieth century was a center of the new spirit in anatomy. [57] Founded in the first decades of the nineteenth century by Caspar Wistar of the University of Pennsylvania the Institute was until the 1890's primarily a museum of anatomical specimens. At that time, Professor Wistar's grand-nephew, General Isaac Jones Wistar, set up endowments, eventually totalling over $3,000,000, which provided the means for an expanded range of activities, including the establishment of research laboratories. Of the ten members of an Advisory Board organized for the Institute in 1905 it is significant that eight were anatomists.

The Wistar Institute has played an important role in the publications of the Association. The *American Journal of Anatomy* and the *Anatomical Record*, which began publication in 1901 and 1906 respectively, were founded by members of the Association to provide information about anatomists and present their research findings. These journals were initially published under the auspices of the Anatomical Journal Trust, a holding organization with three anatomists acting as trustees. In 1908 the two journals were leased to the Institute and in 1920 the trustees outrightly conveyed them to the Institute. The Trust was continued as a Memorial to Professor Minot, however, and was not finally wound up until 1948 when its funds were granted to the Association. Since 1908, therefore, the Wistar Institute has supported the Association's work by providing media for the publication of American anatomical research.

Control of scientific policy and choice of editors, however, has always resided in the Association. The arrangement has been beneficial to the latter by relieving the research men of the financial and routine editorial burdens associated with publication.

From its founding until 1919, the Association usually had its annual meetings during the last week in December. At that time they were shifted to March or April. The meetings have been held in all sections of the country with a medical school, research institute, or university playing host. They are normally three-day affairs and include the usual presentation of papers and demonstrations, transaction of business, including election of officers, and social intercourse among the members. Attendance at these meetings in the past few years has numbered about 1,000 persons.

Membership in the Association is open to persons working in anatomical or cognate sciences who possess the M.D. or Ph.D. or their equivalent and who have published on an anatomical subject. The policy of electing to membership persons distinguished in a cognate field has been followed from the beginning; such members include surgeons, pathologists, zoologists, physiologists, anthropologists, and even one artist. Honorary members from abroad have been from time to time included. Because of its selective policy growth has been slow but steady and presently numbers approximately 1,300 members.[58] The Association's Secretary conducts its business from an office at the School of Medicine, University of Pennsylvania, Philadelphia, Pennsylvania.

AMERICAN MATHEMATICAL SOCIETY

Prior to the founding of Johns Hopkins University in 1876 there was very little study, research, or writing in abstract mathematics in the United States. At that time the English mathematician Professor J. J. Sylvester began teaching at Hopkins, and his students, plus those who had begun to study at the German universities, provided a nucleus of trained mathematicians which resulted in this country in increased interest in the subject and in the establishment of such mathematical journals as the *American Journal of Mathematics* and the *Annals of Mathematics*.[59] It is against this background that, in 1888, six members of the mathematics department at Columbia University, led by a young mathematics instructor, Dr. Thomas S. Fiske, organized the New York Mathematical Society. By 1890 the members, who had increased to 22, decided that they wished to publish a journal which would be devoted to critical articles and reviews and provide news of mathematical interest. In order to accomplish this it became obvious that it would be necessary to broaden and increase the membership in order to sustain the proposed publication. Circular letters were sent to mathematicians in other sections of the country outlining the proposal and inviting them to join the Society, with the result that membership jumped to 174 in 1891, and the first number of the monthly *Bulletin, American Mathematical Society,* appeared at that time. By 1894 membership had increased to such an extent, and on a nationwide basis, that the name of the Society was changed to its present American Mathematical Society.[60]

In 1900 the Society began publication of the bimonthly *Transactions* containing mathematical articles presented at its meetings; in 1940 *Mathematical Reviews,* a review journal which is international in its circulation and coverage; and in 1950, the *Proceedings.* The latter journal contains material of a business and news nature that formerly appeared in the *Bulletin.* The Society has recently engaged in an extensive translation program of foreign mathematical books and articles, particularly Russian, and has also, from time to time, sponsored the publication of books, special surveys, memoirs, reviews and similar material.[61]

Throughout its history the Society has been primarily interested in pure research and writing in mathematics, with the teaching of mathematics a subsidiary interest. The reverse of this is true of its sister society, the Mathematical Association of America. In furtherance of its stated purpose, "The encouragement and maintenance of an active interest in mathematical research," the Society has, through the years, been the recipient of nine different funds. Prizes and other awards made from these funds have been an incentive to mathematical research.

Recent activities of the Society include the coordination and conducting of summer mathematical institutes; maintenance of a national register of mathematicians; and the translation of Russian mathematical articles. An achievement of the Society has been its provision of a medium whereby mathematicians from all over the country could stay in touch with one another. This has been facilitated by its publications and by the meetings held under its auspices. In addition to those scheduled in January and August in conjunction with the meetings of the Mathematical Association of America, the Society for Industrial and Applied Mathematics, and similar organizations, it has sponsored irregular ones in different sections of the country.

Three prizes are awarded by the Society: the Bocher Memorial Prize in Analysis; the Frank Nelson Cole Prize in Algebra and the Frank Nelson Cole Prize in the Theory of Numbers. Each of these prizes is awarded every five years for a significant mathematical research publication.

Ordinary membership is open to professionally qualified mathematicians.

Contributing, institutional and corporate membership is open to individuals and organizations interested in furthering the work of the Society. The total membership is approximately 7,200.[62] The Executive Director of the Society, assisted by a fairly large staff, administers its affairs from headquarters at 190 Hope Street, Providence 6, Rhode Island.

GEOLOGICAL SOCIETY OF AMERICA

Prior to the nineteenth century there were no serious geological studies made in this hemisphere. Thomas Jefferson was interested in vertebrate paleontology and Benjamin Silliman did have some interest in certain aspects of geology, but it was not until 1809, with the publication of William Maclure's "Observations on the geology of the United States, explanatory of a geologic map," American Philosophical Society *Transactions*. Philadelphia, 1809, Volume 6, pp. 411-428, that America produced a study of note. Turning to the colleges and universities, it was not until the 1830s and '40s that courses in geology were offered and it was at this time, on April 2, 1840, that the Association of American Geologists was formed. The Association was the first national society in America devoted solely to the earth sciences and it was the ancestor of the Geological Society of America. The Association was organized because of the need for coordination among New York, Pennsylvania, and New England geologists whose state survey work often carried them across state lines.

In 1843 the newly founded Association widened its scope and its name was changed to the Association of American Geologists and Naturalists. By 1847 a movement took place to broaden the membership and activity still further and, as a result, the Association was enlarged in 1848 into the American Association for the Advancement of Science, with Geology and Geography as Section E of the new Association.

From 1848 to 1881 geologists participated actively in the affairs of the Association and ten of their number served as presidents during the period. By the latter date there was some sentiment expressed for the creation of a separate society, sentiment stemming from dissatisfaction with the Association practice of holding summer meetings plus a desire to emulate other specialized societies formed or in the process of formation. Although a committee to consider the matter had been set up and there was some correspondence, action was delayed until 1888, largely because of a reluctance to do something that might embarrass the Association. This objection was met by a plan whereby the officers of Section E of the Association would be the same as those of the projected society and the meetings of the Section and society would be held jointly. The separate American Geological Society, was therefore, organized on August 14, 1888 on that basis; at its next annual meeting on August 28, 1889, changing its name to the Geological Society of America.

In advancing the science of geology in America, the Society recognized the importance of publication from the beginning of its existence. A committee on publications was named at the 1888 organizational meeting and the establishment of the then quarterly and now monthly *Bulletin* followed the next year. This publication includes the records of meetings of the Society and the papers presented there. Since 1933 an annual, *Proceedings* Volume has also been published as well as intermittent special *Papers and Memoirs*.

Winter meetings of the Society, scheduled in recent years in October or November, have always been a practice. From 1902 to 1908 these meetings were held jointly with the American Association for the Advancement of Science being discontinued on the latter date because of the problem of accommodation. Beginning in 1926 joint meetings have been scheduled intermittently with the Association and with other societies such as the Mineralogical Society of America and the Society of Economic Geologists. These meetings have been held in all sections of the country, usually in the large cities.

During the period 1897-1899 a Cordilleran Section of the Society was created for members in the Far West and in 1947 a Rocky Mountain Section and a Southeastern Section were added. These sections have provided an additional stimulus and source of information for members in their respective regions. In this connection it should be noted that the Society has been instrumental in the creation of several similar organizations including the Paleontological Society, the Mineralogical Society of America, and Society of Economic Geologists. Also, the Geological Society of America had a hand in the 1948 creation of the American Geological Institute.[63]

In carrying on its activities the Society is in a unique position in comparison to the majority of the learned societies due to the fact that in 1931 it was named the recipient of the $3,884,345 Penrose Bequest by the late Dr. R. A. F. Penrose. Dr. Penrose also gave the Society his personal library and provided funds for the Penrose Medal which, in addition to other medals and prizes, is awarded by the Society.

Membership in the Society began with 112 Fellows. Since that time, membership as a Fellow has been on an elective basis from among workers and teachers in geology. In 1947 status as members was extended to those persons interested in geology but not meeting the qualifications for Fellow. Although the constitution provided for contributing members, distinguished foreign scientists, it was not until 1909 that the first of this group was named, and their number has never been over 58 of a total membership today of about 1,700 Fellows and 3,700 members. Women were admitted to the Society at an early date and several have served in official capacities.[64] The Secretary's office is located at 419 West 117th Street, New York 27, New York.

AMERICAN SOCIETY OF ZOOLOGISTS

As one contemporary zoologist has aptly stated, "The history of the American Society of Zoologists is interesting, charming and a little confusing."[65] Much of this confusion can be traced to the series of changes that took place in the Society during its formative period and to conflicting statements of facts about the Society by succeeding writers. Where it has proven impossible to clarify such conflicts, the account which follows presents the differing interpretations.

The Society originated in December, 1890 as an offshoot of the American Society of Naturalists,[66] which was holding its annual meeting in Boston, Massachusetts. This offshoot, the American Morphological Society, was organized because a significant number of biologists and zoologists interested in certain aspects of comparative anatomy, particularly animal morphology, could not find a congenial and stimulating association within the then existing learned societies. The founders, numbering some 20 persons, were mainly professors of biology and zoology in colleges and universities, and the first president was a professor in an institution of higher learning.[67]

By 1899 the Society had fused with several groups of naturalists and its name was changed to the Zoological Society of America. In 1902 this Society was reorganized, with a new constitution; a new name, Society of American Zoologists; and with an Eastern and Western Branch. The following year, 1903, the name was changed to the American Society of Zoologists. The records do not reveal the reasons for these changes in name. Finally, in 1913, the two branches, which had been holding separate annual meetings and a joint one every third year, merged and formed the organization much as it exists today.[68]

Activities of the Society have included efforts towards the holding of the 1907 International Zoological Congress in this country, the creation of various committees to examine and report on the teaching of zoological sciences at the high school and college level, and, during the World War I period, assistance in creating and promoting the newly formed Division of Biology and Agriculture of the National Research Council. Members of the Society, in cooperation with those of the Botanical Society of America, played a major role in the creation in 1922 of the Genetics Society of

America. In this connection, it should be noted that the Society, although apparently many members favored the move, did not join the movement for the creation of the Federation of American Societies for Experimental Biology. Latterly, however, the members of the Society have cooperated with such organizations as the Federation, the American Institute of Biological Sciences, the National Institutes of Health, the Office of Naval Research, and the National Science Foundation. It has also sponsored Summer Institutes for College Teachers, held regional conferences, and has prepared and distributed over 38,000 booklets describing career possibilities in the biological sciences.

Meetings have been held annually since the reorganization of 1902-03 in various cities over the United States. In recent years the Society has met with the American Institute of Biological Sciences at the end of the summer and with the American Association for the Advancement of Science immediately after Christmas. The meetings consist of the usual conduct of business, presentation of papers and scientific demonstrations. Until 1960, the proceedings of these meetings have been published as supplements in the *Anatomical Record;* beginning in 1961 they will be published in the *American Zoologist.* Also, since 1919, the American Society of Zoologists has assumed editorial responsibility for the *Journal of Morphology,* published by the Wistar Institute, and many of the members' papers are presented therein. At the same time an arrangement was made whereby members were given a choice of all of the journals published by the Institute.[69] In recent years, a *Newsletter* has been sent out irregularly by the secretaries of the Society. A movement is afoot at the present time to develop this publication into a regular, quarterly Society publication.

Membership in the Society has always been selective and, at the present, there are four categories; members, restricted to those who have scientific training equivalent to the doctorate and actively engaged in the field of zoology; student; emeritus; and corresponding. The latter category includes distinguished foreign scientists whose number may not exceed one per cent of the number of members. The total membership is approximately 2,000. The Secretary's office is at Goucher College, Baltimore 4, Maryland.[70]

BOTANICAL SOCIETY OF AMERICA

Although the official date for the organization of the Botanical Society of America, Inc. is 1906, the Society actually originated in 1894. This apparent discrepancy is accounted for by the fact that on the former date the Botanical Society of America merged with the Society for Plant Morphology and Physiology, founded in 1896, and the Amerian Mycological Society, founded in 1903, to form the Botanical Society of America, Inc. A history of the latter, therefore, must concern itself with the history of the three merging organizations.

The oldest of the group, the Botanical Society of America, grew out of the American Botanical Club, organized in 1883 as a segment of the American Association for the Advancement of Science. At the 1892 meeting of the Club, a ten-man committee was named to consider and report on the feasibility of an entirely separate botanical society. Strange as it may seem, in 1893 eight members of this committee, including the chairman, reported unfavorably on the proposal; one favored it but did not submit any procedure to carry it through; the final member, Dr. C. R. Barnes, stated that he was unable to agree with the majority report. He offered a report favoring the creation of a separate society which contained rather detailed specifications for carrying it out, and his report was thereupon adopted by a two-thirds majority of the members of the Club.

Acting upon Barnes's plan, 25 botanists were subsequently invited to become charter members of the Botanical Society of America and from this group a committee was designated to draft a constitution. The committee, among other constitutional provisions, recommended that membership should be restricted to "American botanists engaged in research, who have published work of recognized merit," and that persons elected to membership should actively participate in its program or forfeit membership. The proposed constitution also called for relatively high admission fees and dues. In 1894 the constitution, with the above provisions included, was adopted.

Because of these stringent membership regulations and the policy of the Society of holding summer meetings, opposition developed from botanists along the Atlantic seaboard resulting in the creation in 1897 of the Society for Plant Morphology and Physiology, and in 1903 of the American Mycological Society. By the latter date, however, many leading botanists were regretting this fragmentation and were urging a union of all botanists. Committees to consider such a union were named and their recommendations for a merger were crowned with success at a December, 1906 meeting in New York City. A new constitution was adopted by the members of the three societies and the resulting organization adopted the name, the Botanical Society of America, later incorporated under the laws of the State of Connecticut.

Since 1906 the Society has played an important role in the botanical sciences. It has concerned itself with the teaching of botany and has sponsored many symposia on the subject; it has been active in the formation of committees to study various aspects of botanical research and employment opportunities in the field; it aided the defense efforts in World Wars I and II and, during the former war, assisted in the creation of the National Research Council. More recently, it has sponsored summer institutes of botany under grants from the National Science Foundation and, in 1956, established the Certificate of Merit which is awarded annually to an outstanding botanist.

The publications of the Society include the *American Journal of Botany,* which has been published monthly, excepting August and September, since 1914 and the recently established (1955) *Plant Science Bulletin.* The former contains articles and monographs by botanists and occasionally papers presented at the annual meetings of the Society. The latter is devoted to news and notes of interest to all workers in the field of botany.

Although the annual meetings have been held all over the United States and Canada, early in its history in conjunction with meetings of the Association for the Advancement of Science, but more recently with the American Institute for Biological Sciences, the Society has seen fit to create five geographical sections in various parts of the United States which meet intermittently.

Membership has climbed from an original 119 at the time of fusion in 1906 and now numbers about 2,400, including regular members, graduate students, and some 36 corresponding members elected from among distinguished foreign botanists.[71]

A recent development in the botanical field and one of particular interest to the Botanical Society was its establishment in 1958 of a committee to consider the need for and possible formation of a national organization to be called the Federation of Plant Sciences. This organization, if established, would unite the 35,000-40,000 plant scientists of the country, now scattered among a number of specialized botanical societies, into a single unit within the American Institute of Biological Sciences.[72] The office of the Society's Secretary is located at the University of Texas, Austin 12, Texas.

AMERICAN ASTRONOMICAL SOCIETY

Because of the fact that they were few and scattered, early attempts by astronomers to form a national learned society devoted solely to astronomy met with failure, although the *Astronomical Journal,* one of the publications of the present day American Astronomical Society, was founded as early as 1849 by Benjamin Apthorp Gould. It was not until several conferences of astronomers, held at the Yerkes and Harvard observatories in 1897, 1898, and 1899, that a national society finally emerged, bearing the name Astronomical and Astrophysical Society of America. This name was changed in 1914 to the American Astronomical Society but the purpose of the organization has continued to be the advancement of astronomy, astrophysics and related branches of science.

Although the Society has stimulated interest and research in astronomy through various funds and prizes and its standing committees have facilitated work in such areas as meteors, comets, and variable stars, its main activities have been the holding of meetings for members and the publication of various journals.

For the first ten years of its existence the Society did not have a publication of its own, depending upon such journals as *Science* and *Popular Astronomy* to print accounts of its meetings and other material pertaining to astronomy. In 1909 all of this material which had been previously published was gathered together in Volume 1 of the Society's *Publications*. This policy of intermittently gathering such material together for the *Publications* was followed until 1943 when Volume Ten brought the series to a close. At that time the Society took over the publication of the previously mentioned *Astronomical Journal* and the news and material about the Society and astronomy have subsequently appeared there. The Society has also established close relationships with the *Astrophysical Journal* selecting its editorial board from nominees proposed by the University of Chicago.

Initially the Society met annually; since 1950 this has been increased to three times a year. Over 50 per cent of the meetings have been in cities located in the Northeast, with the remainder being scattered over the United States and Canada. They are usually centered at some college or university with an observatory and over 20 of them have been held in conjunction with the meetings of the American Association for the Advancement of Science. Attendance is usually about 150 to 300 persons.

Qualification for membership in the Society has always been predicated upon the preparation of "an acceptable paper upon some subject of astronomy, astrophysics, or selected branch of physics." While this rule has been liberally interpreted, it has been used to bar those obviously insufficiently informed from admission to the Society; in doubtful cases, the secretary has referred papers to referees for their decision.

In 1961, responding to the growth of interest in astronomy outside of professional circles, the Society established two new classes in addition to the basic (full) membership. Junior Membership (with reduced dues), for those under 26, and Associate Membership are now open to students and to any other person with a serious interest in astronomy. These classes share all privileges and responsibilities with Members except those of office-holding and of presenting papers to the Society without sponsorship. Corporate and Emeritus memberships are also offered, but an earlier class of Life Membership has been discontinued. Not more than once each year, one foreign astronomer may be designated for honorary membership, and since 1910, 30 distinguished astronomers from abroad have been accorded this honor.

Until recent times growth of membership has been relatively slow. In 1899 there were approximately 113 charter members; by 1922 membership had increased to 370; it is now about 1,200.[73] The Secretary of the Society is located at the University of Illinois, Urbana, Illinois

AMERICAN PHYSICAL SOCIETY

During the latter decades of the nineteenth century, although physics had become a highly developed discipline in Europe, in America it was still slowly emerging as a separate branch of natural philosophy. One of the first professors of physics in an American university, and incidentally the first president of the American Physical Society, Henry A. Rowland of Johns Hopkins, was not appointed until 1876. The locus at that time for the presentation and discussion of reports and papers of the slowly growing group of American physicists was Section B of the American Association for the Advancement of Science. Sentiment gradually developed for a separate society devoted solely to physics and in 1899 the American Physical Society was founded. The man who took the lead in the creation of such a society and who subsequently received the appellation "Father of the American Physical Society" was Professor Arthur Gordon Webster of Clark University.[74] Although Webster, as chairman of an *ad hoc* committee, did take the lead in sending out the invitations which resulted in the organization meeting at Columbia University on May 20, 1899, Professors Ernest Merritt and Edward L. Nichols of Cornell University and the afore-mentioned Professor Rowland were also responsible for the first meeting and the organization of the Society. About 40 physicists attended this meeting, and committees were there appointed to draw up a constitution which was subsequently presented and adopted at the second meeting of the Society on October 28, 1899.

Since its beginning the Society can point to many achievements. At its fourth annual meeting it appointed a Committee to draft and present a petition to Congress to endorse a proposed Bureau of Weights and Measures. The Society's interest plus the efforts of this Bureau's first director, Dr. S. P. Stratton, resulted in its metamorphosis into the present-day National Bureau of Standards. This initial close relationship has been maintained through the years; the Society for several decades held its

Washington meetings in a room in the Bureau's building that had been designed with that purpose in mind. In 1931, the Society was one of four organizations responsible for the creation of the American Institute of Physics.[75]

The Society sought to stimulate interest in and discussion of various aspects of physics by the creation of various divisions devoted to particular aspects of the subject. At present there are six in existence: Electron, High-Polymer, Solid State, Fluid Dynamics, Plasma, and Chemical. It has also encouraged, for the same reasons, the setting up of sections throughout the country; presently there are four. Indeed, a resolution to this effect was adopted at the Society's very first meeting. Prizes and awards have also been offered. The Bell Telephone Laboratories, for instance, gave $50,000 to the Society to endow the Oliver E. Buckley Prize, given annually since 1952 for outstanding research in solid-state physics performed in the United States or neighboring countries.

In the matter of publications, the present day official organ, the *Physical Review,* antedated the Society by six years since Professor Nichols of Cornell University founded it in 1893. Although the Society initially published nine issues of its own quarterly *Bulletin,* it was discontinued in 1903 because it was reaching only a small number of subscribers and at a high cost, and because an arrangement had been worked out with Nichols and the *Review* whereby Society material would be printed therein and members would receive it at a reduced rate. Furthermore, representation by the Society on the Board of Editors of the *Review* followed almost immediately. In 1913, as membership increased, complete editorial and financial control of the journal was transferred from Nichols and Cornell University, which had provided continuous financial backstopping for it, to the Society.[76] Since then the Society has published this periodical, now a semi-monthly, containing the results of original research from all over the world; it is one of the world's largest learned journals devoted to physics. For the last few years it has been supplemented by another journal called *Physical Review Letters* containing short communications dealing with new discoveries or topics of current interest in rapidly changing fields of research. The *Bulletin* has been revived and contains abstracts of papers presented at the meetings of the Society and official notices to its members. The current quarterly *Review of Modern Physics* was first published in 1929.

Annual meetings of the Society took place in conjunction with those of the American Association for the Advancement of Science until 1940. Since the latter date this practice was abandoned. In addition to the annual meeting, usually in larger cities of the Northeast and Midwest, five to eight meetings are held each year in other parts of the United States, and occasionally in Canada or Mexico.

Reflecting its small membership, the number of persons in attendance at the Society's earlier meetings usually totaled about 50 persons and the program of any one of the first 12 meetings never contained more than seven papers. Since World War I there has been a consistent rise of membership in the organization and the content, variety, and length of the annual meetings and five to eight other meetings held during a year has expanded proportionately.

Soon after the foundation of the American Physical Society two categories of membership, Fellow and Member, were established. The former was reserved for scientists who contributed to the advancement of physics by independent, original research, or rendered some other special service to the cause of science. At present about one-seventh of the total of approximately 17,000 members are designated as Fellows.[77] The Secretary of the Society has offices located at Columbia University, New York 27, New York.

AMERICAN SOCIETY FOR MICROBIOLOGY
(Formerly Society of American Bacteriologists)

The catalytic agent in the creation of this Society, and a man who figured prominently in the creation of several others, was Dr. Franklin P. Mall. It was at his suggestion, at an 1898 meeting of the American Society of Naturalists, that Drs. A. C. Abbott, H. W. Conn, and E. O. Jordan set themselves up as a committee to proceed with the organization of a bacteriological society. Letters were sent out by the three in the fall of 1899 to prominent bacteriologists informing them of the projected society and requesting their attendance at the forthcoming annual meeting of the American Society of Naturalists. Fifty-nine persons were in attendance at the organizational meeting of the Society of American Bacteriologists on December 28-29, 1899 at Yale University. Dr. William T. Sedgwick was named president of this first American society devoted solely to bacteriology. The three organizers above were elected respectively Vice-President, Secretary-Treasurer, and member of a governing Council.

The object of the new Society, as stated in its original Constitution, was "the promotion of the science of bacteriology, the bringing together of American bacteriologists, the demonstration and discussion of bacteriological methods, and the consideration of subjects of mutual interest." Although subsequent revisions made this statement of purpose more explicit, one of the major accomplishments of the Society has been that it established bacteriology as a fundamental discipline and yet left its members considerable latitude in their range of interest. For example, the extension of the interest of many members into the field of microbiology was accomplished within the framework of the Society and some of its major contributions to the advancement of science have been in the microbiological area. This development, furthermore, resulted in the 1960 change in the name of the Society to its present American Society for Microbiology and the designation of an Executive Secretary, whose offices are located in Detroit, Michigan.

The Society has contributed to the organization and support of the American Institute of Biological Sciences which was organized as a cooperating agency in 1947 to advance the biological sciences. It has shared in the management of the American Type Culture Collection and has aided in the preparation of various bacterial classification systems.

Another contribution of the Society has been its publications. The monthly *Journal of Bacteriology* is the best-known and oldest, appearing in 1916. A year later *Abstracts of Bacteriology* was established to be merged, in 1925, with other publications of similar nature in *Biological Abstracts.* More recently (1936-1937) *Bacteriological Reviews* and a *News-Letter,* now called *Bacteriological News,* have been added to the list of publications, and, in 1955, the bi-monthly journal *Applied Microbiology* was established.

Annual meetings of the Society have been held since its founding, with the exception of three years during World War II. They have taken place all over the United States and attendance, which has been on a constant rise, now includes 3,000 to 3,600 persons. A feature of these meetings is the presentation of the Eli Lilly and Company Award in Bacteriology and Immunology. There is also the usual presentation of scientific papers and social intercourse among members. In addition to these annual meetings, each of 33 local branches of the Society hold at least two meetings annually. Beginning with four branches located in the Northeast, there was little activity among them until, in 1934, they were given representation on the governing Council and encouraged in other ways. They have subsequently increased in number and activity and are now located in all sections of this country and abroad.

Membership in the Society was originally restricted to those persons who had performed and published research in bacteriology, and was limited to a set number. In 1913, and to a greater extent in 1916, because of increasing interest among students plus a desire to make the newly established *Journal of Bacteriology* available to as many as possible, these restrictions were abolished and membership was opened to all persons interested in furthering the objectives of the Society. In 1959, however, this policy was changed and new membership is now limited to persons holding a bachelor's degree or possessing the equivalent in training or experience. In addition to the usual Active Members, there are Honorary Members —restricted to eminent, elected scientists; Corresponding Members—distinguished foreign investigators; Student Members; Emeritus Members; and Sustaining Members—research and industrial organizations interested in aiding and furthering the work of the Society. The latter group comprises approximately 100 of a total membership of over 6,200.[78] The offices of the Society's Executive Secretary are located at 19875 Mack Avenue, Detroit 36, Michigan.

AMERICAN ASSOCIATION OF PATHOLOGISTS AND BACTERIOLOGISTS

The year 1901 saw the establishment of this organization. The Association grew out of a desire on the part of certain members of the Association of American Physicians for the formation of a society devoted to experimental science as represented by pathology and bacteriology. Although there was a significant cleavage in the Association on the matter, opposition being based on the grounds that the proposed society would duplicate and weaken existing ones, Dr. William T. Councilman and Dr. Harold C. Ernst took the lead in drafting and circulating a letter among some 40 colleagues asking for support of the proposed organization. The view that a new society was needed prevailed and an organizational meeting was called for and held on April 30, 1900 in Washington, D. C. At this meeting, attended by some 15 persons, a motion was passed calling for the creation of a new society and a committee was appointed to draw up a constitution. At a follow-up meeting, held in New York City on January 26, 1901, the constitution presented by this committee, which called for the creation of the American Association of Pathologists and Bacteriologists, was adopted; officers were elected, Dr. Councilman, President, and Dr. Ernst, Secretary; and a governing council was named.

In addition to the presentation of scientific papers and demonstrations, the first scheduled meeting of the new Association, held in Boston April 5th and 6th, 1901, resulted in discussions about an official journal. Secretary Ernst proposed that the title of the *Journal of the Boston Society of Medical Sciences,* of which he was editor, be changed to the *Journal of Medical Research* and be made the publication medium of the Association. Although alternative suggestions were made, his proposal carried. This *Journal,* with most of its financial support coming from the Association, remained its official publication until 1924 when it was superseded by the Association's present monthly, the *American Journal of Pathology.* These journals contain papers and reports on pathology and bacteriology, and the proceedings of the annual meetings of the Association, together with other news about it and its members.

The "Path and Bac," as it is familiarly called by its members, has not engaged in many joint operations with other societies; has not affiliated with other organizations, such as the American Association for the Advancement of Science; and has not engaged in any licensing or evaluating activities. Nevertheless, the Association has endorsed certain measures which it thought would benefit the pathological and bacteriological sciences. In 1938, for instance, it recommended passage of a bill by Congress that would have provided adequate housing for the Army Medical Museum and Library and, in 1946, it sent a representative before a Congressional Committee to testify in favor of appropriations for the Army Institute of Pathology.

The reluctance to engage in joint operations has not extended to the Association's annual meetings. They have often been held in conjunction with other scientific societies, such as the American Association of Immunologists, and, although the Path and Bac is not a member of the Federation of American Societies for Experimental Biology, meetings have usually been scheduled immediately prior to or after those of the Federation. At an early period the tradition was established of holding meetings where a medical school, rather than a hotel or resort, could host the affair. Such meetings have been held all over the United States and several in Canada. Since 1928 one portion of the meeting has been devoted to some particular debate evoking topic, thus, appropriately, calling for a referee at the meetings.

The Association has set up the unusual and highly personalized Gold-Headed Cane Award. Patterned on a similar award made since the eighteenth century by the Royal College of Physicians in London, the Association's Award was established in 1919. At that time, a gold-headed cane was awarded Dr. Ernst, in recognition of his long service as Secretary, with the provision that upon his death or relinquishment the cane would revert to the Association for further award. A total of ten men, all distinguished scientists, have been the proud possessors of the cane, the incumbent being Dr. George H. Whipple. At the present time, the cane is on display at the Armed Forces Institute of Pathology together with a list of the former holders.

Membership in the Association rests upon nomination by two members accompanied by the presentation of evidence of the accomplishment of creditable research in pathology or bacteriology and an indication of continuing productivity. Proposals to create honorary or other types of membership have consistently been rejected. Although membership is open to foreigners, and some 50 are presently members, they are required to have spent a significant period of study in the United States and meet all of the other requirements for membership. Partially as a consequence, the growth in membership has been a slow but steady one, and presently membership is about 1,000. The Association's roster, however, includes practically all of the outstanding pathologists and bacteriologists of the country. The Secretary's office is located at the University of Kansas Medical School, Kansas City, Kansas.[79]

ELECTROCHEMICAL SOCIETY

The American Electrochemical Society, forerunner of the Electrochemical Society, Inc., was created in 1902, developing out of the burgeoning world-wide scientific interest in the relationship of chemistry and electricity. At approximately the same time the American Society was being organized, similar ones such as the Bunsen Society of Germany (1894) and the Faraday Society of England (1903) were springing into existence. Interest in the formation of such a society in America was the result of a belief on the part of a small group of Philadelphia engineers and chemists that their needs were not being met by then existing learned and scientific societies. This group, led by Joseph W. Richards, Carl Hering, and C. J. Reed, made the initial move in the formation of the Society by sending out a circular letter to some 30 persons presumed to be interested in electrochemistry, calling for an organizational meeting on November 1, 1901 in Philadelphia. Eleven persons attended this meeting and it was there decided that if the names of 75 persons pledging to become members could be obtained, the Society should be formed. Antedating the formation of the Society, a Committee on Membership to carry through on this matter was named as well as one to prepare for the next meeting and one to prepare a constitution. Also, it was at this initial meeting that the name American Electrochemical Society was adopted, not to be changed until the Society was incorporated as the Electrochemical Society in 1930.

Responses to a polling letter to prospective members was unexpectedly and overwhelmingly favorable, 337 membership pledges were received from 36 states and eight foreign countries, and another organizational meeting was called and convened in Philadelphia on April 3, 1902 with 52 persons present. Officers were elected; a constitution was adopted; and some 20 scientific papers were presented at this first formal meeting. Since this meeting the Society has continually sought to stimulate interest and research in electrochemistry. It has sponsored essay and other publication contests and various members have endowed research and publication awards to be administered by it. The following divisions dealing with major aspects of electrochemistry have been established: Battery, Corrosion, Electric Insulation, Electrodeposition, Electro-organic, Electronics, Electrothermics and Metallurgy, Industrial Electrolytic and Theoretical Electrochemistry. Each of these divisions is responsible for its own programs at the semi-annual meetings held by the Society.

During the first decade of its existence, because of financial considerations, serious thought was given to printing the Society's papers and reports in another learned journal. The proposition was not acted upon, however, and the Society has published its own semi-annual *Transactions* from 1902 until 1948. At that time it was superseded by the monthly *Journal* which, in addition to papers and reports, provides more news about the Society and its members. Much of the value of these journals, according to one past president of the Society, is that they provide a compendium of investigations, successful and unsuccessful, that may prove of value to later investigators.

Another medium whereby members stay abreast of the activities of their colleagues is the semi-annual meetings. These meetings, held for four-day periods in the spring and fall, are the occasion for the presentation and discussion of papers; social activity; and the usual attention to business affairs of the Society. Also, the Society, as early as 1904, encouraged the development of regional Sections in the United States and abroad. Nineteen of them now hold periodic meetings and complement the work of the national organization.

Originally there was only one class of membership in the Society and it was open to all who had a scientific interest in electrochemistry. Through the years the membership regulations were revised, and now there are three different categories of regular membership, active, associate, and student, turning upon qualifications and age; plus emeritus, honorary, life, patron and sustaining membership. Over 90 per cent of the present membership of 3,200, however, falls into the regular active category.

Initially members were almost all from the Northeastern section of the United States, particularly New York and Pennsylvania. With the passage of years, however, the membership has become more diversified geographically. The Society includes and has included, as members, practically all of the scientific, educational and industrial leaders in the electrochemical field. It maintains administrative offices, under the direction of an Executive Secretary, at 30 East 42nd Street, New York 17, New York.[80]

AMERICAN SOCIETY OF BIOLOGICAL CHEMISTS

The American Society of Biological Chemists, Inc., founded in December, 1906, was an offshoot of the American Physiological Society, organized 19 years before, in 1887. At the time the latter Society was created, biological or physiological chemistry as it was then called, had relatively few devotees. The period 1887-1906 saw an increase in the number of interested scientists and a corresponding increase in the sentiment that the chemical side of physiology was of equal importance with physical or so-called 'pure' physiology. It is against this background of the relative emphasis to be placed on these categories of physiology that the discussions attendant on the formation of a new society centered; for when the subject was broached many physiologists maintained that their discipline was a broad study of function, and that to divorce physiological chemistry from it would not only weaken the American Physiological Society, but also physiology as a science. These objections were heightened by the problem of where, exactly, did physiological or biological chemistry fit into the academic structure: within the department of physiology or chemistry? New discoveries in biochemistry opening new fields of inquiry and accellerating interest in it as a speciality finally culminated in 1905 in several events that led to the formation of a new society. Conspicuous among them were the creation of a biochemical section of the American Chemical Society and the founding of the *Journal of Biological Chemistry* by Drs. John J. Abel and C. A. Herter. The establishment of the *Journal* by these gentlemen was followed, the next year, by their successful launching of the American Society of Biological Chemists. Dr. Abel sent out a circular letter to a group of biological chemists in October, 1906 calling for a meeting which was subsequently held on December 26th in New York City with 29 persons present. It was at this meeting that a provisional scheme of organization was adopted and the Society came into being.

The *Journal of Biological Chemistry,* while it was not controlled by the Society until later, was always closely tied to it because Drs. Abel and Herter had founded both. Although the original idea for the founding of the *Journal* appears to have been Abel's, they were one in their belief in the project, and Herter carried it through to completion by setting it up as a non-profit corporation in New York State; managing and co-editing it with Dr. Abel; and, apparently, defraying its initial deficits out of his own pocket until his death in 1910. His untimely demise resulted in a crisis for the *Journal* that was met by various economies in publication; the creation of a supporting Christian A. Herter Memorial Fund by relatives and friends of Dr. Herter; transfer of the publication offices to quarters in the Rockefeller Institute, where they remained until 1925; and a campaign to increase the numbers of subscribers by offering sets of excess back numbers free with new subscriptions. As a result, the *Journal* was continued as an independent publication of the Society, although several organizations, including the Amercan Chemical Society, had offered to take over its publication. It was not until 1919 that the Society assumed full responsibilities for the *Journal*. Changes in the constitution were made at that time which provided for the *Journal's* continuation as a corporation but controlled by the Society since the latter had acquired all of the corporation's stock. Finally, in 1942, because of the possible imposition of a New York State income tax, the corporation was dissolved and stock and assets, including the Christian A. Herter Memorial Fund, were turned over to the American Society of Biological Chemists, Inc.

Among the Society's achievements, it can be recorded that it was a member of the three-Society conference committee which resulted in the creation of the Federation of American Societies for Experimental Biology in 1913. The Society has been active in furthering research in bio-chemistry. Its Committee on Protein Nomenclature, for example, cooperated with a committee of the American Physiological Society in making a report on that subject. Its outstanding achievement, however, according to Dr. Russell H. Chittenden, past-president and chief historian of the Society, has been its publication of the *Journal of Biological Chemistry* which contains the abstracts of papers read at the annual meetings, other papers and reports, and news about the Society and its members.

The annual meetings of the Society took place during the last week in December until 1925. The date of meeting was changed at that time and subsequent meetings have been held in the spring. They have provided the usual media where members present papers to be judged by their peers and get acquainted with one another. They have been convened all over the United States and Canada.

In 1906, 81 persons constituted the charter membership of the Society. Since that time membership has been opened to biological chemists who have conducted and published original investigations in the field and who are nominated by a member. Such nominations must then be endorsed by the governing Council and receive a majority vote in a general session of the Society. Until 1961 there was only one class of membership in the Society with the exception of a brief period from 1922 to 1925 when a few "clinical members" were admitted. In 1961 honorary membership was opened to distinguished foreign scientists. Their number, however, may not exceed five per cent of the present approximately 1,700 members of the Society. Also in 1961, because of a recent rapid growth in membership (approximately 100 new members are now being added each year) and in order to stimulate the recruitment and training of biochemists at the graduate level, the Society plans to name a full-time Executive Secretary shortly. For the present, its offices are located at the University of Florida, Gainesville, Florida. [81]

ENTOMOLOGICAL SOCIETY OF AMERICA

Although the first seven decades of the nineteenth century saw the organization of many local entomological societies, the first national one to be organized in the United States was the Entomological Club of the American Association for the Advancement of Science. Set up in 1875, this Club functioned until 1891 when it was discontinued because of the 1889 organization of the American Association of Economic Entomologists. The Association, which was first known as the Association of Official Economic Entomologists, restricted its membership to those in the U. S. and Canadian Departments of Agriculture and their Experiment Stations. It soon modified this requirement; its membership rapidly expanded; and it began to hold meetings, publish a Proceedings, and engage in other activities.

With the establishment of the Association and the suspension of the Club, those entomologists who were not interested in the primarily economic side of entomology were bereft of an organization. In 1906 they organized the Entomological Society of America to meet their needs, and Professor J. H. Comstock of Cornell Unversity was elected the first president.

One of the first activities of the newly founded Society was the founding, in 1908, of a journal, the *Annals*. It is noteworthy that the Association, which had been publishing its Proceedings in *Insect Life* and similar publications, in the same year established its own official publication, the *Journal of Economic Entomology*.

There was always a close connection between the two societies; they cooperated extensively and often held joint meetings. Through the years, therefore, sentiment developed for a merger of the two. In 1949 a joint committe was established to consider the matter, and in 1953 the societies were consolidated as the Entomological Society of America.[82]

An important feature of the new organization is the Sectional grouping that was developed under the 1953 Constitution. These include: a) General Entomology; b) Insect Physiology and Toxicology; c) Insect Biology; d) Medical and Veterinary Entomology; e) Insect Control, Extension, and Regulatory Entomology; and f) Chemical Control Investigations.

The first two Sections, and much of the third, cover the fields of interest of the pre-consolidated Society, the fourth is of interest to the pre-consolidated Society and Association, while the last two are predominanptly in the field of interest of the latter. These Sections form the basis, in the consolidated Society, for: representation upon the Governing Board; control of the various publications of the Society; and the arrangement of program. They are so weighted as to reflect the predominating interests of the academic or economic-professional groups. In other words, the Sections are the structural method whereby the differing and yet related interests of these two groups within the consolidated Society have been balanced and protected.

One of the accomplishments of the consolidated society and its predecessors has been in the publication area. In addition to the *Annals* and *Journal,* both of which were continued after consolidation, a monthly *Bulletin,* containing items of current and general interest to the members, was established in 1955. Also, the Society published the *Thomas Say Foundation Monographs; Entoma,* a magazine devoted to pest control; an annual *Index of American Economic Entomology;* since 1955, it has cooperated in the publication of an *Annual Review of Entomology;* and in 1959 it inaugurated publication of the irregular *Miscellaneous Publications.*

Another activity of the Society has been the organizing and conducting of annual meetings, in most of the major cities of the United States. They have usually been held in conjunction with those of other groups, such as the American Association for the Advancement of Science, and have provided a forum and a meeting place for entomologists.

Branches were organized by both predecessor societies. Their number has been retained and expanded by the existing Society, and the five present-day branches cover the United States, Canada, and Mexico. Their activities parallel those of the national society and provide a local and regional point of contact for all entomologists.

In the consolidated society, the ratio of economic-professional entomologists to those with a more academic interest is approximately two to one. There are four classes of membership: active, all persons engaged in entomological work and approved by the governing board; honorary, distinguished entomologsts who must be nominated and elected—they are limited in number to two per years and cannot exceed 15 at any one time; student; and emeritus. The total membership is presently about 4,300. The administrative offices of the Society, headed by an Executive Secretary, are maintained at 4603 Calvert Road, College Park, Maryland.[83]

AMERICAN SOCIETY FOR PHARMACOLOGY AND EXPERIMENTAL THERAPEUTICS

The American Society for Pharmacology and Experimental Therapeutics, Inc., was the direct outgrowth of the interest of Dr. John J. Abel in pharmacology.[84] Following a six-year period of study in the leading German and French medical schools, he returned to the United States in 1891 to become the first fulltime professor of materia and therapeutics at the University of Michigan. Abel's work marked the beginning of pharmacology as an independent discipline in the universities of the United States. In 1893 he received an appointment as Professor of Pharmacology at Johns Hopkins University and worked at that institution until his retirement in 1932.

Soon after his return from abroad, Dr. Abel saw the need for a learned society devoted to pharmacology and experimental therapeutics, and he was primarily responsible for calling the organizational meeting for such a society in Baltimore, Maryland, on December 28, 1908. At that time the 18 people in attendance adopted provisional articles of agreement which called for the formulation of a permanent constitution. Officers were elected, Dr. Abel being named President, and he announced that arrangements had been made for the publication of a monthly *Journal of Pharmacology and Experimental Therapeutics.*

The following year a permanent constitution was adopted and a Corporation, composed of Drs. J. J. Abel, R. Hunt, and C. Voegtlein, was formed and began publication of the *Journal.* This arrangement, with Dr. Abel as Editor, prevailed until 1933 when Dr. Abel and the Corporation voluntarily transferred control of the *Journal* to the Society. At that time a new Editor and Editorial Board was named to take charge of the publication. It was also voted then that the front cover of the *Journal* should contain a statement that it was founded by Dr. Abel. In addition to the *Journal,* the Society has published, since 1949, the quarterly *Pharmacological Reviews.*

The Society was one of those instrumental in forming the Federation of American Societies for Experimental Biology. The Society administers the John J. Abel Prize in Pharmacology, donated by Eli Lilly and Company, and the Torald Sollmann Award in Pharmacology, sponsored by Wyeth Laboratories, for outstanding research in this area; and holds semi-annual meetings to facilitate communication among members.

Membership in the Society includes Active investigators in pharmacology and experimental therapeutics, Honorary Members and Corporation Associates, and presently totals about 1,000.[85] The Secretary's office is located at the George Washington University Medical School, Washington 5, D. C.

PALEONTOLOGICAL SOCIETY

The Paleontological Society was an offshoot of the Geological Society of America and has always maintained close contacts with the latter organization. The first move for a society separate from the older organization occurred at the latter's 1907 meeting when a committee of nine men, headed by Charles Schuchert, met to discuss the possibility. It was agreed that a letter would be circularized seeking opinion from paleontologists on such matters as the proper nature of the proposed society, its relationship to the Geological Society of America, and publication policy. Thereafter, a meeting was called to be held on December 31, 1908 in Baltimore, and at this meeting, attended by 34 charter members, the Society was formed and an executive committee was named and given powers to proceed with its organization. At a subsequent meeting on February 13, 1909, a proposed constitution was ratified by this committee and a joint conference was held with the Geological Society to define the relationship between the two. It was decided that the Paleontological Society, although independent, would be affiliated with and form a section of the Geological Society of America and that the latter, to the limit of its financial ability, would provide facilities for publishing the research papers and other material of the paleontologists. During this same year inclusion in membership was offered to all of the members of the existing Society of American Vertebrate Paleontologists. Since a large number of members availed themselves of this offer, the latter Society went out of existence in 1910, to be resurrected in 1940-41 as the Society of Vertebrate Paleontology. Thus, by the end of 1909, the Paleontological Society had grown to 96 members and included most of the paleontologists of North America.

The original constitution provided for four classes of membership: Fellows, persons who had published paleontological works and who had been elected Fellows of the Geological Society of America; members, persons with an interest in paleontology; correspondents, distinguished foreign paleontologists elected to membership; patrons, persons bestowing gifts or favors upon the Society. Originally only Fellows could hold office within the Society; in 1949 because of a belief that this rule was discriminatory, Fellows were merged with the regular members. Numerical growth has been slow and membership presently numbers about 900 persons.

From 1909 to 1935 the Society published its proceedings and papers in the *Bulletin* of the Geological Society of America. In the meantime, in 1926, because of the growth of the oil industry and the realization of the value of the application of paleontology to oil discovery, the Society of Economic Paleontologists and Mineralogists was organized. The following year this Society began publishing the annual *Journal of Paleontology*. In 1935 an arrangement was worked out between the two societies whereby the short papers and records and activities of the Paleontological Society were henceforth to be published in the *Journal,* while the proceedings, monographs, and other lengthier material were to be published by the Geological Society of America.[86] Furthermore, the *Journal* was changed to a bi-monthly because of additional financial support provided by the Geological Society of America and the American Association of Petroleum

Geologists. Thus, the *Journal of Paleontology* today, is as described on its cover: "A *publication* of The Society of Economic Paleontologists and Mineralogists *and* The Paleontological Society *with the generous support and cooperation* of The American Association of Petroleum Geologists *and* The Geological Society of America." Since this arrangement took place, some 72 volumes of paleontological monographs have been published in addition to numerous articles and notes.

In addition to this close cooperation in publication, the same situation prevails in regard to annual meetings. The Paleontological Society has always held its meetings with the Geological Society of America, and as kindred organizations came into existence, they were also included. Members tend to cross societal lines at these meetings and attend sessions which most interest them. The place and dates of meetings are arranged jointly, usually being the first week in November in one of the larger cities of the United States.

Since its founding, the Paleontological Society and its members have contributed much to the study of fossils in particular and to geological and zoological advancement in general. One outstanding achievement was the development of improved techniques for the preservation of fossils, including the use of various acids to free silicified fossils from stone, and better methods of illustrating them for publication. The Society has provided a forum where the change in species concept was aired. More recently, it was a joint sponsor with the Paleontographical Society of London and the Society of Economic Paleontologists and Mineralogists, of the project, under the direction of Dr. Raymond C. Moore, which resulted in the classic *Treatise on Invertebrate Paleontology*. The Society also lent support in 1941 to the revival of the International Commission on Zoological Nomenclature, and in 1948 to the establishment of the American Geological Institute.[87] The office of the Society's Secretary is at Harvard University, Cambridge 38, Massachusetts.

AMERICAN SOCIETY FOR EXPERIMENTAL PATHOLOGY

At the turn of the century a small group of scientists recognized the increasing importance of experimental procedures in the field of pathology. The initiative in the formation of a society to develop this aspect of pathology was taken by Drs. Richard M. Pearce and S. J. Meltzer. In 1913, shortly after the Federation of American Societies for Experimental Biology had been founded, these two, who believed that a society devoted to experimental pathology should be established for inclusion in the new Federation, wrote to seven of their colleagues suggesting such a course. Following their initial approval, an additional 16 pathologists of note were invited to become, with the original nine, charter members of the proposed society. At a subsequent meeting at the Hygienic Laboratory of the U. S. Public Health Service in May, 1913 the American Society for Experimental Pathology was brought into being and Dr. Pearce was elected its first president.[88]

The constitution which was adopted by the Society specified that its object was "to bring the productive investigators in pathology, working essentially by experimental methods, in closer affiliation with the workers in other fields of experimental medicine." It was agreed at the original meeting that the Society should initially restrict its membership to 40 persons. During its early years the membership, consequently, was very limited and it was not until 1924 that it was opened more widely to experimental pathologists. At the present time the Society numbers approximately 700 members.

In 1913, shortly after its formation, the Society applied for and was admitted to membership in the Federation of American Societies for Experimental Biology. Since that time it has held annual meetings as a constituent member of the Federation. Many of the papers presented there have been published in abstract form in the *Proceedings* of the Federation. In 1956 the *A.M.A.(American Medical Association) Archives of Pathology* became the official journal of the American Society for Experimental Pathology. The reasons for this move were presented in an editorial which stated in part: "The members of this important organization of pathologists, after careful deliberation, voted to accept the offer of affiliation voted to them by the *A. M. A. Archives of Pathology*. They did so, presumably, because of their belief that experimental pathology had attained a stature warranting a more definite recognition in the general field of pathology. Rather than deciding to establish a journal of their own or to affiliate with a specialized type of journal, many of them preferred to join forces with a journal already devoted to the publication of diversified types of paper in the broad field of pathology."[89]

The present Secretary of the Society conducts its business from quarters at the University of North Carolina, Chapel Hill, North Carolina.

AMERICAN ASSOCIATION OF IMMUNOLOGISTS

In 1912 Dr. Gordon J. Synnott first broached the idea of organizing a "Society of Vaccine Therapists" to be composed of men who had worked under Sir Almroth E. Wright, St. Mary's Hospital, London. This membership restriction was shortly lifted so as to include other men who had worked in equally famous European laboratories and the name of the proposed organization was changed to the more inclusive "The American Association of Immunologists." A meeting was held in May of 1913 in

Washington, D. C., followed by one on June 19, 1913 in Minneapolis which marked the creation of the Association with some 50 charter members. At a meeting in Atlantic City on June 22nd of the following year, the details of organization were completed. It was here also at this meeting that mention was made of the pending setting up by Dr. Arthur F. Coca of a *Journal of Immunology* modeled after the German *Zeitschrift für Immunitatsforschung*. The Association thereupon voted that Dr. A. P. Hitchins, chairman of its governing council, be authorized to represent it in negotiation with Dr. Coca regarding the proposed journal. Dr. Hitchins and other members believed that if such a journal were established without reference to the Association it would be a handicap to its future development. In the meantime, Dr. Coca had been negotiating publication arrangements with the Williams and Wilkins Company of Baltimore, and a representative of that publishing firm was included in the conference which developed. Also included at this conference, held in New York City on October 7, 1915, were Dr. Hitchins and several other representatives of the Association and several representatives, including Dr. Coca, its president, of the New York Society of Serology and Hematology.[90] At this conference it was agreed that the two societies would produce, as their official organ, a publication to be known as the *Journal of Immunology*. Dr. Coca was selected as Managing Editor, and an Advisory Board and a Board of Editors, of many of the leading scientists interested in immunology in the United States and abroad, was provided for. Financial and editorial problems were ironed out at this and subsequent meetings, including the underwriting by several interested members of an expected operational deficit. Publication of the *Journal of Immunology* was begun in 1916 and publication under that name was continued down to 1944 when, because it was believed that the name did not indicate its scope, the title was changed to the *Journal of Immunology, Virus-Research, and Experimental Chemotherapy*. This name proved so unwieldy, however, that it was eventually changed back to the original and present *Journal of Immunology*. Dr. Coca served as Managing Editor under varying titles until 1948 when he resigned and was promptly elected Honorary President.

The *Journal* has probably been the major achievement of the Association because it has provided a medium whereby workers in serology, virology, epidemology, immunochemistry, and other immunological fields can publish their findings. In recent years the *Journal's* reports and articles on viruses have been of particular interest and importance. Another medium of communication among members has been the annual meetings. Up until the approximate time that the Association joined the Federation of American Societies for Experimental Biology in 1942, it usually met with the American

Association of Pathologists and Bacteriologists; since that time it has, of course, met at the same time and place with its sister societies of the Federation.

Active membership in the Association is open to those scientists with a record of published research in some phase of immunology, and there are some 30 emeritus members. Its growth has been a selective and gradual one, its membership today numbering about 600. The Association has an office at 630 West 168th Street, New York 32, New York.[91]

ECOLOGICAL SOCIETY OF AMERICA

A possible ecological society composed of botanists and zoologists was first suggested by Professor Robert H. Wolcott of the University of Nebraska in a letter dated March 27, 1914 to Professor V. E. Shelford of the University of Chicago. In his letter Professor Wolcott stressed field work as one of the main reasons for organizing such a society and, in order to facilitate such work at meetings, he advocated the restriction of membership to the Mississippi Valley area. In reply to this letter, Professor Shelford, while agreeing, broached the possibility of making the society a national one. He also stated that others favored the plan and had urged that "the thing be started" at the AAAS meeting in Philadelphia in December, 1914. Accordingly a group composed of some 20 men met at that time and an organizing committee was set up. Correspondence carried on through 1915 by this committee resulted in another meeting in December in Columbus, Ohio at which the Ecological Society of America was founded. A constitution was adopted, officers were elected (Professor Shelford being named the first president), and it was agreed that the newly formed Society would meet the following December in conjunction with the AAAS meeting at that time in New York City.

Activities of the Society include the establishment of the George Mercer Award, made annually to the writer of an outstanding paper on ecology, and the creation and work of such Committees as Ecology, Radioecology, and Physiological Ecology and Microenvironment. The Committee on Preservation of Natural Conditions concerned itself with the conservation and preservation of wildlife, forest, and certain other natural preserves. It was a continuous committee from 1917 to 1946 and was a powerful force for the preservation, in their pristine state, of such areas as the Yellowstone National Park. In 1946 the Natural Resources Council and the Ecologists Union were formed when the Ecological Society of America adopted the policy of not attempting to influence legislation. From that time on the Society has worked through these two groups on conservation problems. In 1950 the Ecologists Union became The Nature Conservancy.

The major publication of the Society is the quarterly *Ecology*. Such a journal was seriously discussed by members in 1917, but it was not until 1919, largely through the efforts of Barrington Moore and Norman Taylor that this was achieved. These gentlemen also arranged for the owners of *Plant World* to transfer their rights, including subscription lists, to the Society with the only proviso that the cover of *Ecology* should carry the words "Continuing the *Plant World*." Finally, Taylor, who at the time was a staff member of the Brooklyn Botanic Garden, was able to secure its financial backing and the Garden continued to cooperate in the publication of *Ecology* until 1948. Since that time Duke University Press has cooperated with the Society in its publication.

Publications of the Society also include a quarterly *Bulletin*, published continuously since 1917, containing general news about the Society, abstracts of papers presented at the national meetings, and every three or four years a Special Directory Number with names and addresses of all members; and *Ecological Monographs*, which contains longer papers on ecological topics. The latter has been published quarterly since 1931.

Meetings were held annually with the American Association for the Advancement of Science until 1947 when the American Institute of Biological Sciences was formed. Since that date the Society has continued to participate in the AAAS meetings but the annual business meeting and field trips have been scheduled to coincide with the annual meetings of the AIBS which normally is held in late August. These meetings of the Society have been devoted to the usual presentation of papers, official business, and social affairs.

Membership is divided into four categories: active, sustaining, associate, and life, the vast majority of the present 2,200 total being in the first category. The Secretary of the Society has offices at Michigan State University, East Lansing, Michigan.[92]

MATHEMATICAL ASSOCIATION OF AMERICA

The prime movers in the founding of the Mathematical Association of America, in 1915, were Professors W. D. Cairns, E. R. Hedrick and, particularly, H. E. Slaught. It was Slaught who, in 1907, took over the editorial direction and management of the *American Mathematical Monthly*, established in 1894 by B. F. Finkel. Through Slaught's efforts a number of colleges and universities began to provide financial support for the *Monthly*, and the quality of its contents was improved. Also, increasing attention was given to articles of interest to teachers as contrasted with researchers in mathematics. This trend in the magazine which he directed buttressed a developing sentiment that, although the needs of those interested in pure mathematical research were being met by existing organizations, the broad field of collegiate mathematics, and particularly its teaching aspects, was being overlooked. At the April, 1914 meeting of the American Mathematical Society, a committee was organized by Slaught and his associates to call this matter to the attention of the Society. Early in 1915 this committee made a report to the governing council in which it urged the Society to take over publication of *The American Mathematical Monthly*. The governing Council and Society at large took the position that, while the area of activity of the *Monthly* was valuable, it seemed unwise to take over its publication. The Society did, however, encourage the founding of a separate organization for this purpose.

Thereupon the committee issued a call for an organizational meeting to be held in Columbus, Ohio on December 30, 1915. Approximately 100 persons attended this meeting which resulted in the creation of the Mathematical Association of America. Hedrick was elected president; Cairns, Secretary-Treasurer, a position which he occupied until 1942; Slaught was named "Manager" of the new society and when the *American Mathematical Monthly* was acquired in 1916 as the Association's offical publication, he was retained as an editor. He continued in these positions until his death in 1937. Because of the prominent role he played in the organization of the Association and in its activities, Slaught was honored in various ways over the years. Elected President in 1919, in 1933 he was made honorory president for life with the privilege of life membership, and the 1938 publication of the *Monthly* was dedicated to him and featured two articles in memory of him.[93]

The Association, in addition to the *Monthly,* also arranged for the publication of mathematical papers of a historical nature in the *Annals of Mathematics*. This arrangement, which provided for a subsidy from the Association to the *Annals,* was continued from 1916 until 1943. In 1925 funds for the publication of the *Carus Mathematical Monographs* were obtained from Mrs. Mary H. Carus. Mrs. Carus supplied funds for the first four volumes in this series but succeeding ones, presently numbering 13, have been published with appropriations provided by the Association. The Association has also published various reports of its committees and, the year after Slaught's death, a committee was appointed to study its overall activities. Among other recommendations it urged the publication of a series of pamphlets in honor of Professor Slaught. The Association adopted this recommendation and the first issue of the *Slaught Memorial Papers,* after delays due to World War II, appeared in 1947.

For many years the Association has held an annual meeting in January and a summer meeting in August. They have often been convened in conjunction with the American Mathematical Society and similiar organizations. A feature of the summer meetings is the series of Earle Raymond Hedrick Lectures on topics of current mathematical interest. These meetings have been scheduled all over the United States and Canada. In addition to the general meetings, the Association has established 27 sections in the United States which hold one- and two-day meetings for members in their locale. Their programs parallel those of the national meetings, consisting of papers, discussions and social activities.

Other past and present activities of the Association include: the work of its various committees, including the famous National Committee on Mathematical Requirements which studied and reported on the whole problem of mathematical education at the secondary and collegiate levels; its sponsorship of visiting lecturers for secondary schools and colleges; and its establishment of various awards and prizes for outstanding mathematical papers.

Membership is open to anyone interested in the field of mathematics. From 1,045 charter members the Association has grown to over 9,000 members, resident in all the states of the Union and including more than 500 residing in foreign countries. The Secretary maintains offices at the University of California, Davis, California.[94]

AMERICAN GEOPHYSICAL UNION

Soon after the establishment of the National Research Council in 1916, the then chairman of that organization, Dr. George E. Hale, and Dr. Louis A. Bauer, a geophysicist associated with the Council, agreed that the time was ripe for the establishment of a committee or group, within the framework of the Council, devoted to geophysics. They included in the latter term such subjects as geodesy, geological physics, meteorology, terrestrial magnetism and electricity, seismology, and oceanography. It was to bridge the gaps between these closely related subjects and to provide a point of contact for them that a new group was urged.

The initial reaction of the National Research Council was that such a need could be suitably met by the merging of geophysics with an existing geography committee. This was accomplished. A short time later, however, geophysics received a separate status by being included in a new Division of Physics, Mathematics, Astronomy, and Geophysics. So matters rested until the conclusion of World War I when the accompanying reorganization of the Council brought up the question of naming representatives to it from the various divisions. Those segments of divisions, such as Physics, Mathematics, etc., with national societies could easily dispose of the problem by referring it to them. The geophysicists, with one or two exceptions, simply did not have national societies in their major areas of concern. This problem plus a related one, the creation of an American Section of the proposed International Geophysical Union, was met by the appointment of a committee to consider it. On March 4, 1919, Dr. R. S. Woodward, the chairman, made a report which outlined a method whereby the American Section could be constituted. The report also stated that "The earth is at once the subject and the object of many sciences. Of these the most important are Astronomy, Geodesy, Geology, Meteorology, Seismology, Terrestrial Magnetism, Terrestrial Electricity, Tides and Volcanology." It added that "progress in the future is most likely to result from active cultivation of the borderlands that now serve to distinguish, but only indefinitely, the several fields of geophysics," and recommended, in conclusion, "that in order to promote research and discovery in geophysical science in general, steps be taken by the American Section of the International Geophysical Union toward the formation of a new society to be called the American Geophysical Society."

Approval was soon given for the formation of an American Section and it was set up. This Section was also designated as the Geophysics Committee of the Division of Physical Sciences within the National Research Council and the establishment of a geophysical society was referred to it. As the result of numerous meetings to consider the matter, the members of the composite Section-Committee recommended that it be reconstituted as the American Geophysical Union and that this Union be made a separate Committee of the National Research Council. On December 20, 1919 these proposals were approved by the Council. By 1921 the organizational structure had so evolved that the Union played a dual role, *viz.* the Executive Committee of the American Geophysical Union had become the Committee on Geophysics of the National Research Council and the Union, as a whole, became the American National Committee of the International Geodetic and Geophysical Union. From time to time there has been discussion of the creation of a completely separate geophysical society, but the relationship described above has remained the same to date. This is undoubtedly due to the fact that the American Geophysical Union, although sponsored by and an integral part of the National Academy of Sciences-National Research Council, became for all practicable purposes an independent learned society.

The American Union made an initial contribution to science by the leading role its members played in the first organizational meeting of the International Union at Brussels in 1919. Since that time, in furthering its stated purpose of promoting "the study of problems concerned with the figure and physics of the Earth, to initiate and coordinate researches which depend upon international and national cooperation, and to provide for their scientific discussion and publication," the American Union has from time to time sponsored expeditions to various parts of the globe for studies ranging from the oceans depths to the highest mountains; from the coldest to the hottest surfaces of the earth; and to outer space. Many of these expeditions were in cooperation with national and international governmental agencies, scientific institutions and societies, and universities. More recently, officials and members of the American Geophysical Union were responsible to a large degree, for the intiation and success of the highly publicised International Geophysical Year (IGY).

Since 1920, the Union has published the *Transactions*. Published annually and usually in several parts until 1945, and as a bi-monthly from 1945-1958, it contains the scientific papers, discussions, and reports presented at the annual and regional meetings. From 1930 to 1955, an economical feature of this publication has been the use of an off-set printing method. Starting in 1959, the *Transactions* were changed to a quarterly containing information of general interest to geophysicists but excluding purely scientific papers. At the same time it was superseded as a learned journal by the Union's monthly *Journal of Geophysical Research*. The Union has also published many maps and charts and special studies dealing with specific geophysical subjects such as the bibliography of American hydrographic literature.

Annual meetings or assemblies of the Union have taken place every year since 1920. They are scheduled for the spring of the year, usually for a three- or four-day period, and they have always been held in Washington, D. C. Starting in 1961, a second annual meeting was being held in the West; the first such meeting was held in December at the University of California, Los Angeles, (UCLA). Since 1939 a feature of the annual meeting has been the awarding of the William Bowie Medal to a distinguished geophysicist. An increasing number of regional meetings have also been called and, since 1919, the Union has provided representatives at the usually triennial meetings of the International Union.

All of the foregoing activities have done much to gain recognition for geophysics as a scientific profession. Attesting this fact has been the creation, in 1951, of a formal Section of Geophysics within the National Academy of Sciences that presently numbers 31 members.

Membership in the American Geophysical Union was originally restricted to 65 persons. This limit was raised to 75 in 1922 and to 100 in 1928; in 1930 limitation as to membership was removed and from that time forward the Union, which had previously been supported by annual contributions from the National Research Council, became largely self-supporting from dues and other sources. Membership has steadily increased to its present approximate 6,300. In addition to regular membership, open to persons engaged in geophysical research, the Union has associate membership, open to persons interested in geophysics but not qualified for regular membership; corresponding membership, for nationals of other countries; and corporation membership. Executive offices are located at 1515 Massachusetts Avenue, N.W., Washington 5, D. C.[95]

AMERICAN METEOROLOGICAL SOCIETY

The organization of the American Meterological Society in 1919 resulted from a concern about the future of meteorological science following the ebb of interest in it, particularly by the United States government, after World War I. Professor Charles F. Brooks of Harvard University, noting the sharp reductions in the 1919 governmental appropriation for the *Monthly Weather Review,* felt that an organization should be set up to counteract this development. He took the lead in the matter by discussion and correspondence with academic colleagues, government workers and others and, in August, 1919, it was he who announced that an organizational meeting for an American Meteorological Society would be held in St. Louis on December 29th of that year. At this meeting a constitution and by-laws, modeled after those of the American Physical Society, was adopted; immediate affiliation of the new Society was arranged with the American Association for the Advancement of Science; officers were elected, Professor Robert DeCourcy Ward of Harvard University being named the first president; and by January, 1920 the Society counted 586 members.

The monthly *Bulletin* of the Society, under the editorship of Professor Brooks from 1920 to 1936, has been published continuously and contains meteorological papers, reviews, notes and correspondence. The demands for world-wide knowledge of weather conditions during World War II resulted in 1944 in the establishment of the bimonthly *Journal of Meteorology,*[96] to be devoted to technical articles at the professional level. Following the war, *Weatherwise,* a popular, nontechnical bimonthly for amateurs as well as professionals, was established. The Society has also sponsored the periodic publication of *Meteorological Monographs* and *Meteorological Abstracts and Bibliography.* The former contains articles of a long or detailed nature, while the latter includes abstracts of articles and bibliographical information on meteorology. In addition, the Society has published various volumes, the best known being the *Compendium of Meteor-*

ology (1951) containing over 100 articles on all phases of meteorology.

The Society has established various awards to spur research and writing in meteorology. These include, among others, the Meisinger, Carl-Gustaf Rossby, Charles Franklin Brooks, and Father James B. Macelwane Awards, and cover all facets and levels of meteorological work. The Society presently sponsors a guidance service, visiting lecturer program, employment service, and professional directory in its efforts to aid meteorologists and to make a career in the field more attractive.

Throughout its history the Society has cooperated at the international level by way of publication, meetings and conferences, and, since 1951, it has sponsored the translation of foreign language articles and journals in its field.[97] In this, as in all of its other activities, the Society has been aided by the work of various committees, now numbering approximately 20.

Of special note in the history of the Society was the reorganization of 1944-46. It grew out of greatly magnified but similar problems to those facing meteorological workers during and after World War I and had the following results. While retaining the Society's academic and "pure research" interest, it effectually merged it with a greatly expanded professional or applied interest by rearranging the grades of membership; expanding publication facilities, commented on above; and establishing the office of Executive Secretary. This office has grown physically from a few rooms to its present day quarters in a historic house overlooking Boston Common, and performs a wide variety of services for all who are interested in meteorology.

Membership in its formative years was about equally divided between meteorologists and those interested in it as a subsidiary interest. During the span of time between the two World Wars the membership grew from its original 600 to 2,883 at the end of 1945. From the latter date to the present it has surged to over 7,700. Ten per cent of this total membership resides outside the United States, and about ten per cent are women.

There are now five grades of membership: corporation, open to organizations interested in the advancement of meteorological knowledge; professional, persons possessing requisite qualifications or experience; member, persons actively interested in meteorology; students, collegians actively engaged in the study of meteorology; and associates, persons engaged in the study of and amateurs interested in the subject. The professional and member grades comprise about 5,200 persons, corporation members number 85, while the student and associate members comprise the remainder.

Annual meetings, in December or January, have been held in various cities in the United States and Canada and are devoted to the usual reading of papers, discussions, official business, and social activities. The Society has also sponsored or participated in many national and international meetings and conferences. In June, 1958, for instance, it participated in the celebration of the fortieth anniversary of the Polar Front Theory in Norway and in April, 1960 arranged for the Eighth Radar Weather Conference in San Francisco, California. In addition, some 62 local branches have been organized by members. These branches serve as hosts to conferences and provide an additional means of communication about meteorological subjects. They are presently located in over 30 states and several foreign countries.[98] The headquarters of the Society are located at 45 Beacon Street, Boston 8, Massachusetts.

AMERICAN SOCIETY OF PARASITOLOGISTS

Although Dr. Joseph Leidy, famous biologist and paleontologist of the nineteenth century, did pioneer work in parasitology and has been called the "Founder of American Parasitology,"[99] in the United States scientific interest in parasitology as a separate discipline dates from the turn of the twentieth century. Scientists, such as Drs. C. W. Stiles of the U. S. Public Health Service, C. A. Kofoid of the University of California and H. B. Ward of the University of Nebraska and later the University of Illinois, were engaged at that time in parasitological research and, in the case of Drs. Kofoid and Ward, were training graduate students in the subject. In the decade prior to the founding of the American Society of Parasitologists (1924) scientists of the Zoological Division, Bureau of Animal Industry, of the U. S. Department of Agriculture became increasingly active in the area of parasitology. During this same period, too, the School of Hygiene and Public Health at Johns Hopkins University was created (1918) and endowed by the Rockefeller Foundation and in the 1920's it supplied increased numbers of parasitologists and public health officers.[100]

The need for a publication outlet for this research activity in parasitology had resulted in September, 1914 in the establishment of the *Journal of Parasitology* by Dr. Henry B. Ward. Dr. Ward was influenced in founding the *Journal* by his graduate training in Germany and by the establishment in 1908 in England of *Parasitology,* by Dr. George H. F. Nuttall, which pointed up the necessity for a similar journal in this country.

In 1910, four years prior to the publication of the first issue of the *Journal,* the Helminthological Society of Washington, or the "Helmsoc" as it was called by its members, had been organized by a group of parasitologists in the Washington-Baltimore area. A number of the leaders in the Helmsoc were among those active in the affairs of the *Journal* and the latter, with its first volume, Vol. 1, No. 2, December, 1914, assumed publication of the *Proceedings* of the Society which had previously been published in *Science*.[101]

Despite the problems caused by World War I, including the loss of contact with scientists of the Central Powers, the *Journal* was a success and the number of subscribers during the first ten years after its founding continually increased. As has been related, the same period saw a corresponding increase in the number and activity of parasitologists all over the country. Because of these developments, a belief gradually formed among parasitologists, particularly those members of the Helminthological Society of Washington,[102] that a national organization was needed. In the spring of 1924, therefore, a self-constituted committee of parasitologists from the Baltimore-Washington area, consisting of Drs. R. W. Hegner, Eloise B. Cram, B. H. Ransom and W. W. Cort sent out letters of inquiry as to views on such a development. The favorable responses resulted in this committee's drawing up a constitution for the proposed society and the scheduling of an organizational meeting in Washington, D. C. on December 30, 1924. This meeting, attended by 32 persons, saw the adoption of a constitution formally organizing the American Society of Parasitologists. Dr. Henry B. Ward was elected the Society's first president, and Drs. S. T. Darling and W. W. Cort, Vice-President and Secretary-Treasurer respectively. Since Dr. Ward also served *ex-officio* on the Council for the first year and as an elected member of the Council for the next four years and continued as proprietor and editor of the *Journal of Parasitology,* it was natural that the new Society and the *Journal* established a cooperative relationship. Announcement of the organization of the Society was published in the *Journal,* as well as the program and abstracts of papers and other material presented at subsequent annual meetings. Despite this cooperative effort, however, many leaders in the Society felt that it should have its own official publication, and a committee was appointed as early as December, 1927 to consider the matter. Dr. Ward was reluctant to relinquish control of the *Journal* until he was satisfied as to the stability of the Society. By 1932, with a membership which had climbed to about 600 persons, he was convinced and in that year made a gift of the *Journal* to the Society and at the same time resigned as editor. Dr. Ward was spontaneously elected to serve on the editorial board and a provision was made at the time of transfer that the cover of the *Journal* would thereafter always carry the legend, "Founded by Henry Baldwin Ward."[103]

On the occasion of the transfer, the Council of the Society appointed an editorial committee consisting of Dr. W. W. Cort, Chairman, and

Drs. Robert W. Hegner and Francis M. Root. In addition, an eleven-man Editorial Board, diversified as to the various phases of parasitology and representative of the different sections of the country, was appointed.[104] This editorial control structure has been continued to the present day with the difference that, in 1958, the Chairman was designated Editor, and various Assistant Editors were named. Also, following the transfer, the *Journal* changed from a quarterly and became, as it is today, a bi-monthly periodical.

In addition to publishing the *Journal,* the Society can point to other achievements by its officers and members in the advancement of parasitology. The work of Dr. Richard P. Strong in tropical diseases, and Dr. Charles W. Stiles in zoological nomenclature are examples. In recent years, World War II provided a dramatic backdrop for the achievements of American parasitology with the need to combat the parasitic diseases encountered on fighting fronts throughout the world, particularly in the tropical areas of the Pacific. The Society played an important role in organizing and aiding various war-time "crash" programs to speed up knowledge of and ability to cope with these diseases.

Over the years, the Society has been affiliated with the American Association for the Advancement of Science, the National Academy of Sciences — National Research Council, and the American Institute of Biological Sciences. It's first representatives to the AAAS, Drs. George R. LaRue and E. E. Tyzzer, were named in December, 1933. At the December, 1936 meeting the NAS-NRC invitation to become affiliated with its Division of Biology and Agriculture was approved. It was subsequently voted that Dr. Robert W. Hegner serve as the first representative of the Society to the NRC.

The Society was one of 27 biological groups represented, in the person of Dr. W. E. Price, at the April 11, 1947 meeting in Washington, D. C. which resulted the next year in the formation of the American Institute of Biological Sciences. Since that time, it has worked closely with the Institute on the translation of Russian parasitological books and journals, the preparation of career booklets for those interested in a career in parasitology, and other projects.

In 1940 the Society established an Endowment Fund of approximately $1,000 to undertake special projects of long range value and to serve as the nucleus for future gifts. This Fund has grown slowly, as the result of accretions from interest, but it has provided a continuous financial cushion for the Society in the event of an emergency.[105] More recently, in 1958, the Society ordered the design of an official seal and established the Henry Baldwin Ward Medal for meritorius work in parasitology.

The latter honor is sponsored by the pharmaceutical firm of **Parke, Davis and Company.** The laureate receives in addition to the medal, and engraved certificate of award, the sum of $1,000, and the defrayment of expenses to the annual meeting where the award is presented.[106]

The annual meetings of the Society, following the organizational one, were held during the last week in December in conjunction with the meeting of the AAAS. Since the creation of the American Institute of Biological Sciences in 1948, meetings have been scheduled in the late summer or early fall, with the member societies of that organization or of the American Society of Tropical Medicine and Hygiene. The latter organization has many overlapping interests and members with the ASP. These meetings have been held all over the United States and feature the usual reading of scientific papers, transaction of business, and social foregathering of the members.

Following intermittent discussion in the 1940's and 50's of the establishment of regional affiliates of the Society, the 1957 Constitution called for the establishment of such branches under conditions outlined in Article VI of that document. Subsequently, in 1958 and 1959, the Southern California Parasitologists, the Midwestern Conference of Parasitologists, and the Helminthological Society of Washington applied for and were accepted as affiliates of the Society.

Membership in the American Society of Parasitologists originally consisted of only two classes: active, open to anyone interested in parasitology; and, foreign honorary, open to distinguished foreign parasitologists. Qualifications were gradually tightened, however, so as to include among active members only those with adequate academic backgrounds and a record of activity in the field. In 1940, the number of foreign honorary members was restricted to a total of 12 persons at any one time, no two so elected coming from the same foreign country in the same year, and requiring the unanimous vote of the Council. In the same year, honorary life membership was created, limited to a total of five persons at any one time and with the requirement that they be over 60 years of age and receive the unanimous vote of the Council.

The Constitution adopted in 1957 eliminated both foreign honorary and honorary life membership and substituted for them honorary and emeritus membership.

Honorary membership is open to distinguished parasitologists abroad or at home, not active members of the Society. Their number may not exceed 15, and not more than three may be elected in any one year. Election requires the unanimous vote of the Council and a three-fourths vote of active members at a regular business meeting. Emeritus membership is open to all retired parasitologists who have rendered distinguished service to the Society for a period of not less than 20 years, and their number may not exceed one per cent of the number of active members at the time of election. The election procedure for emeritus members is the same as that followed for honorary members.

Emeritus members are exempt from the payment of dues but are accorded all of the rights and privileges of active members. Honorary members must pay regular dues in order to be afforded these privileges. The membership of the Society in all categories, in 1960, totalled approximately 1,000 persons. The Secretary's office is at the University of Illinois, Urbana, Illinois.[107]

AMERICAN INSTITUTE OF NUTRITION

This organization was the outgrowth of an increasing interest in the field of nutrition by certain members of the American Society of Biological Chemists and their desire, expressed as early as the 1920 meeting of the latter Society,[108] that a journal devoted to nutrition be founded. Dr. John R. Murlin, late Professor of Physiology at the University of Rochester, took the lead in this movement which culminated, in 1928, in the incorporation of the American Institute of Nutrition for the express purpose of publishing the *Journal of Nutrition*. Ownership of this *Journal* was vested in Dr. Murlin and four other incorporators, subsequently increased to 12, and Mr. Charles C. Thomas of Springfield, Illinois acted as publisher. The new *Journal* proved to be a success from the standpoint of the large number of manuscripts and papers received for publication; however, in the early stages of its establishment it suffered economic hardships. In 1933, therefore, the corporation turned to the Wistar Institute of Anatomy and Biology, which because of its endowment was in a position to absorb deficits, and negotiated an agreement with the Institute to publish the *Journal*, with the provision that a learned society would sponsor the *Journal* and that all members would be required to subscribe for it. The American Institute of Nutrition was thereupon reorganized in 1934 as a membership society, with 178 original charter members; and, once founded, the society voted the foregoing requirement for membership. Dr. Murlin continued as Editor of the *Journal* until 1939. He was succeeded by Dr. George W. Cowgill until 1959. The present editor is Dr. Richard H. Barnes, Cornell University.

The monthly *Journal of Nutrition*, the only publication in the United States and Canada devoted solely to this field, has been one of the achievements of the Institute. Another contribution of the Institute to the science of nutrition has been the annual meetings it has held since 1933.

Until 1940, they were held prior to and at the place of meeting of the Federation of American Societies for Experimental Biology. In that year, the Institute became affiliated with the Federation, subsequent annual meetings have been held with the other member societies.

The American Institute of Nutrition served as host and sponsored the Fifth International Congress on Nutrition held in the United States in September, 1960. This international conference was attended by approximately 2,300 nutritionists, of whom nearly 600 were from 67 countries other than Canada and the United States.

In recent years the Institute has cooperated on nutritional problems and programs with governmental agencies and such organizations as the Division of Biology and Agriculture of the National Research Council, and nominates members for the U. S. National Committee of the International Union of Nutritional Sciences.

The Institute has established several awards in the field of nutrition, including the Borden Award and the Osborne-Mendel Award for outstanding research contribution in the field of nutrition. In 1958 ten members were given a Fellows Award in recognition of their outstanding service in research in the field of nutrition. Thereafter, three members have been chosen as Fellows each year.

Standards for admission to membership have always been high, approximately 95 per cent of the present members having either a Ph.D. or M.D. degree. The Institute has grown from an initial 178 members to about 750 in 1960. In 1960 the Division of Clinical Nutrition was established. The Institute has the following categories of membership: active, which includes foreign members who comprise about five per cent of the total membership; and honorary, which were elected for the first time in 1960. These honorary members are distinguished individuals of any country who have contributed to the advance of the science of nutrition.[109] The Secretary of the Institute has offices at the National Institutes of Health, Bethesda 14, Maryland.

ECONOMETRIC SOCIETY

Section I of the constitution of this organization, founded in 1930, specifies that: "The Econometric Society is an international society for the advancement of economic theory in its relation to statistics and mathematics. The Society shall operate as a completely disinterested, scientific organization without political, social, financial, or nationalistic bias. Its main object shall be to promote studies that aim at a unification of the theoretical-quantitative and the empirical-quantitative approach to economic problems and that are penetrated by constructive and vigorous thinking similar to that which has come to dominate in the natural sciences. Any activity which promises ultimately to further such unification of theoretical and factual studies in economics shall be within the sphere of interest of the Society."[110]

Although two Europeans of the nineteenth century, Leon Walras and Antione A. Cournot, had engaged in and urged such study, it was not until the twentieth century that their vision was fulfilled. By 1912, several decades prior to the creation of the Society, a small number of men in Europe and the United States were interested in furthering the line of study advocated by Walras and Cournot. At that time Professor Irving Fisher of Yale University made an unsuccessful attempt to get the American Association for the Advancement of Science to create an organization devoted to such study. Although Wesley C. Mitchell, Arthur L. Moore and a few others were interested, it was not until 1926-27, as the result of the activities of Professor Charles F. Roos of Princeton University and Professor Ragnar Frisch of the University of Oslo, that the earlier seed which Fisher planted bore fruit.

It is interesting that these men on opposite sides of the Atlantic arrived at the same conclusions at approximately the same time. The development that prompted Roos in this direction was his attempt to get a technical paper published in 1926-27. He offered it to an American economics journal and the editor replied that he would publish it if the mathematical and statistical aspects were deleted; an inquiry to a mathematical journal brought an offer to publish if the economic and statistical aspects were eliminated; similarly, a statistical journal offered to publish if the mathematical and economic aspects were deleted. In desperation, Roos in the spring of 1928, appealed to Professor Edwin B. Wilson of Harvard University, who was then a member of the Executive Committee of the American Association for the Advancement of Science. The upshot of the matter was the creation of Section K in the Association, to be devoted to the development of economics and sociology as sciences, with Roos as Secretary.

During this same period, in Europe, Professor Frisch, in an exchange of correspondence with European colleagues, was urging the creation of an Econometric Society; suggesting the names of persons who might be interested in such a society and, as early as September 4, 1926, in a letter to Professor Francois Divisia of the Ecole nationale des Ponts et Chaussees, Paris, France, suggested the establishment of a periodical to be called "Econometrica." In the spring of 1928 Frisch came to the United States under the auspices of the Laura Spelman Rockefeller Memorial and in the course of his stay met Professor Roos. They found themselves in agreement as to the need for an Econometric Society and they decided to try to enlist Professor Fisher's support. The latter, although sympathetic to the idea, was inclined to be pessimistic because of his earlier experience, and said that he would cooperate only if 100 supporters could be found. After three days, Roos and Frisch came up with only 70 names but this so far exceeded Fisher's expectations that he agreed to cooperate anyway. After a year of discussion and consultation with others, the three then circulated letters to those likely to be interested in the proposed society and they received a favorable response. Thereupon the three sent out invitational letters to attend an organizational meeting to be held in Cleveland, Ohio on December 29, 1930. The meeting was called at that time and place in order to hold it in conjunction with several other learned societies meeting there. Twelve Americans and four Europeans attended this meeting at which a tentative constitution was adopted and Professor Fisher was elected President and Professors Roos and Frisch were elected members of a nine-man governing Council of the Society.

While the Econometric Society was being formed, Alfred Cowles III, an investment counselor of Colorado Springs, Colorado, had become interested in the failure of forecasters to call the turn on the great depression of '29 and had finally decided, in 1931, to stop his business activity and engage in research on the possibility and feasibility of economic forecasting. During the summer of 1931, Cowles discussed several aspects of such research with Professor Harold T. Davis of Indiana University. In the course of their conversations Davis suggested that Cowles should get in touch with the officials of the newly-formed Econometric Society because he believed that the Society's and Cowles' interests were similar. He also suggested that Cowles might want to underwrite some of the activities of the Society, including publication of a journal if such proved to be the case. Cowles contacted President Fisher and discussed these possibilities with him, Roos, and several other leading American members and they agreed to indorse his proposals. Objections, however, were raised by the European members who desired to know more about Cowles and his proposals before concurring. Cowles replied by writing Frisch, designated by the Europeans as their representative, to come to Colorado Springs as his guest to discuss the matter. The outcome of their week long meeting was that Frisch became satisfied as to the disinterested and scientific basis upon which Cowles was making his proposal, and in January of 1932 joined with Fisher and Roos in recommending its acceptance.

Cowles' proposal was as follows: "Cowles would set up a research organization in Colorado Springs to be known as the Cowles Commission for Research in Economics; the Econometric Society would sponsor the

Cowles Commission; the Cowles Commission would be guided by an Advisory Council appointed by and from the Econometric Society, and Cowles would underwrite the cost of publishing a journal for the Society."[111]

From February, 1932, when the Society accepted this proposal, to 1955 its activities were intertwined with those of the Commission. Upon the founding of the Society's official journal, *Econometrica,* Frisch was chosen the editor and Cowles the circulation manager as well as treasurer of the Society and joint offices of the Society and Commission were maintained from 1932 to 1937 in Colorado Springs. By the latter date, the office's distance from major academic centers plus a change in Cowles' personal affairs due to the death of his father forced a move to Chicago where a mutually advantageous relationship was worked out with the University of Chicago. In 1955 the offices of the Society were moved to Yale University.

Since its founding, the Society and its members, aided by its affiliation with the Cowles Commission, have played an influential role. Professor Fisher made important contributions in the area of money and banking; Professor Harold Hotelling in mathematical statistics; the activities and research of Professors Joseph A. Schumpeter, Wesley C. Mitchell, and John Maynard Keynes, respectively fifth, sixth and seventh presidents of the Society, have received world-wide acclaim.

Membership in the Society developed at a rapid rate. Beginning with 16 in 1930, it grew to 163 in 1931, 671 in 1939 and today stands at approximately 1,600. Early in its career the Society was faced, however, with the problem of maintaining continuing contacts with economists, mathematicians, and statisticians and yet not "opening" the Society to a host that might, by press of numbers, destroy its character. This problem was solved by creating two categories of membership: regular and Fellows. The latter are charged with the general control and direction of the Society and are restricted to those who have knowledge and experience in economics, mathematics, and statistics or who are particularly distinguished in one or two of these fields. Although there have been some modifications of this criteria, the basic features have been retained and today there are only 120 Fellows of the Society.

Reflecting its international complexion, Europe initially led North America in membership. From 1938 on, however, the number of North American members increased and today comprises about 60 per cent of the total, and Europe, about 30 per cent. Because of this international membership and its international origins, the practice developed and has been maintained of alternately naming Presidents of the Society on one side of the Atlantic and Vice-Presidents on the other. Also, although all members realized the advantages of holding one annual international meeting, it was soon decided that pecuniary considerations made this impossible, and so the Society adopted the practice of holding separate European and American meetings. Members present at the time on either continent are welcome to attend. The American meetings have been held in September and December, usually in conjunction with the meetings of the American Economic or Statistical Associations, and follow the usual programmatic scheme of papers, discussion, and business. The European meetings, although several have taken place in such cities as Paris and Rome, have also been held in smaller university towns.[112]

The office of the Secretary of the Society is located at Yale University, New Haven, Connecticut.

GENETICS SOCIETY OF AMERICA

Founded in 1931, this organization was the outgrowth of the Joint Genetics Sections of the American Society of Zoologists and the Botanical Society of America. The Joint Genetics Sections was set up in December, 1921 following an annual meeting of the AAAS and was organized on the basis of proportional official representation from both of these societies.

With the passage of time, it became apparent that many geneticists, not members of either of the existing societies, desired a common meeting ground with their fellow geneticists. There was some dissatisfaction among geneticists within the Joint Sections, too, with the prevailing arrangement. In 1927 therefore, a committee was appointed by the Joint Genetics Sections to consider the kind of organization which could best meet the need of all American geneticists. As the result of this committee's study and subsequent reports, it was resolved in 1931, at an AAAS meeting in New Orleans, that the Joint Genetics Sections be reorganized as an independent Genetics Society of America. A constitution was adopted; the first officers were elected; and the Secretary was instructed to extend a cordial invitation to all geneticists to join the new society.

The Genetics Society of America retained its close connection with the AAAS and, more recently, with the American Institute of Biological Sciences. The old arrangement with the Wistar Institute whereby abstracts of the papers presented at meetings of the Joint Sections were published in the *Anatomical Record* was ended and an agreement was made to publish them in the *American Naturalist*. This arrangement prevailed until 1937 when the abstracts were transferred to *Genetics* and all subsequent ones have been published in that periodical. An official publication of the Society, *Records,* has appeared annually since 1932 and contains information of interest to geneticists in general as well as details of the business of the Society. In 1961 the Society voted to take over the publication of *Genetics* which on January 1, 1963 will become its official organ.

With the exception of the World War II years, annual meetings have been held since 1932, usually in conjunction with the AAAS. In addition, the Society has called a number of other meetings of a special nature, including summer and international ones. In 1950, for example, it cosponsored, in conjunction with the AIBS, a golden jubilee meeting on genetics at Ohio State University which resulted in the publication of *Genetics in the 20th Century,* a book containing essays on the subject by leaders in the field.

Membership is open to those persons interested in genetics. They must be recommended by two members and elected by the Executive Committee. The Society has grown from an initial 338 to its present 1,200 members.[113] Its Secretary's office is at the California Institute of Technology, Pasadena, California.

INSTITUTE OF MATHEMATICAL STATISTICS

The Annals of Mathematical Statistics, founded by Professor H. C. Carver of the University of Michigan in 1930, antedated the formation of the Institute of Mathematical Statistics by five years. During this period *The Annals* was affiliated with the American Statistical Association. By 1935, however, Professor Carver and a small group of persons interested in mathematical statistics became convinced that the existing mathematical and statistical societies did not meet their particular needs. Accordingly, during the joint meeting of the American Mathematical Society and the Mathematical Association of America in Ann Arbor, Michigan on September 12, 1935, this group discussed and adopted a constitution creating the new society and elected Professor H. L. Rietz, then of the State University of Iowa, its first president. By 1941, aided by a subvention in 1938 of $4,000 from the Rockefeller Foundation, the Institute was a going concern and able to assume full editorial and financial responsibility for *The Annals;* a responsibility which Professor Carver had previously shouldered.

Since its founding the quarterly *Annals* has presented articles containing new results in statistical theory and methodology, probability and related fields. In addition, since 1948 a Committee on Special Invited Papers periodically selects and publishes expository papers that are of particular interest and merit. Another publication of the Institute is a series entitled *Statistical Research Monographs* which provides a means of publication for articles, because of size, content or both, that are impracticable for other media. A contribution of the Institute in 1955 was its editing and resultant publication by McGraw-Hill Book Company of *Selected Papers in Statistics and Probability by Abraham Wald.*

In furthering its stated purpose of encouraging the development, dissemination, and application of mathematical statistics, the Institute has designated members to serve on inter-society committees, councils and other scientific groups such as the American Association for the Advancement of Science, and the National Research Council. It has established the Rietz Lecture, named for its first president, and every second year designates a distinguished scientist to deliver it. Also, since 1956 the Institute has presented, at each Annual meeting, a sequence of three or four one-hour expository lectures by one lecturer, on some phase of work in progress which is of considerable interest to members. The specialist selected to present the lectures has sufficient time to develop his material in some detail and thus makes it accessible to people not particularly conversant with his specialty. This series of annual lectures is called the Wald Lectures in honor of Abraham Wald.

The Institute, since 1935 has scheduled annual meetings for all members, usually in the fall and in conjunction with the meetings of the American Mathematical Society and the American Statistical Association. The programs of these meetings consist of the typical presentation of research papers, addresses of a more general nature, the transaction of business, and dinners and other social affairs. Also, since 1949, informal groups in the Eastern, Central and Western Regions of the United States have held annual meetings of their own, each under the aegis of an Associate Secretary, and have provided additional means of communication and intercourse among members with reduced travel costs.

Membership is open to all persons interested in mathematical statistics and includes primarily students and faculty members in colleges and universities and persons in government and industry. The membership is international, although 80 per cent is concentrated in the United States. Members of outstanding reputation and accomplishment may be elected Fellows, a distinction presently held by 168 members. In addition, there is provision for retired members and institutional members. The latter comprises organizations desirous of contributing $100 or more annually toward the support of the work of the Institute. The total membership is presently about 2,300.[114] The Secretary maintains an office at the University of North Carolina, Chapel Hill, North Carolina.

ASSOCIATION FOR SYMBOLIC LOGIC

The major objective of the Association for Symbolic Logic has always been to bring together mathematicians and philosophers interested in problems of logic. Prior to the organization of the Association, in 1935, mathematicians interested in problems of foundations and philosophers interested in symbolism did not have an effective medium for publication or means to bridge the gap that existed between them. Early in the 1930's a group of philosophers—mathematicians, including Professors C. A. Baylis, Alonzo Church, H. B. Curry and C. J. Ducasse, became convinced that the situation warranted the creation of a medium of publication for papers devoted to symbolic logic, papers that were not always welcomed by the existing philosophical or mathematical journals. Professor Ducasse took the lead in the matter and at the 1935 annual meeting of the American Philosophical Association's Eastern Division at Columbia University he presented a plan to organize an Association for Symbolic Logic with the express purpose of underwriting a learned journal. Enough interest was generated so that Professor Ducasse drew up a constitution and he was elected the first president of the new Association. In 1936 the quarterly *Journal of Symbolic Logic* was established with Professors Alonzo Church and C. H. Langford as editors.

The *Journal* is generally conceded to be the major accomplishment of the Association and, in addition to presenting articles, reviews, and notes, it is the medium whereby the bibliography of all known publications on symbolic logic since Leibnitz (1666) has been presented. This bibliography, published in 1936 (Volume 1, No. 4, of the *Journal*), with additions and corrections in 1938 (Volume 3, No. 4, of the *Journal*), is supplemented by a continuing review section which has kept it up to date. The bibliography and the review section have been the almost single-handed work of Professor Alonzo Church. The *Journal* is financed largely from membership dues, but subventions have been received from various universities and, more recently, it has received support from UNESCO through the International Council of Scientific Unions. It publishes articles in English, French, and German and the *Journal* is currently printed in the Netherlands.

Membership in the Association is open to all who are interested in symbolic logic. Approximately one-third of its 600 members live abroad.

Meetings are usually held in December. In addition to addresses by invited speakers, they provide a forum for research reports of members. These meetings are often held in conjunction with the American Mathematical Society or the Eastern Division of the American Philosophical Association. Also, the Association maintains close contact with and is a member of the American Association for the Advancement of Science, the National Research Council, and the International Union of History and

Philosophy of Science.[115] The business office of the Association is located at 190 Hope Street, Providence 6, Rhode Island.

The idea of a geochemical society originated with a small group of earth scientists headed by Drs. Earl Ingerson and John A. S. Adams. These men felt the need of a society devoted to the application of chemistry to the solution of geological and cosmological problems. Discussions by the group were held in 1955 at the annual meetings of the Society of Economic Geologists and the American Geophysical Union, and a decision was reached to hold a formal meeting at the November, 1955 New Orleans meeting of the Geological Society of America. At that time the Geochemical Society was organized; officers were elected, and a committee to formulate a constitution was named.

The following year, at a November, 1956 meeting, a constitution was adopted and the Society was incorporated in the District of Columbia. Also, an agreement was reached with the Pergamon Press whereby *Geochemica Acta* was established as the official journal of the Society. The Press retained financial control while the Society exercised editorial control of the publication. Since 1956 the Society has also published *Geochemical News* which provides notices, book reviews, etc., of interest to members. With funds provided by the National Science Foundation, the Society has recently engaged in an extensive translation program of Russian journals and books in the geochemical field. Several books and journals have already been published under the program, and more are underway.

The committees of the Society have been active: the Standards Committee aided in a project conducted by the National Bureau of Standards to supply standard samples for isotope abundance; the Research Committee has compiled and explored a world-wide list of possible geochemical research projects; an Education Committee has been making a study in that area; and an Organic Geochemistry Group was organized in November, 1959.

Annual meetings are held in conjunction with the November meeting of the Geological Society of America. The Geochemical Society also cooperates with other organizations in holding national and international symposia. In 1956, for example, it cooperated with the International Geological Congress in its meeting in Mexico; in 1959 it sponsored, at Coonamessett, Massachusetts a conference on the geochemistry of carbonates.

Membership is open to all persons with a sincere interest in the purposes of the Society who can give evidence of scholastic or practical attainments in the physical sciences. Total membership includes about 2,400 persons from over 50 different countries; about one-third of the members are from outside the United States. Many of the governing Council officers, including presidents, have been elected from among these foreign members.[116] The office of the Secretary of the Society is located at the Carnegie Institution of Washington, 2801 Upton Street, N.W., Washington 8, D. C.

CHAPTER III

COUNCILS AND SOCIETAL INSTITUTES

All of the national learned societies heretofore discussed are members of one or more of the groupings commonly labelled "councils" or "institutes." The councils are national in scope and, together, cover all aspects of the higher learning. They are the American Council on Education, the National Academy of Sciences-National Research Council, the American Council of Learned Societies, and the Social Science Research Council.[1]

The societal institutes, also named associations and federations, while national in scope, are groupings of learned societies in general areas or disciplines, although several include individuals as well as societies in their membership. In the natural sciences they include the American Association for the Advancement of Science, the Federation of American Societies for Experimental Biology, the American Institute of Physics, the American Geological Institute, and the American Institute of Biological Sciences. Although, as has been pointed out, the American Association for the Advancement of Science does have an interest in certain aspects of the social sciences, such as the history of science, similar institutes in the humanities and social sciences have not developed. The American Council of Learned Societies and the Social Science Research Council through their commissions and committees, and organizations such as the American Academy of Political and Social Science[2] and the National Academy of Design,[3] have, up to the present time, met the needs for cooperation among workers in these areas. There does appear, however, to be some contemporary sentiment for their creation. Societies such as the Metaphysical Society of America and the American Studies Association are certainly oriented in this direction.

THE COUNCILS[4]

Each of the four councils, to a greater or lesser degree, was an outgrowth of World War I. As that war heralded the United States as a world power, so the creation of these councils marked the organization for research and higher learning at the national and international level. In varying degrees, the learned societies have figured in their activities.

AMERICAN COUNCIL ON EDUCATION

Among the four councils, the American Council on Education occupies a pivotal position. It is "a *council* of national educational associations;

120

organizations having related interest; approved universities, colleges, teachers' colleges, junior colleges, technological schools, and selected private secondary schools; state departments of education, city school systems and private school systems; selected educational departments of business and industrial companies; voluntary associations of higher education in the states; and large public libraries."[5]

The Council was organized in 1918 by 11 national educational associations to coordinate the work of educational institutions and organizations during World War I. Membership was soon expanded to include: other educational associations, which together with the original 11 were designated *constituent* members; *institutional* members, that is, colleges and universities; and *associate* members, organizations with interests related to those of the Council.

The membership of the Council today is approximately 1,189 consisting of 142 national and regional associations, and 1,047 educational institutions. To it belong many of the other educational associations, including two of the three other councils, the National Research Council and the American Council of Learned Societies, as well as the American Association for the Advancement of Science, the American Institute of Physics, and the National Education Association. Although it strives to improve education at all levels, the Council has placed particular emphasis on higher education.

The Council is primarily financed by dues from its member organizations, by grants from foundations and individuals, and by payments from government contracts for special activities relating to education. The total budget for the calendar year 1960 was $1,083,494.37.

The Council operates through its staff and commissions and committees. Some of these, such as the Special Committee on Athletic Policy and the Committee on Aviation Education, have been organized on an *ad hoc* basis for specific purposes and limited periods of time. Others, such as the Commission on Government Relations (formerly the Committee on Relationships of Higher Education to the Federal Government), have had a long continuous service. The Commission on Government Relations has a membership representing a broad cross-section of American colleges and universities. Representatives of other educational organizations act as consultants to the Commission. This broad representation has enabled it to provide a consensus on educational matters affecting higher education and the Federal Government. Congressional committees and other government agencies seeking information have consistently requested this Commission's advice in such areas as veterans educational benefits, Reserve Officer Training Corps programs, Federal support for housing and academic facilities, Federal fellowship and student aid programs, etc. The Council's

Commission on International Affairs performs similar functions in its area of interest.

The Council maintains a press, one of its "best sellers" being *American Universities and Colleges*. Periodicals include the quarterly *Educational Record,* established in 1920, which presents articles primarily on phases of higher education, and *Higher Education and National Affairs,* an occasional bulletin which aims to report significant government, Council, and other national activities to educational institutions and organizations. Both of these publications are distributed free to members of the Council.

The annual meetings of the Council, which have been held alternately in Washington and Chicago, provide a sounding board for educational problems and are attended by educators from all over the United States and abroad.

Dr. Samuel P. Capen (1919-22) and Dr. Charles R. Mann (1923-34) were the Council's first two directors. Dr. George F. Zook assumed the presidency in 1934, having previously been United States Commissioner of Education. Dr. Zook served until 1950 and was succeeded by Dr. Arthur S. Adams, formerly president of the University of New Hampshire. In 1961, Dr. Adams retired and Dr. Logan Wilson, formerly President and Chancellor of the University of Texas, was chosen to head the Council.

Although the learned societies did not participate in the creation of the American Council on Education and, compared to their number and activities in the other councils, their role has not been as important, through the years there have been some very productive relationships between the ACE and a few of the learned societies.

Membership in the ACE has always been open to all of the learned societies upon application from them and approval by the Council but the number included in the Council's constituent membership has always been very small, and only five are presently constituent members.[6] Of this total, all save one are societies devoted to the humanities or social sciences. This paucity of numbers appears to be partially attributable to the fact that, with the exception of the Mathematical Association of America, which was included as a constituent member from 1946 to 1953, all of the member learned societies have had associate membership status. As such, the societies are constitutionally not permitted to cast votes on matters affecting policy, finances, officers, etc. The ACE's primary concern has been with the provision of a forum for the discussion and solution of broad educational problems; the maintenance of liaison between its membership, particularly its institutional members, and the federal government; and the conduct of studies and dissemination of findings bearing on these matters. Conversely, the other three Councils restrict their activities and efforts to matters relating respectively to the humanities, natural sciences, and social sciences and thus present more of an attraction to the particular societies. The dues of associate members in the ACE are considerably less than those charged the other categories: $50.00 per year as compared to $200.00 for constituent members and from $75.00 to $300.00 for institutional members, depending upon type of institution and enrollment. The associate members are entitled to nearly all of the benefits flowing from Council membership, *viz.,* representation at the annual meetings, publication discounts, representational and information services, etc. Some learned societies, such as the American Historical Association and the Modern Language Association of America, have found the ACE a willing partner or sponsor in movements for educational betterment. As early as 1920, for instance, the Modern Language Association of America requested the Council "to appoint a commission to study the position of modern languages in the American educational system and to assume financial responsibility therefor."[7] Out of this request there developed, in 1928, the establishment of the Council's Committee on Modern Languages. Through the succeeding decades, until its termination in 1955, this Committee made a number of contributions to the solution of language problems, particularly in the teaching of English as a foreign language. Much of its success was undoubtedly due to the effective working relationship between the ACE and MLA developed by Dr. Robert H. Fife, chairman of the Committee during the major portion of its existence.

However, the small number of member learned societies, the fact that they are all associate members and therefore the least influential in forming policy, and the fact that they act as independent units with little or no coordination between them makes for their having little influence on the ACE. The reverse of this is, of course, also true. Reflecting this loose relationship, only a few publications in which the learned societies have figured have been published by the ACE. To summarize, of any of the four councils, the American Council on Education has the least developed relationship with the learned societies.

The offices of the Council are located at 1785 Massachusetts Avenue, N. W., Washington, D. C.

NATIONAL ACADEMY OF SCIENCES-NATIONAL RESEARCH COUNCIL

The National Research Council also grew out of World War I, although its parent organization, the National Academy of Sciences, extends much further back into history. In order to comprehend the function of the National Research Council it is necessary to understand the history and role of the Academy.

The precursors of the National Academy of Sciences were two national societies founded in 1840, the National Institution for the Promotion of Science and the American Society of Geologists and Naturalists. The purpose of both was the advancement of science, but the first was an association with a broad membership, scientific and lay, while the second was composed almost wholly of professional scientists. After a brilliant and auspicious beginning supported by men of affairs and scientists from all over the country, the National Institution languished and finally died in 1861 because of changes in the political scene and a resultant refusal on the part of Congress to come forward with the necessary financial support. The American Society of Geologists and Naturalists continued its existence but, in 1848, changed its name and purpose to become the all-inclusive American Association for the Advancement of Science.[8]

The National Institution and the American Association paved the way for the National Academy of Sciences because scientists active in those organizations saw the need for an Academy. Alexander Dallas Bache, for instance, who became the first president of the Academy, in an 1851 presidential address to the American Association for the Advancement of Science, stated that "an institution of science supplementary to existing ones is much needed to guide public action in reference to scientific matters."

Bache, who was head of the United States Coast Survey, and Admiral Charles H. Davis, head of the Navy's Bureau of Navigation, were the two persons directly responsible for the establishment of the National Academy of Sciences. Davis, in 1863, conceived the idea of a scientific advisory commission to the Navy to aid it in the solution of technical problems. This Commission composed of Bache, Davis, and Joseph Henry, head of the Smithsonian Institution, was set up by Navy Secretary Gideon Welles on February 11, 1863. Almost immediately the plan for a broader academy occurred to Davis, and he and Bache and several other scientific figures succeeded in gaining Congressional and Presidential approval for its creation.[9]

The National Academy of Sciences was chartered on March 3, 1863, to meet the need of the government for competent, objective advice on scientific matters. The charter provides that "the Academy shall, whenever called upon by any department of the Government, investigate, examine, experiment, and report upon any subject of science or art, the actual expense of such investigations, examinations, experiments, and reports to be paid from appropriations which may be made for the purpose, but the Academy shall receive no compensation whatever for any services to the Government of the United States."[10]

The membership of the Academy, originally restricted to 50 persons, has always been a select group. Through the years, with the growth of the country's population the limitation on the number of members was periodically increased and, in 1950, removed. Officers and members have always insisted, however, on rigorous standards for election to membership and there is a limitation of 35 persons who can be elected members in any one year. As a result, although there are at present approximately 600 members of the Academy, such membership is considered one of the highest scientific honors.

During the decades between the Civil War and World War I, the Academy carried on its work through the appointment of committees to analyze and report on scientific problems. With the outbreak of war in 1914, however, the scientific leaders of the country realized that a better method for organizing the scientific and technical competence of the country was needed if the United States became involved. In 1916, therefore, led by George E. Hale, director of the Mount Wilson Observatory, William H. Welch of Johns Hopkins University, and Ambrose Swasey, a Cleveland, Ohio, engineer, the Academy offered its services to President Woodrow Wilson and the government. As the result of his acceptance, urged on apparently by his close friend and advisor, Col. E. M. House,[11] the National Research Council was created in 1916 as an operating arm or agency of the Academy and contributed materially to the war effort. As a result, several months before the armistice, on May 11, 1918, President Wilson issued Executive Order No. 2859 requesting the Academy to perpetuate the Council as a permanent body. The general purpose of the Council, as stated in that order, was "to stimulate research in the mathematical, physical, and biological sciences, and in the application of these sciences to engineering, agriculture, medicine, and other useful arts, with the object of increasing knowledge, of strengthening the national defense, and of contributing in other ways to the public welfare."[12]

The major portion of the membership of the Council is made up of representatives of the learned and technical societies of the country which are invited to nominate representatives for appointment by the President of the Academy. Originally designated by approximately 40 societies, those named in this way now total about 175 persons from some 110 societies.[13] There are, in addition, a number of members-at-large and a number of representatives from government agencies. The total membership of the National Research Council is presently about 250.

Reflecting the utilitarian aspect of its origin and *raison d'etre,* technical and professional societies have always adhered to the Research Council;

indeed, the Engineering Foundation of New York sustained the Council during the first year of its existence. Thus, although the division between basic and applied science is always a shifting and somewhat arbitrary one, only 29 of the 110 adhering societies in the Research Council can be classified as learned societies, the remainder being professional societies in the areas of medicine, agriculture, engineering, etc.

In the decades since World War I, the Academy and the Research Council have increasingly meshed and they have come to be designated the Academy-Research Council. In effect, the Academy members have come to act as trustees or a large board of directors for the Research Council. The executive body of the two groups is a Governing Board composed of the eleven-member Council of the Academy and the (8) Chairmen of the eight Divisions of the National Research Council.

The undertakings of the Academy-Research Council are carried out by these eight divisions operating through boards and institutes, committees, sub-committees, panels, and special *ad hoc* groups. There are also several inter-divisional offices, such as the Office of Scientific Personnel and the Office of International Relations. The pattern of organization has intentionally been left flexible to meet the needs of widely varying scientific problems.

A staff of approximately 150 executive and professional employees is maintained by the Academy-Research Council. Until the 1950's the Academy and the Research Council had, respectively, a President and a Chairman, the latter acting as chief administrative officer for the Council. At that time, these offices were gradually merged and Dr. Detlev W. Bronk, President of The Rockefeller Institute, was designated President of the combined Academy-Research Council. A new full-time post, Executive Officer, was also created and its present occupant is Dr. S. D. Cornell.

In 1962 Dr. Bronk was succeeded as President of the NAS-NRC by Dr. Frederick Seitz, Professor of Physics in the University of Illinois.

It would be futile to attempt to list all the contributions of the Academy-Research Council to scientific advancement. An outstanding example is the fellowship program of the NRC's Office of Scientific Personnel, headed by Dr. M. H. Trytten. Begun more than a quarter of a century ago with grants from the Rockefeller Foundation, the fellowship program has since benefited from the financial support of such corporations, foundations, and learned societies as the Radio Corporation of America, Merck and Company, the Eli Lilly Research Laboratories, the Carnegie Corporation of New York, and the American Chemical Society. The National Science Foundation has, since its beginning, requested that the Academy-

Research Council, through its Office of Scientific Personnel, select the scholars who should receive the many fellowships it awards.

Officials of the Academy-Research Council have always been aware of the important role played by the societies within the larger organization. In 1920 James R. Angell, then Chairman of the Research Council, had this to say: "The personnel of societies such as these being, in theory at least, chosen for merit in the form of scientific accomplishment, evidently sustains a relation of peculiar potential value to the scientific development of our democracy. It is clear that only from this group, formed by natural processes of segregation, can be expected any considerable and uninterrupted contribution to the methods of human progress . . . . The Council is built on the foundation of the national scientific societies, upwards of forty being represented in our constituency. It is their instrument, so far as they choose to use it, for the promotion of research, and especially, where this is practicable and desirable, for the promotion of cooperation among research agencies."[14]

Very recently, President Bronk recognized the societies' importance to the Council by inaugurating, in 1958, a meeting of several days for all members of the Council. Held subsequently in 1959 and 1960, it is planned that henceforth one will be held each year. These meetings, which have been remarkably well attended, provide a means of inter-communication between the societies and the Academy-Research Council. Broad, inter-disciplinary scientific problems have been discussed and scientific leaders from all over the world have addressed the plenary and sub-sessions.

Of the four councils, the Academy-Research Council has had, by far, the largest operating budget. The 1958-59 annual report shows that "during the year ended June 30, 1959, the activities of the Academy and Research Council . . . resulted in total income from all sources of $12,310,262 and total expenses for all purposes of $12,310,262."

This report also shows that the United States government provided about 70 per cent of the income, while approximately 20 per cent came from foundations and other private concerns and 10 per cent from investments.[15]

The learned societies adhering to the Council exercise far more influence on the NAS-NRC than the constituent member learned societies of the ACE exercise on that Council. In the case of the Academy, although there is no official connection between them, the societies would appear to exercise a considerable indirect influence and *vice versa* because the Academy's members are made up over-whelmingly of individuals who are active in the affairs of their various learned societies. There is, too, some degree of over-lapping with Academicians serving as societal representatives on the Council.

In the case of the National Research Council, as has been pointed out, there is an official connection and the adhering societies provide representation to the Council. Although the adhering societies pay no dues to the Academy-Council, their representatives are a considerable factor in determining Council policy and they either form or designate members of the various committees and commissions which are created to carry out the projects inaugurated by this policy. Publications growing out of these projects are, consequently, usually of interest to members of the learned societies.

The headquarters building of the Academy-Research Council is located at 2101 Constitution Avenue, N.W., Washington 25, D. C.

AMERICAN COUNCIL OF LEARNED SOCIETIES

One of the associate members of the American Council on Education, the American Council of Learned Societies was organized at approximately the same time, 1919, as the ACE. Both organizations grew out of World War I, although for dissimilar reasons; whereas the ACE had been created by a group of educational associations to aid the allied war effort, the ACLS was organized by the following 12 learned societies shortly after the war ended:

American Philosophical Society
American Academy of Arts and Sciences
American Antiquarian Society
American Oriental Society
American Philological Association
Archaeological Institute of America
Modern Language Association of America
American Historical Association
American Economic Association
American Philosophical Association
American Political Science Association
American Sociological Society

The initiative in calling the organizational meeting in Boston for September 19, 1919, rested with the officers of the American Academy of Arts and Sciences and the American Historical Association. An immediate purpose of the new organization was to provide representation in the Union Académique Internationale (International Academic Union) in the absence of an official organization, similar to a European academy, to represent the United States abroad. It was exactly this absence of such an organization and the many attendant difficulties facing any attempt to create one that resulted in the plan for creating a federative Council from among existing organizations.[16]

From its original list of 12, the ACLS has periodically added other societies to its roster, so that by 1960 it was composed of 30 constituent societies.[17] Membership in the Council has always been highly selective, requiring a three-fourths vote of all the members at an annual meeting. Although discreet initiative has undoubtedly been taken by the Council on some occasions, a requisite for application by non-member organizations has always included extensive dossiers outlining the history, purpose, membership, financial condition, publications, etc., plus extensive conversations with Council officials. While the ACLS has always maintained that it was impossible to formulate specific criteria for the admission of new constituent societies, a 1950 statement on the matter postulates that a prospective constituent society should be concerned with the advancement of humane learning, be national in its membership, and should be able to demonstrate that it is stable and active.[18]

The Council originally consisted of two delegates from each of the constituent societies, but in 1946-47 a revision of the by-laws reduced the number of delegates from two to one. At the same time a Board of Directors, consisting of 12 members, in 1957 enlarged to 13 members, was created as a part of the Council and voted broad powers to manage the funds and affairs of the ACLS. The Board, which meets eight or more times a year, has been able to develop a continuity of policy based on the needs of the ACLS and the humanities as a whole rather than the sometimes differing interests of the individual societies. Several members-at-large, persons of broad competence in the humanities, have also been selected annually since the reorganization. It should be noted, however, that the practice of naming members-at-large will be discontinued when present members have served out their terms of office.

The delegates from the constituent member societies have always been named on the basis of criteria set up by the societies. Members of the Board of Directors and members-at-large are elected by the delegates. Officers of the Board are elected by the Council.

In addition to the above representation, a conference of secretaries or executive officers of the constituent societies has regularly met at the annual meetings of the Council. From 1925 until 1946 the conference was on an *ad hoc* basis; at the latter time it became a permanent adjunct of the ACLS. It considers the many problems of mutual concern to the societies, particularly those involved in the operation of respective executive offices, exchanges ideas, and reports the results of its deliberations to the Council for needed action.

From its beginnings and through the years the ACLS has continued to represent the humanities internationally by providing delegates to the annual meetings of the International Academic Union. In addition, however, the promotion of humanistic studies in the United States became one of its major concerns at a very early period. The outstanding fruits of this early activity were: the publication of the *Dictionary of American Biography* (DAB), the second supplementary volume of which appeared in 1958; the *Linguistic Atlas of New England* (the published portion of the *Linguistic Atlas of the United States and Canada*); and various grants-in-aid and research programs in the humanities.

Even before the 1930's the ACLS had begun to engage in many activities designed to broaden the scope of humanistic knowledge and research. It was, for instance, laying the groundwork for the study of the Middle East, the Far East, and Russia that was to prove so valuable to the nation in World War II. When this national emergency arose, the Council was prepared to make a unique contribution by identifying the linguistic, intelligence, and other specialists who were necessary for the prosecution of war in areas totally unfamiliar to all but a handful of Americans. In addition, the ACLS aided in devising ways and means to train other persons as specialists in these areas in the shortest possible period of time. The contribution of the ACLS in these endeavors was wholehearted and note-worthy but was not widely publicized nor fully appreciated.

The ACLS, both in its relations to its constituent societies and in its programs, usually has operated at the college and university level, although in recent years the relevance of more general matters has been recognized with increasing frequency. Although it does receive dues from its constituent societies, its chief means of support has continued to be grants from philanthropic foundations and, on a number of occasions, government contracts. The present annual budget (1960) of the ACLS is about $1,000,000.

The program of the ACLS comprehends a variety of activities and interests, among which are: the support of fundamental scholarly research through programs of fellowships and grants-in-aid; an investigation of the problems of scholarly publication; efforts toward increasing our participation in international scholarly conferences; sponsorship of small conferences; encouragement of the humanities in the secondary schools; increase of public understanding of the humanities; and development of teaching materials for little-known languages.

All of the above activities are carried on by a small executive staff with the help of an extensive system of committees. In recent years there has been an increasing number of joint committees with the Social Science Research Council.

In 1957, Frederick Burkhardt, former president of Bennington College, was made executive head of the ACLS, with the title of president. Former executive directors were Waldo G. Leland, who assumed office in 1924 and became director emeritus in 1946; Richard H. Shryock; Cornelius Kruse; Charles E. Odegaard; and Mortimer Graves.

The 1957-58 reorganization of the executive offices was accompanied by a shift in location of its headquarters from Washington, D. C., to New York City.

The American Council of Learned Societies has always been influenced by its member societies to a much greater extent than was the case with the ACE or NAS-NRC. The ACLS was the direct outgrowth of common action by a group of societies. Even though the 1946-47 reorganization resulted in the creation of a governing Board of Directors which was one step removed from the elected representatives of the societies, these same representatives vote on who is elected to the Board. Furthermore, from the beginning, the conference of secretaries of the societies met annually within the Council's larger annual meeting. The conference may recommend measures to the Council which, although not mandatory for action by the latter body, are carefully considered. The dues paid by all of the societal members, although only $35 to $100 per annum, depending upon the size of membership, are in contrast to the little or none paid by members of the other councils. Practically all of its publications have been of direct interest to one or more societal members. Furthermore, the ACLS has attempted to aid its member societies by interceding with the foundations and other groups for financial aid for projects carried out by the individual societies rather than the Council. To summarize, the American Council of Learned Societies appears to have had a close and intimate relationship with its member societies.

Headquarters of the Council are at 345 East 46 Street, New York, N.Y.

SOCIAL SCIENCE RESEARCH COUNCIL

The initial recommendation for the creation of a Social Science Research Council came from the Committee on Political Research of the American Political Science Association in 1922.[19] The stated purpose of the proposed Council included the development of research in the social sciences, encouragement of the establishment of institutes for social science study and other specific suggestions. The subsequent deliberations of the incorporating group that organized the "permanent" Council in 1923-24, however, led to its incorporation with a broader statement of purpose and the selection of specific appropriate means for advancing research in the social sciences was left flexible to meet future needs. This flexibility has been a primary factor in the Council's successful operation which has changed over the years as the interests of social scientists have altered.

Underlying the reasons for the creation of the SSRC were the influences of World War I upon the individuals who founded it. Their awareness of the social problems that would arise from advances in the natural sciences and technology and of the consequent need for understanding human behavior in the light of these advances led them to provide a mechanism for interdisciplinary effort and cooperation.[20]

The Social Science Research Council was incorporated in the State of Illinois on December 27, 1924. Its original incorporators represented the American Political Science Association, the American Economic Association, the American Sociological Society, and the American Statistical Association. In the following year they were joined by representatives appointed by three other learned societies, the American Historical Association, the American Anthropological Association, and the American Psychological Association.[21] The membership of the corporation consists of all former and all current members of its governing Board of Directors. Thus, the Council was created by social science scholars and has been governed by them.

The relationship between the Council and its associated societies has been one of cooperation on matters of mutual interest but with complete independence on both sides. The only formal relationship is that the societies select, from slates proposed by the Board of Directors of the Council, a large proportion of this same Board. Consequently the 30-member Board is composed of 21 members selected in this way, and the remaining 9 Directors are selected at large, without restriction, by the Board. Although some critics maintain that this is a non-democratic procedure, the reason for this development appears to be the necessity for getting men on the governing Board who are not only respected by their fellow academicians but who are also known to be willing to engage in the time-consuming work entailed in election to membership. It is significant that the ACLS after some 40 years of representation based on direct nomination by the societies has now adopted several features of this procedure.

In advancing social science research the SSRC has, in general, been interested in the analysis of problems and the development of plans of research in various social science areas, and the administration of a program of fellowships or grants to individuals or groups of individuals for their research projects in the social sciences. Since inception the Council has carried out its program through a flexible committee system. Virtually all business clears through the Council's Committee on Problems and Policy before going to the Board or its Executive Committee. Committees have, from time to time, been constituted for specific considerations and terminated at the conclusion of their usefulness. Others have been of continued existence. The committees, presently numbering about 30, have generally been of two types, those connected with research planning and appraisal, and those concerned with the planning and administration of the Council's fellowships or grants.

The Council's Committee on Political Behavior is an example of a committee of the first type. Since 1949 it has been this Committee's task to analyze the possibilities of applying worthwhile empirical techniques in other fields to research in political science. Two examples of the second type are the Committee on Social Science Personnel, with responsibility for the development of research workers in all the social sciences and administration of the Council's research training fellowship program, and the Committee on Grants-in-Aid, with a program of grants for projects undertaken by mature scholars of established competence. The latter committees have been in operation since 1933 and 1926 respectively.

Another aspect of Council activity has been the occasional stimulation of research in an area where it is needed but not being undertaken. The Committee on the Near and Middle East, for instance, was set up in 1951 and reconstituted in 1955 to develop plans for research on contemporary problems in that area. Another instance is provided by the establishment in 1956 of the Committee on National Security Policy Research to stimulate research on problems bearing on national defense since 1939.

The SSRC, while operating in a cooperative relationship with its associated societies, receives no dues from these societies. Its chief sources of revenue are grants from philanthropic foundations and income from capital investment funds provided it by some of these foundations. The 1960 annual budget of the SSRC was about $1,500,000.

Originally the chairman of the Board of Directors served as the executive officer of the Council, but since 1929 a separate executive officer has been named: E. B. Wilson, statistician, 1929-31; R. S. Woodworth, psychologist, 1931-32; Robert T. Crane, political scientist, 1932-45; Donald R. Young, sociologist, 1945-48. Dr. Young's successor and the President today is Dr. Pendleton Herring, political scientist.

The SSRC is similar to the ACLS in that its publications and other activities are of interest to the members of its associated societies. Through the years the SSRC has been relatively more interested in programs sponsored and conducted by itself than was the case with the ACLS, which was founded directly by its member societies and has always been much concerned with societal projects and problems. It must be said, however, that the ACLS appears to be veering more and more towards the SSRC position.

In conclusion, it seems that the SSRC is not as closely related to its associated member learned societies as the ACLS, but somewhat more than is the case with the NRC, and a great deal more than is the case with the ACE.

Headquarters of the SSRC are located at 230 Park Avenue, New York, New York.

SOCIETAL INSTITUTES

AMERICAN ASSOCIATION FOR THE ADVANCEMENT OF SCIENCE

Three converging and overlapping forces led to the founding of the American Association for the Advancement of Science in 1848. These were the possibilities for scientific advancement inherent but not realized in the ill-starred National Institution for the Promotion of Science organized in the 1840's; the movement for a broadening of the area of operation of a then existing society, the Association of American Geologists and Naturalists; and the formation, at York, England in 1831 of the British Association for the Advancement of Science.

After Washington became the national capital in 1800-1801 various attempts were made to establish a national learned society or institution there. A United States Military Philosophical Society held a meeting there in 1808. The Metropolitan Society was organized there between 1810 and 1815 and, in 1816, this became the Columbian Institute for the Promotion of Arts and Sciences. Daniel Webster, John C. Calhoun, Henry Clay, John Quincy Adams, and many other prominent figures of the day participated in its activities. By 1840 the Columbian Institute had metamorphosed into the National Institution for the Promotion of Science. This organization was projected as a national one and included eight sections devoted to various branches of learning. It was incorporated by Act of Congress at that time and received Congressional appropriations of money in 1841 and 1842. In 1844, it held a national scientific congress in the capital which was attended by many of the nation's scientific and political leaders. The American Philosophical Society, the Association of American Geologists and Naturalists and several other organizations were associated with it in this noteworthy enterprise. Despite this auspicious beginning, inept management and shifting political tides worked the

National Institution's undoing and, in 1861, it was swept into oblivion by the Civil War.

The effect of the National Institution and, particularly, its congress of 1844, was not lost on the Association of American Geologists and Naturalists. Men prominent in the latter organization had been active in the former and they saw the benefits to be achieved from an all-inclusive scientific association. Accordingly, as early as 1845, it was announced at an Association meeting that "a constant effort has been made to counteract the impression that the objects of the Association are exclusively geological or directed to those cognate subjects only which have a direct bearing upon that subject." In 1847 further moves were made to enlarge the membership and scope of the Association. Finally, on September 20, 1848, at a meeting in Philadelphia, the name was changed to the American Association for the Advancement of Science and the constitution was revised. The "Rules" (constitution) was certainly borrowed from that of the British Association for the Advancement of Science, established earlier. Louis Agassiz, newly arrived from England and one of three members of the constitutional drafting committee, was familiar with the organization and work of the British Association and probably copied its constitution.[22]

Since its founding the AAAS has held meetings in all parts of the country, though tending to concentrate on the larger cities on the East Coast. It has engaged in scientific publication, the *Proceedings* being published from the beginning while the weekly *Science* and the *Scientific Monthly* were established in 1900 and 1915 respectively. They were both continuously published until 1958 when the *Monthly* was merged with *Science*. More recently, the *AAAS Bulletin,* a monthly publication with articles of historical and general interest, was published from March, 1942 through December, 1946.[23]

The Association has offered membership to all persons interested in any aspect of science. In this regard it is quite similar to other learned societies and institutes. It differs from them, however, in its all-inclusive disciplinary character. Its relationship to the learned societies has been historically conditioned, too, by the Association's being the spawning ground of societies and not *vice versa*.

Originally membership in the AAAS and the programs at the annual meeting were divided into rather fluid sections. The constitution of 1874, however, provided for two definite sections: Mathematics, Physics, and Chemistry (A), and Natural History (B). This set a precedent and as science became more specialized and membership increased the number of sections did likewise. There were 9 in 1892; 12 in 1895; and at the present time, 18. They are: Mathematics (A), Physics (B), Chemistry

(C), Astronomy (D), Geology and Geography (E), Zoological Sciences (F), Botanical Sciences (G), Anthropology (H), Psychology (I), Social and Economic Sciences (K), History and Philosophy of Science (L), Engineering (M), Medical Sciences (N), Dentistry (Nd), Pharmacy (Np), Agriculture (O), Industrial Science (P) and Education (Q). Members, upon entering the Association, designate the Section in which they wish to enroll.

The Sections have been a centripetal and centrifugal force within the Association. Created to supply a demand by members for more specialized grouping, there have been numerous examples of members branching out and organizing such independent societies as the Geological Society of America, the Botanical Society of America, American Physical Society, the American Anthropological Association, and the History of Science Society.

It thus became apparent as early as the 1890's that some policy regarding the Sections and their offspring would have to be taken by the Association. A Committee to consider the problem was created in 1895 and as a result of its and other deliberations the learned societies were given "Affiliated" or "Associated" status within the Association by the terms of the Constitution of 1899. During 1901 the affiliated societies were extended representation on the legislative Council; their representatives now form a majority of that body of approximately 400 scientists. The AAAS, therefore, originated as an individual membership society and it was not until the development of a great number of learned societies after the Civil War that the question of its relationship to them arose. By deliberate action of the Association, such societies were invited and did become affiliated with it. Although they do have a considerable influence within the Association, because of its tremendous number of individual members, with greatly varying interests, and the vast number of sections and committees set up within the Association's structure, this influence has been diffused. The Association, more so than any other societal institute, is in the delicate position of balancing the sometimes conflicting objectives and desires of groups of individual members and the learned societies.

In addition to the members associated with it through the almost 300 affiliated societies and academies,[24] the Association's own membership has grown from an original 461 to 1,004 in 1854; 1,030 in 1879, after a drop as a result of the Civil War; 2,000 in 1883; 4,000 in 1903; 11,000 in 1920 and approximately 60,000 today. Although five different types of membership are provided for, *viz.,* annual, life, sustaining, honorary and emeritus, the main distinction in membership, since 1874, has been between that of ordinary members and Fellows. The latter are elected because of merit and are the only members that can be elected to the legislative Council. There are presently about 15,000 Fellows.

In addition to the Council, the organizational structure of the AAAS includes a thirteen man Board of Directors, which acts as the legal representative of the Association and performs the functions of an executive or governing committee, and an Executive Officer, Dr. Dael Wolfle.

Besides the Affiliated societies, the AAAS has provided for the creation of autonomous divisions which receive financial support in the form of remission of a part of members' dues. In 1915 the Pacific Division was set up, in 1920 the Southwestern and Rocky Mountain Divisions, and in 1951 the Alaskan Division. Although the airplane has facilitated travel and made it much easier for members from other sections to attend meetings in the East, these divisions are still very active; they hold their own meetings, elect their own officers, and utilize the Association's journals to make announcements. They have undoubtedly been another significant factor in making the Association one great union of scientists and learned societies.[25]

The activities of the Association are conducted from a recently completed office building at 1515 Massachusetts Avenue, N. W., Washington 5, D. C.

FEDERATION OF AMERICAN SOCIETIES FOR EXPERIMENTAL BIOLOGY

The Federation of American Societies for Experimental Biology was organized by delegates from the American Physiological Society, the American Society of Biological Chemists, and the American Society for Pharmacology and Experimental Therapeutics on December 31, 1912. The primary purpose of the new organization was the arranging of joint meetings of these societies for the presentation of scientific papers to their members.

The following year the American Society for Experimental Pathology was formed, applied for and was admitted to membership in the Federation. Since that time only two other societies have been admitted to membership, although more than that number have applied. These two were the American Institute of Nutrition in 1940 and the American Association of Immunologists in 1942.[26] Criteria for membership in the Federation have included: concern with the biological sciences, particularly its biomedical aspects; non-duplication of functions of member societies; and a record of stability and scholarship, as evinced by sufficient members, fiscal responsibility, and a significant publication program.

Originally the Federation was a loosely-knit organization with executive functions vested in an Executive Committee composed of the President and Secretary of each member society. It was found at an early date, however, that one person could best handle programming of the meetings and, until 1946, this task was performed by Dr. D. R. Hooker. In 1947 a new full-time position, that of Executive Officer, was created and augmented functions were assigned that officer. Dr. Milton O. Lee, then editor of the *American Journal of Physiology,* was the original person named as Executive Officer, a position which he still holds. In 1952, a new Constitution and By-Laws were adopted and the Federation was incorporated on January 19, 1954, in the District of Columbia, with a Charter that broadened its purposes and objectives. In 1958, the Federation was further reorganized and an Advisory Committee was created, composed of one representative from each Society, which meets regularly and reports to the Federation's Board. This Executive Board, in turn, is composed of three delegates from each of the six societies.

The Federation serves more than 6,600 members of its six societies. Its primary contributions to the members and the societies have been threefold: facilitating personal contact between investigators in the biological and medical sciences by means of the annual meeting (at the April, 1960 annual meeting, in Chicago, there was a registered attendance of 11,000 persons and more than 2,600 papers were presented); performing other functions, such as the holding of symposia, etc., in which the societies can operate more effectively as a group than as individual units; and the publication of the *Federation Proceedings.* Put out as a quarterly since its origin in 1942 but changed to a bi-monthly publication in 1962, this journal was established in order to publish a consolidated program of the meetings of the Federation member Societies, abstracts of papers presented at these meetings, symposia and other papers, and a directory of members of the Societies of the Federation.[27]

Headquarters of the Federation are located at 9650 Wisconsin Avenue, N. W., Washington, D. C.

AMERICAN INSTITUTE OF PHYSICS

This organization came into being in 1931 as a means to preserve communication among physicists as a whole in the face of the dispersal of physicists into an increasing number of special fields. Leaders in physics were aware that other groups, such as the chemists, had solved this problem by structuring the different special fields as divisions or sections within one central society. The American Physical Society's Committee on Applied Physics, however, explored this plan and rejected it in favor of an "Institute of Physics" which would allow individual societies to retain their autonomy. Acting upon a December, 1930 Report on the Committee calling for the establishment of such an "Institute" and led by Drs. Karl T. Compton and George B. Pegram, the American Physical Society, the Optical Society of America, and the Acoustical Society of America formed a joint committee which met at Columbia University on February 27, 1931. Pursuant to recommendations adopted at that meeting, these organizations agreed to establish the American Institute of Physics. A Governing Board, composed of three members from each society, together with three from the Society of Rheology which had been invited to join the Institute, held its first meeting on May 3, 1931, in Washington, D. C. Shortly thereafter, on January 27, 1932, the newly formed American Association of Physics Teachers was admitted as a founder society with the other four.[28]

Office space in New York City and initial support for the newly-formed Institute was provided by the Chemical Foundation, a non-profit New York organization. By 1932 a constitution had been adopted which stated that the objective of the AIP was "the advancement and diffusion of knowledge of the science of physics and its application to human welfare" and that "to this end it is part of the purpose of this corporation to undertake, among other measures, the publication of scientific journals devoted wholly or mainly to physics and related sciences; to serve the public by making available to journals, newspapers, and other channels of public information reliable communications as to physics and its progress; to cooperate with local, national and international organizations devoted to physics; to promote unity and effectiveness of effort among all those who are devoting themselves to physics by research, by application of its principles, by teaching or by study; and to foster the relations of the science of physics to other sciences and to the arts and industries."

Except for a temporary, legalistic interval at the time of incorporation, the AIP had no individual members of its own; it acted through its Governing Board as a service organization for the founder societies. In 1946 the constitution was changed so as to provide that members of the individual societies were automatically members of the Institute; associate membership in the Institute alone was provided for those not desiring to join a particular society; representation on the Governing Board was changed so that it depended upon the membership of each society and three members-at-large were elected from the entire AIP membership.

In January, 1958, the constitution was further amended to provide for a new class of membership, the associate member society, in addition to existing member society and affiliated societies. The two present associate member Societies are the American Crystallographic Association and the American Astronomical Society, each of which elects one director to the AIP Governing Board. The prior individual associate membership was dropped and election of the three directors-at-large was made the responsibility of the Governing Board itself. The Governing Board presently numbers 25 persons; five each from the American Physical Society and the American Association of Physics Teachers; four each from the Optical Society of America and the Acoustical Society of America; two from the Society of Rheology; one each from the American Crystallographic Association and the American Astronomical Society; and three directors-at-large.

Other classes of membership are the student sections, which at the close of 1960 numbered 105, and the corporate associates, some 175 corporations, institutions and laboratories whose annual dues contribute toward the support of the Institute's program.

Publication of the journals of its member societies has, from the beginning, been a major activity of the Institute. Thus, the *Physical Review* and *Review of Modern Physics* as well as its *Bulletin* are published for the American Physical Society. The Institute publishes the *Journal of the Optical Society of America; Journal of the Acoustical Society of America; Noise Control;* the *American Journal of Physics* for the American Association of Physics Teachers; and the *Astronomical Journal* for the American Astronomical Society. Ownership and editorial control of these publications have been retained by each of the Societies, but the Institute handles routine publication matters. The Institute, in its own name, publishes and edits the *Review of Scientific Instruments, Journal of Chemical Physics, Journal of Applied Physics, The Physics of Fluids, Journal of Mathematical Physics,* and *Physics Today.* The latter journal is a news and communication medium rather than a technical one and has a circulation in excess of 30,000.

Recently, the AIP has engaged in an extensive translation program of Russian language journals and occasionally books dealing with physics, this program being carried on under grants from the National Science Foundation. It sponsors the publication of other books from time to time; cooperates with the British publishers of *Physics Abstracts;* and, with the advice of its Committee on Publishing Problems, engages in several aspects of documentation research.

In addition to publishing activities, the Institute carries on a program designed to advance physics and to serve the public interest through physics. Its education program is concerned with strengthening education in physics at all levels and has included such projects as a visiting physicist program for high schools, colleges and universities, the design of physics buildings, course content improvement, construction of teaching apparatus, and the preparation of career booklets. The public relations program is directed toward promoting a wider public understanding of physics. In addition to setting up press rooms and news conferences at member society meetings, the Institute has held seminars for science news writers to provide them with background information essential to an understanding of rapidly advancing fields of physics, so that they may better interpret physics to the layman. Other activities include manpower studies, services rendered to its societies, and operation of a free placement service for the use of employers and of physicists seeking jobs. The Institute holds an annual meeting of its corporate associates as well as an annual assembly of society officers and Governing Board members. Also it cooperates with other organizations in sponsoring conferences in interdisciplinary fields.

From 1931 until 1957 Dr. Henry A. Barton was Director of the Institute. His successor and the present Director is Dr. Elmer Hutchisson. From a membership in the five founding societies of an estimated 3,500, the number of physicists represented by the Institute now numbers approximately 25,000, exclusive of the associate member and affiliated societies and the corporate associates. From an initial budget of approximately $60,000, the Institute's financial operation for 1960, including various accounts of the member societies, totalled about $3,000,000.[29]

Both the American Institute of Physics and the Federation of American Societies for Experimental Biology were the direct outgrowth of the need by certain societies for a central organization. Member societies of the Federation elect three delegates to the Governing Board which controls it. The same procedure is followed by the Institute except that the number of such delegates is dependent upon societal membership and there are several members-at-large. Publications in both institutes are an important part of their activities and in both they are split—some controlled by the institute, others published for convenience by the institute but controlled by a member society.

Headquarters of the Institute are at 335 East 45th Street, New York, New York.

AMERICAN INSTITUTE OF BIOLOGICAL SCIENCES

This Institute developed from the same impetus that had, at an earlier period, spurred the creation of the American Institute of Physics, and caused the American Chemical Society to alter itself so as to take on a variety of additional activities. That is, the need for a central organization which could serve physicists, chemists, or in this case biologists, as a whole. The catalyst in bringing this about for the biological sciences was the Academy-Research Council. Although there had been discussion for a number of years within the Division of Biology and Agriculture of the Council about the possibility and even desirability of an institute, it was not until a November 21, 1946 conference at the National Research Council of a Committee on the Proposed Institute of American Biologists that definite plans for promoting such an institute were laid and agreement was reached that it should be discussed further at the forthcoming December meeting of the American Association for the Advancement of Science.

At the December, 1946 meeting of Section G of the AAAS a "Symposium on Proposed Plans for Union Involving Workers in the Biological Sciences" was held. Papers on the need for a national organization were read by Drs. Robert F. Griggs, R. E. Cleland, and H. R. Tukey and subsequently a follow-up meeting was called by the National Research Council to be held in Washington on March 18, 1947. This meeting included 14 biologists of note and constituted itself the Advisory Committee for an American Institute of Biological Sciences. An agreement was reached at this meeting to establish an organizing board composed of one member from each member society of the Division of Biology and Agriculture of the Research Council, and a sub-committee was appointed to prepare a tentative constitution for the board. On April 11, 1947, this organizing board met and adopted a provisional constitution calling for the establishment of the American Institute of Biological Sciences within the framework of the Research Council. It also recommended that the AIBS be launched upon ratification of the constitution by 10 of the 27 societies to be invited to become members and that control of the new organization be vested in a Governing Board composed of representatives of the prospective society members. By the end of 1947, 12 societies[30] had accepted membership, and the Institute came into being at a February 20, 1948, meeting at the National Research Council. An executive committee of the Governing Board was named and this committee was authorized and subsequently chose Dr. Clarence J. Hylander as the first Executive Secretary of the new organization.[31]

In 1955, although the AIBS has continued to maintain close liaison with the Academy-Research Council through its officers, committees, and executive staff, it severed its official connection with the Council and became an independent, non-profit organization, incorporated in the District of Columbia.

Since its inception in 1948 and reorganization in 1955, the AIBS has expanded in membership and activities. Its membership in all categories is now estimated to be over 80,000. It is composed of 23 member societies[32] national learned and professional societies concerned with the advancement of the biological sciences; 20 affiliate societies, similar regional societies; and 18 associate societies, organizations interested in contributing to the support of the AIBS. In addition, since 1955, individual membership has been provided for, although persons who are members of the adhering societies are considered members of the AIBS as well. The member and affiliate societies pay dues based on their membership, while the associate societies make varying contributions but not less than $200 per year. The various classes of individual membership, with the exception of honorary members, also call for the payment of dues.

The budget for the operation of the Institute has increased proportionately to its membership. From an initial one of about $17,000, in 1960 it was in excess of $2,000,000. Only a small portion of this amount was contributed by the societies, the remainder being grants and funds from government agencies, foundations, and other organizations. Also, the staff, under the supervision of Dr. Hiden T. Cox, Executive Director, has been increased and presently numbers about 100 persons.

The increase in Institute activities is due to the many additional projects it has undertaken in addition to its initial ones of sponsoring meetings of the biological societies and the publication of the *AIBS Bulletin* and other media of interest to biologists. The Institute has, in the past decade, organized and conducted a visiting lecturers program for high schools and colleges; engaged in an extensive translation program of Russian biological journals; cooperated with the National Science Foundation in the maintenance of a national register of biological scientists; made an extensive biological science curriculum study in 1959-60; sponsored closer contacts with international biological organizations and foreign scientists; and a host of other projects.[33]

These projects were developed by groups of biologists working within the framework of the AIBS. They were undertaken in the belief that they would work toward the betterment of biology. They reflect the belief— a belief which has been held by the AIBS since its founding days—that they are projects which small societies in the field could not undertake by themselves.

Main offices of the Institute are maintained at 2000 P Street, N. W., Washington, D. C. Suboffices are located in Baltimore, Maryland; Kansas City, Missouri; and Boulder, Colorado.

AMERICAN GEOLOGICAL INSTITUTE

It appears that an address before the 1942 annual meeting of the American Association of Petroleum Geologists by Dr. Carey Croneis sparked the movement for the creation of an American Geological Institute. In his address,[34] Croneis stated that geologists occupied a very low academic status. He attributed this status to an inept public relations attitude on the part of geologists and urged this as a compelling reason for the establishment of an American Geological Association or Institute. On April 10, 1943, a meeting to discuss Dr. Croneis's proposal was held at Fort Worth and was attended by more than 100 geologists from a majority of the national and regional geological societies. The upshot of this meeting was endorsement of the proposal and the naming of an organizational committee. This committee met in Chicago on August 20-23, 1943 and drafted a report of a tentative constitution and statement of purpose for the proposed organization which was submitted to 11 national geological organizations.[35] A meeting attended by representatives from 9 of these societies was subsequently held in New York on October 22, 1944 and, although there appears to have been some sentiment for the reorganization of the Geological Society of America to provide the services envisioned, it was generally agreed that a federation of societies was a better alternative. Thereupon, the name American Geological Institute was decided upon for the proposed organization and a revised constitution was adopted to become effective upon ratification by 7 of the 11 national societies designated as eligible to be founding members.

The record of events for the year following the New York meeting is obscure. Developments took a new course, however, with the calling of a meeting for October 12 and 13, 1945, by Dr. W. W. Rubey of the National Research Council, to be sponsored jointly by the Council and the Geological Society of America. In addition to the 11 societies previously enumerated, the Canadian Institute of Mining and Metallurgy, and Section E (Geology and Geography) of the American Association for the Advancement of Science, as well as the National Research Council participated in this meeting. A number of suggestions were made as to the type of geological organization to be formed: a trial organization, in the form of an informal council of geological societies; that Section E of the AAAS be used as a cooperating agency; that the Division of Geology and Geography of the National Research Council establish a Committee or Commission of geological societies as a Division function. Two committees were next set up to consider the problem and prepare reviews and reports on the matter. Finally, on May 2, 1947, at the annual meeting of the Division of Geography and Geology of the National Research Council, Dr. Detlev W. Bronk called the attention of the geologists to the AIBS, being created under Council auspices, and indicated that a similar arrangement for geologists would meet with Council approval. A subsequent meeting of the various geological societies on October 27, 1947 resulted in their falling in line with this plan and a revised constitution with an explanatory covering letter was sent out to the societies in December of 1947. The founding meeting of the AGI was then held in Washington on November 15, 1948 after the ratification of the constitution by the societies and after more than six years of planning, discussion and debate.[36]

Although the Institute was established, it was June 1, 1949 before the first Executive Director, Dr. David M. Delo, assumed his office and then on only a half-time basis; it was not until 1953 that the position was made a full-time responsibility. Furthermore, the financial situation of the new organization was shaky because of a constitutional provision, Article IX, No. 2, which stated that: "No Member organization shall be subject to assessment in any amount for any purpose." This provision plagued the Institute through the early 1950's and it was not until after the present Executive Director, Dr. Robert C. Stephenson, assumed office in 1955 that a regular contribution pattern by the member societies to the Institute developed but still on a voluntary basis with annual review by the contributing societies. In 1956 the Board of Directors voted that basic costs of the office and staff of the Institute should be the responsibility of the member societies. The total cost of Institute operations has always, however, exceeded the dues paid by the member societies and the difference has been annually made up by contributions from the Committee of One Hundred, leaders in the geological field, who each contribute $100 annually to Institute support, the Committee of One Thousand, each member contributing $10 annually, and from Industrial Associates, industrial organizations interested in supporting the Institute.

The governing body of the AGI is the Board of Directors, composed of two directors from each member society and two from the Academy-Research Council. Although the latter does provide directors, is *ex officio* represented on the executive committee, and handles the funds of the Institute, it does not control the Institute. There has been some sentiment, however, for an easing of the ties that do bind the organizations and, since 1959, the AGI has been planning toward eventual independence of the Academy-Research Council.

The membership of the American Geological Institute is composed of learned societies and technical and professional organizations.[37] It does not hold open, annual meetings, its policies being formulated and carried through by periodic meetings of the Executive Committee plus recommendations of standing and special committees and the staff. Activities carried on by such means include: formulation of a long-range program for education in the earth sciences; maintenance of an inventory of available geologists; and the providing of counsel and guidance to government agencies. Other activities of the AGI include the publication of the *Geo Times,* a news-periodical appearing eight times a year, *Geo Science Abstracts,* and since 1958, the *International Geological Review,* a periodical devoted to the translation of foreign geological articles, particularly Russian ones. Complete translations of the *Doklady* and *Isvestiya* (Geology Series) of the Academy of Sciences of the U.S.S.R. are also published by the Institute.

The Executive Director and administrative staff of the American Geological Institute are located at 1155 Sixteenth Street, N. W., Washington, D. C. but the mailing address of the Institute is 2101 Constitution Avenue, N. W., Washington 25, D. C.[38]

CHAPTER IV

RELATIONSHIP TO PHILANTHROPIC FOUNDATIONS

A foundation may be broadly defined as a privately endowed, tax-exempt, eleemosynary organization which has been established to provide financial support for projects useful to society.[1]

Organizations meeting the above definition can be found in the history of ancient Egypt and the city-states of Greece. Plato, for instance, established an academy which endured for centuries. In the early Christian era, many Roman emperors established foundations for the relief of the poor. With the advent of Constantine, the first Christian emperor, all public and private giving for worthy causes was channelled through the Church, which throughout the mediaeval period administered many endowments for hospitals and schools, the sick and the indigent.

Excluding such institutions as colleges, hospitals, learned societies, etc., there were relatively few foundations created in America prior to the twentieth century and most of these were limited in size and scope. It is true that Benjamin Franklin set up various endowments, as did Stephen Girard and James Smithson; and, in the nineteenth century the Peabody and Slater Funds were established. It remained for the great industrial leaders of the late nineteenth and twentieth century U. S. A., such as John D. Rockefeller, Andrew Carnegie and, later, Henry Ford and others, to create the heavily endowed and wide-ranging institutions which are synonymous with the present day term foundation. Their action spurred the creation of a host of foundations so that estimates of the total number presently in existence in the United States range from 6,000 to 13,000.

Foundations fall into two broad types or categories: grant-making and operating, although some combine both. The former make grants to individuals or organizations to carry out their programs while the latter carry on their work with their own staffs, occasionally engaging non-staff members to carry out specific studies. In this respect they are more similar to colleges or universities than their grant-making brethren.

The vast majority of the smaller foundations, those with endowments of less than $10,000,000, devote their funds almost wholly to palliative and charitable purposes at the local level. By contrast, a majority of the larger foundations, those with assets in excess of $10,000,000 and now numbering approximately 175, operate in a wide number of fields and in a variety of ways. A preponderance are most active in the fields of education, social welfare, and health or some combination of the three. Also, an increasing number believe that their grants should be for preventive as opposed to palliative purposes. Out of this belief has developed the foundation operating principle of "venture capital," based on the premise that foundation assets, with a pioneering capacity usually difficult to achieve within more restricted organizations, should be primarily devoted to the novel and experimental in an effort to expand the bounds of man's knowledge.[2]

Many of the large foundations, because of their similar interests and a common devotion to the expansion of knowledge, bear a similarity to the learned societies, councils, and institutes. The category into which these organizations fall is, therefore, in some instances a somewhat arbitrary one. Some authorities, for example, have classified the American Philosophical Society as a foundation because of its sizeable endowment and its grants program.[3] Also, the fact that all of these organizations can change and some have changed their methods of operation makes it difficult to place them in definite categories. Nevertheless, it would appear that the main features differentiating the foundations from the learned societies, councils and institutes is that they: a) are not membership organizations, restricted or open, and b) are not set up or created by other organizations to perform a considerable number of functions for them. It is on the basis of these distinctions that this writer has categorized the foundations and studied their relationships to the other organizations.

In ascertaining the relationship between the foundations and the learned societies, councils and institutes, it is apparent that gifts or grants of money flowing from the foundations to the other organizations for certain projects and programs and the number, size, type and purpose of such grants form the tangible links between them.

The initiation of the request for funds for these projects and programs varies. Some projects are proposed by foundation officials to individuals or groups within the learned societies, councils or institutes; the reverse is perhaps the more usual procedure. Special projects tend to fall in the former category. Proposals by the societies, councils, and institutes generally involve requests for general support, publication aid, or travel funds to national or international meetings. This is not always the case, of course. The 1930 Commission on the Social Studies of the American Historical Association, for instance, was initiated at the special request of a group of historians within that organization and resulted in a grant from the Carnegie Corporation of New York to the Association to sustain the Commission's program.

The sections which follow are the result of a study of the extent and character of the flow of foundation funds to the learned societies, councils and institutes. All of the financial figures given represent the awards made by the donor to the recipient organization, and no account is taken of the relatively small amounts which occasionally reverted to the donor if the funds were not expended for the specified project. Also it should be noted that payments on many of the larger grants were spread out over a number of years. Data were derived from the annual and special reports of all of these organizations and the replies to questionnaires and letters submitted to them.

LEARNED SOCIETIES

The Carnegie Corporation of New York, various Rockefeller philanthropies including the Rockefeller Foundation, the General Education Board, and the Laura Spelman Rockefeller Memorial, and the Ford philanthropies, including the Ford Foundation and the Fund for the Advancement of Education have rendered, by far, the major portion of foundation aid to 58 learned societies.[4]

The histories of the Carnegie Corporation, founded in 1911, and the Rockefeller Foundation, founded in 1913, are remarkably similar in their first decades of operation in that up to and including World War I, they made very few grants to the learned societies. After the war a gradual pattern of grants to them developed, characterized in both cases by support for the general administration of certain societies; aid for publication of books, learned journals and other periodicals; and assistance in defraying the travel costs for their representation at international meetings.

Specific analysis of the Carnegie Corporation operations from its beginning to the year 1960 shows that it aided some 23 learned societies, 18 of them active in the humanities and social sciences and 5 in the natural sciences. Total aid granted during the period to all 23 amounted to approximately $1,257,075, less than one-half of one per cent of the total amount of about $300,000,000 appropriated by the Corporation. One of the largest grants was $67,500 in 1931 to the American Political Science Association for its general support; the smallest, $1,000, in 1940, to the Econometric Society for research and publication purposes. There were a total of approximately 100 grants made to the societies during the five decades. Two special projects were supported by the Corporation for a number of years. They were the art program, carried on through grants totaling about $200,000, to the College Art Association of America in the 1920's and '30's, and the support of approximately $350,000 provided the Commission on Social Studies of the American Historical Association.

The grants provided the College Art Association were designed to aid the Corporation's broad-scale program in this area by the Association's stimulation of art competition, conduct of art exhibitions, and publication of journals devoted to art. The project involving the American Historical

Association was initiated by a group of historians headed by Dana C. Munro and including Charles A. Beard, Isaiah Bowman, Guy S. Ford, Charles Merriam, and Carleton J. H. Hayes. It was carried on in the midst of the great depression of the 30's and resulted in a controversial series of volumes culminating in a final Conclusions and Recommendations which four members of the study group refused to endorse, primarily because of differences over political and economic views expressed therein.

From its inauguration in 1913 until 1929, the Rockefeller Foundation restricted its activities primarily to work in medicine and public health on an international scale. This policy was pursued because of initial misunderstanding and criticism of the Foundation's efforts outside these areas plus a belief by Dr. Frederick W. Gates, one of the chief organizers of the Foundation and an influential advisor to Mr. John D. Rockefeller, Sr., that medical research and education was, by far, the best way for the Foundation to expend its funds. In 1929 a reorganization took place which broadened the area of interest of the Foundation to include all of the natural sciences as well as the humanities and social sciences. Programs in the latter area were taken over from the Laura Spelman Rockefeller Memorial, which was consolidated with the Foundation. At the same time, it was decided that the General Education Board would concentrate its activities in education, while the Foundation would engage in research including educational research.

Since 1929, the Rockefeller Foundation has aided some 13 learned societies; 8 active in the humanities and social sciences and 5 in the natural sciences. Aid granted to these societies during the period amounted to a total of approximately $900,000, .13 per cent of the grand total of approximately $711,550,000 awarded by the Rockefeller Foundation during the period. One of the largest grants was $140,000 in 1957 to the American Historical Association for its South Asia program, the smallest, $1,000, in 1929, to the Bibliographical Society of America for support of its publications. The Foundation made a total of 36 grants to the 13 societies during the years 1929-1960.

A special and continuing program of the Rockefeller Foundation is the grants it has made to learned societies to enable them to invite scholars in various foreign areas and disciplines to the United States for research and teaching. The Association for Asian Studies, the American Historical Association, the American Economic Association, and the Genetics Society of America have each received grants to carry out such programs in Southeast Asia, Latin-America, and Russia. This program is in addition to the regular series of fellowships for foreigners administered directly by the Foundation.

Another special project, since 1952, has been the teaching of modern languages in the United States. A total of $160,500 has been appropriated to the Modern Language Association of America to enable it to conduct surveys of modern language education in the United States and to develop methods and prepare material for better and more efficient methods of teaching these languages.

From its establishment by John D. Rockefeller in 1902 until the termination of its active program in 1956, the General Education Board appropriated in excess of $322,000,000 to aid education in the United States. Over 50 per cent of this total was appropriated for the Southern States, to uplift the educational facilities of that section, the remainder being used for educational ventures all over the country. A total of four national learned societies received aid from the Board during its period of activity. The American Association of Pathologists and Bacteriologists, in the 1920's, received $45,000 toward the support of its *Journal;* the Mathematical Association of America, during the period 1918-1938, received $61,300 for various studies of the mathematics curriculum in the secondary school; in 1937 and 1938, $7,500 was appropriated to the Botanical Society of America for a study of the first year college course in botany; and, in 1940-41, $2,625 was provided the American Political Science Association for several projects in civic education and the social studies. The total amount of money involved in aid provided these four societies was $116,425.

Between 1918 and 1929 the Laura Spelman Rockefeller Memorial disbursed approximately $74,000,000. During this period the American Historical Association and the American Psychological Association received grants totalling $55,000 and $76,500 respectively. Those to the former were primarily for conference and publication purposes. Those to the latter were made towards the support of the Association's *Psychological Abstracts Journal* and were payable over an eleven-year period beginning in 1926.

Although it was organized in 1936, the Ford Foundation did not engage in the large scale activities characteristic of the Carnegie Corporation of New York and the Rockefeller Foundation until a reorganization which took place in 1950. At that time, as the result of a tremendous increase in funds, which placed it first in size among all foundations, it completely reorganized its program. Previously confined to the local and palliative giving typical of smaller foundations, the new program, arrived at by a special study group named by Henry Ford II and directed by H. Rowan Gaither, Jr., called for activities on a global scale and in the best "venture capital" tradition.[5] As a consequence, it was at this time that Ford Foundation grants to learned societies began.

During the ten year period from 1951-1960 the Ford Foundation made grants to 12 learned societies, only two of which operated primarily in the natural sciences. The total amount of aid granted by it to these learned societies amounted to approximately $2,800,000;[6] less than three-tenths of one per cent of the total of approximately $1,300,000,000 appropriated during the period. Thirty-five individual grants ranged in size from $717,-000 to the American Political Science Association for its program of Congressional Fellowships for selected individuals who are temporarily attached to the offices of U. S. Congressmen and Senators and Congressional Committees, to a $3,896 grant to the American Historical Association for the expenses of foreign historians attending meetings in this country.

In its record of grants, although the Ford Foundation followed the Carnegie Corporation of New York and Rockefeller Foundations' pattern of providing aid for publication and the travel costs of attendance at international meetings, the Ford Foundation does not furnish a single instance of general support for any one of the learned societies. Rather it has been prone to support special projects such as the modern language program of the MLA; the aforementioned Congressional Fellowship program of the American Political Science Association; and the Service Center for Teachers of History of the American Historical Association. The Center is designed to improve the teaching of history at all levels by providing bibliographic tools and other information to those in the field. Another project of the American Historical Association which has received considerable aid was that connected with the microfilming and editing of various German historical documents, particularly those of the Hitlerian and World War II period.

To summarize, the Carnegie Corporation of New York, the Rockefeller Foundation, the General Education Board, the Laura Spelman Rockefeller Memorial, and the Ford Foundation have provided aid of approximately $4,615,000 to 20 out of 29 humanistic-social science societies and approximately $590,000 to 9 out of 29 natural science societies. The total amount of aid rendered by them to these 29 learned societies receiving grants was, therefore, approximately $5,205,000.

The same relative pattern of giving of the Rockefeller, Carnegie, and Ford philanthropies emerges from an examination of some 19 other foundations which have provided aid to the learned societies. Only 5 of the 19 foundations provided aid totalling $124,000 to 5 societies operating in the natural science areas, whereas 15 of the 19 foundations provided aid totalling $564,010 to 15 societies operating in the humanistic-social science areas.

The Lilly Endowment, the Bollingen Foundation and the Asia Foundation were among the most active foundations supporting humanistic and social science societies. The first of these contributed $30,000 towards the general expenses of the American Antiquarian Society during the period 1946-53; $329,000 during the period 1937-60 toward the Bibliographical Society of America's preparation and publication of editions of the *Bibliography of American Literature;* and $10,000 to the Modern Language Association of America in 1957 for the purpose of locating certain manuscripts.

The Bollingen Foundation in the 1950's made a total of $40,110 available for publication purposes to the following six societies: the American Philosophical Association, $2,000; the American Society for Aesthetics, $1,500; the Archaeological Institute of America, $500; the College Art Association of America, $1,300; the Society of Biblical Literature and Exegesis, $30,000; the American Folklore Society, $4,810.

The Asia Foundation made grants totalling $29,500 to the following five societies in the 1950's to aid the societies defray membership costs of Asians in the societies, provide for their travel to societal meetings, or for other activities of the societies: the American Anthropological Association, $5,000; the American Historical Association, $2,500; the American Philosophical Association, $4,000; the American Sociological Association, $7,500; the American Studies Association, $10,500.

Eleven foundations in the late 1940's and 1950's have provided sums totalling $120,400 to eight learned societies for publication purposes, studies conducted by the societies, or general expenses. Names of the foundations and societies and specific amounts of aid rendered are listed below:

Avalon Foundation	American Historical Association	$29,000
Creole Foundation	American Philosophical Association	$ 1,500
John Simon Guggenheim Memorial Foundation	Mediaeval Academy of America	$ 2,500
Samuel H. Kress Foundation	College Art Association of America	$ 9,500
Littauer Foundation	Mediaeval Academy of America	$ 6,000
Matchette Foundation	American Society for Aesthetics	$ 3,400
Old Dominion Foundation	American Historical Association	$36,000
Overbrook Foundation	American Historical Association	$ 5,000
Presser Foundation	American Musicological Society	$ 5,000
Russell Sage Foundation	American Sociological Association	$ 6,000
Wenner-Gren Foundation	American Anthropological Association	$16,500

In addition, the Commonwealth Fund, in 1926-27, made a grant of $5,000 available to the Modern Language Association of America for a special study project of the Association.

The following six humanistic-social science learned societies do not appear to have received aid from any philanthropic foundation: the American Numismatic Society, the American Oriental Society, the Association of

American Geographers, the Metaphysical Society of America, the Renaissance Society of America, and the Society of Architectural Historians.

By way of contrast 17 of the 29 natural science learned societies do not appear to have received a grant from any philanthropic foundation. These seventeen include: the American Association of Anatomists, the American Association of Immunologists, the American Astronomical Society, the American Physical Society, the American Physiological Society, the American Society for Experimental Pathology, the American Society for Microbiology, the American Society for Pharmacology and Experimental Therapeutics, the American Society of Biological Chemists, the American Society of Parasitologists, the American Society of Zoologists, the Ecological Society of America, the Electrochemical Society, the Geochemical Society, the Geological Society of America, the Institute of Mathematical Statistics, and the Paleontological Society.

Only five foundations other than the members of the Rockefeller, Carnegie, Ford groups appear to have provided grants to five natural science learned societies. The largest of these was $100,000 granted the American Chemical Society in 1958 by the Alfred P. Sloan Foundation for the filming of two college chemistry courses.[7] The Asia Foundation made a grant of $2,500 to the American Geophysical Union in 1960 to provide membership fees in the Union for scientists from Asian countries; the Daniel and Florence Guggenheim Foundation made a grant of $5,000 in 1944 to the American Meteorological Society to aid it in the establishment of its executive offices; the Carus Foundation contributed $3,000 to the Association for Symbolic Logic at an unspecified time towards publication expenses; and the Cowles Foundation, during the period 1955-1959, contributed $13,500 for the general purposes of the Econometric Society.

To summarize, of the approximate total of $5,893,000 provided some 35 learned societies by some 30 foundations, over 88 per cent was provided by Rockefeller, Carnegie, or Ford philanthropies. Of the total, 88 per cent was provided to 23 humanistic-social science learned societies, whereas only 12 per cent of the total was provided to 12 natural science societies.

THE COUNCILS

AMERICAN COUNCIL ON EDUCATION

For the first few years of its existence, the American Council on Education had very limited relationships with the philanthropic foundations. Called into existence and financially sustained by a group of educational organizations for the purpose of aiding the defense effort in World War I, it was not until the late 1920's that appreciable sums began to flow from the foundations to the American Council on Education. During that period there were three major projects sponsored by the foundations: a series of modern language studies, an educational finance inquiry, and a program of international activities. The first of these was financed by a series of grants from the Carnegie Corporation of New York amounting to some $250,000. The second was financed by a group of foundations, including the Commonwealth Fund, the Milbank Memorial Fund, the Carnegie Corporation of New York, and the General Education Board, and made extensive studies of the financing of education at all levels. Total funds expended on this project during the '20's were approximately $450,000. The program of international activities, supported by grants totalling approximately $120,000 from the Commonwealth Fund and the Laura Spelman Rockefeller Memorial, involved the maintenance of offices in Western European countries which provided liaison for U. S. nationals with the academic personnel and universities in that area. This project was terminated in 1927-28 when the newly created Institute of International Education began operations.

The period from 1929 to the advent of World War II was characterized by a fluctuating but over-all steady increase of funds to the ACE from, primarily, two foundations, the General Education Board and the Carnegie Corporation of New York. In addition to the general support they rendered the Council of approximately $450,000, these same two, plus a few others, provided the necessary funds for a score of special projects of the Council, including studies of college teaching and teachers; surveys of secondary school systems; educational finance inquiries; the use of radio and film as education media; and general education. The American Youth Commission, set up by the Council in the midst of the great depression to study the problems facing American youth, was primarily financed by funds flowing from the General Education Board through the Council. Various educational surveys conducted by the United States Office of Education were largely financed through the Council. With the coming of World War II there was a diminution in the flow of funds and the various projects referred to above were carried forward on a reduced scale. Expanded, of course, were the informational and other services concerning education and the war effort. It was at this time that the Council's bulletin *Higher Education and National Affairs* was established with the aid of a subvention from the Carnegie Corporation of New York.

Following World War II there was a substantial increase in the number and size of grants from the philanthropic foundations to the ACE. By the 1950's such grants were running in excess of $1,000,000 annually. They came from some 35 foundations, ranging in size from the very largest to the very small. With the exception of two general support grants of $150,-000 each from the Rockefeller Foundation and the Carnegie Corporation of New York in 1950, and a number of smaller ones for the same purpose from a few smaller foundations, almost all of these grants were for special educational projects similar to those of the pre-war period.

The total amount of foundation aid made available to the ACE from its beginning in 1918 to 1960 was approximately $12,000,000. Of this total over 90 per cent was for special projects while the remainder was for general support of the Council. In this connection, successive officials of the Council have all expressed the conviction that it would be best if the central office, containing the permanent staff and secretariat of the organization, were supported entirely by dues received from members thus obviating the need for making requests for general support grants from the foundations. By the 1950's, through a modest increase in dues charged members, plus receipts from administrative fees, this situation was about achieved.

Various Rockefeller and Carnegie philanthropies, including the General Education Board, the Laura Spelman Rockefeller Memorial, the Rockefeller Foundation, the Rockefeller Brothers Fund, the Carnegie Corporation of New York, the Carnegie Foundation for the Advancement of Teaching, and the Carnegie Endowment for International Peace, have provided the ACE with approximately 70 per cent ($8,400,000) of the total monetary aid it has received from foundations. Ten per cent ($1,200,-000) has been provided by some 25 other foundations such as the Kellogg Foundation, Lilly Endowment, and Grant Foundation. The remaining 20 per cent ($2,400,000) has been supplied, entirely in the 1950's, by the Ford Foundation and its Fund for Adult Education and the Fund for the Advancement of Education. The bulk of the money appropriated by these Ford philanthropies was for the support of activities in educational television, particularly the Joint Commission on Educational Television, popularly known as the JCET, for which the Council acted as its fiscal agent.

Although there are some instances where the foundations made joint grants to the ACE, the vast majority have been unilateral. Joint grants usually resulted where projects calling for sizeable sums of money made it imperative that more than one foundation finance them, where general support was being rendered the Council for its central office, or where a grant had been made by one foundation with the stipulation that additional sums must be secured from others.

The vast majority of the special projects financed by the foundations have been carried out by the regular or special staff of the Council and under the auspices of one of its commissions or committees. Occasionally, as in the case of several grants for the United States Office of Education, funds have been provided to the Council for the use of other agencies. Regarding the tripartite relationship of the foundations, councils and learned societies, there is no apparent instance of foundation funds being utilized jointly by the Council and a learned society or societies, or of being provided the Council for use by a learned society. This is not to say, of course, that Council Committees and staff have not often consulted with officers and members of various learned societies. There are many instances where this has occurred and, indeed, members of some committees have been selected because of their connections with certain societies, connections which would enable them to bring to bear a distillation of expert information on one or more specialized fields of knowledge.

NATIONAL ACADEMY OF SCIENCES-NATIONAL RESEARCH COUNCIL

The National Academy of Sciences from its founding during the Civil War to World War I had become largely honorific. This fact, plus the pre-World War I lack of concern of the new twentieth century foundations with such organizations as the Academy, militated against the development of relationships between them. It was not, therefore, until the mobilization of scientific effort called for by the events of 1916-18 that the Academy and foundations were brought together. The fruit of this juncture was the National Research Council, for the Council was created in 1916 by funds supplied by the Engineering Foundation and the Carnegie Corporation of New York. Sustained by additional grants from the Corporation and the Rockefeller Foundation, and small appropriations for work done for the Signal Corps, it was not until 1918 that President Wilson authorized the first of several larger governmental grants to it. Immediately following the war, the Council was placed on a permanent basis within the Academy and, in 1919, the Carnegie Corporation of New York appropriated $5,000,000 for the erection of a building to house the Academy-Council and an endowment to maintain it.

The post-war role of the Council evolved as the result of discussion and actual operation. In 1919 President George Vincent of the Rockefeller Foundation suggested to the NRC's Robert A. Millikan and a group of fellow scientists the creation of a central institute of science comparable to the Rockefeller Institute for Medical Research. Millikan and a majority of the scientists rejected this idea, maintaining that such centralization would be inimical to the advancement of science. While no definite action concerning the Council's post-war structure was taken as a result of discussion incidental to this plan, it did result in the Council's inaugurating a series of post-doctoral fellowships financed by the Rockefeller Foundation.[8]

The importance of these fellowships, aside from their impact on science and the individuals selected, was that, together with other special projects financed by Rockefeller and Carnegie philanthropies, they became the major operating function of the NAS-NRC between the two World Wars. Begun with an initial grant of $50,000 in 1919 for fellowships in physics and chemistry, they were gradually extended to include medicine, the biological and physical sciences, anthropology and psychology, and agriculture and forestry. By the time the Rockefeller Foundation began to curtail this fellowship program in the 1950's some 1,500 young scientists had participated in it at a cost in excess of $5,000,000. The various NRC boards of selection and the Foundation worked in close harmony. For example, European fellows selected for work in this country received advice and aid from the Council and the Foundation while American fellows working abroad were similarly aided by the various foreign offices of the Foundation.

Other Rockefeller philanthropies providing aid to the Council during the 1920's and '30's were: the Laura Spelman Rockefeller Memorial, the General Education Board, and the International Education Board. Diverse projects receiving aid included: reseach in population problems, including migration research; surveys of schools for the deaf; studies of child development; sponsorship of lecture tours of distinguished foreign scientists; and technical studies in various disciplines, physics, astronomy, etc.

The Carnegie Corporation of New York also supplied funds for specific projects including some fellowships; research and study on the preservation of books and records; scientific aids to learning; and problems of human heredity. It tended, however, to concentrate its grants upon general support of the Academy-Council and for the work of its divisions and committees.

Although the Rockefeller and the Carnegie philanthropies supplied about $10,000,000 or about 50 per cent of the total funds received by the NAS-NRC during the period 1918-1941, there were a number of other foundations which made important grants during that time. In addition to the Engineering Foundation, these included the Chemical Foundation, the John and Mary R. Markle Foundation, the Russell Sage Foundation, and the Commonwealth Fund. The latter organization made an emergency grant of $12,000 in 1919 which was described in the Council's annual report for that year as preventing a "grave catastrophe."

Regardless of the source of aid for the projects of the Academy-Council, they were carried out almost entirely by the various divisions and committees of the NRC. These in turn were composed primarily of representatives of the various technical and learned societies. Therefore, rather than acting as a central institute of science or a scientific arm of government supported by government funds, the Academy-Council's primary function became that of an impartial and unbiased council for American science, at home through its divisions and committees and abroad through representatives in the International Research Council, later the International Council of Scientific Unions.[9]

There are only a few instances of foundation support of learned societies through the Academy-Council or of joint participation by the three in a mutual effort. During a nine-year period from 1925 to 1934 the General Education Board and the Rockefeller Foundation made approximately $165,000 available to the Academy's Committee on Funds for Publication of Research which aided the learned journals of 16 learned societies and the American Institute of Physics. The Institute was provided funds to enable it to carry through on its program of publication for a number of physics journals. The grants to the learned societies never exceeded a few thousand dollars each and were designed to: (a) aid in the publication of good material that had been accumulated at a rate faster than the journals could afford to publish, (b) aid newer journals that appeared to have a promising future, or (c) aid those journals desirous of expanding their scope or content.[10]

Another instance of mutual collaboration involved the Office of Scientific Personnel. Set up within the Academy-Council during World War II at the request of the government as a temporary office, a movement to continue the Office because of its usefulness to various societies was initiated by these societies toward the close of the war. Subsequently, the Academy-Council, with the financial aid of such groups as the American Mathematical Society, the Mathematical Association of America, the American Chemical Society, the American Psychological Association, and the American Institute of Physics, contributed to the initial support of the office. It was not until later, as its activities broadened, that additional and joint support was forthcoming from the foundations.

World War II saw a change in the role played by the foundations vis-a-vis the Academy-Council. The Carnegie Corporation of New York and the Rockefeller Foundation provided hundreds of thousands of dollars for the necessary working capital to initiate preparedness projects during the years 1939-41. This capital was needed because the government during this period was unable, because of statutory restrictions, to supply it. Following United States involvement in the war this difficulty was surmounted and ever-increasing amounts of money flowed from the government to the Academy-Council.

Because of this deep involvement with government contracts, many of them of a classified nature, the fact that the Academy-Council was until the 1950's a bifurcated organization, and the sheer amount of money involved, it is more difficult to ascertain the nature of the income of the NAS-NRC than is the case with the other three national councils. It appears, however, that the total income of the Academy-Council was about $120,-000,000 for the period 1918-1960. The total amount of aid rendered to it by all of the foundations during the same period appears to have been approximately $30,000,000 or about 25 per cent of the total. In assaying the role of particular foundations, it appears that the various Rockefeller and Carnegie philanthropies have supplied about 80 per cent of such aid, the remainder being scattered among some 25 other foundations.

From 1946 to the present, foundation funds have been an ever smaller part of the total income of the Academy-Council. Despite this development these same funds are just as important as they were when they constituted a larger portion of that income. This is because foundation financial support forms one of the major bases upon which the Academy-Council is able to maintain its objective position in regard to the government and government sponsored projects.

Partly as a result of the realization of the continued need for such funds, partly as the result of a tremendous increase in Council activities, and partly as a result of an increase in the number of foundations, the base of foundation support of the Academy-Council has shifted from the relatively few of the pre-World War II period to more than 25 such organizations since the war. In addition to the continuing, although relatively diminished, aid of the Rockefeller and Carnegie philanthropies, grants were provided by large foundations such as the Ford Foundation, the Milbank Memorial Fund, and the Alfred P. Sloan Foundation and smaller foundations such as the Meyer, Tasdon and Coolidge Foundations.

AMERICAN COUNCIL OF LEARNED SOCIETIES

The Carnegie and the Rockefeller philanthropies were the first foundations to render support to the American Council of Learned Societies. During the period 1925 through 1960 the Rockefeller Foundation gave about $4,560,000 to the Council, most of it in the 1930's and 1940's.[11] Of this total approximately $1,400,000 was for general support; $1,100,000 for Council projects, including those of committees on Latin-American and Far Eastern Studies; $1,400,000 for fellowships and grants-in-aid; $500,000 for various publications, such as the *Linguistic Atlas of New England, Dictionary of American Biography,* and *Current Digest of the Soviet Press;* and $100,000 for the holding of conferences.

The Carnegie Corporation of New York gave about $1,665,000 to the Council during the same period.[12] Of this sum, the Corporation appropriated about $700,000 for general support; $500,000 for projects, including the holding of conferences; and approximately $465,000 for fellowships and grants.

The Ford Foundation, during the period January, 1950-November, 1960, provided the ACLS with about $4,337,000. Of this sum, $2,637,000 was for general support, approximately $700,000 was for various projects, particularly Near and Far Eastern language studies; $200,000 was for various publications; $300,000 for fellowships and $500,000 for participation in international conferences. In December of 1960, the Ford Foundation made two grants, one of $2,500,000, and one of $5,670,000 to the ACLS. These grants are unique, being the largest in the Council's history, and are a tremendous earnest of the interest of the Ford Foundation in the humanities.

In announcing these grants President Burkhardt stated[13] that the $5,670,-000 grant was for the basic program of the ACLS including fellowships, grants-in-aid, and travel grants, planning and development; and staff and organizational functions of the central office.

"The new Ford grant," President Burkhardt concluded, " gives ACLS greater financial stability than it has enjoyed in the past and for a decade frees the Council's Directors and Executive Staff from perennial concern over income for the central establishment and essential program. Forty years of ACLS history have been more often marked by depression than by boom, and with a minuscule endowment of $100,000 the Council has always been dependent on foundation support. A grave crisis in 1955 led to a vigorous drive for aid, and in the following year, five-year grants from the Ford Foundation and the Carnegie Corporation of New York met the office budget and, augmented by other grants, financed an expanded program. These Ford and Carnegie grants run through 1961-62 and the new ten-year Ford grant just announced covers the period from 1962-1972."

President Burkhardt also stated in the same issue of the ACLS *Newsletter:*

"The grant of $2,500,000 is designed to increase Europe's understanding of America by assisting European universities to strengthen their teaching and scholarly resources in American Studies.

"To this end the ACLS will formulate a fellowship program under which European scholars will study American subjects in the United States on one or two-year grants. It will also establish and if necessary fill professorships in American Studies at European universities. In the selection of Fellows and the establishment of university posts, priority will be given American history and literature without excluding political and social institutions.

"Europe's interest in American Studies has increased markedly since World War II, and inquiries have indicated that there will be no dearth of able candidates for the Fellowships among the younger scholars of Western Europe and that a number of European universities are prepared to establish academic posts in American Studies with short-term financial guarantees. It is estimated that some fifteen of them will be set up in the next two or three years. The number of Fellowships is expected to be thirty or forty a year with an average grant, covering travel, dependents, and university fees, of about $9,000."

In addition to the funds from the Rockefeller, Carnegie, and Ford philanthropies, the ACLS has received subventions amounting to about $550,000 from some 17 other foundations. The largest of these grants include: $100,000 in 1950-52 from the John and Mary R. Markle Foundation for faculty fellowships; $220,000 from the Bollingen Foundation, and $76,000 from the Houghton Foundation for general support, this support by the former of $20,000 annually from 1947 through 1957, and the latter from 1955 through 1958, helped to sustain the ACLS at a very crucial period in its history; and a very recent (1960) award from the Charles E. Merrill Trust for fellowships to enable selected high school foreign language teachers to study one year abroad.

The smallest of these awards included one of $500 from the Coolidge Foundation in 1942 for the publication of a Malay Handbook and a $238 grant from the China Foundation in 1938 for a Bibliography of Northeastern Asia.

The total of all foundation aid provided the ACLS from its beginnings through 1960 totals approximately $20,000,000.

SOCIAL SCIENCE RESEARCH COUNCIL

At the time of its founding in 1922-24 the Social Science Research Council had no clear-cut concept of the method by which it should operate. The consensus appears to have been that any projects undertaken by it would be of a coordinating nature and on a volunteer basis. There also seems to have been little anticipation of the substantial research funds which would flow to it from the philanthropic foundations.

The initial grant from a foundation to the Council was one in 1924 of $18,000 from the Laura Spelman Rockefeller Memorial for a study of the social aspects of human migration. This grant, and a subsequent one of $2,500 from the same source for a study of international news and communication, had an important effect on the Council. The setting up of committees to facilitate the conduct of these studies placed it in the mainstream of social science research activity and served as a precedent for the future operations of the Council. Thus, for about three decades, it has been Council policy to serve principally in an advisory or facilitating capacity and it does not directly administer research projects except when no other competent sponsor exists.

Throughout the 1920's the Memorial contributed a total sum of about $2,600,000 to the Council. Approximately $1,500,000 was for general administration and projects. In addition to giving the Council a considerable degree of flexibility at a time when it was most needed, this money provided the funds for a paid staff which, by 1926, because of the increase in the number of projects undertaken, had become a necessity. The Memorial also granted $500,000 for the establishment of a *Journal of Social Science Abstracts,*[14] approximately $490,000 for various fellowships, and about $75,000 for the support of summer research conferences.

When the Memorial terminated its activities in the early '30's several other Rockefeller philanthropies, the General Education Board, the Spelman Fund, and the Rockefeller Foundation, began to provide financial aid for numerous purposes. The first two, because of concentrations of interest elsewhere, provided sums of only about $300,000 between the years 1931-1935, for graduate fellowships and several study projects. The Rockefeller Foundation, on the other hand, has been a principal contributor to the Social Science Research Council. During the period 1929-1960 it has appropriated approximately $12,000,000 to the Council. Fellowships and grants-in-aid programs conducted by the Council account for approximately $4,800,000 of this sum. The great majority of these awards were granted for work in all of the fields of the social sciences. Some, however, were restricted to specific areas, such as agricultural economics, and, recently, political theory and legal philosophy.

Various studies and research projects, conducted primarily by committees of the Council, such as the Committee on Public Administration, received subventions amounting to about $3,000,000. These studies range all the way from small ones, $1,500 for a 1933 study of retail prices and $1,230 for a 1934 study of statistics of payroll attachments, to intermediate ones, $45,000 in 1946 for research on housing problems, to large ones, $300,000 in 1940 for research in economic history. For planning purposes and conferences connected with these studies the Rockefeller Foundation made subventions amounting to about $1,500,000. It also made grants of about $300,000 for the preparation and publication of several books and for the purchase and distribution of books and periodicals to foreign libraries following World War II.

To administer all of the foregoing activities obviously required an administrative staff commensurate with the attached responsibilities. From

1939 through 1950, therefore, the Rockefeller Foundation provided $495,-
000 toward the Council's general administrative expenses. Furthermore,
in 1951, it endowed it with a sustaining fund of $1,500,000 from which
the interest only could be expended until the lapse of ten years. The Council, however, expends the interest and manages the fund as it sees fit.

Including a $25,000 grant from the Rockefeller Brothers Fund in 1953
for research in psychiatry and the social sciences, and various sums which
the Council has received from the Rockefeller Foundation as a fiscal agent
for other agencies, the total financial aid received by the Social Science Research Council during the period 1924-1960 from all of the Rockefeller
philanthropies amounted to approximately $15,000,000.

The pattern of Council support followed by the Carnegie Corporation
of New York is generally that followed by the Rockefeller Foundation,
but it differs in timing and in the relative amounts for specific purposes.
Whereas the Rockefeller Foundation began to provide aid for fellowships in
the late 1920's, it was not until 1947 that the Carnegie Corporation com-
menced. Since that time, however, it has approached Rockefeller munifi-
cence with grants of almost $3,000,000 for fellowships. Support for studies
and research projects was initiated by the Corporation in 1931, within a
year of the date first undertaken by the Foundation, and has continued
down to the present. Within the total of almost $1,100,000 for these proj-
ects, there appears the same range in size and purpose that prevailed in
the Rockefeller grants. Similarly, sums of approximately $375,000 and $1,-
000,000 were respectively provided for conferences and general support.
Joint grants by both foundations for the same purpose are only to be found
in a few instances out of a total of hundreds.

Including $10,000 granted the Council by the Carnegie Foundation for
the Advancement of Teaching and various sums from the Carnegie Corporation to be administered by the Council as fiscal agent, these two foundations granted a total of approximately $5,500,000 to the Social Science Re-
search Council during the period 1926-1960.

The new colossus of the philanthropic world, the Ford Foundation, follows the pattern of the Rockefeller and Carnegie philanthropies in grants
to the Council for research development and fellowships, appropriating approximately $3,700,000 and $2,000,000, respectively, for those purposes
during the period 1950-1960. In other respects, however, the Ford Foundation departs from the older foundation practices. It provided only $450,-
000 for conferences and institutes and only $250,000 for general Council
support, the latter sum in one appropriation in 1955. Two separate funds set
up by the Ford Foundation, the East European Fund, and Resources for
the Future, have also had dealings with the SSRC. The Fund made $45,000

available to the Council, which acted as fiscal agent jointly with the ACLS, for the publication of the *Current Digest of the Soviet Press*. Resources for the Future transferred $5,000 to the Council as its share in the cost of a conference held by a Council committee.

Thus, beginning at the relatively late date of 1950, the Ford philanthropies in the short period of ten years, have provided the Council approximately $6,400,000.

Although not in the same category with the philanthropic giants, the Russell Sage Foundation has been a noteworthy and consistent supporter of the Social Science Research Council. Annually, from 1925 through 1947, it made grants of a few thousand dollars toward the Council's general administrative expenses and, by the latter date, they totalled $87,000. Since that time, it has appropriated $71,250 to the Council for projects in the Foundation's major fields of interest, the relationship of the social sciences to professions such as medicine, and studies based on census data.

Eight other foundations, the Commonwealth Fund, the Maurice and Laura Falk Foundation, the General Electric Foundation, the Grant Foundation, the John and Mary R. Markle Foundation, the Julius Rosenwald Fund, the Scripps Foundation for Research in Population Problems, and the Twentieth Century Fund have appropriated about $630,000 in grants to the Council. They span the period 1926-1960, vary in size from $1,000 to $150,000, and are for general support, studies, and fellowships.

The total financial support provided the Social Science Research Council by all of the foundations from its beginnings through 1960 amounts to approximately $27,000,000.

Societal Institutes

Relative to the councils, the five societal institutes have received little aid from the foundations. The Federation of American Societies for Experimental Biology and the American Geological Institute have not received any foundation grants during their entire period of existence, and the total aid granted the three other institutes by some seven foundations totals about $1,000,000. Furthermore, over 90 per cent of this amount was received in the period from 1950 to 1960.

Several reasons account for this relative lack of financial support. Prior to the 1950's there was not the near crisis atmosphere in American science which was produced by the rise to scientific eminence of the Soviet Union. At the same time that this crisis did occur various agencies of the government were prepared to support research and other activities of the institutes with large sums of money. Many foundation executives apparently felt that several of the institutes had long been able to finance their projects from their own resources and, therefore, did not need foundation aid. Strengthening this attitude was the view that member societies supporting these institutes, particularly the Federation, were composed of what were, relatively, well to do scientists. Finally, pharmaceutical and medical supply houses as well as industrial concerns had developed an early interest in the institutes and many of them provided sums of money toward their general and special support.

Nevertheless, as the succeeding analysis of each of the institutes receiving foundation grants shows, although small in number and size these grants have often been forthcoming at crucial points. For, as is true in other areas of foundation activity, the private foundation with its greater freedom and flexibility can put sums of money, and quickly, into very valuable and timely projects which, for one reason or another, cannot find support elsewhere.

AMERICAN ASSOCIATION FOR THE ADVANCEMENT OF SCIENCE

The relationship of the AAAS with the philanthropic foundations has been a very recent development and restricted to nine foundations, some large, some small. The first grant from a foundation was one of $1,000, in 1924, from the Commonwealth Fund for a study of the place of science in education. During the period 1930-1938 the General Education Board and the Carnegie Corporation of New York supplied the Association with some $17,000 in general support of its educational program. In the 1950's the Rockefeller Foundation made grants totalling about $48,000 towards the payment of expenses connected with the holding of the Gordon Research Conferences. The Westinghouse Educational Foundation, in the 1940's and 1950's, supplied funds of approximately the same amount for science writing awards. A few other foundations, such as the Wenner-Gren Foundation for Anthropological Research, supplied smaller sums for publication and other purposes.

Since 1954 about 60 per cent of the grants made to the Association have been for the purpose of holding various scientific meetings and conferences. The remainder has been for special projects such as awards for newspaper and magazine science writing and provision of scientific books for certain foreign areas. Among the projects, probably the most noteworthy has been the Carnegie Corporation's support of approximately $550,000 towards the Association's program for improvement in the teaching of science and mathematics in the secondary schools, and this aid forms by far the largest portion of the total sum of approximately $722,000 supplied the Association by all of the foundations.

In all of the Association's projects, there was no instance of foundation funds flowing through it to a learned society. There was only one instance of dual foundation support of a project, that of the costs of a Parliament of Science, approximately $18,000, defrayed by the Rockefeller Foundation and the Alfred P. Sloan Foundation.

To summarize, throughout the period of its existence foundation funds have played a relatively minor role in the operation of the Association. Its present day operating budget of approximately $2,000,000 is largely derived from membership fees, subscription and advertising revenues, interest on invested funds, and grants from the National Science Foundation.

AMERICAN INSTITUTE OF PHYSICS

The American Institute of Physics, although its expenses for the first two or three years of its existence were defrayed by the Chemical Foundation, has received relatively few grants from philanthropic foundations. The Rockefeller Foundation provided funds in 1945 in the amount of $29,300 to aid the Institute in initiating a program to provide a new kind of income for journal publication by charging authors' institutions a fixed amount per page. This page charge now contributes a large annual sum toward the costs of publication of the physics journals. In 1957, the Ford Foundation provided $15,000 for the AIP's future physicist fund. In 1957 also, the Fund for the Advancement of Education granted $52,750 for studies related to the improvement of physics teaching, such as TV and film evaluation. The Educational Facilities Laboratories, an organization established in 1958 by the Ford Foundation to conduct research and other activities on educational facilities, including buildings, in that year made a $75,850 grant to the Institute to prepare an informative book for the guidance of institutions planning new physics buildings.

The Rockefeller and Ford Foundations and several other foundations provided smaller sums to the AIP for other purposes but the total amount of foundation aid rendered the Institute from its inception to 1960 is but a small fraction of its total income during that period.

AMERICAN INSTITUTE OF BIOLOGICAL SCIENCES

The American Institute of Biological Sciences has also received very little aid from the private philanthropic foundations. The Rockefeller Foundation appropriated $40,000 to it in 1952 for general support over a three-year period. This came at a time when the Institute was still struggling and really needed support but, since that time, this same foundation has made only two small grants to defray the travel expenses of several biologists. The Asia Foundation made two similarly small grants in 1959 and

1960 for the same purposes. The only other foundation making a grant to the AIBS during its entire history was the Ford Foundation. In 1958 it awarded the Institute $172,191 for the development and production of a motion picture film of a basic biology course for high school use. Thus, the total dollar amount of all foundation funds awarded the AIBS through 1960 has been approximately $212,000.

CHAPTER V

RELATIONSHIP TO GOVERNMENT, INDUSTRY AND UNIVERSITIES

Prior to World War II the United States government,[1] industrial, and university support of the national learned societies, councils and institutes, and indeed of research in general, was relatively small. For example, one estimate of the total national expenditure in 1938 for research and development amounted to only $264,000,000 of which industry supplied 67 per cent, government 18 per cent, universities 11 per cent, and foundation and other sources 4 per cent.[2] At that time the major portion of government and industrial research funds was used to support their own projects conducted in their own laboratories and only a very limited amount was placed with outside agencies, principally colleges and universities. In this pre-war period, the National Academy of Sciences-National Research Council was the only organization among those included in this study which received any appreciable amount of government and industrial funds. The American Council on Education was the only one receiving significant sums from the universities and colleges.

With the mobilization of scientific and intellectual manpower called for by World War II and the resultant achievements of scientists, culminating in the atomic bomb, a tri-fold revolution took place in the sponsorship of research and development in the United States. First, total spending for such purposes since 1938 has continually increased. By 1953 it was calculated that it totalled about $5,000,000,000 annually, and by 1960, about $12,000,000,000 annually. Second, the relative position of governmental and industrial support has been reversed, with government now supplying approximately 66 per cent of such funds, industry about 25 per cent and the universities, foundations and other sources, the remainder.[3] Third, a considerable number of government agencies, particularly the National Science Foundation,[4] developed the practice on a wide-spread scale of the placing of research grants and contracts with organizations outside the government, including our national learned societies, councils, and societal institutes.[5]

LEARNED SOCIETIES

The total amount of financial aid rendered 32 out of 58 learned societies, by governmental agencies, appears to be about $5,600,000; nearly all of this sum since World War II.[6]

Since its organization in 1950 through 1960 the National Science Foundation has supplied a total of approximately $4,300,000 to 19 of the 29 natural science learned societies and a total of approximately $450,000 to 7 of the 29 humanistic and social science societies. This aid represents, by far, the largest amount of government aid to all of the learned societies; it accounts for about 83 per cent of the total, the remainder of $800,000 being supplied by some 8 other governmental agencies.

The Mathematical Association of America and the American Mathematical Society have been the recipients of the largest amounts of aid from the National Science Foundation. The former has received approximately $1,000,000 in grants and contracts, during this decade, while the latter received approximately $850,000. The purpose for which this aid was rendered included $430,000 to bring distinguished mathematicians as lecturers and visiting scientists to our colleges and secondary schools, almost all of these funds being appropriated to the Mathematical Association of America, and $375,000 to provide for the translation and publication of foreign mathematical publications, almost all of these funds being appropriated to the American Mathematical Society. Approximately $600,000 was appropriated for the use of both societies in conducting studies and engaging in other means for the improvement of instruction in mathematics at the college and secondary school level. $310,000 was appropriated for conferences and meetings of both societies, $73,000 for a register of mathematicians, and $71,000 for international travel grants was granted to the American Mathematical Society.

Four societies—the American Meteorological Society, the American Chemical Society, the American Physiological Society, and the American Geophysical Union—have received grants totalling about $400,000 each from the National Science Foundation. Although the proportions are somewhat different with the first three societies, the NSF grants to them were made for approximately the same purposes as were those to the American Mathematical Society and the Mathematical Association of America. The American Geophysical Union shows a different pattern; NSF grants to it were almost wholly for translation and publication purposes with a few smaller grants for special studies and symposia.

The American Astronomical Society received support totalling about $200,000 for translation and publication purposes, visiting scientists, and special studies programs, and the Botanical Society of America and the Geochemical Society about $100,000 each for similar purposes.

Ten societies received aid totalling about $370,000 from the National Science Foundation. The American Physical Society received about $70,000, primarily for support of its publication program; the Institute of Mathematical Statistics, approximately $70,000 for its publication program and the conduct of summer institutes in its area of interest; the Genetics Society of America, about $60,000 to aid it in defraying the costs of its sponsorship of the 10th International Congress of Genetics and for the work of its Committee on the Maintenance of Genetic Stocks; the Entomological Society of America about $50,000 to defray the costs of U. S. participation in the 11th International Congress on Entomology, and for its publication program; the American Institute of Nutrition about $45,000 towards the costs of U. S. participation in the 5th International Congress on Nutrition; the Ecological Society of America a $24,000 grant for a committee of the Society to review the present status of the ecological sciences; approximately $17,000 to the American Society of Zoologists, primarily for conferences and studies in the zoological sciences; $17,000 to the Electrochemical Society, for two special studies in its area of interest; a $9,690 grant was made to the American Society for Microbiology to enable it to prepare a career information booklet; and a $3,410 grant to the American Society of Parasitologists to enable it to prepare a cumulative index to the *Journal of Parasitology*.

Five other government agencies have, through the years, supplied a total of $168,000 to eight natural science learned societies; among this number were three societies that had not received aid from the National Science Foundation. The Office of Naval Research in the late 1940's and 1950's provided grants of: about $10,000 to the American Physiological Society for research and travel purposes; $20,000 to the American Physical Society for publication purposes; and $5,000 to the Electrochemical Society for research and travel purposes. The Office of Scientific Research of the Air Force during the same period made grants of: about $10,000 to the American Physiological Society for research purposes; and $4,000 to the Electrochemical Society for travel purposes. The U. S. Public Health Service made a $30,000 grant in 1960 to the American Society of Biological Chemists for the activities of its Educational Affairs Committee. The Department of Agriculture made two grants totalling $5,000 to the Entomological Society of America for publication purposes. Finally, the National Institutes of Health have appropriated a total of $89,100 to the following societies, on the dates, in the amounts, and for the purposes listed: 1956, the American Physiological Society, $6,000 for a conference; 1959, the Entomological Society of America, $10,000 for publication purposes; 1958-59, the American Institute of Nutrition, $13,000 for an International Congress of Nutritionists; 1959, the American Association of Anatomists, $45,000 for an International Congress of Anatomists; 1960, the American Society of Parasitologists, $1,100 for U. S. attendance at the 1st International Congress of Trichinellosis; and, during the late 1950's, the American Society for Pharmacology and Experimental Therapeutics, $14,000 for the work of its Educational Affairs Committee.

Seven natural science societies have apparently not received financial aid from any agency of the government. They are: the American Association of Immunologists, the American Association of Pathologists and Bacteriologists, the American Society for Experimental Pathology, the Association for Symbolic Logic, the Econometric Society, the Geological Society of America, and the Paleontological Society.

The total amount of governmental aid supplied the 29 humanistic-social science societies is approximately $1,150,000. Approximately $900,000 of this amount, however, was provided 7 societies which are almost wholly of the social sciences.

The National Science Foundation has provided the American Psychological Association with $224,380 for preparation of a register of psychologists, a program of visiting scientists in our colleges and universities, conferences, and toward support of the 14th International Congress of Psychologists.

The American Anthropological Association received $97,340 for a program of visiting scientists in our colleges and support of the 5th International Congress of Anthropology and Ethnology.

The National Science Foundation has made grants to the American Statistical Association, totalling $26,000, for publication purposes; the History of Science Society of $51,000 for studies and conferences and support of the 10th International Congress for the History of Science; the Association of American Geographers of $15,000 for travel purposes.

The American Political Science Association estimates that it has received approximately $30,000 from various government agencies for projects it has conducted for them. The American Historical Association estimates that it has received government aid annually since 1890, in the amount of $5,000 to $10,000 by subsidization through the Smithsonian Institution of various printing costs. At $7,500 per year, the total of such aid from 1890 through 1960 would be about $450,000.

One humanistic society, the Modern Language Association of America, has received considerable support from the Office of Education of the United States Department of Health, Education, and Welfare. Grants totalling $224,000 were made by the Office to the Association in 1959 for special studies and research in the teaching and other aspects of foreign language study. The American Philosophical Association received a grant in 1950 of $8,500 from the National Science Foundation for the translation of certain publications by Polish logicians and the Association for Asian

Studies received a grant of $25,530 from the Foundation in the same year for a special study dealing with China.

Nineteen of the 29 humanistic-social science learned societies do not appear to have received financial aid for any purpose from any government agency. These 19 are: the American Antiquarian Society, the American Economic Association, the American Folklore Society, the American Musicological Society, the American Numismatic Society, the American Oriental Society, the American Philological Association, the American Society for Aesthetics, the American Sociological Association, the American Studies Association, the Archaeological Institute of America, the Bibliographical Society of America, the College Art Association of America, the Linguistic Society of America, the Mediaeval Academy of America, the Metaphysical Society of America, the Renaissance Society of America, the Society of Architectural Historians, and the Society of Biblical Literature and Exegesis.

Industrial aid to the learned societies, as compared to that provided by the foundations and government is, with one exeception,[7] negligible and usually confined to support of a society whose interests coincide with those of the grant-making industry. Moreover, the total of about $339,000 in aid provided by these industrial concerns is confined almost wholly to the natural science societies. Ten of the 29 natural science societies received aid totalling about $300,000 whereas only three of the 29 humanistic-social science societies, the American Anthropological Association, the American Political Science Association, and the Association of American Geographers, received aid amounting to $39,000.[8]

Various industrial concerns have rendered aid to the ten natural science societies in the following amounts: the American Astronomical Society, $20,000; the American Geophysical Union, $26,900; the American Meteorological Society, $6,000; the American Physical Society, $67,500; the American Physiological Society, $1,250; the American Institute of Nutrition, $17,850; the American Society for Experimental Pathology, $3,000; the American Society for Microbiology, $76,000; the American Society for Pharmacology and Experimental Therapeutics, $70,000; and the Genetics Society of America, $6,480.

Examples of the grants from industrial firms, and their purposes, are those of the Bell Telephone Laboratories and the Hughes Aircraft Company to the American Physical Society for prizes to physicists; the Bendix Aviation Corporation and United Air Lines to the American Meteorological Society to aid it establish its executive offices; and the Parke-Davis Company to the American Society for Experimental Pathology to provide funds for an annual research award.

Any comment on financial aid rendered the learned societies by colleges and universities is similar to observations concerning an iceberg: by far the greater proportion of it cannot be seen.

The colleges and universities of the United States make an inestimable contribution to the learned societies by providing released time to faculty members serving as officers of societies, office space, and clerical help.

Instances of actual financial aid by colleges and universities to learned societies include the following: New York University's subvention of $1,500 to the American Physiological Society to publish the results of a conference held by the Society; the University of Pennsylvania's contribution of $5,000 annually, for the past several years, toward the support of the American Studies Association; the receipt by the Mediaeval Academy of America of $8,000 from two educational institutions to provide for publication of books in its area of interest; and the Wesleyan University Press has provided approximately $30,000 to aid the American Academy of Arts and Sciences publish its journal, *Daedalus.* Some 100 colleges and universities are currently making cash subsidies to the support of the learned journals of the following societies: the American Society for Aesthetics, the American Studies Association, the Association for Symbolic Logic, the College Art Association of America, the Institute of Mathematical Statistics, and the Metaphysical Society of America.

An officer of one learned society, Dr. B. R. Stanerson, Deputy Executive Secretary of the American Chemical Society, in a very interesting article,[9] calculates that the services rendered his Society by members serving on committees would have cost the Society about $1,000,000 in the period 1951-58. Since a great many of the committeemen of this and other societies are faculty members, and this is only one society, albeit one of the larger ones, some insight into the total college and university contribution to the learned societies can be gained.

THE COUNCILS

NATIONAL ACADEMY OF SCIENCES-NATIONAL RESEARCH COUNCIL

The National Academy of Sciences was organized during the Civil War as the Government's science advisor and was called upon during that war to aid in the scientific matters connected with its prosecution. As has been pointed out previously, the wording of the Academy's congressional charter gives it an official connection with the United States government and it and its operating arm the National Research Council have received more governmental support than any other learned society, council, or institute, in all cases for services rendered by the Council to the government.

After the Civil War scientific activity in the Academy sponsored by the government practically ceased; it seldom called on the Academy for advice, and the Academy became primarily an honorific membership society which administered certain funds bequeathed to it. The Academy's Annual Report for 1880, for instance, listed a total of only 30 projects and investigations conducted for the government up to that time. Indeed, during the first 50 years of its existence, 1863-1913, only 53 committees of inquiry were appointed at government request. Of this total, the following branches of government were represented thus: Congress—8; President—2; Treasury Department—24; Navy Department—8; War Department—5; State Department—2; Agriculture Department—2; Interior Department—2.[10] Toward the close of the century, however, government bureaus began to turn more to the Academy for advice and furnished it funds to carry on research. In 1896-97, for instance, the Department of the Interior was instrumental in providing the Academy with $24,000 to enable a special committee to report on policy regarding the national forests of the United States. As late as 1910, however, a well-known American historian in commenting upon the Academy, stated: "The old American Association for the Advancement of Science, popular before the war, failed to meet; but in lieu of its meetings and in imitation of the famous French Academy and the Royal Society of London, Congress incorporated the National Academy of Sciences, a close corporation of fifty men, which held a few secret meetings and then failed ignominiously, lacking entirely in popular support."[11]

With the advent of World War I and the creation of the Academy's National Research Council there was a sharp but temporary increase in activities involving the Academy-Council and government. Several hundreds of thousands of dollars for research and other activities was provided by the Council of National Defense and the various arms of the War and Navy Departments. The cessation of hostilities saw the end of this activity and from that time until the beginnings of World War II government support of Council activities was limited to the State Department, the Department of Agriculture, and the Bureau of Standards.

From 1920 through 1931 the dues of the NRC in the International Research Council and the various international subsidiary Unions were paid almost entirely by government funds out of State Department appropriations. Although cut out during the depression years 1932-34, these funds were subsequently restored and have been so paid to the present time, currently amounting to approximately $65,000 per year.

The Department of Agriculture through the 1920's and '30's supplied thousands of dollars annually to the Council's Highway Research Board for research in various aspects of highway construction. For the Bureau of Standards, the Council acted as fiscal agent for various projects conducted by the Bureau.

Set up in World War I to coordinate government scientific activity, the NRC barely got started before the war ended. Because it was already in existence and on the scene and with the mission described above, it would appear that the Council would be the logical choice for such a role in World War II. This did not materialize for two reasons: First, the difficulty regarding funding of government research contracts referred to in Chapter IV, and second, in the two decades between the wars the Council was little used by government and, consequently, had developed along civilian lines. The necessary alterations in organization and personnel to make it a suitable vehicle for primarily military research would have been too slow a process for the emergency confronting the nation. Consequently, while certain divisions of the NRC, particularly the Medical Division and Committee on Strategic Minerals and Metals, did play such an overseeing role in World War II, an entirely new scientific organization, the National Defense Research Committee (NDRC), merged later into the Office of Scientific Research and Development (OSRD), was created within the executive branch of the government to coordinate much of the war-time scientific activity.[12]

The critical role played by the OSRD in World War II did not diminish the importance of the Academy-Council to the war effort, and during the war years 1941-46, some $4,000,000 were channelled to the Academy-Council through the OSRD and other government agencies. At the peak of the war such funds constituted approximately 75 per cent of the Council's total annual income and were allocated to all of its scientific divisions. The War Department provided funds for research in Quartermaster Corps problems, aircraft production, and protection against bombing. The Civil Aeronautics Authority awarded large-scale contracts in connection with the selection and training of aircraft pilots. Scores of other government agencies requested aid for such diverse projects as nutrition and food research, optical properties of laminated glass, sound control, and the availability of scientific and technical personnel. Although still little known, the vast operations which led to the production of the atomic bomb were triggered by recommendatory results of an initial survey as to its feasibility by a 1941 Academy committee. A parallel committee, the top-secret one on biological warfare, was activated on a request by the

Secretary of War and supervised the vast research effort in this area throughout the war period.

The post-war era, because of the Cold War, the increasing reliance on research for scientific breakthrough, and the termination of the OSRD, saw no diminution but rather a steady increase in the government research contracts placed with the Council. New agencies, such as the Atomic Energy Commission and the National Science Foundation, allocated sizeable sums to it while older ones increasingly called on it for assistance and advice. Thus, for the fiscal year ending June 30, 1960, of a total budget in excess of $15,000,000, government funds accounted for about $10,-000,000 or approximately 70 per cent of the total.

Based on examination of the fiscal reports of the Academy-Council for the entire period 1918-1960, it received $60,000,000, or about 50 per cent of its total income of $120,000,000, from government sources. Over 80 per cent of this $60,000,000 came to it as the result of projects entered into during World War II and the period since that time. Compared to its present day multi-million dollar government income, a statement pointing out the increase in government projects in the Academy's 1941 Annual Report, pp. 44-45, points up the even greater change in the role played by the government *vis-a-vis* the NRC since World War II: "A comparative analysis of annual expenditures in the Council for the past 5 years shows certain significant trends. The administrative costs have risen over 20 per cent, while the total amount of money handled has increased over 80 per cent. . . . The marked change in the proportion of these financial operations has been in the funds handled (under contract) for government projects. This figure increased from $65,793.95 in 1936-37 to $355,153.68 in 1940-41, over five-fold."

Prior to World War I, industrial support of the NAS-NRC was practically negligible. With the creation of the National Research Council, however, various industrial firms began to grant it funds. The Bell Telephone System was a pioneer. In 1918, it made an award of $25,000 to the Council for its general support at a time when such aid was sorely needed. Other firms, such as Corning Glass Works, Corn Products Refining Company, E. I. Du Pont de Nemours and Company, General Electric Company, General Motors Corporation, Merrell-Soule Company, and Texas Gulf Sulphur Company made grants throughout the 1920's for fellowships, research projects and other purposes.

It appears that from World War I to the great depression of the 1930's industrial support of the NAS-NRC probably amounted to about $1,500,-000.[13] Such support reached its highwater mark in 1930 and then began a drastic retreat. Table 4, presents financial information as to the period

1929-1942 for the National Research Council and graphically illustrates this development.

TABLE 4

INDUSTRIAL SUPPORT OF NATIONAL RESEARCH COUNCIL, 1929-1942[a]

Year	Total NRC Expenditures	Total Expended by NRC for Projects and Fellowships[b]	Received by NRC From Industrial Organizations for Projects and Fellowships[b]	Industrial Organizations Per Cent of NRC Expenditures for Projects and Fellowships[b]
1929	$ 882,030	$724,045	$195,099	27
1930	958,536	798,498	242,515	30
1931	1,004,615	838,249	132,406	11
1932	942,178	780,147	64,354	8.2
1933	833,914	689,873	35,173	5.1
1934	811,578	713,785	20,790	2.9
1935	669,877	574,383	17,921	3.1
1936	523,832	228,846	7,225	3.1
1937	474,284	241,167	6,487	2.7
1938	498,809	274,584	5,430	1.9
1939	557,648	328,740	6,099	1.8
1940	630,166	412,850	5,870	1.0
1941	853,802	627,110	8,143	1.0
1942	1,085,131	829,235	7,983	.09

a Source: Annual Reports of the National Academy of Sciences-National Research Council, 1929-1942.

b From 1936 on these figures are for research projects only.

The total amount of industrial support to the Academy-Council during the period 1931 through 1942 did not exceed $500,000.

From 1943-1946 government funds annually supplied 50 per cent or more of the total income of the NRC. In one year, 1945, such funds formed 72.9 per cent of the total. Industrial support was negligible during this period.

Following World War II, industrial firms stepped up their outlays to the NAS-NRC. Much of this increased activity was in the form of sub-contracts from industrial firms who held prime research contracts from the government. Approximately $8,000,000 flowed to the Academy-Council during the period 1947-1960 from industrial sources.

During the entire period 1918-1960, the total amount of industrial support rendered the Academy-Council was approximately $10,000,000. There were a few appropriations made for special awards and some for general support but over 90 per cent of this sum appears to have been appropriated for special research projects and fellowships, usually within the area of interest of the company.

To summarize, industrial support of the NAS-NRC has been subject to fluctuation because of economic conditions and, compared to foundation and even governmental support, does not appear to be as flexible and divorced from self-interest.

Although there are close ties between the universities and the NAS-NRC, its officers, members, committee personnel, and representatives on the Research Council are connected with such institutions, and many of its projects are carried out on campuses, there is no official connection between the universities and the NAS-NRC, and university support of the NAS-NRC has seldom taken the form of direct financial support. Rather, the substantial support these institutions have rendered has been of an indirect nature, the release of faculty time on a certain project, for example, or the provision of space and equipment with which to carry out such a project.

The Annual Report of the National Research Council for 1920, p. 38, records such an instance, noting that out of expenditures of about $60,000 to investigate the fatigue phenomena of metals, the University of Illinois had contributed the equivalent of $6,000 in manpower, laboratories, and equipment. This was one project in one year; multiplied over the years it can be seen that, while it is impossible to ascertain exactly how much such support came to, it must have run into hundreds of thousands of dollars, perhaps millions.

AMERICAN COUNCIL ON EDUCATION

By contrast with the National Academy of Sciences-National Research Council, the American Council on Education has had a direct and official connection with the colleges and universities since 1919 when they were admitted as institutional members. Furthermore, these institutions, in 1960 numbering some 1,047 members out of a total of 1,189 have since provided well over 50 per cent of the membership fees of the Council. In recent years most of its officers have been university officials. The majority of its projects have been of direct concern to higher education, and some of them have been conducted on college and university campuses with the indirect but tangible benefits enjoyed thereby. Thus, although the constitution of the American Council on Education states: "The Council was organized to meet national needs in time of war and will always render patriotic service," during the first World War the Council met these national needs on a consultative basis to the various government agencies concerned with the role of education in the war effort, and no government funds were supplied to the Council for its aid and advice.

Its budget for the first few years of its operation was less than $25,000 annually and supplied almost entirely by dues from its members. From that time until 1941 the Council's income came primarily from membership fees or foundation grants. By way of illustration, the president's annual report for 1930, p. 210 states: "An analysis of the receipts and expenditures of the Council made at the request of the U. S. Office of Education shows that from 1918 to 1930 the Council received in membership fees and other sources of general income a total of $379,188.61 and in grants from foundations a total of $885,408.22. We have expended in the same period $1,240,291.72."

In other words, during the period from 1918-1930, out of a total income of approximately $1,250,000 all but about $25,000 came from membership fees and similar general income sources or foundation grants.

It was not until 1941 that the first instance of money supplied the ACE by government is recorded. At that time the War Department allotted $15,000 for the use of the Council's Cooperative Test Service. This money was to be used by the Service for the construction of tests to assist the Army in its selection of warrant officers.

During World War II the Council conducted other personnel studies for the Army and was similarly reimbursed. The Civil Aeronautics Authority commissioned the Council to conduct research with respect to several of its programs and, for the Office of Coordinator of Inter-American Affairs, it initiated a program of assistance for certain South American schools which involved aid in the selection of teachers, preparation of teaching materials, and general support. The latter program eventually developed into the Council's Inter-American School Service which, since the war, has functioned with the cooperation and support of the Department of State. At the present time the Service serves as a clearinghouse of financial assistance and educational advice for approximately 300 schools in Latin America. These bi-national schools were established in the Latin-American countries to supplement the various national elementary and secondary school systems. In addition to other activities, the Director of the Service sponsors intermittent regional and general conferences of the school directors and assists them in recruiting teachers, etc. The present annual budget for the Service is now about $250,000 per year, of which $180,000 is used for direct grants to schools.

Many of the other present day ACE activities conducted for the government grew out of similar requests for services during the war. Advice and the preparation of material for the U. S. Armed Forces Institute and the Department of Defense's Office of Armed Forces Information and Education has been a continuing function. The Council operates, under a contract with the Department of Defense, a Commission on Accreditation of Service Experiences whose publication and consulting services are widely used by university and government officials. Similarly, the Council has accepted contracts from the Navy Department for various studies and surveys, particularly in the personnel area.

Since World War II the Council has contracted with the Department of State to operate the Leaders and Specialists Program which annually brings to the United States some 400 leaders in all walks of life and from some fifty different countries. Established in 1954, for the past three years this program has had annual budgets in excess of $700,000. In addition to the State and Defense Departments, the Department of Health, Education, and Welfare, the Economic Cooperation Administration, the Office of Civil and Defense Mobilization, the United States Information Agency, the Tennessee Valley Authority and others have provided funds for various studies and projects of an educational nature.

The total income of the ACE from 1918 to 1960 amounted to approximately $26,000,000. Total government funds received by it from 1941 to 1960 amount to approximately $10,000,000. For the past few years such funds have accounted for over 50 per cent of its annual income.

In comparison to that of the universities and government, industrial support of the ACE has been minuscule. One of its first grants from business concerns, and incidentally the largest of its kind, was that of $125,000 in 1944 by eight motion picture companies for the work of the Council's Commission on Motion Pictures in Education.

In 1948 such industrial giants as American Telephone and Telegraph Co., E. I. Du Pont de Nemours Co., General Motors Corp., B. F. Goodrich Co., R. H. Macy Co., and Socony-Vacuum Oil Co. made grants of $150 each to support a study of placement services for college graduates being made by the Council's Committee on Student Personnel Work. Grants of a similar nature include one in 1947 by Brandon Films for the expenses of printing the proceedings of a conference on visual aids; one in 1952 by the International Business Machines Corporation for the costs of printing the program for a National Conference on Women in the Defense Decade; and one each from the Fuller Brush Co., General Dynamics Corporation, and General Mills, Inc. for the holding of a conference to study the relationships between the United States and Canada. Each grant from these corporations was for $250.

Nearly all other financial aid from corporations received by the ACE has been towards the general support of and various activities of its Inter-American School Service which aids some 300 American sponsored schools in certain Latin American republics.[14] Some 25 corporations, from 1952-1957, supported the Service program for schools in Cuba with grants ranging from $50 to $3,000 and totalling about $30,000. Seven companies, in 1957, provided about $8,000 to the Service for such schools in Colombia, and the Ford Motor Co., in 1960, gave $20,000 for those in Argentina. The Service received from about $1,000 to $3,000 each from seven other corporations for schools in Mexico, Venezuela, Colombia and Ecuador. The total of such aid was about $10,000. Also, in 1957, ten companies supplied about $5,000 for the expenses of a conference in Washington on the problems of the American sponsored schools in Latin America.

The total amount of money supplied by United States corporations to the Service for these American sponsored schools in Latin America, therefore, was approximately $75,000.

Industrial or corporate support of the American Council on Education's activities has never achieved the size or range of support it has received from other sources. Almost without exception, those grants which it has received have been for purposes which appear to have been of direct or indirect benefit to the donor company or its employees. Furthermore, although some 50 different companies have made grants to the Council during the period from 1919-1960, amounting to a total of about $200,000, most of them have been in the $100 to $500 range.

AMERICAN COUNCIL OF LEARNED SOCIETIES

AND

SOCIAL SCIENCE RESEARCH COUNCIL

Relative to the National Academy of Sciences-National Research Council and the American Council on Education, the total amount of governmental financial support flowing to the American Council of Learned Societies and Social Science Research Council has been small. Of the two, the ACLS has received the largest amount, approximately $2,500,000, and well over 75 per cent of this sum was granted to it for the conduct of intensive training in certain foreign languages during and immediately following World War II. The approximately $2,000,000 thus appropriated came from the Department of State, the then War and Navy Departments, and the Council of National Defense. The remaining approximately $500,000, with the exception of a $6,000 grant from the National Science Foundation in 1957, came from the Department of Health, Education, and Welfare for programs to improve instruction in critical foreign languages. The impetus for these appropriations was the post-Sputnik scare which resulted in the passage of the National Defense Education Act.

The Bureau of the Census of the Department of Commerce has provided by far the largest amount of governmental money to the SSRC, for studies involving census data. Between 1950 and 1960, six contracts amounting to $173,900 were made for that purpose. The National Science Foundation, with grants in 1958 and 1959 amounting to $35,900, supported a conference on the history of quantification in the sciences, the distribution of certain Chinese scientific translations to various libraries, and a conference dealing with certain aspects of linguistics and psychology. A 1957 grant of $17,462 from the National Institutes of Health, for a seminar on aphasia and a 1960 one of $29,325 for the support of the Council's Committee on Socialization and Social Structure, completes the total governmental support of about $250,000 to the SSRC up to and including the year 1960.

Direct industrial and university support of the ACLS and SSRC has been minuscule. The ACLS has received about $39,000 from the Arabian American Oil Company and several publishing firms for publication purposes and $36,000 from the Corning Glass Company for a special conference. The SSRC has received a few awards, one of $1,000, for example, from the Lord and Taylor Company, but the total from industrial sources does not reach $5,000. Thus, both Councils have received a sum total of less than $100,000 from industrial sources during their entire period of existence.

Turning to the universities, the situation for the ACLS and the SSRC is similar to that of the NAS-NRC. All of these Councils draw overwhelmingly from academicians for membership on their working committees, and portions of many research projects are conducted in university offices and laboratories. While the Councils do defray the direct cost of participation in such activities, travel costs involved, etc., the indirect value of such expert advice is incalculable.

It goes without saying that such activities by academicians are of inestimable value to the Councils and, indeed, to the entire academic community. In other words, it is a nice question whether they are giving aid to the Councils, the Councils aid to them, or whether what is involved is instead a joint effort by all.

SOCIETAL INSTITUTES

AMERICAN ASSOCIATION FOR THE ADVANCEMENT OF SCIENCE

The third annual meeting of the newly formed American Association for the Advancement of Science was held in 1850 in Charleston, S. C. The expenses of this meeting, including the printing of the *Proceedings* resulting therefrom, were paid for by the city of Charleston. The President and other officers of the Association, in noting this generosity, stated that this action aided in the elimination of political and economic friction between the North and South, and implied that it might be wise for other cities to continue the practice. The suggestion bore fruit, and from that time down to the Civil War, various cities, Cincinnati, Cleveland, and others, in which meetings were held, defrayed such costs.

This support provides the first instance, albeit at the local level, of governmental support of the AAAS.

The Association resumed operations after a temporary cessation of activities during the Civil War, but the early form of local governmental aid was not continued and the costs of meetings and publication were henceforth met from its own revenues.

Throughout the nineteenth century, although the AAAS was the only national organization encompassing all of science and with membership open to all, it remained a relatively small organization. Its membership in that century never exceeded 2,045 and its income and expenditures never exceeded $12,000 per annum.

Following World War I there was a considerable increase in income and membership, and a corresponding one following World War II. It was not, however, until 1955, with the convening of an International Arid Land Meeting in New Mexico, that United States government funds were provided the AAAS. The costs of that meeting were met by grants of $10,000 each from the National Science Foundation and the Rockefeller Foundation, together with smaller ones from the Department of State, UNESCO, and local business groups.

Since 1955 the National Science Foundation has provided additional aid to the Association, amounting, through 1960, to a total of about $2,-100,000. Of this sum, all but about $400,000 has gone to develop and support traveling libraries of books about science and scientists. At their point of highest activity, these libraries circulated during the year among some 1,700 high schools and 800 elementary schools throughout the United States. Expenses of meetings and conferences, fellowships, and several special projects, such as a study of the qualification and teaching load of secondary school teachers of science and mathematics, and a symposium on the sciences in Communist China, were the purposes for which the other grants were made.

Industrial support of the AAAS has been sporadic and has never been sought on an extensive scale. In 1959, 15 industrial firms supplied funds totalling $11,200 towards the holding of an International Oceanographic Congress under Association auspices. Since 1953 a local committee on arrangements for the Association's annual meetings has secured gifts for that purpose from industrial sources. Such annual contributions for the past eight years have averaged about $9,000 and the total amount of such contributions has been approximately $70,000.

The annual Gordon Research Conferences of the AAAS are somewhat uniquely aided by industrial supporters. In the 1930's and '40's about 58 industrial firms supplied $1,000 each toward the purchase of a building on an island off the Maryland coast where these Conferences were held. In 1949 this property was sold, but the Conferences were continued and the proceeds from the sale were used as an endowment to cover a portion of the costs. In a sense, industry is, therefore, continuously providing limited support for the Conferences.

The American Association for the Advancement of Science is similar to the other four societal institutes in that it has received little or no direct financial aid from colleges and universities.

FEDERATION OF AMERICAN SOCIETIES FOR EXPERIMENTAL BIOLOGY

Until 1953 the Federation of American Societies for Experimental Biology did not receive any substantial amounts of aid from the Federal government. At that time the National Science Foundation made a grant to it of $11,400 for advisory services and counsel in the general field of biology. Subsequent grants, through 1960 totalling approximately $163,000, were made for the same purpose, for a register of experimental biologists, and for the support of symposia and other special projects.

The National Institutes of Health, during the period 1957-1960, awarded about $112,000 to the Federation for travel grants to international conferences and research projects in biology and for a survey of manpower needs in the biological sciences. Two other grants from governmental agencies were received in 1959; one of $10,000 from the U. S. Air Force's Office of Scientific Research and the other of $5,000 from the U. S. Army's Quartermaster Corps' Research and Equipment Command, both being for conferences on research on human acclimation to cold. Thus the approximate total funds received by the Federation from governmental agencies is about $300,000.

Although the Federation has, from time to time, benefited from minor grants for special purposes from industrial firms, the major grant received from this source was in 1954. At that time the Federation purchased its present quarters at 9650 Wisconsin Avenue, Washington, D. C., and 16 pharmaceutical and allied firms, plus four individuals made gifts totalling $24,000 for remodeling purposes.

AMERICAN INSTITUTE OF PHYSICS

From its founding in 1931 through 1956 the American Institute of Physics received few grants or contracts from the government. Those received were primarily from the Office of Naval Research and the Atomic Energy Commission, and they amounted to about $75,000.

In 1957 the Institute received an award of $18,300 from the Atomic Energy Commission for a study of publishing problems in physics. This award was supplemented in 1958 and 1960 by grants totalling $138,400 for similar purposes from the National Science Foundation. By the latter date the Institute had in addition received approximately $850,000 from the Foundation for other publication projects, over 80 per cent of this sum being budgeted for the translation and publication of Russian language journals and books.

The National Science Foundation also awarded the Institute grants amounting to about $192,000 for a program enabling outstanding domestic and foreign physicists to visit our colleges and high schools and stimulate the teaching of physics therein; $59,000 was appropriated for an apparatus drawing project and other programs for the general improvement of physics teaching. The Foundation also made $27,000 available for the preparation and publication of booklets to encourage the youth of the nation to choose physics as a career and approximately $22,000 for conferences, seminars and other projects devoted to special aspects of physics. Since 1958, under NSF contracts amounting to $72,800, the Institute has maintained the Physics and Astronomy Sections of the National Register of Scientific and Technical Personnel.

Other than the Atomic Energy Commission and the National Science Foundation, the only other government agency making awards to the Institute was the Air Force's Office of Scientific Research. It made grants totalling $93,500 for a three year period from 1958 through 1960 toward the support of a new journal, *The Physics of Fluids*.

During the entire period 1931-1960 a total of four government agencies made grants to the Institute which totalled approximately $1,500,000.

Industrial support of the American Institute of Physics has always been an important factor. Beginning in 1935 the Institute opened its ranks to Corporate Associates who have since aided the Institute significantly in furthering its work. These Associates now number some 175 corporations including, for example, Aluminum Corporation of America, Bausch and Lomb Incorporated, the Dow Chemical Company, General Electric Company, General Motors Corporation, Libbey-Owens-Ford Glass Company and

Shell Development Company. In addition to this type of support, several corporations have sponsored special projects for the Institute. In 1958 the Institute expanded its communication program between academic physicists and the industrial world and inaugurated an annual Corporate Associates' meeting which has developed into a valuable forum for representatives of industry and university physicists.

AMERICAN INSTITUTE OF BIOLOGICAL SCIENCES

Total income from all sources of the American Institute of Biological Sciences from 1948 through 1954 amounted to less than $200,000. Since the latter date, however, of the five societal institutes the AIBS has received the largest amount of financial support from the government. The National Science Foundation alone has provided it with approximately $3,700,000 from 1955 through 1960. This sum was appropriated through the years for the following purposes: $2,031,000 for the support of an Institute committee engaged in a study looking toward the best curriculum for the biological sciences; $750,000 for the translation and publication of various Russian periodicals and books in the biological sciences; $265,000 for other publications; $230,000 for a national register of biological scientists; $220,000 for a visiting lecturers program; $81,000 for the holding of or travel to various international congresses and meetings; $60,000 for conferences on various biological problems; $48,000 for the production of two college undergraduate biology course television films; and $17,600 for general support. In 1955 the AIBS requested and received this last sum from the National Science Foundation with an understanding that the money would be used to ease the transition of the Institute to a status independent of the National Academy of Sciences-National Research Council and that such a request would not be renewed.

Also in 1955, the AIBS entered into a continuing contract with the Navy's Office of Naval Research for certain basic research in the biological sciences. By 1960 money granted under this contract totalled about $400,000. During this period a sum of about the same magnitude was provided by the Atomic Energy Commission for publication and lecture purposes and certain curriculum studies. Both of these government agencies, together with the Department of Health, Education and Welfare, the Public Health Service, including the National Institutes of Health, and the Army's Chemical Corps and the Air Force's Materiel Command, have contributed amounts totalling about $235,000 toward the support of conferences sponsored by the AIBS; travel and other expenses connected with international congresses and meetings; and the preparation and publication of various articles and books dealing with biology.

The total amount of government support provided the American Institute of Biological Sciences from 1955 through 1960 amounts to approximately $5,000,000, almost all for support of specific projects.

Industrial associates, some 18 firms interested in furthering the work of the AIBS, have contributed several thousand dollars annually towards its general support.

AMERICAN GEOLOGICAL INSTITUTE

In 1953 the American Geological Institute received its first government award of $3,750 towards the preparation of a glossary of geologic terms. This grant, and all succeeding ones received by the Institute through 1960, were from the National Science Foundation. During this period a total of 23 awards amounting to $635,995 were made by the Foundation to the AGI. Approximately 50 per cent of this amount was for publication purposes, including the translation and publication of foreign periodicals; 20 per cent for the inauguration and continuation of a register of earth scientists; and 20 per cent for a visiting geological scientists program whereby selected earth scientists, including distinguished foreign ones, visited various colleges and universities for specified periods. The remaining 10 per cent was for special projects such as a teaching development program for geology and for general support of the Institute. In connection with this last item, $23,000 was granted to the Institute by the NSF in 1956-57 as emergency support for its general operations. It was understood at the time that such support would not be continued and was given with the understanding that Institute officials would secure other means of support, an understanding which was successfully met.

The National Science Foundation funds form approximately 50 per cent of the 1948-60 total income of about $1,200,000 of the Institute. Of the remainder, it received about $155,000 from two member societies, the Geological Society of America and the American Association of Petroleum Geologists; eleven other member societies and various miscellaneous sources contributed about $236,000; various individuals gave $120,000, these were primarily members of the Committee of One Hundred, members who agree to pay $100 a year towards the support of the Institute; and $54,000 was received from Industrial Associates. Industrial support of the AGI centers around the latter. These Associates are organizations, primarily oil companies and including the Amerada Petroleum Corporation, Arabian Oil Company, Arabian American Oil Company, Creole Petroleum Corporation, Gulf Oil Corporation, Humble Oil Company, Phillips Petroleum Company, Shell Oil Company and various affiliates of the Standard Oil Corporation, who are interested in the geological sciences, realizing that they have a vital stake in maintaining the quality and strength of U. S. geological manpower, and believing that financial support of the Institute will aid such maintenance. The industrial support since its inception in 1953 has been wholly in the form of grants for general support of the Institute.

Chapter VI

INTERNATIONAL RELATIONS

International relations, those relationships transcending national boundaries, have traditionally been conducted in the politico-military-economic sphere. The historical record of these relationships is to be found in the negotiation of innumerable treaties beginning with the rise of the ancient seats of civilization in the Middle and Far East and extending down to the present day. In the Western World, the city states of Greece and the Roman Empire negotiated with other nations and empires. Medieval Europe witnessed, through the constant jockeying for position by vying kingdoms under the unifying influence of an all-encompassing Church, the growth of groups of people with a common international outlook which, through the centuries, laid the basis for much of modern formal diplomatic relationships.

During this ancient and medieval period, in addition to the development of a rudimentary diplomatic code, there appeared various leagues of a military-economic nature which can be viewed as a primitive form of international organization. The various military leagues and councils of ancient Greece and Republican Rome, the confederation of the Swiss cantons, and the Hanseatic League are examples of this type of organization. It must be noted, however, that all of these groupings united people of similar backgrounds and were accomplished under the stress of military and economic necessity.

The sixteenth, seventeenth, and eighteenth centuries, which saw the ending of the dream of a revived Roman Empire, coterminous with the Protestant Reformation, the Industrial Revolution, and the emergence of the modern state system, witnessed the development of rapidly shifting alliances of various states which did indeed transcend national boundaries, contain many of the seeds of present-day international organizations, and form part of the evolution of the sovereign state system which ultimately produced the vital need for international organizations. It was not, however, until the Napoleonic period that the clear-cut idea of sovereign nation-states cooperating in various ways emerges and the Congress of Vienna (1815), which closes that period, is generally conceded to be the event which ushers in the period of modern international relations. For, in addition to settling many purely diplomatic and military problems, for example diplomatic representatives at a given post should take precedence in terms of their seniority, it led to the establishment of specific channels for international consultation and ushered in concern for other than politico-military-economic affairs. The great powers at Vienna, for instance, made a joint declaration looking forward to the end of the slave trade and, in 1823, the British and Foreign Anti-Slavery Society was organized in London and proceeded to hold in 1840 the first of the modern international conferences. During the next decade it was followed by international conferences called by organizations devoted to world peace, religious questions, and prison reform. All of these organizations and conferences were humanitarian in their motives, however, and it is not until 1853, with the convening of the first International Statistical Conference that we have a meeting devoted to what was, in large part, an intellectual or scientific subject matter. From this point on the number of international intellectual organizations and their international conferences or congresses proliferates at an astonishing rate.[1] Today, out of slightly more than 2,000 such organizations founded since 1815, there are more than 1,500 still in existence. By the beginning of the 20th century these organizations were holding international conferences at the rate of approximately 100 per year, by 1920 this figure doubled, and it has since doubled again so that such conferences now average about 400 per year.[2]

During the 100 years from 1815 to 1915, the relationship of the existent American learned societies to the international intellectual organizations was informal and irregular. In most cases it consisted of participation by interested individuals, acting also as representatives of the existing learned societies, in various sporadic and intermittent international conferences called during the period. Examples of the latter include those devoted to chemistry at Geneva in 1892; Social and Economic Sciences at Bordeaux in 1907; Botany and Horticulture at Brussels in 1864; History at Chicago in 1893; Religious Science at Stockholm in 1897; and Mathematics at Chicago in 1893. The vast majority of the approximately 5,000 such meetings during the period 1815-1915 were sponsored by private, nongovernmental groups.[3] There was usually no provision made for succeeding meetings; no permanent secretariat was provided to carry on between them; and expenses were usually met on a temporary, one-shot basis. Finally, there was a great deal of either over-lapping and duplication or fragmentization in various learned disciplines. In chemistry, for instance, there were five different international organizations dealing with that subject, while in astronomy almost a score of independent bodies dealt with specialized aspects of the subject and thus hampered consideration of major problems spanning several segments of the science.

It was not until the post-World War I period that there emerged two permanent international organizations beneath whose aegis took place a concerted development of permanent international organizations devoted to specific disciplines, capable of coordinating research in inter-disciplinary problems, and formed with the express intention of convening meetings periodically. These two organizations were the International Research Council and the International Academic Union.

The International Research Council was organized as the result of dissatisfaction with the International Association of Academies;[4] the war-time scientific collaboration of the Allies, particularly that between the United States and Great Britain, which resulted in a belief that a permanent organization should be created to continue this scientific intercourse; and a desire to reorganize the existing international learned and scientific organizations so that they could perform in a more efficient and effective manner. This sentiment for a new over-all scientific organization culminated in the Royal Society's call for a Conference on International Scientific Organizations to be held in London on October 9, 1918. Belgium, Brazil, France, Great Britain, Italy, Japan, Serbia, and the United States were represented at this conference.[5]

The American delegates thereto introduced the basic plan upon which the International Research Council was erected. They proposed the organization of a National Research Council in each country represented which would be a federation of the major scientific organizations therein. The International Research Council, in turn, would be a federation of all of these National Research Councils. Following intervening consultation and discussion, a second conference was called by the French Academy of Sciences to be held in Paris from November 26th to November 29, 1918. In addition to delegates from the countries mentioned previously, Poland, Portugal, and Rumania sent representatives to this conference. Following the preparatory work of a provisional executive committee which met in Paris in May, 1919, the formal organization of the Council took place at a meeting in Brussels, July 18-28, 1919. The governing statutes, adopted there, specified that the International Research Council would consist of the following adhering countries: Belgium, Brazil, United States of America, Great Britain, Australia, Canada, New Zealand, South Africa, Greece, Italy, Japan, Poland, Portugal, Rumania and Serbia. Each of them could join the Council by naming delegates from a national research council or similar organization or, in a few instances, directly by its government. The governing body of the Council, the General Assembly, would consist of these same delegates from adhering countries. The international scientific Unions, those in existence and those projected, were not afforded official representation in the Assembly, although these Unions, composed of the principal national learned societies within specific and general areas of scientific knowledge, were to be the principal agencies through which the Council was to act. It was agreed that the legal home of the Council should be Brussels. Voting rights and financial support were based on scales of 1 to 5 and 1 to 8 respectively, both proportional to the populations of the adhering countries. It was agreed that, following adherence by three countries, these statutes should come into force on 1 January 1920 and remain in force until 31 December 1931. Finally, the objects of the International Research Council were, as formulated at this meeting:

"1. To coordinate international activities in the various branches of science and its applications.

"2. To encourage the formation of international associations or unions needed to advance science.

"3. To guide international scientific activities in fields where no adequate organization exists.

"4. To establish relations with the governments represented in the union for the purpose of interesting them in scientific projects."[6]

It can be seen from this latter statement that the primary tasks of the Council were ones of coordination and organization. In line with this mandate, there was organized at the Brussels meeting the International Astronomical Union, the International Geodetic and Geophysical Union, and the International Union of Pure and Applied Chemistry. By 1938 four additional scientific Unions had been established: the International Scientific Radio Union, the International Union of Pure and Applied Physics, the International Geographical Union, and the International Union of Biological Sciences. After World War II, seven more groups were added. The latter include the International Mathematical Union, the International Union of Biochemistry, the International Union of Crystallography, the International Union of the History and Philosophy of Science, the International Union of Physiological Sciences, the International Union of Theoretical and Applied Mechanics and the International Union of Geological Sciences. Each of these 14 unions[7] is composed of appropriate national learned societies and these societies, together with the national councils and other national organizations, now constitute representation from 45 countries all over the globe.

From the beginning the Unions had a powerful influence on the International Research Council; as time went on, however, they became dissatisfied with what they maintained were undue restrictions on their freedom of action. A particular bone of contention was that the Unions, under the existing statutes, were not allowed to accept a country as a member if it did not belong to the Council. This, of course, precluded the former Central Powers from participation in activities of the various

Unions as well as the Council. Although the General Assembly of the Council voted, in 1926, to invite Germany, Austria, Hungary, and Bulgaria to join the Council and the Unions, they were slow to act on the invitation[8] and the Unions became increasingly restive. In the face of incipient revolt, led by certain members of the International Astronomical Union, a Commission on Statutes was appointed in 1928 to consider revision of the statutes, due to lapse in 1931 unless renewed. In June, 1931, this Commission reported to a meeting of the General Assembly that it believed that the Council should become an emanation of the Unions and that its name should be changed to the International Council of Scientific Unions. The statutes implementing this change were unanimously adopted. The chief particular changes, in addition to the change in name, were:

1. The General Assembly was to consist of delegates from the international Unions instead of from the national research council or similar organizations only and, instead of the vote according to population, each national organization was given one vote and each Union, three votes.

2. The Executive Committee of the General Assembly would be formed to a large extent by delegates from each of the Unions.

3. Each of the Unions was given complete autonomy in the management of its affairs, including admitting members irrespective of whether or not the country applying to it was a member of the ICSU.

4. Financial contributions were based on a flat rate for each country plus, for the first time, contributions from each of the Unions.

From this time on, the ICSU was a true federation of international scientfic unions and, although having governmental connections, it became and is a non-governmental organization.[9]

Although the relationship of the national learned societies to their respective national research councils, to the international Unions, and to the International Council of Scientific Unions varies from country to country, the relationship of such organizations in the United States is fairly representative of that of the more populous and scientifically advanced countries.

The official connection between the national learned societies in the United States and the International Council of Scientific Unions and the associated Unions is through the National Academy of Sciences-National Research Council. Repsonsibility for the selection of members of "national" committees of the National Research Council, those committees representing the scientists of the United States in matters involving national participation in the International Council and Unions, rests with the appropriate divisions of the National Research Council. The divisions, however, are predominately made up of representatives of the national learned societies of the particular disciplines concerned. Indeed, the statutes of some of the national committees specify representation from one or more national learned societies. In all cases, however, there is provision for members-at-large to enable the national committees to benefit from others in government, industry, universities, etc. As the national committee is the body most likely to be aware of those taking an active part in the national and international activities in its disciplinary area, the recommendation of members of the national committee concerning its future membership also is given much weight. In practice, it is never a case of the national committee or any other group imposing its will but rather a process of exchanging suggestions, followed by general acceptance of a slate from which the President of the Academy-Research Council designates future members.

Thus, although many of the national learned societies send representatives to the international congresses which are periodically held by the Unions and the International Council, the Academy-Research Council occupies the pivotal position vis-a-vis the International Council of Scientific Unions and the Associated Unions. In addition to being the national body representing the United States on the International Council, it adheres to 13 of the 14 associated Unions of the ICSU and recommends official representatives to these Unions. The exception in this case is the International Union of Theoretical and Applied Mechanics which has a U. S. national committee organized outside the framework of the Academy-Research Council. The chairman of the IUTAM, however, always participates in meetings of the various other national committees, there has always been friendly cooperation between the IUTAM committee and the other national committees, and, in effect, it functions as one with them. The internal organizational structure through which these activities are conducted is the Academy-Research Council's Office of International Relations. In many matters of policy, especially where coordination is needed, the national committees act through this Office. Since these committees also have a dual function as committees within the technical divisions of the Academy-Research Council, however, they are free to deal directly with agencies abroad about scientific matters of a technical nature requiring no coordination.

An organization which is somewhat a counterpart to the International Council of Scientific Unions in the humanities is the International Academic Union[10] and the creation of the former organization undoubtedly inspired sentiment for a similar one in the humanities.

Scholarly groups, set up in the United States and Great Britain, to study and make recommendations for a just peace following World War I were composed largely of humanists and, upon the convening of the Peace Conference in Paris following that war, they were in an advantageous and unprecedented position to create such an international organization. The French Academie des Inscriptions et Belles Lettres initiated the movement for its establishment by inviting in March, 1919 the major humanistic learned societies of the Allied nations to send delegates to a conference to be held in Paris in May, 1919. Representatives from Belgium, France, Greece, Italy, Japan, Rumania and the United States attended this conference, drew up the plan for the establishment of an International Academic Union, and agreed to hold another conference in Paris in October. At this conference, attended by delegates from 11 countries, including in addition to those in attendance at the previous conference (with the exception of Rumania) Denmark, Great Britain, Holland, Poland, and Russia, the plan of organization for the Union was perfected and adopted.[11] The former Central Powers, which had been excluded by statute from participation in the International Research Council until 1926, were not specifically excluded from joining the proposed International Academic Union, but invitations to join the new organization were simply not extended to them. It was not, therefore, until the late 1930's that such an invitation was forthcoming and Germany and Austria joined the organization.

The structure of the International Academic Union corresponded to that of the International Research Council-International Council of Scientific Unions in that each participating country was entitled to representation. Such representatives were to be chosen by the recognized national academy or grouping of learned societies of each country. These representatives were the governing body of the Union and elected its administrative officials. The permanent secretariat was located at the Palais des Academies in Brussels and it is there that the delegates meet annually to discuss and decide upon the general program to be followed by the Union.[12]

Financial support for the regular, administrative expenses of the International Academic Union has always been supplied by the members. In a few instances, such expenses have been defrayed by the respective governments of the home countries of the national societies or academies represented in the Union. The United States of America has never assumed such expenses and they have always been met from the funds of the American Council of Learned Societies.

By way of contrast, the governments of the majority of the countries represented in the ICSU, including the United States of America,[13] have assumed the administrative costs of participation therein. Both Unions have depended upon other sources of aid, including foundations and national academies, for the various special projects they have undertaken.

At the same time that the International Research Council and the International Academic Union were being organized, the League of Nations was being brought into existence. Reflecting the legalistic approach embodied in the various articles of the Covenant of the League of Nations, there was no express provision in that document for the creation of cultural and scientific organizations which could have provided material aid in the League's stated object of promoting "international co-operation" and the achieving of "international peace and security." There was, rather, great emphasis upon juridical, political, and economic measures to ensure such objectives. This is not to say that attempts had not been made to provide for international intellectual and scientific cooperation. The Belgians, particularly, had been in the forefront in advocating such measures but were consistently voted down. Despite this situation, at the very first Assembly of the League, Henri Lafontaine of Belgium, founder of the Union of International Associations, again urged the creation of appropriate facilities under League auspices for the coordination of the intellectual and scientific activities of all nations with the view of contributing to the ensurement of world peace. The Assembly, as the result of favorable pressure from continental European countries and the Latin-American countries with whom they had cultural ties and with the precedent of the creation of similar organizations in the economic field, succumbed and turned the matter over to the League Council with its blessing. After discussion, the Council, on May 15, 1922, set up a 12 man group (finally enlarged to 19) called the International Committee on Intellectual Cooperation charged "to examine international questions regarding intellectual cooperation."

Although the original 12 man committee had a distinguished chairman, Henri Bergson the French philosopher, and included such outstanding figures as Mme. Marie Curie, Albert Einstein, and Robert Millikan, it was provided grossly inadequate funds for its work and, after several meetings, the members finally turned to the national governments for support. The French government thereupon came forward to the Committee and the League with a proposal in 1924 which envisioned the establishment of an Institute of Intellectual Cooperation with a headquarters building in Paris and adequate funds for its operation to be provided by France. In September, 1924 the move was approved by the Council and Assembly of the League and an arrangement was made whereby the Institute was to operate as an independent agency under the control of the Committee. A special section of the League secretariat was designated to coordinate its activities with those of the Institute. In 1926 the League afforded the Institute and Committee, which it called the International Organization for Intellectual Cooperation, the same official status as similar organizations in other fields. In 1928 the Italian government established the Institute for the Unification of Private International Law and the International Educational Cinematographic Institute. The International Studies Conference, although an autonomous group, cooperated throughout the period between the two World Wars with these Institutes and the International Committee in a variety of activities. These included, in general, the interchange of information between universities and libraries, and, in particular, service as a coordinating center for the chief international learned and scientific organizations.[14]

From the foregoing, it is obvious that the International Organization for Intellectual Cooperation of the League of Nations with its Committee, various Institutes, and affiliated groups had much in common with the IRC-ICSU and the IAU. While there was some limited contact between this arm of the League and the two international learned organizations, it was not until July 9, 1937 that a formal agreement was reached between the League and the ICSU. Under the terms of this agreement the ICSU was to act in an advisory capacity to the International Institute of Intellectual Cooperation on all scientific problems presented to it while the ICSU was to consult with the Institute "on all international questions concerning the organization of scientific work."[15] The Institute helped to organize one international study meeting with the ICSU and two of its associated Unions, and then came World War II and the cessation of all such activities.

A similar agreement between the International Academic Union and the Institute was never reached.

Although throughout the interim period between two World Wars the United States had not officially joined the League of Nations, it did have an observer there. There existed also the connection between the United States and the League via the international organizations described above. Nevertheless, it was true that the country whose president (Wilson) had taken the lead in the founding of the League had never legally sanctioned it. This despite the fact, acknowledged even by critics of the League, that a considerable segment of the American people and perhaps even a majority were in favor of joining the organization. Against this background, the overwhelming majority of the leaders of the United States determined from the outset of World War II that a new organization of states dedicated to peace must rise from that awful conflict. It was President Roosevelt who coined the phrase, the United Nations, at a meeting in Washington in January, 1942, of 26 states united against the Axis powers. While the United Nations Declaration, resulting from that conference, dealt more with the waging of the war than with the forging of peace, it was a giant step along the way and it and the Teheran Declaration of December 1, 1943 were to culminate, in August, 1944, with the calling of the Dumbarton Oaks Conference in Washington. This Conference had been preceded by months of consultation between the United States Democratic administration and the Republican opposition to ensure that a latter day Wilson-Lodge battle did not develop. Following bipartisan domestic agreement, liaison was arranged with British and Russian officials and drafts of what type peace organization should be created were circulated before the Conference. By prior mutual consent it was agreed that the moribund League of Nations should not be resuscitated but that an entirely new organization should be set up.

The agreements reached at the Dumbarton Oaks Conference and the subsequent Yalta Conference of 1945 saw the creation of the main features of the United Nations as we know it today. The final Conference in San Francisco, which opened on April 25, 1945, was sponsored by the United States, Great Britain, Russia, China, and France, and resulted in the drafting of the charter of the United Nations.[16]

The role of the U. S. learned societies, councils, and societal institutes in the creation of the U. N. was quite different from that which they played in the creation of the League of Nations. While it is probably true that the vast majority of the leaders in these organizations were in favor of the League and United States adherence to it, the fact remains that the Councils had come into existence contemporaneously with the League, and were, therefore, not in a position to bring their influence to bear in favor of it. The American Association for the Advancement of Science and the Federation of American Societies for Experimental Biology were the only societal institutes in existence, but they were still small-scale organizations with a limited outlook on other than purely scientific matters. Also, as has been pointed out, the learned societies' primary concern in international affairs was convening of and attendance at sporadic international congresses, much of it on a personal rather than official basis. Consequently, only a few officials of these organizations endorsed the concept of the League of Nations and worked actively for it. By way of contrast, many of the leaders in these organizations were active in the establishment of the United Nations. For example, Dr. George F. Zook, then President of the American Council on Education, with representatives from 42 other non-governmental organizations, was invited by the

State Department to be a consultant at the San Francisco Conference where his and their advice and recommendations were welcomed.

The part played by persons identified with such organizations in the creation of the United Nations Educational, Scientific, and Cultural Organization (UNESCO) is even more pronounced. The background for this participation is to be found in the dissatisfaction in United States educational, scientific, and cultural circles with the delayed, desultory, and inadequate operation of the International Committee on Intellectual Co-operation following World War I. Prior to the calling of the San Francisco Conference there had already been considerable discussion by educational and cultural leaders centering in war-time London. The United States in 1943 sent observers to the Council of Allied Ministers of Education (CAME) meeting there and, in 1944, upon invitation by this body, the United States State Department agreed to send an official delegation headed by Representative (later Senator) J. William Fulbright. The subsequent meeting, which opened in London on April 5, 1944, resulted in the drafting of a proposal for the creation of an educational and cultural organization within the framework of a projected United Nations, but occupying a semi-independent position. The proposals resulting from the Dumbarton Oaks Conference later in the year did not specify the creation of such an organization. Continuous pressure was brought to bear, therefore, on the American delegation to the San Francisco Conference by United States educational and cultural leaders for its inclusion in any charter adopted for world cooperation. The following resolution adopted by the Executive Committee of the American Council on Education, a copy of which was sent to each member of the delegation at San Francisco, is representative of this sentiment:

"In accordance with opinions expressed in ballots from representatives of 59 constituent organizations belonging to the American Council on Education, the Executive Committee of the Council, meeting in Washington, May 4, 1945, strongly urges the American Delegation at the San Francisco Conference to support specific provisions for an international office of education and cultural relations as an integral part of an international organization. Provision for this office will give due recognition both to the importance of cultural interchange in the maintenance of world peace and to the role of education in promoting this interchange. It will, moreover, avoid the great confusion which for twenty years prior to the outbreak of the present war has resulted from the division between two international organizations of responsibilities for the closely related fields of education and intellectual co-operation."[17]

Consequently, Article 71 of the resultant Charter of the United Nations adopted at that Conference stated:

"The Economic and Social Council [of the United Nations] may make suitable arrangements for consultation with non-governmental organizations which are concerned with matters within its competence. Such arrangements may be made with international organizations and, where appropriate, with national organizations after consultation with the Member of the United Nations concerned."

The Economic and Social Council (ECOSOC), which is on a par with the Security Council, the Trusteeship Council, and the International Court of Justice, at an early date began making arrangements that "went further in extending to non-governmental organizations opportunities for presentation of their views than have ever been granted to such groups by any national government."[18] Such arrangements were the granting of consultative status to some 300 organizations which have a basic interest in the area of work of ECOSOC. This status entitles these organizations to send representatives to attend the meetings of the Council and its subsidiary Commissions; submit written documents and oral statements to it; in certain instances, introduce items into the agenda of Council and Commission meetings for consideration; and, in short, express their views on all matters being considered.

Probably the best known organization resulting from the Article 57 directive of the U. N. charter to ECOSOC is the United Nations Educational, Scientific, and Cultural Organization (UNESCO).

The November 1-16, 1945 London Conference for the Establishment of UNESCO was the result of this directive and it was there that delegates from 43 countries hammered out and adopted the constitution for UNESCO.

The relationship that non-governmental organizations, such as the International Councils, should bear to UNESCO was one of the major issues debated at this Conference. The point at issue was the relative status that governmental and non-governmental representatives should have in UNESCO and particularly in the annual General Conference, UNESCO's large governing group. Some nations, particularly France, argued for a tri-partite annual General Conference composed of the representatives of governments, and of non-governmental national commissions, and international Unions and Councils. It was finally resolved that governments only should be represented in the General Conference with the right to vote but that non-governmental representatives might attend as observers. In partial deference to the defeated viewpoint, however, it was agreed that, although the Executive Board should be chosen from among governmental representatives at the General Conference, those so elected should thenceforth function as individuals responsible only to the General Conference and were to be free agents as regards their own country and free to express the viewpoint of the non-governmental organizations with which many were associated. This system, with its built-in conflict of interests, was obviously foredoomed to failure and, in 1954, following a 1952 resolution to have the General Conference meet biennially rather than annually, the Conference voted to amend the UNESCO constitution so that Board members were *de facto* as well as *de jure* representatives of their respective governments. The relationship of UNESCO to non-governmental organizations, therefore, is through the consultative status it has granted to some 147 intellectual international organizations already in existence and those which it has helped to create.

Since the natural sciences, through the International Council of Scientific Unions, already had a strong and viable organization which united most areas of natural science activity, a mutually satisfactory relationship was easily worked out between UNESCO and the ICSU whereby the latter became the coordinating center for the 14 international scientific Unions (scientific members) and 45 national scientific organizations (national members). The latter group is composed of the national academy or research council of each country and, failing these, the government itself. UNESCO has provided the ICSU and its members $2,955,201 during the period 1946-1960. These funds were used for conferences, travel, research, publication, etc. The ICSU sponsorship of the International Geophysical Year of 1957-58, aided by funds and personnel supplied in part by UNESCO, is probably the most striking example of the work in which both have been involved.[19]

In the humanities the situation was not as clear cut as in the natural sciences. Many scholars felt that the International Academic Union did not have an effective secretariat and, of more importance, was not sufficiently representative nor wide enough in scope for the post-war humanistic field. To take one example, the International Committee of Historical Sciences, established in 1926 at Geneva, had members in over 40 countries and an active program of publications and meetings. It had never affiliated with the IAU and, following World War II, was preparing to continue its separate existence. At the UNESCO General Conference in Paris in 1946, therefore, a resolution was adopted which called for a broad survey of the status of the philosophic and humanistic studies and the relationship that UNESCO should bear to them. Following subsequent correspondence and conferences, it was resolved by the special Committee appointed for the survey that UNESCO propose to the various international humanistic organizations that they federate into a council similar to the ICSU. The General Conference of UNESCO, which met in Mexico in November, 1947, concurred in this recommendation and instructed the Director-General to proceed by the establishment of a Preparatory Commission composed of representatives of the following organizations: the International Academic Union, the International Federation of Philosophic Societies, the Permanent International Committee of Linguists, the International Committee of Historical Sciences, and the International Committee on Folk Arts and Folklore.[20] A meeting of this Commission was held at UNESCO House, Paris, from September 8 to 11, 1948. The draft constitution, which was adopted at that meeting, provided for the creation of an International Council for Philosophy and Humanistic Studies (ICPHS).

The first meeting of the Assembly of the ICPHS was held in Brussels from January 18-21, 1949. At this meeting the draft constitution was adopted, which officially brought the Council into existence, and which specified where its headquarters would be located (Brussels).

Although the ICPHS is similar in structure and purpose to the ICSU, it differs from the latter in that it does not have a dual structure, i. e., it does not have national members but only Union members. For example, the United States adheres to the ICSU through the National Academy of Sciences-National Research Council and the Unions. The American Council of Learned Societies, which is a counterpart to the NAS-NRC in the humanities, however, does not adhere to the ICPHS but only to the International Academic Union. The comparative relationships are roughly as described below:

TABLE 5

RELATIONSHIP OF THE COUNCILS AND UNIONS TO THE INTERNATIONAL COUNCIL OF SCIENTIFIC UNIONS AND THE INTERNATIONAL COUNCIL FOR PHILOSOPHY AND HUMANISTIC STUDIES.

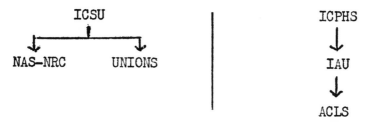

Because of its prominence, the International Academic Union was ensured one-third of the total number of votes and delegates on the

Council and two-fifths of the total number of votes and delegates in the governing Assembly. The other Unions would be equally represented in the remaining proportions. At the first meeting of the Assembly, therefore, the IAU was represented by ten delegates and the remaining Unions by three each. Thus, the IAU occupies a unique position among the member Unions of the various international Councils operating in collaboration with UNESCO.

The major portion of the expenses of the surveys and work of the Preparatory Commission and of various meetings incident to the creation of the ICPHS were defrayed by UNESCO. It has continued to provide funds for various activities of ICPHS and, up to 1960, had appropriated $2,163,445 for such purposes. These activities include primarily the coordination of a multitude of research projects, some of them extending back to the period before World War II. UNESCO has also provided financial and administrative aid to the Council in its conduct of international meetings and toward the publication of several humanistic studies.

At the initial meetings, which resulted in the creation of the ICPHS, discussion was had as to the relationship this international Council should bear to social science organizations. It was noted that international organizations of social scientists in several disciplines did not yet exist and that existing ones were apparently not yet ready to affiliate with an international organization like the ICPHS. It was agreed that the door to join should be left open for them, but the consensus was that no official action should be taken by the Council to initiate the matter.

UNESCO had recognized the organizational problem posed by social science organizations at its beginnings. Five months after its creation in 1946, it decided to devote special effort to the clarification of the international status of the social sciences, particularly regarding individual disciplines therein. Following such steps, the creation of international organizations in these disciplines was envisaged. UNESCO, therefore, provided material assistance to the efforts which culminated in the formation in 1949 of the International Sociological Association, the International Political Science Association, and the International Economics Association and, slightly later, the International Association of Legal Science, the International Union of Scientific Psychology, and the International Union of Anthropological and Ethnological Sciences. The creation of these Unions and the resulting exchange of views between them was the basis for the formation, in 1952, of the International Social Science Council with headquarters in Paris.[21]

This international Council corresponds in the social science field to the ICSU and ICPHS. The ISSC is more like the latter than the former in that it is composed primarily of representatives from autonomous, non-governmental, international organizations. It differs from each of the other Councils, however, in its organizational structure. The ISSC is composed of 18 distinguished social scientists serving for three year terms, but it is self perpetuating, two-thirds of its members being appointed by it on the recommendation of the member international social science Unions while the remainder are chosen directly by it. Due concern is given, however, to equitable world-wide and disciplinary coverage.

Assisted by advice from the International Social Science Council, UNESCO has aided the social sciences by providing funds for the establishment of Regional Cooperation Offices, social science documentation, and the execution of international or inter-cultural research projects. It has supported various research projects and provided funds for the publication of various works sponsored by the member Unions of the Council. In 1949, moreover, it helped to found the *International Social Science Bulletin,* a quarterly designed to be the link between UNESCO and ISSC and its Unions plus providing news and authoritative articles of interest to the international social science community. The sums appropriated for these purposes by UNESCO during the period 1952 through 1960 amount to $275,600.[22]

While officials and members of the Social Science Research Council play an important advisory role in the ISSC and its member Unions, the SSRC has no official connection with the ISSC corresponding to that of the NAS-NRC and ACLS to the ICSU and ICPHS. Similarly, the American Council on Education, although it has initiated and sponsored projects designed to promote better international understanding and relations in the area of higher education, has no official connection with the International Association of Universities, set up under UNESCO's auspices in 1950.

The three international Councils, the International Council of Scientific Unions (ICSU) in the natural sciences, the International Council for Philosophy and Humanistic Studies (ICPHS) in the humanities, and the International Social Science Council (ISSC) in the social sciences, with the differences noted, occupy roles in the international field analogous to the various national councils in the domestic field, particularly the three of the United States.[23] They serve as coordinating and cooperating agencies for their member organizations. They have paralleled our national councils by the creation, in 1959, of a Committee of Liaison of International Organizations. They and their adhering Unions are dependent upon an outside agency, the United Nations or its subsidiaries, for the major portion of their operating funds. Finally, they have not discouraged but rather encouraged their member organizations to deal directly with UNESCO, believing, as do the United States national councils, that such freedom and flexibility makes for greater viability on the part of all.[24]

CHAPTER VII

RETROSPECT AND PROSPECT

Conceived in Europe at the approximate time our modern age was being born, the learned societies or their counterparts have since spread throughout the world, including the United States of America. The Eighteenth century *alter egos* to the British Society and French Academy in the new world were the American Philosophical Society and the American Academy of Arts and Sciences. It is generally conceded that these two societies, one situated in New England and one in the Middle Atlantic region, have had a continuous culturally beneficial effect on the United States in that they have provided a common meeting ground for outstanding natural scientists, social scientists, humanists, and men of affairs. They have also provided a measuring device for intellectual achievement through their honorific membership, effected cross-fertilization between disciplines because of their interest in all fields of knowledge and, latterly awarded small but strategic grants for promising research projects.

The criticism of these societies is that they tend to be dominated by Eastern residents. Critics admit that the two societies have broadened their membership geographically so as to include significant numbers of members from other sections of the country but they maintain, nevertheless, that this dominance does exist and that in selecting new members, outstanding men from other sections of the country are often overlooked. These critics allege, furthermore, that the sheer physical location of these societies in the Northeastern section of the country aids the cause of science and learning there but is less stimulating to the rest of the country.

Dismissing the establishment of percentage sectional categories as defeating the purpose of such honorific societies, these critics maintain that the only feasible remedy for this situation is the establishment of several new societies in other sections of the country of a similar nature but still electing members on a national basis. These might include Southern, Mid-Western, and Western societies with names appropriate to the history and culture of these sections.

Proponents of these measures argue that European countries have long maintained similar sectional-national societies and this in the face of much smaller total and vastly smaller intellectual populations than the United States. They also argue that if these newer societies were maintained on the same honorific basis as the two older ones, they, too, would have a national as well as sectional lifting effect on the morale of intellectual workers.

Support for such societies, it is maintained, should come in large measure from the states within the section while a smaller proportion should be provided by the federal government. Individuals and industrial firms in the section might also contribute to their support.[1]

Turning to the learned societies which developed in late nineteenth and early twentieth century U. S. A., we find that they were contemporaneous with our burgeoning universities and expanding cities. The former were modelled on the German universities with their emphasis upon original and intensive investigation in narrowly limited areas of research. Thus, our changing universities and specialized learned societies complemented each other in their development. At the same time, the large cities made it possible for those pursuing the same interests to meet conveniently. In other words, the specialized learned societies were largely the product of the same technological and scientific advancement which made possible the development of our urbanized and industrialized civilization and it is significant that they were all organized in cities, primarily the larger ones on the Atlantic seaboard. It is interesting that consequential criticism alleging overgrowth and congestion of our specialized societies and of our cities developed at approximately the same time, in the 1930's. One foremost contemporary critic of our present day cities maintains, however, that "the greatest justification for metropolitan congestion" is that it fostered the origination of voluntary associations such as the learned societies.[2]

Be this as it may, the specialized learned societies are characteristically our own—i. e., they are professional and specialized but with membership open to all interested persons. These two attributes of the societies are conceded to be the touchstones from which all their blessings have flowed. Because of their specialized nature they have provided a common meeting ground for those, particularly college and university professors, interested in one discipline or subdiscipline, and the publications and special projects they have sponsored have served the same purpose. At the same time, because of their non-exclusive character, they have served to lessen the gap between these professionals and the lay men in their areas of interest. As a consequence, they had an incalculable part in transforming the United States from a still predominantly rural and semi-frontier nineteenth century nation, which looked askance at intellectuals in general and the "absent-minded professor" in particular, to one which accords ever increasing respect to those engaged in intellectual pursuits.

These societies have made a tremendous contribution to the advancement of learning in the United States by providing a focus for particular divisions and sub-divisions of the humanities, social sciences, and natural sciences through sponsorship of learned journals and other publication media; convening of annual meetings where members exchange views and become mutually stimulated by one another; and the awarding of prizes and grants for research and publications.

Also, these societies have been almost solely responsible for elevating various disciplines from an amateurish to a professional status. Numerous examples of this development can be noted in the individual histories of these societies.

In all of the contributions and achievements made by these societies, the role played by their executive officials and committee members has been a prominent, and even preeminent, one. There is nothing but praise for administrators and administration of all of the learned societies. Whether a large, medium, or small society, the compensation of officials has always been relatively modest. As a consequence, the majority of these officials have been dedicated men who have been elected to office after long periods of activity in the scholarly area of the society's concern. The rapport which thus naturally exists between administrators of the societies and its members undoubtedly explains the successful administration of these societies.

In the twentieth century, with the advent of World War I, there came into being the four national councils, primarily the result of increasing American involvement internationally but also due to the need for organizations prepared to span the gaps between various disciplines and, increasingly, acquainting the humanists, social scientists, and natural scientists with the rationale and problems besetting each group.[3] Similarly, the societal institutes which developed in the first half of the twentieth century were interdisciplinary in nature. More recently, in the third decade of the twentieth century, there emerged learned societies which are not honorific and which are interdisciplinary in approach and thus different from those of either the eighteenth or nineteenth centuries.

Prior to World War II, it appears that, with the possible exceptions of the councils, the role of these organizations in international affairs was negligible. Their problems and difficulties during this period were primarily ones of coordination with governmental and intergovernmental organizations. Since World War II a fairly complete and highly improved organizational structure for each of the major areas of learning has been effected and the problems of coordination have to a large degree been resolved within the framework of the United Nations. Reasonably adequate funds for operations within these structures have been forthcoming from private organizations including foundations, national governments, and international organizations such as UNESCO. It is still somewhat early, however, to say whether or not these problems have been permanently allayed. Certainly a continuing major problem is the intransigent and belligerent position taken by some officials and delegates of the Soviet Union and its satellites while in attendance at international meetings.[4]

In the last three decades there has been increasing dissatisfaction with the multiplicity of our national learned organizations and the alleged fragmentizing effect that they have had on science and the arts. At the same time, dissatisfaction is voiced with a number of 'giant' societies which include in their membership those interested in all the different aspects of a broad general field of knowledge. In other words, on the one hand there is dissatisfaction because a small number of devotees of one aspect of a general field of knowledge are drifting apart from the main stream of that knowledge by their creation of a specialized society. While on the other hand there is dissatisfaction with organizations composed of thousands of members who, it is alleged, break up into small coteries and are, similarly, cut off from the new streams of knowledge. It is alleged, too, that such large societies make it difficult for men with interests in a particular aspect of the larger field to develop the meaningful relationship which persists in the smaller specialized societies.[5]

These problems of size and fragmentization in turn raise internal problems for the specialized learned societies. With more members and more specialization all except the very smallest societies are confronted with such problems as the best method of holding annual and other meetings, a sound publication program and effective administration.

The traditional method of holding meetings is the scheduling, over a two to five day period, of a series of papers to be read during the day, and more formal dinner meetings, social hours, etc., in the evening, usually concluded by a business session. Increasing criticism of this method is being advanced, particularly by younger members of the societies. Some, and they are quite serious, say that the majority of the papers read are not worth hearing and even less worthy of publication.[6] It would be far better, it is urged, if the learned societies and universities would recognize that the primary value of the annual meetings to most members is the intellectual and social contact between members on an informal, conversational basis. If agreement on this point were reached then programs could be arranged by the assignment of daytime meeting rooms according to major fields of interest but with no presentation of papers. The evenings could be reserved for a few such presentations and the highest standards of excellence could be maintained for these.

Publications of the specialized learned societies have also come in for criticism. It is argued that many articles published in their learned journals are in the nature of mediaeval disputations as to how many fairies can dance on the head of a pin. Paradoxically, it is maintained that the natural science publications have become the worst offenders in this regard and that abstracts of their flood of minutiae have become an indispensable item for the large natural science societies. The remedy proposed is for the societies to publish only material that has a broad perspective and consists wholly of original findings supplemented by published lists of current research being conducted in the field.

Defenders of the specialized societies and the departmental structure of our universities argue that the specialization inherent in them has proved to be the only sound and feasible system whereby neophytes can gain an intensive and thorough grounding in their specialties. They maintain that it is only on the bedrock of this grounding that the superstructure of genius can be erected and that previous attempts to alter this method have always resulted in intellectual mediocrity.

The councils and societal institutes have not been faced in the same degree with these problems and questions confronting the learned societies. Since they have been effective in spanning disciplines and even broader areas of knowledge, specialization has *ipso facto* not been an issue with them. Although they have had, at various periods, to curtail some of their activities for lack of funds,[7] their primary problem has been their relationship to their constituent or member societies at one echelon and to the foundations, government, industry and universities at the other. Since they occupy an intermediary position between the two, they have adopted a variety of measures to ensure good relationships at both echelons. Most of them hold regular annual meetings wherein the societies are represented; they consult the various societies as to the makeup of working committees; some provide financial aid for societal projects; and all provide a locus for intersocietal projects and other matters of interest to a number of societies.

The relations of the councils and institutes with the foundations have probably been better and more productive than with government or industry. Since the larger foundations have provided varying amounts of financial aid to these organizations over long periods of time, it is natural that a very congenial relationship has developed between them. This is not to say, however, that they always see eye to eye. On the matter of overhead expenses on grants by the foundations, for instance, there has always existed a considerable difference of opinion. The foundations generally take the position that they should not assume overhead costs at all or only a very modest per cent of such costs. The government position on this point has been more in line with council and institute thinking, i.e., various government agencies providing aid to them either allocate full overhead costs on sponsored projects or percentages of up to about 25 per cent on them.[8]

Government support, however, is not as flexible, more bound by red tape, and is hampered by security restrictions. Also, there has always been opposition to the government becoming the principal or sole means of support of these organizations because it might eventually lead to too much governmental control of them. These problems of governmental support were brought home to the scientific community in late 1962 by the National Institute of Health's tightening of its control policies in regard to its grantees and, more forcibly, the allegation by the National Science Foundation of misuse of its grant funds by the American Institute of Biological Sciences and the complications brought to light in ensuing discussions between the NSF and the Institute. The primary disadvantage of industrial support appears to be that it is relatively small and has a tendency to be restricted to projects which are of direct interest to the industry providing support.

The learned societies, and to a lesser extent the societal institutes, have had few direct relationships with government and industry and foundations until recently and those which have developed are primarily the result of concern with our defense posture.[9] The societies and institutes have tended to follow the patterns set by the councils and consequently there has been relatively little disagreement about policy in their relationships.

Turning back to the alleged fragmentization of knowledge, which accompanied the rise of specialized learned societies, closely tied up with this problem is that of the relationship between the natural sciences, social sciences, and humanities.[10] That is, are these societies driving a divisive wedge between these general areas of knowledge and polarizing the natural scientists from the humanists and social scientists and, although to a lesser extent, creating a similar problem for the latter two?

A powerful contributing factor to the divisiveness and lack of understanding between the natural scientists on one hand and the humanists-social scientists on the other is the imbalance in the financial and material support rendered in the two areas. The natural science societies, councils and institutes receive relatively great sums of money from governmental, and industrial sources while their counterparts in the humanities and, to a lesser extent, in the social sciences, are forced to rely primarily on the foundations.

This imbalance in interest and support is in large measure the result of the *zeitgeist* of our age which has led us to elevate natural science to the status of a religion. But the preeminent thinkers of today have realized that man with his materialistic science has not achieved omniscience and that something may yet be said for the spiritual and humanistic. This relatively new skepticism of our intellectual leaders is gradually sifting down to the rank and file of the intelligentsia. It appears inevitable, therefore, that as this skepticism grows our humanistic and social sciences will gain in favor and support.

The large foundations have had the perspicacity to render continuous support to the humanities and social sciences and in the face of the above imbalance they have actually in the last decade curtailed their activities in the natural sciences as the government and industrial aid in this area was increased.

Industrial support, with a very few exceptions, such as support of certain societal institutes, has not been an important factor in outside support for the learned organizations and what there is of it has been restricted to the natural sciences and to organizations having kindred interests with the industrial sponsor. It should be said, however, that businessmen, particularly those identified with big business, are increasingly aware of the importance of humanistic and allied organizations to the industrial sector of our civilization. It may be, therefore, that industrial support will become of significance in the future.

Committed to the venture capital concept of operation, foundations traditionally withdraw after an experimental period of support. Despite the recent long-range support by the large foundations, particularly the Ford Foundation, of the humanistic and social science societies and councils, the problem is sure to be one that will become more acute at the termination of such support unless the public, its elected officials, and industrial and social leaders, make the same change in attitude towards financial support of humanistic and social science activities which they previously have made toward the natural sciences. It is an interesting historical commentary on this point that whereas in Galileo's Italy, when learned societies were first developing, governmental financial support was available for much that is encompassed today in the humanities but such support was practically non-existent for the rudimentary natural sciences.

In the past there was opposition to appeals for aid from the federal government and industry on the grounds that such aid inevitably meant control and that of the most pernicious sort, thought control. Those opposed maintained that natural scientists could accept such aid because theirs was an exact science which did not admit of influence, i. e., $2 + 2$ is clearly and demonstrably $=$ to 4, no matter who finances the process by which the answer is reached.

Today there is practically a consensus among academicians that the natural sciences are becoming more and more inexact, despite which the natural science organizations have thus far maintained their independence, in the face of increasing governmental and industrial support. Proponents of increased governmental or industrial aid for the humanities and social sciences believe that, as a minimum, the federal government and/or industry should supply the societies and councils active in these areas with funds for fellowships and annual subsidies for publication of journals, administration, and travel and expense funds to attend national and international meetings.[11] At the same time, they argue that the humanistic-social science councils should be provided with annual capital funds which they could draw upon at their discretion as promising opportunities for research or other projects presented themselves.

They cite, in support of their position, the fact that such aid has been provided, albeit piecemeal, by several of the larger foundations with no apparent loss of independence by either party.[12] Furthermore, and they appear to be on unshakeable ground, they point to the fact that since 1890 the U. S. government through the Smithsonian Institution has defrayed the costs of the printing of the annual reports and other documents of the American Historical Association. It is conservatively estimated that this support has provided that learned society with what amounts to an annual subsidy of from \$7,500 to \$10,000 a year. More recently, with the passage in 1957 of the National Defense Education Act, several of the humanistic learned societies, such as the Modern Language Association of America, have received governmental financial support for the conduct of such programs as the improvement of scholastic instruction in modern foreign languages. Since few academicians would argue that such support has resulted in a diminution in the freedom and independence of the American Historical Association or the Modern Language Association of America, why, it is contended, should support at least of publication, travel, and administration, not be provided for the remaining learned societies? If it is in the national interest to promote our general cultural development by aiding a few national learned societies, why not aid all, and also the councils and societal institutes? However, if there is to be increased financial support from government and industry for these organizations then there must be effective safeguards erected to maintain their free and independent operational status.

An indication of developing governmental concern for the general scientific and cultural health of the nation was the creation of the National Science Foundation. This governmental entity was consciously created and patterned after the private foundations to support men and projects operating on the frontier of knowledge. It has a great degree of freedom in its methods of operation, relies on expert advice to aid it in making grants, and has supported many innovative projects in the best 'venture capital' tradition. It is significant that the NSF, which initially restricted its grants almost entirely to individuals and organizations active in the natural sciences, is showing an increasing interest in the social sciences, including, for instance, such subjects as the history and philosophy of science.

The preferential government support of our natural science organizations has been not only a result of our contemporary reverence for science but also, of course, the pressure of the Cold War with Russia. It has become apparent with the passage of time that this conflict is being increasingly waged on the ideological front as well as on the scientific-technical front. A particularly forceful expression of this viewpoint is to be found in a recent address by Professor Whitney J. Oates: "Two distinguished colleagues of mine, one an economist and the other a physicist, recently addressed a letter to a United States Senator, who is an influential member of two highly important Senate Committees. I beg your permission to quote two or three sentences from this letter: 'Let us recall that it has often been said that the World War of 1914 was won by the chemists, that of 1939 by the physicists. Even though one of us is a physicist, we are equally convinced that the conflict which we are facing will be won by the philosophers and other representatives of the Humanities. The conflict, in fact, may not be an armed one, but may be fought for the loyalties of the population in all countries of the world. It will be won by the country which can inspire enthusiasm in the populations of other nations and induce its own population to make sacrifices and endure hardships in order to maintain its way of life. For this type of warfare we are inadequately prepared, even though potential strength in this type of warfare is infinitely greater than that of authoritarian countries.' "[13]

In the light of the foregoing controversy over specialization, imbalance in support, and national needs, it appears that the specialized learned societies will, in the near future, undergo considerable change. The development and growth of the councils and societal institutes and even other learned societies to span specific disciplines, which has become the avowed mission of our two oldest learned societies, and criticisms of over-specialization in our institutions of higher learning[14] show a shift away from specialization.

There are four major trends in the present day development of the learned societies, councils and institutes:

First, their ever-increasing involvement or concern with international affairs. This is evidenced by the sheer statistical increase in the official participation by such organizations in international meetings, symposia, projects, etc.

Second, a growing awareness that at the same time that they and the United States become more and more involved in international affairs, they, as organizations, must serve the national needs. Disciplines, for example, such as language and linguistic studies, which would have been deemed highly esoteric even thirty years ago are now recognized by all as highly important to our national well-being.

Third, agreement that the humanistic and social science societies and councils must receive much greater financial support from the federal government and industry. It is only from these sources that funds sufficient for future needs can be obtained.

The fourth trend is the increase in the number and scope of activities of learned organizations specifically created to bridge what are, increasingly, artificial barriers between disciplines which in the nineteenth century were considered separate and sufficient unto themselves.

These trends are, of course, closely interrelated. If one views them in that light and then if one considers the simultaneous development of the specialized learned societies of the late nineteenth and early twentieth centuries with the characteristic politico-socio phenomenon of our age, the rise of the large city, it appears that a similar phenomenon is taking place, one step removed, at the present time. That is, the meshing of specialized societies with each other, with councils and institutes, the creation of societies spanning various disciplines, and the modification or elimination of departmental barriers in many universities may portend the emergence of new and effective politico-socio world organizations which would tend to break down national and other barriers on that plane. The ever-growing international involvement of all of the organizations and agencies previously discussed, learned societies, councils, institutes, foundations, government, industry, and universities, is a strong indication that this is the case and that we are on the threshold of such a movement.

A very interesting development in the last connection, and one that provides a fitting conclusion to this study has been the creation of a score of unique twentieth century institutes which have few points of similarity to the existing national or international learned societies, councils, societal institutes, or universities. Because of their pioneering and innovative character, their proponents maintain that they are the twentieth century counterparts of the sixteenth and seventeenth century learned societies. They advocate the creation of more such private and public institutes, strategically located, in order to bring together, from a variety of disciplines, the best brains of the nation and the world to work on broad problems cutting across traditional disciplinary barriers.

They cite the activities of the following private (non-governmental controlled and supported) and public (governmental controlled and supported) institutes, in various fields, as examples of what they endorse: Private—The Brookings Institution (Economics, Political Science, and Government); Rockefeller Institute[15] (Medicine and Public Health); Wistar Institute of Anatomy and Biology (Biology); Graduate Research Center of the Southwest (Research in all of the natural sciences); and the Center for the Study of Democratic Institutions[16] (Political Science and Philosophy); Public—Armed Forces Institute of Pathology (Pathology); and National Institutes of Health (Research in all aspects of medicine and health in over a score of sub-institutes). In addition to these public and private institutes there are a number that appear to fall somewhere in between these categories. Some are managed by industrial concerns, for example, Aircraft Nuclear Test Facility, Oak Ridge National Laboratory, and Electronic Defense Laboratories. Others are managed by an educational institution or a group of educational institutions, for example, Lincoln Laboratory, Brookhaven National Laboratory and National Astronomical Observatory. Still others are managed by other nonprofit organizations, not educational institutions, for example, RAND Corporation and Aerospace Corporation. All in this in-between category are largely dependent upon government research contracts for their operation.[17]

The private Institute for Advanced Study at Princeton, New Jersey, presently headed by Dr. Robert Oppenheimer, is probably the best known of these novel organizations. Gathered together there from all over the world, from a multitude of disciplines, and for varying periods of time, is a small congerie of some of the best brains of the twentieth century for the express purpose of "the encouragement, support and patronage of learning—of science, in the old, broad, undifferentiated sense of the word."[18]

What may, however, herald the ultimate in this development was the recent announcement by Alex Faber, a retired Danish industrialist living in Mexico City, of the creation of a series of "sane asylums, where Nobel prize winners and other intellectuals of equal standing can get away from the throng—and think, just think."[19]

REFERENCES

INTRODUCTION

[1] *Historical Scholarship in America.* A Report of the Committee of the American Historical Association on the Planning of Research, Ray Long and Richard R. Smith, Inc., New York, 1932.

[2] Binkley, Robert C., "World Intellectual Organization," *Educational Record,* Vol. XX, No. 2, April, 1939, p. 257.

[3] White, Lyman C., *International Non-Governmental Organizations.* Rutgers University Press, New Brunswick, New Jersey, 1951, p. vii.

[4] The distinction between a learned society and a professional society was, in a few cases, admittedly a fine one. In such instances, decisions as to exclusion or inclusion in this study were arrived at through consultation and correspondence with officials and members of the societies, councils, and institutes and by an examination of their stated purpose, membership, and program of activities.

[5] For example, the National Institute of Arts and Letters and its affiliate the American Academy of Arts and Letters. The Institute was organized in 1898 by the now defunct American Social Science Association (see p. 234, Reference 19 of Chapter III). The Academy was founded in 1904 by the Institute. Membership is limited to 250 persons in the Institute and 50 in the Academy. Only Members of the Institute are eligible for election to the Academy. In addition to elevating eminent scholars to membership, both organizations further their work of stimulating the arts and letters by conferring a variety of awards and honors for distinguished work in these areas.

[6] In the case of several societies, such as the Econometric Society and the Institute of Mathematical Statistics, the question arose as to whether they should be included with the humanistic-social science societies or with the natural science societies since their spheres of interest included disciplines in both areas. It was decided, in such cases, that the Council to which they belonged would be the determining factor. Thus, both of the aforementioned societies, members of the National Academy of Sciences—National Research Council, are included with the 29 natural science societies.

[7] See Appendix A - List of Learned Societies Which are Members of Councils and Societal Institutes, pp. 262-264.

The relationship between the societal members and the various Councils and Institutes varies. Thus, in a very close and formal relationship the societies are designated 'member' societies. Where the relationship is less formal and there is a greater degree of independence or a shading off in the closeness of the relationship on both sides, the societies are designated 'affiliate,' 'affiliated,' 'associate,' 'associated,' or 'adhering,' member societies.

[8] See Appendix B - Date of Founding of 60 Learned Societies, 4 Councils, and 5 Societal Institutes, pp. 265-266.

[9] While it is documented in other pertinent sections, it should be pointed out here that all of the statistics as to monetary assets, financial receipts and expenditures, etc., used in the study, unless otherwise noted, are based on a terminal date of 1960.

CHAPTER I

[1] Hull, L. W. H., *History and Philosophy of Science*. Longmans, Green and Co., London, 1959, p. 146. See also, Wolf, Abraham, *A History of Science, Technology and Philosophy in the 16th and 17th Centuries*. Macmillan and Co., New York, 1935, p. 37.

[2] Note, too, that a mass media magazine can publish an article in the same vein. See Barfield, Arthur O., "The Rediscovery of Meaning," *Saturday Evening Post*, Vol. 234, No. 1, January 7, 1961, pp. 36-37, 61, 64-65.

[3] See Ornstein, Martha, *The Role of Scientific Societies in the Seventeenth Century*. University of Chicago Press, Chicago, Illinois, 1938, especially pp. 53; 110-111; 163; 196-197; and 262. See also, Wolf, Abraham, *A History of Science, Technology and Philosophy in the 16th and 17th Centuries,* especially pp. 54-55; *Some Milestones in the History of Science to 1800.* Linda Hall Library, Kansas City, Missouri, 1956, see particularly, p. 9 and pp. 26-27; and, for an earlier interpretation, Lecky, W. E. H., *History of the Rise and Influence of the Spirit of Rationalism in Europe.* Longman, Green, Longman, Roberts, and Green, 2 Volumes, London, 1865, see particularly Vol. I, pp. 206-385.

[4] For the earliest history of the Royal Society, see Sprat, T., *The History of the Royal Society of London.* 2nd edit., London, 1702. For two more recent histories, see Lyons, Henry, *The Royal Society, 1660-1940.* Cambridge University Press, Cambridge, England, 1944, and Stimson, Dorothy, *Scientists and Amateurs: A History of the Royal Society.* Henry Schuman, New York, 1948. See also, among a series of publications accompanying the Tercentenary Celebration of the Royal Society. Andrade, E. N. da C., *A Brief History of the Royal Society.* The Royal Society, London, 1960; and Moe, Henry Allen, "Tercentenary of the Royal Society," *Science,* Vol. 132, No. 3442, December 16, 1960, pp. 1816-1822.

[5] Up until 1840 the founding date of 1743 was recognized and accepted by members of the Society. In 1840 Peter Stephen Du Ponceau, then president of the Society, contended that it originated in 1727. The basis for his reasoning was that the Junto of the 1750's was a continuation of that of the 1720's. Mr. J. Francis Fisher, in a separate communication to the Society, reasoned otherwise and fixed the founding date at 1743. The question raised was referred to a committee, which reported in 1841 in favor of Fisher's contention that the founding date was 1743. Subsequently, at the Society's 1906 celebration of the bicentenary of Benjamin Franklin's birth, printed matter used at that time listed the 1743 founding date. In 1910, however, another committee to consider the matter was named and reported that it considered the founding date of the Society to be 1727. The unanimous concluding statement of that committee is as follows: "The question whether Franklin was in a proper sense the founder of our Society is not in doubt. He founded the American Philosophical Society in 1743. He founded the Junto of 1727. The development of a junior Junto—if such a thing occurred—was unquestionably due to the impetus of the older Junto; and the change of the local Junto into a Society which included corresponding members from other colonies was a mere broadening of its purpose . . . . it is clear that when Franklin founded his original Junto, he became the founder of the American Society. He is admitted by all to be the founder of the Philosophical Society. Our Society therefore owes its origin to him on both sides."

The report of this committee was accepted by the Society in 1914 and the date of origin on its seal and stationery was ordered changed from 1743 to 1727. This decision never met with wholehearted approval, however, and in 1948 the Society voted to reverse itself, to recognize 1743 as its official founding date, and to change the seal and stationery accordingly. There the matter rests today.

See Dercum, Francis X., "The Origin and Activities of the American Philosophical Society and an Address on the Dynamic Factor in Evolution," *Proceedings, American Philosophical Society,* Vol. 66, 1927, pp. 19-46.

6 See Shryock, Richard H., "The Planning and Formal Opening of Library Hall," and "The Library of the American Philosophical Society," in *Proceedings, American Philosophical Society,* Vol. 104, No. 4, August 15, 1960, pp. 349-356 and pp. 398-403.

7 Conklin, Edwin G., "A Brief History of the American Philosophical Society," *Year Book, American Philosophical Society,* January 1, 1947-December 31, 1947, pp. 7-26. See also Goode, G. Brown, "The Origin of the National Scientific and Educational Institutions of the United States," *Annual Report, American Historical Association, 1889,* Senate Miscellaneous Documents, 51st Congress, 1st Session, Vol. 4, 1889-1890, Government Printing Office, Washington, D. C., 1890, pp. 58, 72, 83, 108-109; Painter, Sidney, "The American Philosophical Society," *The World of the Mind,* Prepared by Broadcast Music Incorporated in association with the American Council of Learned Societies and the American Association for the Advancement of Science, pp. 1-5, hereafter referred to as *World of the Mind;* Franklin, Benjamin, *The Writings of Benjamin Franklin.* A. H. Smyth, edit., Macmillan Company, Vol. 1, New York, 1907, pp. 298-299; and Franklin, Benjamin, *Autobiography.* Edited by Carl Van Doren. New York, Viking Press, 1945.

8 It should be noted that, in 1946, the American Academy of Arts and Sciences sold the bulk of this library, totalling some 62,000 items to the Linda Hall Library, Kansas City, Missouri.

The Linda Hall Library was established in 1945 under the terms of the will of Herbert F. Hall, a Kansas City businessman. With the American Academy's holdings as the base of its collection, this Library has become one of the outstanding scientific and technological reference libraries of the nation.

9 *Blue Book.* Information pamphlet of the American Academy of Arts and Sciences, Boston, Massachusetts, May, 1959, p. 4.

10 *Survey of Learned Societies,* the American Academy of Arts and Sciences, conducted in the 1930's and 1940's for the American Council of Learned Societies by Waldo G. Leland and Mortimer Graves and filed in its offices. Unpublished. Hereafter referred to as *Survey.* See also Shapley, Harlow, "The American Academy of Arts and Sciences," *World of the Mind,* pp. 1-6; and Adams, John, *Works.* C. F. Adams, edit., Boston, Massachusetts, 1851-1856, particularly Vol. IV, p. 302.

11 A group of Virginians led by a Frenchman, the Chevalier Quesnay de Beaurepaire, in 1788 established in Richmond, Virginia an "Academy of Arts and Sciences in the United States of America." This academy had the endorsement of the King of France and the French Academy, after which it was closely modelled. The French Revolution removed its main financial and moral support, however, and, following an unsuccessful attempt by the Virginians alone to maintain the Academy, it failed. See Goode, G. Brown, "The Origin of the National Scientific and Educational Institutions of the United States," *Annual Report, American Historical Association, 1889,* Senate Miscellaneous Documents, 51st

Congress, 1st Session, Vol. 4, 1889-1890, Government Printing Office, Washington, D. C., pp. 59-61.

CHAPTER II

[1] Shipton, Clifford K., "The American Antiquarian Society," *The World of the Mind*, New York, 1959, p. 4.

[2] *Survey*. The American Antiquarian Society; Paine, Nathaniel, *An Account of the American Antiquarian Society*. Charles Hamilton, Worcester, Massachusetts, 1876, pp. 5-7; Brigham, Clarence S., *American Antiquarian Society, Handbook of Information*. Published by the Society, Worcester, Massachusetts, 1909, pp. 7-18; and Edwards, Agnes, "The Library of the American Antiquarian Society," *The Massachusetts Magazine*, Vol. IX, No. 1, January, 1916, pp. 5-14.

See also the various Reports of the Director of the American Antiquarian Society and published in the *Proceedings*. See, particularly, *Proceedings*, April, 1960, pp. 3-11 and October, 1960, pp. 353-370.

[3] *Survey*, American Statistical Association. See also, Kopf, Edwin W., "American Statistical Association," *Proceedings of the Casualty Actuarial Society*, Vol. XI, Part 1, November 20, 1924, pp. 129-131; "American Statistical Association," *AAAS Bulletin*, Vol. 3, No. 8, August, 1944, pp. 63-64; and the following articles by Paul J. Fitzpatrick appearing in *The American Statistician*: "The Early Teaching of Statistics in American Colleges and Universities," Vol. 9, No. 5, December, 1955; "Statistical Works in Early American Statistics Courses," Vol. 10, No. 5, December, 1956; and "Statistical Societies in the United States in the Nineteenth Century," Vol. 11, No. 5, December, 1957.

[4] *Journal of the American Oriental Society*, Vol. 1, 1849, pp. vi-vii.

[5] *Journal of the American Oriental Society*, Vol. 37, 1917, pp. 7-18 and Vol. 45, 1925, p. 392.

[6] *Survey*, American Oriental Society.

[7] *Handbook of Information*. Published by the American Numismatic Society, New York, 1952.

[8] Moore, Frank Gardner, "History of the American Philological Association," *Transactions and Proceedings, American Philological Association*, Vol. L, 1919, pp. 5-32. In the same volume, see also Shorey, Paul, "Fifty Years of Classical Study in America," pp. 33-61; Bloomfield, Maurice, "Fifty Years of Comparative Philology in America," pp. 62-83; and Elmore, Jefferson, "The Philological Association of the Pacific Coast," pp. 84-90. See also *Survey*, American Philological Association.

[9] *Survey*, Archaeological Institute of America. See also, Johnson, Jotham, "The Archaeological Institute of America," *The World of the Mind*, pp. 1-5.

[10] Kraft, Charles F., "The Society of Biblical Literature and Exegesis, A Short Descriptive Article," Mimeographed, 2 pages, 1956. See also, "Transactions and Memorabilia of the Fiftieth Anniversary Meeting of the Society," *Journal of Biblical Literature*, Vol. L, 1931, pp. i-lxxx; and Goodenough, Erwin R., "The Society of Biblical Literature and Exegesis," *The World of the Mind*, pp. 1-5.

[11] Long, Percy W., "The Association in Review," *Publications of the Modern Language Association of America*, hereafter cited as *PMLA*, 1948 Proceedings, Vol. LXIV, Supplement, Part 2, March, 1949, p. 1.

12 *PMLA,* Vol. LXXI, No. 2, April, 1956, p. 31; *PMLA,* Vol. LXVIII, No. 2, April, 1953, pp. 65-78; Stone, George W., Jr., "The Beginning, Development, and Impact of the MLA as a Learned Society," *PMLA,* Vol. LXXIII, No. 5, Part 2, December, 1958, pp. 23-44. See other articles and papers of historical interest in this Seventy-Fifth Anniversary Issue of *PMLA,* edited by George W. Stone, Jr.

13 Long, Percy W., "The Association in Review," *PMLA,* 1948 Proceedings, Vol. LXIV, Supplement, Part 2, March, 1949, p. 8.

14Parker, William R., "The MLA, 1883-1953," *PMLA,* Vol. LXVIII, No. 4, Part 2, September, 1953. pp. 3-29. See also Brown, Carleton, "A Survey of the First Half-Century," *PMLA,* Vol. XLVIII, Supplement, 1933, pp. 1409-1422; and Pound, Louise, "Then and Now," *PMLA,* Vol. LXXI, No. 1, March, 1956, pp. 3-13.

15 For a brief history of the Association see p. 234, Reference 19 of Chapter III.

16 For an early history of the *Review,* see Jameson, J. Franklin, "The American Historical Review, 1895-1920," *The American Historical Review,* Vol. XXVI, October, 1920, pp. 1-17.

17 Jameson, J. Franklin, "The American Historical Association, 1884-1909," *The American Historical Review,* Vol. XV, No. 1, October, 1909, pp. 1-20. See also "Report of the Organization and Proceedings," *Papers, American Historical Association,* Vol. I, No. 1, G. P. Putnam's Sons, New York, 1885, pp. 5-44; *Annual Report, American Historical Association,* 1920, pp. 73-74; and *Survey,* The American Historical Association.

18 "Charter and By-laws of the American Economic Association," *American Economic Review,* Vol. XXXII, No. 3, Supplement, September, 1942.

19Ely, Richard T., "The Founding and Early History of the American Economic Association," *American Economic Review,* Vol. XXVI, No. 1, Supplement, March, 1936, pp. 141-150. See also *Information Pamphlet.* Published by the American Economic Association, Evanston, Illinois, 1954; and Jameson, J. Franklin, "The American Historical Association, 1884-1909," *The American Historical Review,* Vol. XV, No. 1, October, 1909, p. 6.

20 Leach, MacEdward, "American Folklore Society," *Standard Dictionary of Folklore, Mythology, and Legend.* Edited by Maria Leach. Volume I, Funk and Wagnalls Company, New York, 1949, pp. 48-49. See also, *Survey,* American Folklore Society and Gayton, Anna H., "The American Folklore Society," *The World of the Mind,* pp. 1-6.

21 See Fernberger, Samuel W., "American Psychological Association, 1892-1942," *Psychological Review,* Vol. 50, No. 1, January, 1943, pp. 33-60. See, in this same Semi-Centenary issue, Vol. 50, No. 1, pp. 7-79, of the American Psychological Association, ten other articles dealing with various aspects of the Association's development.

22 See, in addition to Fernberger, Samuel W. *loc. cit.,* Fernberger, Samuel W., "The American Psychological Association; A Historical Summary, 1892-1930," *Psychological Bulletin,* Vol. XXIX, 1932, pp. 1-89; Wolfle, Dael, "The Reorganized American Psychological Association," *The American Psychologist,* Vol. I, No. 1, January, 1946, pp. 3-6; and Wolfle, Dael, "The American Psychological Association," *AAAS Bulletin,* Vol. 5, No. 3, March, 1946, pp. 23-24.

23 Gardiner, H. N., "The First Twenty-Five Years of the American Philosophical Association," *Philosophical Review,* Vol. XXXV, March, 1926, pp. 145-158. See also, *Survey,* The American Philosophical Association.

24 Stocking, George W. Jr., "Franz Boas and the Founding of the American

Anthropological Association," *American Anthropologist,* Vol. 62, No. 1, February, 1960, pp. 1-17. See also, *Survey,* Americal Anthropological Association; Boas, Franz, "The American Ethnological Society," *Science,* New Series, Vol. XCVII, January 1, 1943, pp. 7-8; Eggan, Fred, "The American Anthropological Association," *AAAS Bulletin,* Vol. 2, No. 5, May, 1943, p. 38; and Stout, D. B., "American Anthropological Association," *Dictionary of Folklore, Mythology, and Legend.* Edited by Maria Leach. Vol. 1, Funk and Wagnalls Company, New York, 1949, p. 43.

[25] *Fellow Newsletter.* Vol. 2, No. 1, January, 1961, pp. 2-3.

[26] This class has never been used and it will probably be eliminated shortly.

[27] For further information on the publications of the American Anthropological Association, see de Laguna, Frederica, edit., *Selected Papers From the American Anthropologist, 1888-1920.* Evanston, Illinois, 1960.

[28] Reeves, Jesse S., "Perspectives in Political Science, 1903-1928," *The American Political Science Review,* Vol. XXIII, No. 1, February, 1929, pp. 1-2.

[29]"Constitution of the American Political Science Association," *The American Political Science Review,* Vol. XXXVII, No. 1, February, 1943, p. 131.

[30] *Survey,* The American Political Science Association.

[31] Constitution of the Bibliographical Society of America, Supplement to the *Papers* of the Society, Vol. 34, Second Quarter, 1940, p. 92.

[32] Van Hoesen, Henry B., "The Bibliographical Society of America—Its Leaders and Activities, 1904-1939," *The Papers of the Bibliographical Society of America,* Vol. 35, No. 4, December, 1941, pp. 177-202. See also, Jackson, William A., "The Bibliographical Society of America," *The World of the Mind,* pp. 1-5.

[33] The American Geographical Society of New York was founded in 1852 as the American Geographical and Statistical Society, but the name was changed to the present one in 1871 when its charter was amended so as to drop its statistical interest and to provide for a permanent abode in New York City. Since 1910 the Society has owned and maintained a building at Broadway and 156th Street, adjacent to the site of the American Numismatic Society's Building, which houses offices and exhibition rooms and a library containing approxmately 150,000 volumes and 275,000 maps and atlases. In addition to providing research facilities, the Society conducts a School of Surveying, a Department of Hispanic-American Research, and publishes an extensive series of periodicals, books and maps. It has been called upon by state and national governments on numerous occasions for assistance in providing the solution to boundary disputes. Membership in the Society is open to all interested parties, but it has remained small, numbering about 4,000 today and restricted primarily to the New York-Middle Atlantic area. *See Booklet of Information.* Published by the American Geographical Society of New York, undated, pp. 1-16.

The National Geographic Society was formed in 1888 because of a belief that non-professionals would be interested in geographic activity. In the same year it began publication of the *National Geographic Magazine,* a monthly that contained non-technical articles about out-of-the way places. The Society succeeded beyond the wildest dreams of its founders. Membership, which entitled one to receive the *Magazine,* soared from 200 in 1888 to about 1,000,000 today.

[34] See the *Handbook-Directory.* Published by the Association of American Geographers, Washington, D. C., 1961, particularly Section A, "Highlights of the History of the AAG: 1904-1960," pp. 1-4 and Section B, "Highlights of the History

of the ASPG: 1943-1948," pp. 4-6. These two sections include the significant published sources on the history of the organization.

For the early history of the organization see, particularly, Brigham, Albert P., "The Association of American Geographers, 1903-1923," *Annals of the Association of American Geographers,* Vol. XIV, No. 3, September, 1924, pp. 109-116 and Colby, Charles C., "Changing Currents of Geographic Thought in America," *Annals of the Association of American Geographers,* Vol. XXVI, No. 1, March, 1936, pp. 5-7; 16-19.

[35] *Survey,* American Sociological Society. See also, "Report and Recommendation of the Special Committee on the Scope of Research of the American Sociological Society," *Publication and Proceedings of the American Sociological Society,* Vol. XXVI, No. 2, June, 1932, pp. 1-39.

[36] Burke, W. L. M., "Early Years of the College Art Association," *College Art Journal,* Vol. 1, No. 4, May, 1942, p. 101.

[37] Sloane, Joseph C., "The College Art Association of America," *The World of the Mind,* pp. 1-5. See also Smith, Holmes, "Problems of the College Art Association," *Bulletin, College Art Association of America,* No. 1, 1913, pp. 6-10; and Hiss, Priscilla and Roberta Fansler, *Research in Fine Arts in the Colleges and Universities of the United States,* Carnegie Corporation of New York, New York, 1934.

[38] "Statutes of the History of Science Society," *Isis,* Vol. 35, 1944, pp. 51-52. See also, Stimson, Dorothy, "History of Science Society," *The World of the Mind,* pp. 1-5.

[39] Bloomfield, Leonard, "Why a Linguistic Society," *Language,* Vol. 1, March, 1925, p. 1. This same volume contains additional information about the founding, early organization, and purpose of the Society.

[40] Marckwardt, Albert H., "The Linguistic Society of America," *The World of the Mind,* pp. 1-5.

[41] Coffman, George R., "The Mediaeval Academy of America: Historical Background and Prospect," *Speculum,* Vol. 1, January, 1926, pp. 5-9.

[42] Whiting, Bartlett J., "The Medieval Academy of America," *The World of the Mind,* pp. 1-5.

[43] For the history of the Council, see Chapter III, pp. 128-131.

[44] Letter dated October 1, 1950 from William J. Mitchell, Secretary, American Musicological Society to Charles E. Odegaard, Executive Director, American Council of Learned Societies, Files of American Council of Learned Societies, New York, New York. See also "Constitution and By-Laws," *Journal of the American Musicological Society,* Vol. II, No. 2, Summer, 1949, p. 138.

[45] The foregoing account of the Society of Architectural Historians, is based, in the main, on an unpublished "Brief Historical Summary" of the Society furnished the author in April, 1960, by Dr. Turpin C. Bannister, Dean of the School of Architecture and Fine Arts, University of Florida.

[46] Pritchard, Earl H., "The Association for Asian Studies, Inc., A Brief History," *Journal of Asian Studies,* Vol. XVI, August, 1957, pp. 679-680; and Crane, Robert I., "The First Ten Years of the Association for Asian Studies, 1948-1958," *Journal of Asian Studies,* Vol. XVII, August, 1958, pp. 657-675. See also, Fairbank, Wilma, "The Association for Asian Studies," *The World of the Mind,* pp. 1-5.

[47] Letter dater November 16, 1949 from George Boas, President, American Society for Aesthetics, to Charles E. Odegaard, Executive Director, American

Council of Learned Societies, Files of the American Council of Learned Societies, New York, New York. See also, "American Society for Aesthetics: Historical Note," *Journal of Aesthetics and Art Criticism*, Vol. IV, No. 1, pp. 60-61.

[48] Information furnished the author by Professor Francis H. Parker, Haverford College, Haverford, Pennsylvania, Secretary-Treasurer of the Society.

[49] *Bulletin of Information*. Published by the American Studies Association, Undated.

[50] "Constitution and By-Laws, Renaissance Society of America," *Renaissance News*, Vol. VIII, No. 1, Part II, Spring, 1955, p. 58.

[51] Bradner, Leicester, "Renaissance Scholarship in America," *Renaissance News*, Vol. VII, No. 1, Spring, 1954, pp. 1-5. See also, "Renaissance Society of America, an account of the Executive Board," *Renaissance News*, Vol. VIII, No. 1, Spring, 1954, pp. 7-11.

[52] For the history of the American Association for the Advancement of Science, see Chapter III, pp. 134-137.

[53] Browne, Charles A., edit., "A Half-Century of Chemistry in America, 1876-1926," *Journal of the American Chemical Society*, Special Issue, Vol. 48, No. 8-A, Easton, Pennsylvania, 1926. This issue of the *Journal* contains thirteen articles. See, particularly, the article by Parsons, Charles L., "The Activities of the American Chemical Society," p. 48.

[54] For a recent and complete history of the American Chemical Society, by its former historian, see Browne, Charles A., and Mary Elvira Weeks, *A History of the American Chemical Society, Seventy-Five Eventful Years*, American Chemical Society, Washington, D. C., 1952. See also Parsons, Charles L., "The American Chemical Society," *AAAS Bulletin*, Vol. 2, No. 4, April, 1943, pp. 29-31.

[55] For the history of the Federation of American Societies for Experimental Biology, see Chapter III, pp. 137-138.

[56] Howell, William H., and Charles W. Greene, *History of the American Physiological Society, Semicentennial, 1887-1937*. Baltimore, Maryland, 1938.
See also, Meek, W. J., "The American Physiological Society," *AAAS Bulletin*, Vol. 4, No. 6, June, 1945, pp. 47-48; Dubois, Eugene F., "Prefatory Chapter, Fifty Years of Physiology in America," *Annual Review of Physiology*, Vol. XII, 1950, pp. 1-7; and Gerard, R. W., "By-ways of Investigators: Thoughts on Becoming an Elder Statesman," *American Journal of Physiology*, Vol. 171, No. 3, December, 1952, pp. 695-703.

[57] For the earlier history of the Wistar Institute see Wistar, Isaac Jones, *Autobiography of Isaac Jones Wistar, 1827-1905; Half a Century in War and Peace*. The Wistar Institute of Anatomy and Biology, Philadelphia, Pennsylvania, 1937. For a more recent history of the Institute see Wistar Institute of Anatomy and Biology, *Biennial Report, 1958-59*, Press of the Wistar Institute, Philadelphia, Pennsylvania, 1959.

[58] Michels, Nicholas A., "The American Association of Anatomists, A Sketch of its Origin, Aims, and Meetings," *Anatomical Record*, Vol. 122, No. 4, August, 1955, pp. 679-714.

[59] The *Journal* was founded in 1878 at Johns Hopkins University and has since been published continuously by that institution with the collaboration, since 1927, of the American Mathematical Society.
The *Annals* was founded in 1884 at the University of Virginia and was published there until 1899. Subsequently Harvard University and later Princeton

University assumed that responsibility. Since 1933 the Institute for Advanced Study has aided Princeton University in publication of the *Annals*.

60 Fiske, Thomas S., "Mathematical Progress in America," *Bulletin, American Mathematical Society*, Vol. XI, February, 1905, pp. 238-246. This article also appears in *Science*, New Series, Vol. 21, February 10, 1905, pp. 209-215.

61 Walker, Gordon L., "Publications of the American Mathematical Society," *Notices, American Mathematical Society*, Vol. 7, No. 2, Issue No. 45, April, 1960, pp. 169-178.

62 Archibald, Raymond C., *A Semicentennial History of the American Mathematical Society, 1888-1938*, American Mathematical Society Semicentennial Publications, Vol. I, History, New York, 1938. See also Richardson, R. G. D., "American Mathematical Society," *Proceedings, Casualty Actuarial Society*, Vol. XI, Part I, No. 20, 1924, pp. 131-133, and Kline, J. R., "American Mathematical Society," *AAAS Bulletin*, Vol. 2, No. 5, May, 1943, pp. 36-38.

63 For the history of the Institute see Chapter III, pp. 143-146.

64 See Fairchild, Herman L., *The Geological Society of America, 1888-1930*. Published by the Society, New York, 1932 and Betz, Frederick, Jr., "The Geological Society of America," *Geo Times*, Vol. V, No. 8, May-June, 1961, pp. 18-23; 46-47. See also Winchell, Alexander, "Historical Sketch of the Organization," *Bulletin, Geological Society of America*, Vol. 1, February, 15, 1890, pp. 1-6; Stevenson, J. J. "Our Society," *Bulletin, Geological Society of America*, Vol. 10, February 26, 1899, pp. 83-98; Hitchcock, C. H., "Supplementary Note on the Organization of the Geological Society of America," *Bulletin, Geological Society of America*, Vol. 21, December 31, 1910, pp. 741-746; and Aldrich, H. R., "The Geological Society of America," *AAAS Bulletin*, Vol. 2, No. 6, June, 1943, pp. 43-44.

65 Excerpts from a Lecture given at an August 27, 1958 meeting of the American Society of Zoologists, held at Indiana University, Bloomington, Indiana. Unpublished. By Dr. H. Burr Steinbach, Department of Zoology, University of Chicago.

66 The American Society of Naturalists was first organized in 1883, and 14 national learned societies are still listed as being affiliated with it. Edwin G. Conklin in his "Fifty Years of the American Society of Naturalists," *The American Naturalist*, Vol. LXVIII, No. 718, September-October, 1934, pp. 385-401, calls it "the old grandmother of scientific societies" and ascribes over a score as owing their origin to it. Because of this splintering development, together with the emergence of new groupings such as the Federation of American Societies for Experimental Biology and the American Institute of Biological Sciences, interest in the American Society of Naturalists has steadily declined and its individual membership today totals about 600 persons.

67 In Bardeen, Charles R., *Anatomy in America*. Bulletin of the University of Wisconsin, No. 115, Science Series, Vol. 3, No. 4, September, 1905, Madison, Wisconsin, the number of founding members is given at 22 and in "Historical Review," *Anatomical Record*, Vol. 11, No. 6, January, 1917, pp. 546-554, the number is given as 26.

There is a similar discrepancy regarding who was the first president of the Society. Bardeen states that Professor C. O. Whitman of the University of Chicago was the first; whereas the "Historical Review" article gives Professor E. B. Wilson of Bryn Mawr College as the first president. The conflict turns, apparently, on whether Professor Wilson, who was elected chairman at the organizational meeting, should on this account be considered the first head of the organization.

[68] This account is based on the lecture, see Reference 65 above, given by Dr. Steinbach. The "Historical Review" article, see Reference 67, states that the Zoological Society of America was founded in December, 1902 and does not mention the organization of a Society of American Zoologists predecessor to the American Society of Zoologists. See also, Conklin, Edwin G., "Fifty Years of the American Society of Naturalists," *The American Naturalist,* Vol. LXVIII, No. 718, September-October, 1934, pp. 385-401.

[69] See "Report of the Committee on Publications, American Society of Zoologists," *Anatomical Record,* Vol. 20, No. 2, January, 1921, pp. 166-169.

[70] For information about recent activities see *Newsletter,* February, 1960, American Society of Zoologists, and Minutes of Executive and Policy Committee Meetings, November 12 and 13, 1959, furnished the author by Dr. Gairdner B. Moment, Goucher College, Secretary of the American Society of Zoologists. See also, *American Society of Zoologists.* Information pamphlet published by the American Society of Zoologists, Undated.

[71] Tippo, Oswald, "The Early History of the Botanical Society of America," *American Journal of Botany,* Vol. 43, No. 10, December, 1956, pp. 852-858. See also Burkholder, Paul R., "The Botanical Society of America, Inc." *AAAS Bulletin,* Vol. 2, No. 8, August, 1943, pp. 61-62.

[72] Wetmore, Ralph H., "Do We Need a National Center for Plant Sciences?" *Plant Science Bulletin,* Vol. 7, No. 2, May, 1961, p. 1-3.

[73] Stebbins, Joel, "The American Astronomical Society, 1897-1947," *Popular Astronomy,* Vol. LV, No. 8, October, 1947, pp. 404-413. See also, in the foregoing issue, Struve, Otto, "The Yerkes Observatory, 1897-1947," pp. 413-417. See also McLaughlin, Dean B., "The American Astronomical Society," *AAAS Bulletin,* Vol. 2, No. 10, October, 1943, pp. 77-78, and Brouwer, Dirk, "One Hundred Years: 1849-1949," *The Astronomical Journal,* Vol. 55, No. 1, December, 1949, Number 1181, pp. 1-2.

[74] For a biography of Webster see Duff, A. Wilmer, "Arthur Gordon Webster— Physicist, Mathematician, Linguist and Orator," *The American Physics Teacher,* Vol. 6, No. 4, August, 1938, pp. 181-195.

[75] For the history of the Institute see Chapter III, pp. 138-141.

[76] For the complete story of this transfer see the *Physical Review,* Vol. 32, First Series, p. 593, and Vol. 1, Second Series, pp. 1 and 61.

[77] Merritt, Ernest, "Early Days of the Physical Society," *The Review of Scientific Instruments,* Vol. 5, New Series, April, 1943, pp. 143-149. See also, Bedell, Frederick, "What Led to the Founding of the American Physical Society," *Physical Review,* Vol. 75, Second Series, May 15, 1949, pp. 1601-1604, and "The American Physical Society," *Physics Today,* Vol. 4, No. 10, October, 1951, pp. 18-19.

[78] Cohen, Barnett, *Chronicles of the Society of American Bacteriologists, 1899-1950.* Williams and Wilkins Company, Baltimore, Maryland, 1950. See also, Parr, Leland W., "The Society of American Bacteriologists," *AAAS Bulletin,* Vol. 5, No. 4, April, 1946, pp. 30-31.

[79] Manuscript history of American Pathology by Dr. Esmond R. Long, Pedlar Mills, Virginia. Dr. Long expects to publish his history shortly. Also, "Summary of the Actions of the Council of the American Association of Pathologists and

Bacteriologists, 1900-1955," compiled by Drs. H. T. Karsner and E. A. Gall, former secretaries of the Association. Unpublished.

[80] Hering, Carl, "The American Electrochemical Society," *Transactions, American Electrochemical Society,* Vol. XI, 1907, pp. 17-41; Burgess, Charles F., "Early Days in our Society," *Transactions, American Electrochemical Society,* Vol. 82, 1942, pp. 16-27; Burns, R. M., "The First Decade; An Account of the Founding and Early Days of the Society," *Journal, American Electrochemical Society,* Vol. 99, No. 1, January, 1952, pp. 9c-16c; Hunter, Ralph M., "The Electrochemical Society—Past and Future," *Journal, American Electrochemical Society,* Vol. 99, No. 7, July, 1952, pp. 155c-157c. Volume 99 of the *Journal, American Electrochemical Society,* is the Fiftieth Anniversary Issue and also contains histories of the Committees of the Society. In addition, it gives incidental information about the founders of the Society and its early days; see also, *Transactions, American Electrochemical Society,* Vol. I, 1902, pp. 1-30.

[81] Chittenden, Russell H., *The First Twenty-Five Years of the American Society of Biological Chemists.* New Haven, Connecticut, 1945. Printed by the Waverly Press, Baltimore, Maryland; see also, Gies, W. J., "American Society of Biological Chemists," *Science,* New Series, Vol. 25, No. 630, January 25, 1907, pp. 139-142; Richards, A. N., Donald D. Van Slyke, and R. J. Anderson, *The Journal of Biological Chemistry, 1905-1953,* privately published, 1953; Clarke, Hans T., "The Journal of Biological Chemistry," *Journal of Biological Chemistry,* Vol. 216, No. 2, October, 1955, pp. 449-454.

See also the following articles on the Fiftieth Anniversary of the American Society of Biological Chemists appearing in *Federation Proceedings,* Vol. 15, No. 2, July, 1956, Luck, J. Murray, "Introductory Remarks," pp. 793-794; "Congratulatory Messages on the 50th Anniversary of the American Society of Biological Chemists," pp. 795-799; Shaffer, Philip A., "Origin and Development of the American Society of Biological Chemists," pp. 800-802; and Richards, A. N., "Journal of Biological Chemistry: Recollections of its Early Years and of its Founders," pp. 803-806.

[82] For details of this consolidation see Linsley, E. G., "Consolidation of the Entomological Society of America and the American Association of Economic Entomologists," *Annals, Entomological Society of America,* Vol. 45, No. 2, June, 1952, p. 359.

[83] For the early history of the American Association of Economic Entomologists and the Entomological Society of America see Osborn, Herbert, *Fragments of Entomological History.* Published by the author, Columbus, Ohio, 1937; Howard, L. O., *A History of Applied Entomology.* Publication 3065. Smithsonian Institution, Washington, D. C., 1930; and Mickel, Clarence E., "The Entomological Society of America," *AAAS Bulletin,* Vol. 2, No. 6, June, 1943, pp. 44-45.

See also "Preface," *Annual Review of Entomology,* Vol. 4, 1959, pp. V-VI.

[84] Note that Dr. Abel was also instrumental in the founding of the American Society of Biological Chemists, see above, pp. 87-89.

[85] Geiling, E. M. K., "Milestones in the Life of John J. Abel," Unpublished paper presented at a Seminar, Army Chemical Center, Edgewood, Maryland, November 13, 1959. Dr. Geiling also furnished the author with excerpts from the minutes of the organizational and first meeting of the American Society for Pharmacology and Experimental Therapeutics.

[86] In 1958, publication of the proceedings was transferred to the *Journal.*

87 See the following articles in a Symposium on Fifty Years of Paleontology, Parts 1-3, in the *Journal of Paleontology*, Vol. 33, No. 3, May, 1959: Newell, Norman D., "Adequacy of the fossil record," pp. 488-499; Just, Theodor, "Progress in Paleobotany," pp. 500-510; Howe, Henry V., "Fifty years of micropaleontology," pp. 511-517. See also the following articles in a Symposium on Fifty Years of Paleontology, Parts 4-6, in the *Journal of Paleontology*, Vol. 33, No. 5, September, 1959: Dunbar, Carl O., "A Half Century of Paleontology," pp. 909-914; Romer, Alfred Sherwood, "Vertebrate paleontology, 1908-1958," pp. 915-925; Cloud, Preston E., Jr., "Paleoecology—Retrospect and Prospect," pp. 926-962. See also, Proceedings of the preliminary and first annual meetings, first constitution and by-laws, and list of first officers and members of the Paleontological Society, *Bulletin, Geological Society of America*, Vol. 21, March 31, 1910, pp.. 69-86, and Vokes, H. E., "The Paleontological Society," *AAAS Bulletin*, Vol. 4, No. 5, May, 1945, pp. 39-40.

88 Correspondence files of the American Society for Experimental Pathology. See also H. T. K. [Howard T. Karsner], "Obituary-Richard Mills Pearce Jr., M.D., 1874-1930," *Archives of Pathology*, Vol. 9, No. 3, March, 1930, pp. 714-716.

89 Cannon, Paul R., "Editorials," *A.M.A. Archives of Pathology*, Vol. 62, No. 3, September, 1956, p. 173.

90 This Society, which had been organized during World War I was soon superseded by the Association, its activities declined, and it was finally voted by the members on July 27, 1920 that the Society be dissolved and merged with the Association, all of its remaining assets being transferred to the Treasurer of the Association on December 1, 1920.

91 Much of the foregoing account is based on Minutes of the American Association of Immunologists made available to the author through the courtesy of Dr. Calderon Howe, Secretary-Treasurer. See also, Coca, A. F., An unpublished historical summary of the *Journal of Immunology*, 1950, made available to the author through the courtesy of Dr. Geoffrey Edsall. See also, Edsall, Geoffrey, "What is Immunology," *Journal of Immunology*, Vol. 67, No. 2, August, 1951, pp. 167-172.

92 See Shelford, V. E., "The Organization of the Ecological Society of America, 1914-19," *Ecology*, Vol. 19, No. 1, January, 1938, pp. 164-166; Taylor, Norman, "The Beginnings of Ecology," *Ecology*, Vol. 19, No. 2, April, 1938, p. 352; Moore, Barrington, "The Beginnings of Ecology," *Ecology*, Vol. 19, No. 4, October, 1938, p. 592; and Dreyer, William A., "The Ecological Society of America," *AAAS Bulletin*, Vol. 4, No. 2, February, 1945, pp. 15-16.

Information about the Society was also furnished the author by Professor John E. Cantlon, Michigan State University and Professor Emeritus V. E. Shelford, University of Illinois.

93 For the life of Professor Slaught, which also provides a great deal of information about the Association, see Dark, Harris Jeremiah, *The Life and Works of Herbert Ellsworth Slaught*. George Peabody College for Teachers, Nashville, Tennessee, 1948. See also Bliss, G. A., "Herbert Ellsworth Slaught—Teacher and Friend," *The American Mathematical Monthly*, Vol. XLV, January, 1938, pp. 5-10; Cairns, W. D., "Herbert Ellsworth Slaught—Editor and Organizer," *The American Mathematical Monthly*, Vol. XLV, January, 1938, pp. 1-4; Cairns, W. D., "Mathematics in Education," *AAAS Bulletin*, Vol. 3, No. 1, January, 1944. pp. 7-8; and Slaught, Herbert Ellsworth, "Retrospect and Prospect for Mathematics

in America," *The American Mathematical Monthly*, Vol. XXVII, November, 1920, pp. 443-451.

For similar references to Professors Cairns and Hedrick, see *The American Mathematical Monthly*, Vol. L, January, 1943, p. 1, and pp. 409-411.

[94] *Bulletin of Information.* Published by the Mathematical Association of America, pp. 1-6, Undated.

[95] Fleming, John A., "Origin and Development of the American Geophysical Union," *Transactions, American Geophysical Union*, Vol. 35, No. 1, February, 1954, pp. 5-46. See also, Bauer, Louis A., "The Organization and Aims of the American Geophysical Union," *Bulletin, National Research Council*, Vol. 7, Part 5, No. 41, January, 1924, pp. 7-18.

[96] Superseded in 1962 by the *Journal of Atmospheric Sciences;* a new *Journal of Applied Meteorology* was inaugurated at the same time.

[97] For a history of the international organization for meteorology see Tannehill, I. R., "The History and Status of the International Meteorological Organization (I. M. O.)," *Bulletin, American Meteorological Society*, Vol. 28, No. 5, May, 1947, pp. 207-219.

[98] See Fortieth Anniversary Issue of *Weatherwise*, Vol. 12, No. 6, December, 1959, containing the following articles: Brooks, Charles F., "The Society's First Quarter Century," pp. 223-230, and Ludlum, David M., "The American Meteorological Society," pp. 231-245. See also, the informational pamphlet, *American Meteorological Society, Its Purposes, Its Activities, Its Organization.* Published by the American Meteorological Society, Undated.

[99] Ward, Henry B., "The Founder of American Parasitology, Joseph Leidy," *Journal of Parasitology*, Vol. 10, No. 1, September, 1923, pp. 1-21.

[100] Fosdick, Raymond B., *The Story of the Rockefeller Foundation.* Harper and Brothers, New York, 1952, p. 42.

[101] This procedure was followed until 1934 when the Helminthological Society of Washington established its own *Proceedings.*

[102] The important role played by members of the Helminthological Society of Washington in the formation of the American Society of Parasitologists is described in "Historical Resume of the Helminthological Society of Washington," *Proceedings, The Helminthological Society of Washington*, Vol. 27, No. 3, December, 1960 (Special Anniversary Number), p. 250.

In this same issue of the *Proceedings*, commemorating the fiftieth anniversary of the Society there appear several other articles bearing on historical aspects of parasitology, together with summaries of remarks delivered at the Fiftieth Anniversary Banquet, pp. 238-241, of a similar nature.

[103] For a more detailed account of this transfer, see Kiger, Joseph C., "The American Society of Parasitologists: A Short History," *Journal of Parasitology*, Vol. 48, No. 5, October, 1962, pp. 641-650.

[104] See Cort, W. W., "Professor Henry Baldwin Ward and the Journal of Parasitology," *Journal of Parasitology*, Vol. 19, No. 2, December, 1932, pp. 99-105.

See also, "Announcement of the Transfer of the Journal of Parasitology to the American Society of Parasitologists," *Journal of Parasitology*, Vol. 19, No. 1, September, 1932, pp. 96-97.

[105] See "The Endowment Fund of the American Society of Parasitologists," *Journal of Parasitology*, Vol. 36, No. 6, Section 2 (Supplement), December, 1950, pp. 50-51.

106 For a detailed description of the seal, see Mueller, Justus F., "The Society Seal," *Journal of Parasitology,* Vol. 46, No. 1, February, 1960, pp. 112-113. See, for a detailed account of "The Award of the First Henry Baldwin Ward Medal," *Journal of Parasitology,* Vol. 46, No. 1, February, 1960, pp. 113-115.

For a picture of the medal and a detailed description of it and how it was made together with an amusing anecdote of the designer's relationship with Dr. Henry Baldwin Ward, and Ward's Natural Science Establishment Inc., there being no connection other than the professional and scientific between the two Wards, see Mueller, Justus F., "The Henry Baldwin Ward Medal," *Journal of Parasitology,* Vol. 47, No. 2, April, 1961, pp. 206-208.

107 See also the following articles in *Journal of Parasitology*: Chandler, Asa C., "The Making of a Parasitologist," Vol. 32, No. 3, June, 1946, pp. 213-221; Cram, Eloise B., "Stepping Stones in the History of the American Society of Parasitologists," Vol. 42, No. 5, October, 1956, pp. 461-473. See also Culbertson, J. T., "American Society of Parasitologists," *AAAS Bulletin,* Vol. 3, No. 6, June, 1944, pp. 47-48.

Information about the Society was also furnished the author by Drs. George R. LaRue, Justus F. Mueller, G. F. Otto, Norman R. Stoll and Horace W. Stunkard.

108 Chittenden, Russell H., *The First Twenty-Five Years of the American Society of Biological Chemists.* New Haven, Connecticut, 1945, p. 75.

109 Information furnished the author by Professor George R. Cowgill, former Editor of the *Journal of Nutrition,* and by Dr. George M. Briggs, Secretary of the American Institute of Nutrition.

See also the following articles in the *Journal of Nutrition:* Murlin, John R., "Editorial-Transfer of the Journal of Nutrition to the Wistar Institute," Vol. 7, No. 3, March, 1934, pp. 365-366; "Proceedings of the First Annual Meeting of the American Institute of Nutrition," Vol. 7, No. 5, Supplement, May, 1934, pp. 1-8; Cowgill, George R., "John R. Murlin—Honor Volume," Vol. 31, No. 1, January, 1946, pp. 3-4; Nasset, E. S., "John Raymond Murlin—Investigator, Teacher, Colleague," Vol. 31, No. 1, January, 1946, pp. 5-12; Deuel, Harry J., Jr., "Biography of Graham Lusk," Vol. 41, No. 1, May, 1950, pp. 3-12.

110 Frisch, Ragnar, "Editorial," *Econometrica,* Vol. I, No. 1, January, 1933, pp. 1-4.

111 *Economic Theory and Measurement; A Twenty Year Research Report, 1932-1952.* Published by Cowles Commission for Research in Economics. Printed at the Waverly Press, Baltimore, Maryland, 1952, p. 10. For the history of the activities of the Cowles Commission see this Report.

112 For the origins and development of the Econometric Society from an American viewpoint see Roos, Charles F., "A Future Role for the Econometric Society in International Statistics," *Econometrica,* Vol. 16, No. 2, April, 1948, pp. 127-134. For the European viewpoint see Divisia, Francois, "La Societe d'Econometrica a Atteint sa Majorite," *Econometrica,* Vol. 21, No. 1, January, 1953, pp. 1-30. See also the previously cited *Economic Theory and Measurement, A Twenty Year Research Report, 1932-1952* of the Cowles Commission for Research in Economics; and Leavens, Dickson H., "The Econometric Society," *AAAS Bulletin,* Vol. 4, No. 7, July, 1945, p. 55.

113 Whiting, P. W., "History and Organization," *Records, Genetics Society of America,* No. 2, 1933, pp. 5-8, and *Records, Genetics Society of America,* No. 3,

1934, pp. 5-7. See also, Kaufmann, B. P., "Genetics Society of America," *AAAS Bulletin,* Vol. 3, No. 7, July, 1944, pp. 55-56.

[114] *An Introduction to the Institute of Mathematical Statistics.* Published by the Institute of Mathematical Statistics, June 15, 1958. See also King, Willford I., "The Annals of Mathematical Statistics," *The Annals of Mathematical Statistics,* Vol. 1, No. 1, February, 1930, pp. 1-2; "Notice of the Organization of the Institute of Mathematical Statistics," *The Annals of Mathematical Statistics,* Vol. VI, No. 4, December, 1935, p. 227; and "The Institute of Mathematical Statistics," *AAAS Bulletin,* Vol. 4, No. 3, March, 1945, pp. 23-24.

[115] *Bulletins of Information.* Published by the Association for Symbolic Logic, 1935, 1938, and 1951. Information about the Association was also furnished the author by Professors C. A. Baylis, Duke University; H. B. Curry, Pennsylvania State University; C. J. Ducasse, Brown University; and S. C. Kleene, University of Wisconsin.

[116] Information furnished the author by Dr. Earl Ingerson, University of Texas, Translations Editor of the Geochemical Society. See also *Bulletin of Information,* published by the American Geological Institute, Washington, D. C., June, 1960.

CHAPTER III

[1] It may be noted that the Social Science Research Council, the American Council on Education, the American Council of Learned Societies, and the National Research Council, in 1944, organized the Conference Board of Associated Research Councils. Membership of the Board is composed of two administrative officers from each of the Councils, and a Secretary. Two main projects of the Board to date have been the Commission on Human Resources and Advanced Training which resulted in Dr. Dael Wolfle's book, *America's Resources of Specialized Talent: The Report of the Commission on Human Resources and Advanced Training.* Harper and Brothers, New York, 1954, and the activities of the Committee on International Exchange of Persons. This Committee cooperates with the Department of State and Board of Foreign Scholarships in the administration of the Fulbright educational program as it applies to university teaching and advanced research.

[2] The American Academy of Political and Social Science was established in Philadelphia on December 14, 1889, to provide a national medium for the discussion of political and social questions. The principal means by which the work of the Academy has been conducted is its publications and meetings. In 1890, the quarterly, later bi-monthly, *Annals* was established and, in the same year, the first meeting was held. From 1890 to 1902 separate issues of the *Annals* were devoted to a number of topics. Since the latter date, however, each volume treats of one subject only and the resulting publications are actually books on a wide variety of political and social topics. Also, in 1902, the symposium device was adopted for the annual meetings and it has become the custom to publish papers presented there as the July issue of the *Annals.*

In addition to its publications and meetings, the Academy also established and grants several research fellowships to selected scholars for work on various political and social problems. One is in honor of the late Dr. Edmund J. James, founder of the Academy and a former President of Northwestern University and the University of Illinois. The other was named for the late Professor Simon N. Patten, also one of the early leaders of the Academy.

Membership in the Academy originally turned on proposal by a member and approval of the governing Council. Today it is open, upon payment of annual dues, to any interested person who receives a written invitation to join. It is interesting to note that the Executive Committee of the Academy, in 1890, declared that the members of the American Association for the Advancement of Science, the American Economic Association, the American Historical Association, and the American Sociological Association, together with a small number of other educational groups, were also members of the Academy. This action was designed to create a functioning and viable membership as early as possible, but the practice was discontinued in the early years as the number of direct subscribers increased. Since that time the Academy has consisted of individual members and institutional subscribers.

From approximately 3,000 members in 1891 the Academy has grown so that at the present time there are approximately 14,000 members, including 1,400 outside the United States. This figure of 14,000 includes 4,500 institutional subscribers.

The foregoing information is based on a *Summarized Statement of Activities, 1889-1927*. Published by the American Academy of Political and Social Science, Undated, and information furnished the author by Dr. James C. Charlesworth, President, American Academy of Political and Social Science.

[3] Founded in New York City in 1825, under the leadership of Samuel F. B. Morse, the National Academy of Design has continued to include in its membership those persons most eminent in the arts of painting, architecture, sculpture, and graphic design. Limited originally to a total of 30 professional artists, the Academy has expanded to permit a total today of 250 Academicians; an unlimited number of Associates; and 7 Honorary corresponding members to be enrolled in its ranks. All three categories of members are subjected to a winnowing nominating process with the Academicians being selected by an exeptionally rigorous competitive process from the ranks of the Associate members.

In addition to the honorific characteristics of the Academy it has, throughout its existence, conducted exhibitions in its galleries, located in its present home at 1083 Fifth Avenue, New York City. The Academy also operates a school of fine arts, with classes in drawing, painting in oil and watercolor, sculpture and a mural workshop. The school has been located, since 1959, at 5 East 89th Street, New York City.

For a recent history of the National Academy of Design, see Clark, Eliot, *History of the National Academy of Design, 1825-1953*. Columbia University Press, New York, 1954. See also, Cummings, Thomas S., *Historic Annals of the National Academy of Design, 1825-1863*. Philadelphia, Pennsylvania, 1865.

[4] This section is partially based on an earlier account by the author. See Kiger, Joseph C., "The Four Councils," *Educational Record,* Vol. XXXIX, October, 1958, pp. 367-373.

[5] *A Brief Statement of the History and Activities of the American Council on Education*. Published by the American Council on Education, Washington, D. C., 1960, p. 1.

[6] See Appendix A - Learned Societies Which Are Members of Councils and Societal Institutes, pp. 262-264.

[7] *Minutes of Executive Committee of the American Council on Education,* February 28, 1920, Page A-2185, Item (f), American Council on Education, Washington, D. C.

[8] Goode, G. Brown, "The Origin of the National Scientific and Educational Institutions of the United States," *Annual Report, American Historical Association, 1889,* Senate Miscellaneous Documents, 51st Congress, 1st Session. Vol. 4, 1889-1890, Government Printing Office, Washington, D. C., 1890, pp. 53-161. See also, Goode, G. Brown, "The First National Scientific Congress and its Connection with the Organization of the American Association," *Proceedings, American Association for the Advancement of Science,* Vol. XL, 1891, pp. 39-47.

[9] Gray, George W., *Science at War.* Harper and Brothers, New York, 1943, pp. 43-66. See also True, F. W., edit., *A History of the First Half-Century of the National Academy of Sciences, 1863-1913.* National Academy of Sciences, Washington, D. C., 1913; and Dupree, A. Hunter, *Science in the Federal Government.* Harvard University Press, Cambridge, Massachusetts, 1957, pp. 115-148.

[10] *Report of the National Academy of Sciences-National Research Council.* Government Printing Office, Washington, D. C., 1959, p. vii.

[11] For a full account of this interesting sidelight on the origin of the National Research Council, see Jewett, Frank B., "The Genesis of the National Research Council and Millikan's World War I Work," *Review of Modern Physics,* Vol. 20, No. 1, January, 1948, pp. 1-6.

[12] *A History of the National Research Council, 1919-1933.* Reprint and Circular Series of the National Research Council, No. 106, National Academy of Sciences-National Research Council, Washington, D. C., 1933. See also Dupree, A. Hunter, *Science in the Federal Government,* pp. 302-330; Gray, George W., *Science at War,* pp. 46-48; Kellogg, Vernon, "The National Research Council," *International Conciliation,* No. 154, September, 1920, pp. 423-430; and Zwemer, Raymund L., "The National Academy of Sciences and the National Research Council," *Science,* Vol. 108, No. 2801, September 3, 1948, pp. 234-238.

[13] See Appendix A - Learned Societies Which Are Members of Councils and Societal Institutes, pp. 262-264.

[14] Angell, James R., "The Organization of Research in Our American Democracy," *Proceedings of the Institute of Medicine of Chicago,* March 5, 1920, pp. 14-15.

[15] *Report of the National Academy of Sciences-National Research Council,* Government Printing Office, Washington, D. C., 1960, p. 106.

[16] Leland, Waldo G., "The International Union of Academies and the American Council of Learned Societies," *International Conciliation,* No. 154, September, 1920, pp. 442-457.

[17] See Appendix A - Learned Societies Which Are Members of Councils and Societal Institutes, pp. 262-264.

[18] "Policy Statement With Regard to Admission of New Constituent Societies to the ACLS," approved by the Council, January 26, 1950, Mimeographed, General Files, American Council of Learned Societies, New York, New York.

[19] Although their names are somewhat similar, the Social Science Research Council has no connection with the American Social Science Association of the late nineteenth and early twentieth century.

The Association was organized in Boston in 1865 by some 300 persons interested in the betterment of society. Its membership included many eminent people, particularly in the New England area, and it patterned itself after the British Social Science Association which had been founded in 1856. The Association, through its publications, meetings, and other activities, was probably one of the principal forces behind social reforms in the nineteenth century. It was very active in the movements for civil service, prison, public health, and educational reform. In addition, the Association figured in the formation of many other organizations, including two learned societies. These included the National Prison Association (1870), the American Public Health Association (1872), the National Conference of Charities (1874), the Association for the Protection of the Insane and the Prevention of Insanity (1880), the American Historical Association (1884), the American Economic Association (1885), and the National Institute of Arts and Letters (1898). The success of the Association in this direction was its own undoing. It had emasculated itself to such an extent that, in 1912, it went out of existence.

See Small, Albion W., "Fifty Years of Sociology in the United States," *The American Journal of Sociology,* Vol. XXI, No. 6, May 1916, pp. 725-727 and "History of the American Social Science Association in a Letter to Its Present Secretary, I. F. Russell, New York, by F. B. Sanborn, of Concord, Massachusetts, a Founder," *The American Journal of Sociology,* Vol. XV, No. 5, March, 1910, pp. 592-595.

[20] *Social Science Research Council Annual Report,* 1945-1946, p. 7; see also its *Decennial Report,* 1923-33, particularly, "A Decade of Council History," pp. 1-18.

[21] See Appendix A - Learned Societies Which Are Members of Councils and Societal Institutes, pp. 262-264.

[22] Goode, G. Brown, "The First National Scientific Congress and its Connection with the Organization of the American Association," *Proceedings, American Association for the Advancement of Science,* Vol. XL, 1891, pp. 39-47. Goode ascribes great importance to the influence of the National Institution and other societies in the creation of the AAAS. For a *contra* view see Fairchild, Herman L., *The Geological Society of America, 1888-1930.* Published by the Society, New York, 1932, pp. 31-37, and Fairchild, Herman L., "The History of the American Association for the Advancement of Science," *Science,* Vol. LIX, No. 1530, April 25, 1924, pp. 365-369. See also Hale, William H., "Early Years of the American Association," *Appleton's Popular Science Monthly,* Vol. XLIX, No. 4, August, 1896, pp. 501-507; Moulton, Forest R., "The American Association for the Advancement of Science - A Brief Historical Sketch," *Science,* Vol. 108, No. 2801, September 3, 1948, pp. 217-218; and Dupree, A. Hunter, *Science in the Federal Government,* pp. 70-75.

[23] This publication was resumed on a quarterly basis in January, 1961 to serve as a news medium about the Association.

[24] See Appendix A - Learned Societies Which Are Members of Councils and Societal Institutes, pp. 262-264.

In addition to 42 learned societies affiliated with the AAAS, the American Geological Institute, the American Institute of Biological Sciences, and the American Institute of Physics are also affiliated with the Association.

[25] "A Brief History of the Association - From Its Founding in 1848 to 1948," *Summarized Proceedings and Directory, 1940-1948,* American Association for the Advancement of Science, Washington, D. C., 1948, pp. 1-19; see also pp. 22-28 and

pp. 62-69 of this volume. See also Fairchild, Herman L., "The History of the American Association for the Advancement of Science," *Science,* Vol. LIX, No. 1531, May 2, 1924, pp. 385-390 and No. 1532, May 9, 1924, pp. 410-415; Mather, Kirtley F., "Geology, Geologists, and the AAAS," *Science,* Vol. 129, No. 1108, April 24, 1959, pp. 1106-1111 and "Historical Sketch," *Directory of Officers and Activities for 1961.* American Association for the Advancement of Science, Washington, D. C., pp. 65-75.

[26] See Appendix A - Learned Societies Which Are Members of Councils and Societal Institutes, pp. 262-264.

[27] *Background Material - Federation of American Societies for Experimental Biology,* Mimeographed. Federation of American Societies for Experimental Biology, Washington, D. C., July 20, 1960.

[28] See Appendix A - Learned Societies Which Are Members of Councils and Societal Institutes, pp. 262-264.

[29] Barton, Henry A., "The Story of the American Institute of Physics," *Physics Today,* Vol. 9, No. 1, January, 1956, pp. 46-60. See also Harrison, George R., "Twenty Years of Age," *Physics Today,* Vol. 4, No. 10, October, 1951, pp. 12-13; this same issue contains brief histories of the American Institute of Physics and its five member societies—see pp. 14-27. See also, Hutchisson, Elmer, "AIP Annual Report, 1959," *Physics Today,* Vol. 13, No. 5, May, 1960, pp. 16-25; Barton, Henry A., and George H. Burnham, "The American Institute of Physics," *Science,* Vol. 97, No. 2512, February 19, 1943, pp. 172-176; and *Bulletin of Information.* Published by the American Institute of Physics, New York, 1960.

[30] American Physiological Society, American Society for Horticulture Sciences, American Society of Parasitologists, American Society of Plant Physiologists, American Society of Zoologists, Botanical Society of America, Inc., Genetics Society of America, Limnological Society of America, Mycological Society of America, Poultry Science Association, Society for the Study of Development and Growth, Society of American Bacteriologists.

[31] Hylander, Clarence J., "The American Institute of Biological Sciences: A Historical Resume," *AIBS Bulletin,* Vol. 1, No. 1, January, 1951, pp. 6-8, and Vol. 1, No. 2, April, 1951, pp. 13-15.

[32] See Appendix A - Learned Societies Which Are Members of Councils and Societal Institutes, pp. 262-264.

[33] Dickson, James G., "American Institute of Biological Sciences, A Progress Report," *AIBS Bulletin,* Vol. IX, No. 1, January, 1959, pp. 15-16, and Cox, Hiden T., "The AIBS After Ten Years," *AIBS Bulletin,* Vol. IX, No. 5, November, 1959, pp. 19-21. See also, *A Decade of Growth in Biology, 1948-1958.* Information pamphlet published by the American Institute of Biological Sciences, Washington, D. C., Undated.

[34] Croneis, Carey, "Geology in War and Peace," *Bulletin, American Association of Petroleum Geologists,* Vol. 27, No. 7, 1942, pp. 1221-1249.

[35] American Association of Petroleum Geologists (AAPG), American Geophysical Union (AGU), American Institute of Mining and Metallurgical Engineers (AIME), Geological Society of America (GSA), Mineralogical Society of America (MSA), Paleontological Society (PS), Seismological Society of America (SSA), Society of Economic Geologists (SEcG), Society of Economic Paleontologists and Mineralogists (SEPM), Society of Exploration Geophysicists (SEGp), and Society of Vertebrate Paleontology (SVP).

36 "Shall Geoscientists Unite," *Geo Times,* Vol. III, No. 3, October, 1958, pp. 6-8 ; 27-29.

37 See Appendix A - Learned Societies Which Are Members of Councils and Societal Institutes, pp. 262-264.

38 "Ten Years of the American Geological Institute, 1948-1958," *Geo Times,* Vol. III, No. 3, October, 1958, pp. 12-17 ; 30-32. See also, Eckhardt, E. A., "More About AGI History," *Geo Times,* Vol. III, No. 3, October, 1958, pp. 22-25.

CHAPTER IV

1 Such organizations as the Armour Research Foundation, the Batelle Memorial Institute, the Mellon Institute, and the Southern Research Institute would not be included in this group. These institutes conduct many basic scientific projects and have made many scientific discoveries, but they are all primarily committed to programs of direct and practical benefit to certain industrial or governmental sponsors.

2 For the historical development of this and other principles see Kiger, Joseph C., *Operating Principles of the Larger Foundations.* Russell Sage Foundation, New York, 1954. See also Andrews, F. Emerson, *Philanthropic ' ɪndations.* Russell Sage Foundation, New York, 1956.

3 See Walton, Ann D., and F. Emerson Andrews, edit., *The Foundation Directory,* Edition 1. Published for the Foundation Library Center by Russell Sage Foundation, New York, 1960, p. 554.

4 These figures do not include the American Philosophical Society and the American Academy of Arts and Sciences since they are concerned with all fields of knowledge, natural sciences, social sciences, and humanities. The former has received about $137,000 in financial aid from the foundations while the latter has received approximately $200,000 in foundation grants.

5 See *Report of the Study for the Ford Foundation on Policy and Program.* The Ford Foundation, Detroit, Michigan, 1949, and the *Annual Reports,* 1951-1952 of the Ford Foundation.

6 The Fund for the Advancement of Education, a Ford philanthropy, made one grant of $5,000 to the American Philosophical Association in 1957 to improve the teaching of philosophy.

7 These figures on foundation giving do not include the income which the American Chemical Society received from the Petroleum Research Fund.

The Fund was set up in 1944 by a group of oil companies and it now has assets in excess of $70,000,000. The income from this Fund, which through 1960 amounted to approximately $12,000,000, has been administered by the Society to support research in various fields of chemistry.

8 Millikan, Robert A., *Autobiography.* Prentice-Hall, New York, 1950, pp. 180-184. See also Dupree, A. Hunter, *Science in the Federal Government,* pp. 305-313.

9 For the history of the IRC-ICSU, see Chapter VI, pp. 192-195.

10 For a report on this aspect of the Committee's work, see *Report of the National Academy of Sciences.* Government Printing Office, Washington, D. C., 1928, pp. 8-15.

11 The General Education Board, a Rockefeller philanthropy, made two grants to the ACLS amounting to $134,000 for general and special purposes; one in 1926, the other in 1945.

The Laura Spelman Rockefeller Memorial made a grant of $15,000 in 1925 and another for the same amount in 1928 for research projects of the ACLS.

Although it lies outside the period covered by this study, it should be mentioned that the Rockefeller Foundation, in 1961, provided $1,000,000 to the ACLS for its general support.

[12] In the 1940's the Carnegie Endowment for International Peace made grants totalling $11,500 to the Council for publication purposes and the Carnegie Institution of Washington one of $1,646 for a historical program at St. Augustine, Florida.

Although it lies outside the period covered by this study, it should be mentioned that the Carnegie Corporation of New York, in 1961, appropriated $650,000 to the ACLS for its general support, fellowships, and grants-in-aid.

[13] *ACLS Newsletter,* Vol. XI, No. 10, December, 1960.

[14] The *Journal* was terminated in 1932 because of its lack of use by social scientists.

CHAPTER V

[1] The various state and local governments have never contributed any significant financial support to these organizations. Throughout this chapter, therefore, unless otherwise noted, government refers to the United States government.

[2] *Science and Public Policy: A Report to the President.* Report of the President's Scientific Research Board, Vol. I, Government Printing Office, Washington, D. C., 1947, p. 10.

[3] *10th Annual Report,* National Science Foundation, Government Printing Office, Washington, D. C., 1960, pp. 138-151; and *Federal Funds for Science.* Vol. IX, National Science Foundation, Government Printing Office, Washington, D. C., 1960, pp. iii-4. See also, *Sponsored Research Policy of Colleges and Universities.* American Council on Education, Washington, D. C., 1954, pp. 24-41.

[4] Created in 1950 by the Federal government for purposes similar to those for which the learned societies, councils, and societal institutes had been set up, i. e., the advancement of science and knowledge, the NSF has dispensed an ever-increasing flow of funds to a number of these organizations.

In addition to the natural sciences, the National Science Foundation has proved of inestimable value to the social sciences and humanities because its expenditures, primarily in the natural sciences, have released other funds for expenditures in such areas as history, art, music, etc.

For the story of this development see Bush, Vannevar, *Science, the Endless Frontier.* Government Printing Office, Washington, D. C., 1945 and successive annual issues, Nos. I through IX, 1950 through 1960 of *Federal Funds for Science.* National Science Foundation, Government Printing Office, Washington, D. C. See also, Price, Don K., *Government and Science.* New York University Press, New York, 1954, and Price, Don K., J. Stefan Dupre, and W. Eric Gustafson, "Current Trends in Science Policy in the United States," *Impact of Science on Society,* Vol. 10, No. 3, 1960, pp. 187-213.

[5] The two administrative methods of placing government funds for research with outside organizations are the contract and the grant. The former is the traditional method for spending these funds and is still the one most extensively

used, particularly for large scale projects. The latter is a fairly recent development borrowed from the private foundations, and permits much more flexibility and freedom to the grantee than the contract. In the face of greatly augmented funds for research, where results are so uncertain, there has been an increasing tendency to permit greater flexibility in those government agencies using contracts and, since 1958, a great number of them have been given discretionary authority as to which form they should use. As a result there appears to be a decrease in the distinction between them; this is clearly apparent in the government contracts and grants placed with the learned societies, councils, and societal institutes. No attempt, therefore, has been made to draw a distinction between them in this study.

It may be noted, also, that the method followed in arranging for these grants or contracts and the procedures followed after they are made, approximates the foundation pattern. In other words, the approach may be either from the grantor or the grantee and a conscious attempt is made to maintain flexibility. Despite this attempt, however, it must be said that government grants and contracts still fall short of the private foundation mark in this regard.

6 These figures do not include the American Philosophical Society or the American Academy of Arts and Sciences since they are concerned with all fields of knowledge, natural sciences, social sciences, and humanities. The former received negligible financial support from the government; the latter approximately $150,000, all from the National Science Foundation, for various studies, conferences and publications sponsored by the Academy in the 1950's.

7 The exception is the approximately $1,200,000 received by the American Chemical Society from various industrial corporations to aid it in the construction of its new headquarters building in Washington.

8 These figures exclude the American Philosophical Society and the American Academy of Arts and Sciences, the former has received no aid from industrial concerns and the latter about $5,000.

9 Stanerson, B. R., "Thanks a Million," *Chemical and Engineering News*, Vol. 37, No. 28, July 13, 1959, p. 114.

10 "National Academy of Sciences to 1917," *AAAS Bulletin*, Vol. 2, No. 7, July, 1943, pp. 52-54.

11 Fite, Emerson D., *Social and Industrial Conditions in the North During the Civil War*. Macmillan Company, New York, 1910. p. 252.

12 For the story of this development see Baxter, James Phinney, 3rd, *Scientists Against Time*. Little, Brown and Company, Boston, Massachusetts, 1946, and Stewart, Irvin, *Organizing Scientific Research for War: the Administrative History of the Office of Scientific Research and Development*. Little, Brown and Company, Boston, Massachusetts, 1948. See also the Academy's *Annual Report*, 1946-47, pp. 1-6.

13 Because of the large number of industrial concerns contributing large and small sums for intermittent periods; their desire, in many cases, to remain anonymous; the secrecy that surrounded many of the projects, particularly during World Wars I and II; and the oft-time difficulty in deciding what constituted an industrial firm, all of the figures presented herein are approximate and no attempt has been made to give total sums appropriated by specific firms or for specific purposes.

14 See above, p. 180.

CHAPTER VI

¹ It was not until after World War I, and in a few cases, World War II, that the term Congress came to be generally applied to international meetings, while International Association, Institute, or, more generally, Union, was applied to the organizations convening and holding the Congress. Prior to that time these terms were often used interchangeably, which leads to much confusion. Thus prior to the organization of the International Mathematical Union in New York in 1950, the organization which sponsored international mathematical congresses was titled the International Mathematical Congress.

For this reason, the terms organization and conference have been used herein until the period following World War I.

² For further statistics and other information see *The 1978 International Organizations Founded Since the Congress of Vienna*. Document No. 7, Union of International Associations, Brussels, Belgium, 1957. Note that this Union of International Associations, established in 1910 at Brussels, had as its primary purpose the study and coordination of all international associations. Despite its impressive history prior to World War I, H. R. C. Greaves, *The League Committees and World Order*. Oxford University Press, London, 1931, credits it with being a major factor in the creation of the League of Nations, it languished after that conflict and practically ceased to exist by World War II. Following that conflict, it was resuscitated through the efforts of Mr. Jules Polain and Mr. G. P. Speekaert and the latter is presently Secretary-General of the organization. In 1951 it was granted consultative status with the United Nations and in 1952 with UNESCO. It has since begun an impressive publication program of which this Document No. 7 is an example.

For the historical background of modern international organizations see Shenton, Herbert N., *Cosmopolitan Conversation*. Columbia University Press, New York, 1933, pp. 23-33; Mangone, Gerard J., *A Short History of International Organization*. McGraw-Hill Book Company, Inc., New York, 1954, pp. 12-66; Schmeckebier, Laurence F., *International Organizations in Which the United States Participates*. The Brookings Institution, Washington, D C., 1935, pp. 314-315; Ware, Edith E., edit., *The Study of International Relations in the United States*. Columbia University Press, New York, 1934, p. 103.

³ *The 1978 International Organizations Founded Since the Congress of Vienna*, p. *x*.

⁴ Delegates from nine European academies met at Weisbaden in October, 1899, and formed the International Association of Academies. By the following year a total of 18 national academies had joined the Association, including all the major European academies and the National Academy of Sciences of the United States. The Association included a Section of Science and a Section of Literature and provision was made for a governing Committee and a general meeting every three years.

The Association, however, was not completely representative of the scientific and cultural interests of those countries comprising it. Furthermore, despite its governing Committee, it had no permanent headquarters or secretariat, and during the intervals between its triennial meetings it was almost inactive. Finally, it was very inadequately financed.

For an account of the organization of the Association, by the then permanent secretary of the Paris Academy of Sciences, see "The International Association of Academies," *Nature*, Vol. LXII, July 12, 1890, pp. 249-250.

5 Since World War I was still in progress, the countries of the Central Powers were not invited to be represented at the Conference.

6 Hale, George E., "The International Organization of Scientific Research," *International Conciliation*, No. 154, September, 1920, p. 436; and Jones, H. Spencer, "The Early History of ICSU, 1919-1946," *ICSU Review*, Vol. 2, No. 4, October, 1960, pp. 169-171.

7 See Appendix C - Members of International Councils, p. 267.

8 Hungary joined the Council in 1927 and Bulgaria in 1931. Germany and Austria apparently never joined the Council during the interwar period although both of these nations, in the 1930's, did provide for adherence to several of the Unions.

9 *Minutes*. Division of Foreign Relations. National Academy of Sciences-National Research Council, Washington, D. C., 1926-1939. See also Jones, H. Spencer, "The Early History of ICSU, 1919-1946," *ICSU Review*, Vol. 2, No. 4, October, 1960, pp. 171-181.

10 This Union is also designated Union Académique Internationale or International Union of Academies.

11 Bidez, Joseph, "L'Union Académique Internationale de Son Origine a 1939," *Coup D'Oeil Sur Les Vingt-Cinq Premierés Sessions du Comite 1920-1950*, Union Académique Internationale, Bruxelles, Belgique, 1951, p. 5.

12 Leland, Waldo G., "The International Union of Academies and the American Council of Learned Societies," *International Conciliation*, No. 154, September, 1920, pp. 442-448. See also White, Lyman C., *International Non-Governmental Organizations*, p. 112, and Ware, Edith E., edit., *The Study of International Relations in the United States*, pp. 42-43.

13 The first of such appropriations was made in 1929 and continued annually until 1932. At that time the Congress ceased to so appropriate and these expenses were met from the funds of the National Academy of Sciences-National Research Council. They were resumed in 1935 and have continued to be appropriated down to the present day. It must be noted, however, that such sums have never been large. Prior to 1960 a statutory limitation prevented United States contribution in excess of $9,000 annually. Since that date the limitation has been raised to $65,000 annually.

14 Davis, Malcolm W., "The League of Minds," *Pioneers in World Order*. Edited by Harriet E. Davis, Columbia University Press, New York, 1944, pp. 240-249. See also, *The Aims, Methods and Activity of the League of Nations*. Secretariat of the League of Nations, Geneva, Switzerland, 1935, pp. 154-164 and Ware, Edith E., edit., *The Study of International Relations in the United States*, pp. 445-453.

15 *Plan of Work 1938*. International Institute of Intellectual Cooperation, Report Number 10, November, 1939, C. A. 60, 1937, p. 17.

16 The following publications, of a non-periodical nature, deal with the background and history of the United Nations: Cheever, Daniel S., and H. Field Haviland, Jr., *Organizing for Peace*. Houghton-Mifflin Company, Cambridge, Massachusetts, 1954; Goodspeed, Stephen S., *The Nature and Function of International Organization*. Oxford University Press, New York, 1949, pp. 3-78; and Nicholas, H. G., *The United Nations as a Political Institution*. Oxford University

Press, London, 1959. See also, Asher, Robert E., and Associates, *The U. N. and the Promotion of the General Welfare.* Brookings Institution, Washington, D. C., 1957, and MacIver, Robert M., *The Nations and the United Nations.* Manhattan Publishing Company, New York, 1959. The latter is the last in a series prepared by the Carnegie Endowment for International Peace and dealing with the relationships of some twenty different countries to the United Nations.

[17] Himstead, Ralph E., "Education and the Peace," *AAUP Bulletin,* Vol. 31, No. 3, Autumn, 1945, p. 467.

[18] White, Lyman C., *International Non-Governmental Organizations,* p. 258.

[19] For the development of the organizational structure of the ICSU and a description of its recent activities see Atwood, Wallace W., Jr., "International Council of Scientific Unions," *Science,* Vol. 128, December 19, 1958, pp. 1559-1561. An earlier article by the same author provides a more general historical sketch of international organizations concerned with research in the natural sciences, see Atwood, Wallace W., Jr., "United States Participation in International Scientific Organizations," *International Associations,* Vol. 4, April, 1956, pp. 242-250. This issue of *International Associations* contains seven other articles devoted to varying aspects of the subject, "International Non-Governmental Cooperation in the United States."

[20] See Appendix C - Members of International Councils, p. 267.

[21] See Appendix C - Members of International Councils, p. 267.

[22] *The First Six Years, 1953-1959, I.S.S.C.* UNESCO, Paris 1959. See also, *The Social Sciences.* Unesco and its Programme. Vol. XII, UNESCO, Paris, 1955, and *Appraisal of UNESCO's Programmes.* UNESCO, Paris, 1960.

[23] UNESCO has created other organizations which have no exact counterpart in the United States. The Council for International Organizations of Medical Sciences, for instance, set up in 1949, plays an important coordinating role for some 50 international medical-biological organizations.

[24] For an interesting discussion of whether or not an international Council should act as the sole intermediary between a member Union and UNESCO, see "Meetings of Representatives of National Social Science Councils and Similar Bodies," *International Social Science Council Bulletin,* Vol. VII, No. 2, 1955, pp. 319-325.

CHAPTER VII

[1] The discrepancy in assets between the American Philosophical Society, approximately $12,000,000, and American Academy of Arts and Sciences, approximately $2,000,000, could also be altered at the same time.

[2] Mumford, Lewis, *The City in History.* Harcourt, Brace and World, Inc., New York, 1961, pp. 551-552.

[3] For example, see Herring, Pendleton, "On Science and Polity," *Items,* Vol. 15, No. 1, Part 2, March, 1961, pp. 1-6 and "The Relationship Between the Humanities and Social Sciences," *ACLS Newsletter,* Vol. XII, No. 3, March, 1961, pp. 3-18.

[4] The actions of certain Soviet officials at the 1960 meeting of the International Congress of Orientalists, wherein several sessions were used as springboards for attacks on alleged American imperialism in the Orient, is an example of this attitude. See "A Report on the Organizational and Political Aspects of the XXVth

International Congress of Orientalists," *ACLS Newsletter,* Vol. XI, No. 10, December, 1960, pp. 3-6.

[5] The specialized learned societies are also bedeviled with what their position should be regarding regional and local societies in their respective disciplines. No clear-cut pattern of action has developed, some societies officially include them, some officially exclude them, and some do both. Thus, the American Historial Association includes as an affiliate the Pacific Historical Association but not the Mississippi Valley Historical Association or the Southern Historical Association.

Attitude and policy regarding local and regional affiliates or branches similarly varies.

[6] How often have academicians fulminated, in recent years, "Why don't we mimeograph the papers, circulate them in advance of the meeting or have them for distribution there, and devote all of our time to the more profitable business of meeting and convening with friends and colleagues in the lobbies and corridors of the hotels?"

[7] An often voiced antidote for this situation is the creation of small endowments or stable annual appropriations from governmental or other sources, to be used at the officers' discretion for emergency appropriations toward projects of a timely nature. Proponents believe that even very small amounts of money, if quickly brought to bear, can have a catalytic effect all out of proportion to their size.

The recent (1957) $60,000 appropriation of the Carnegie Corporation of New York to the American Council on Education for such purposes is pointed to as an example.

[8] Overhead or indirect costs are considered to be those costs arising from the use of facilities, such as libraries, office space, equipment, etc., which the organization receiving a grant must maintain and in some cases enlarge, and which are made use of by the personnel working under a grant. For a discussion of this problem, together with other problems connected with sponsored research, see *Sponsored Research Policy of Colleges and Universities.* American Council on Education, Washington, D. C., 1954.

[9] Several of the natural science societies and institutes, however, have been provided substantial aid by the larger industrial firms, and with no strings attached. Such support seems to indicate that the larger industries are recognizing their indebtedness to scholarly activity for scientific advances.

[10] For three recent works on this question, see Snow, C. P, *The Two Cultures and the Scientific Revolution.* Cambridge University Press, New York, 1959; Barzun, Jacques, *The House of Intellect.* Harper and Brothers, New York, 1959; de Huszar, George, edit., *The Intellectuals.* Free Press, Glencoe, Illinois, 1960— see particularly therein, Holton, Gerald, "Modern Science and the Intellectual Tradition," pp. 180-191. See also, Dupree, A. Hunter, "Public Education for Science and Technology," *Science,* Vol. 134, No. 3481, September 15, 1961, pp. 716-718.

[11] Apropos the latter, it is maintained that considerable governmental aid could be supplied all of the societies and their members by simply allowing such expenses as necessary professional expenses for income tax purposes. Similar expenses are presently deductible for business men attending their conventions and meetings; it does seem illogical that a manufacturer attending a meeting of the National Association of Manufacturers is able to deduct this expense while historians and

astronomers attending meetings of the American Historical Association or American Astronomical Society are unable to do so.

[12] For an interesting discussion of one aspect of this point, see Colvard, Richard, "Foundations and Professions: The Organizational Defense of Autonomy," *Administrative Science Quarterly,* Vol. 6, No. 2, September, 1961, pp. 167-184.

Professor Colvard is presently engaged in a broad scale study of the maintenance of their autonomous and independent position by donors and recipients of foundation aid.

[13] Oates, Whitney J., "An Evaluation of Graduate Work in the Humanities in the Land-Grant Institutions," address at the Centennial Convocation of the American Association of Land Grant Colleges and State Universities, November 15, 1961, Kansas City, Missouri. Mimeographed, pp. 16-17. See also, Lumiansky, Robert M., "Toward a Broader Definition of Federal Responsibility in Education," *ACLS Newsletter,* Vol. XIII, No. 1, January, 1962, pp. 1-6.

An admirable recent summation of the need for such support is to be found in Jones, Howard Mumford, *One Great Society: Humane Learning in the United States.* Harcourt, Brace, and Company, New York, 1959.

[14] Critics of the departmental system in our colleges and universities maintain that this system was the primary cause of specialized learned societies which, whatever their virtue at inception, have become a curse rather than a blessing. As an antidote they advocate the modification of the departmental system and the merging of the specialized societies.

As an example of what should be done at the university level they point to the Massachusetts Institute of Technology which, in its Second Century Program, is constructing five great interdisciplinary research centers where, although the physical facilities will be arranged by disciplines, the research conducted therein will be directed towards the solution of problems that can only be attacked on an interdisciplinary basis.

See Lessing, Lawrence, "MIT and the New Breed of Hairy Ears," *Fortune,* Vol. LXIII, No. 2, February, 1961, pp. 129-135; 172; 176; 178 for an interesting account of this program.

Another example they cite is the recently established Graduate Research Center of the Southwest. Located in Texas between Dallas and Fort Worth, the Center was brought into being to uplift the scientific competence of the entire Southwestern area of the United States. Research objectives rather than departmental or laboratory structure, however, were made the organizational foci. For a detailed statement about the Center, see Berkner, Lloyd V., "Renaissance in the Southwest," *Saturday Review,* June 3, 1961, pp. 42-47. See also, J. L. [Lear, John], "Engineer of the Intellect: John Erik Jonsson," *Saturday Review,* June 3, 1961, pp. 46-47.

[15] In 1954 the charter of the Rockefeller Institute was amended so as to make it a part of the University of the State of New York, with authority to grant advanced degrees. It is significant, however, that the Institute's *1960-61 Catalogue,* in the sections devoted to organization (p. 35) and research (p. 36), makes the points that:

"The Institute is not an aggregate of departments which deal with specialized fields of science and comprise scientific specialists. It is a community of scientific scholars, who are free to follow their interests in any field of scholarship. . . .

"One of the distinguishing characteristics of The Rockefeller Institute is the flexible and personal nature of its organization; it is built around individuals rather than departments. This provides freedom for faculty and students to study and do research in any field of science they choose without regard for the inhibiting restrictions of departmental barriers."

[16] For a description of the Center and its work see, Ashmore, Harry S., "The Thinking Man's Shelter," *Esquire,* Vol. LXII, No. 4, April, 1962, pp. 109-112.

[17] Note that during the presidential campaign of 1960, former Vice-President Richard M. Nixon issued a policy paper entitled, "The Scientific Revolution," Washington, D. C., September 8, 1960, Mimeographed. This paper, which was partially based on the work of a policy planning group of educators, endorsed the general concept of these institutes and advocated their creation in strategic spots all over the country.

[18] *Some Introductory Information.* Institute for Advanced Study, Princeton, N. J., undated pamphlet, p. 1.

[19] *Newsweek,* February 20, 1961, p. 52.

BIBLIOGRAPHY

GENERAL WORKS AND SURVEYS

Learned Journals. Many issues of learned journals, *Proceedings, Transactions, Records,* etc., of the learned societies, councils and institutes were consulted in the course of this study. Articles cited from these journals are included in Section IV of this Bibliography. Material of a more general nature, constitutions, by-laws, lists of officers, etc., when utilized, is not included in this Bibliography but appears as footnote citations in the preceding chapters.

Survey of Learned Societies. The results of an extensive survey of the humanistic-social science learned societies are filed in the offices of the American Council of Learned Societies. Assembled intermittently in the 1930's and 1940's by Waldo G. Leland and Mortimer Graves—this unpublished material is valuable for the historical background and development of these societies prior to World War II. Where information has been extracted from this source, a footnote citation to it has been made and such citations are not reproduced in this Bibliography.

A more general work by Ogg, Frederic A., *Research in the Humanistic and Social Sciences.* The Century Co., New York, 1928, parallels the foregoing *Survey* and is valuable not only for the historical development of the learned societies in all fields, but also for a description of the relationship then existing between them and the councils, institutes, foundations, universities, government and industry.

The World of the Mind. A series of articles for presentation on radio, prepared by Broadcast Music Incorporated in association with the American Council of Learned Societies and the American Association for the Advancement of Science, New York, 1958. The series included a number of historical articles about various learned societies.

Where information has been extracted from this source, a footnote citation to it has been made and such citations are not reproduced in this Bibliography.

Handbook of Learned Societies and Institutions. America. Publication No. 39, Carnegie Institution of Washington, Washington, D. C., 1908. An outdated work that is still valuable, however, for historical reference.

Two books, each published in several editions, were of especial value in the conduct of this study. They are: Bates, Ralph S., *Scientific Societies in the United States.* Second Edition. Columbia University Press, New York, 1958 and *Scientific and Technical Societies of the United States and Canada.* Seventh Edition. Publication 900. Compiled by John H. Gribbin and others. National Academy of Sciences-National Research Council, Washington, D. C., 1961.

REPORTS

American Council of Learned Societies, New York, 1920-1960.
American Council on Education, Washington, D. C., 1920-1960.
Bollingen Foundation, New York, 1945-1958.
Carnegie Corporation of New York, New York, 1922-1960.
Carnegie Foundation for the Advancement of Teaching, New York, 1906-1960.

246

Commonwealth Fund, New York, 1919-1960.

Falk Foundation, Maurice and Laura, Pittsburgh, Pennsylvania, 1933-1960.

Federal Funds for Science. Volumes I through IX, National Science Foundation, Government Printing Office, Washington, D. C., 1950 through 1960.

Field Foundation, New York, 1949-1960.

Ford Foundation, New York, 1951-1960.

Fund for the Advancement of Education, New York, 1952-1959.

General Education Board, New York, 1902-1960.

Laura Spelman Rockefeller Memorial, New York, 1919-1928.

Lilly Endowment, Indianapolis, Indiana, 1950-1960.

Macy Foundation, Josiah, Jr., New York, 1932-1960.

Markle Foundation, John and Mary R., New York, 1935-1960.

Mellon Educational and Charitable Trust, A. W., Pittsburgh, Pennsylvania, 1930-1960.

Milbank Memorial Fund, New York, 1922-1960.

National Academy of Sciences-National Research Council, Washington, D. C. 1863-1960.

National Science Foundation, Washington, D. C., 1950-1960.

New York Foundation, New York, 1949.

Old Dominion Foundation, New York, 1941-1958.

Rockefeller Brothers Fund, New York, 1954-1960.

Rockefeller Foundation, New York, 1913-1960.

Rockefeller Institute, 1960-61 Catalogue. Vol. 5, No. 2, The Rockefeller Institute, New York, 1961.

Rosenberg Foundation, San Francisco, California, 1946.

Russell Sage Foundation, New York, 1948-1960.

Sloan Foundation, Alfred P., New York, 1945-1960.

Social Science Research Council, New York, 1920-1960.

Spelman Fund of New York, New York, 1930-1949.

Twentieth Century Fund, New York, 1930-1960.

Wistar Institute of Anatomy and Biology, Philadelphia, 1958-59.

PAMPHLETS AND BULLETINS

A Brief Statement of the History and Activities of the American Council on Education. Published by American Council on Education, Washington, D.C., 1960.

ACLS Newsletter. Published monthly October through May by the American Council of Learned Societies, 1949-1960.

A Decade of Growth in Biology, 1948-1958. Information pamphlet published by the American Institute of Biological Sciences, Washington, D. C., Undated.

American Meteorological Society, Its Purposes, Its Activities, Its Organization. Published by the American Meteorological Society, Undated.

American Society of Zoologists. Information pamphlet published by the American Society of Zoologists, Undated.

An Introduction to the Institute of Mathematical Statistics. Published by the Institute of Mathematical Statisics, June 15, 1958.

Background Material—Federation of American Societies For Experimental Biology. Mimeographed. Federation of American Societies for Experimental Biology, Washington, D. C., July 20, 1960.

Blue Book. Information pamphlet of the American Academy of Arts and Sciences, Boston, Massachusetts, May, 1959.

Brigham, Clarence S., *American Antiquarian Society, Handbook of Information.* Published by the Society, Worcester, Massachusetts, 1909.

Bulletin of Information. Published by the American Geological Institute, Washington, D. C., June, 1960.

Bulletin of Information. Published by the American Institute of Physics, New York, New York, 1960.

Bulletin of Information. Published by the American Studies Association. Undated.

Bulletin of Information. Published by the Mathematical Association of America. Undated.

Bulletin of Information. Published by the Association for Symbolic Logic. 1935, 1938, and 1951.

Directory of Officers and Activities for 1961. American Association for the Advancement of Science, Washington, D. C., 1961.

The First Six Years, 1953-1959, I.S.S.C. UNESCO, Paris, 1959.

Handbook-Directory. Published by the Association of American Geographers, Washington, D. C., 1961.

Handbook of Information. Published by the American Numismatic Society, New York, 1952.

Information Pamphlet. Published by the American Economic Association, Evanston, Illinois, 1954.

Items. Published quarterly by the Social Science Research Council, 1947-1960.

The Rockefeller Institute, 1960-61 Catalogue. Vol. 5, No. 2, The Rockefeller Institute, New York, 1961.

Some Introductory Information. Institute for Advanced Study, Princeton, New Jersey, Undated.

Summarized Statement of Activities, 1889-1927. Published by the American Academy of Political and Social Science, Undated.

ARTICLES AND BOOKS

Adams, John, *Works.* C. F. Adams, edit., Volumes I-IV, Boston, Massachusetts, 1851-1856.

The Aims, Methods and Activity of the League of Nations. Secretariat of the League of Nations, Geneva, Switzerland, 1935.

Aldrich, H. R., "The Geological Society of America," *AAAS Bulletin,* Vol. 2, No. 6, June, 1943, pp. 43-44.

"The American Physical Society," *Physics Today,* Vol. 4, No. 10, October, 1951, pp. 18-19.

"American Society for Aesthetics: Historical Note," *Journal of Aesthetics and Art Criticism,* Vol. IV, No. 1, pp. 60-61.

"American Statistical Association," *AAAS Bulletin,* Vol. 3, No. 8, August, 1944, pp. 63-64.

Andrade, E. N. da C., *A Brief History of the Royal Society.* The Royal Society, London, 1960.

Andrews, F. Emerson, *Philanthropic Foundations.* Russell Sage Foundation, New York, 1956.

Angell, James R., "The Organization of Research in Our American Democracy,"

Proceedings of the Institute of Medicine of Chicago, March 5, 1920, pp. 1-18.

Appraisal of UNESCO's Programmes. UNESCO, Paris, France, 1960.

Archibald, Raymond C., *A Semicentennial History of the American Mathematical Society, 1888-1938.* American Mathematical Society Semicentennial Publications, Vol. I, History, New York, 1938.

Asher, Robert E., and Associates, *The U. N. and the Promotion of the General Welfare.* Brookings Institution, Washington, D. C., 1957.

Ashmore, Harry S., "The Thinking Man's Shelter," *Esquire,* Vol. LVII, No. 4, April, 1962, pp. 109-112.

Atwood, Wallace W., Jr., "United States Participation in International Scientific Organizations," *International Associations,* Vol. 4, April, 1956, pp. 242-250.

Atwood, Wallace W., Jr., "International Council of Scientific Unions," *Science,* Vol. 128, December 19, 1958, pp. 1558-1561.

Bannister, Turpin C., Brief Historical Summary of the Society of Architectural Historians, Unpublished.

Bardeen, Charles R., *Anatomy in America.* Bulletin of the University of Wisconsin, No. 115. Science Series. Vol. 3, No. 4, September, 1905, Madison, Wisconsin.

Barfield, Arthur O., "The Rediscovery of Meaning," *Saturday Evening Post,* Vol. 234, No. 1, January 7, 1961, pp. 36-37, 61, 64-65.

Barton, Henry A., and George H. Burnham, "The American Institute of Physics," *Science,* Vol. 97, No. 2512, February 19, 1943, pp. 172-176.

Barton, Henry A., "The Story of the American Institute of Physics," *Physics Today,* Vol. 9, No. 1, January, 1956, pp. 46-60.

Barzun, Jacques, *The House of Intellect.* Harper and Brothers, New York, 1959.

Bauer, Louis A., "The Organization and Aims of the American Geophysical Union," *Bulletin, National Research Council,* Vol. 7, Part 5, No. 41, January, 1924, pp. 7-18.

Baxter, James Phinney, 3rd, *Scientists Against Time.* Little, Brown and Company, Boston, Massachusetts, 1946.

Bedell, Frederick, "What Led to the Founding of the American Physical Society," *Physical Review,* Vol. 75, Second Series, May 15, 1949, pp. 1601-1604.

Bennett, Alvin Le Roy, *The Development of Intellectual Cooperation Under the League of Nations and United Nations.* University Microfilms, Ann Arbor, Michigan, 1950.

Berkner, Lloyd V., *Science and Foreign Relations; International Flow of Scientific and Technological Information.* International Science Policy Survey Group, Washington, D. C., 1950.

Berkner, Lloyd V., "Renaissance in the Southwest," *Saturday Review,* June 3, 1961, pp. 42-47.

Betz, Frederick, Jr., "The Geological Society of America," *Geo Times,* Vol. V., No. 8, May-June, 1961, pp. 18-23; 46-47.

Bidez, Joseph, "L'Union Académique Internationale de Son Origine a 1939," *Coup D'Oeil Sur Les Vingt-Cinq Premierés Sessions Du Comite, 1920-1950,* Union Academique Internationale, Bruxelles, Belgique, 1951, pp. 4-11.

Binkley, Robert C., "World Intellectual Organization," *Educational Record,* Vol. XX, No. 2, April, 1939, pp. 256-262.

Bliss, G. A., "Herbert Ellsworth Slaught-Teacher and Friend," *The American Mathematical Monthly,* Vol. XLV, January, 1938, pp. 5-10.

Bloomfield, Leonard, "Why a Linguistic Society," *Language,* Vol. 1, March, 1925, pp. 1-5.

Bloomfield, Maurice, "Fifty Years of Comparative Philology in America," *Transactions and Proceedings, American Philological Association,* Vol. L, 1919.

Boas, Franz, "The American Ethnological Society," *Science,* New Series, Vol. XCVII, January 1, 1943, pp. 7-8.

Bradner, Leicester, "Renaissance Scholarship in America," *Renaissance News,* Vol. VII, No. 1, Spring, 1954, pp. 1-5.

"A Brief History of the Association—From Its Founding in 1848 to 1948," *Summarized Proceedings and Directory, 1940-1948,* American Association for the Advancement of Science. Washington, D. C., 1948, pp. 1-19.

Brigham, Albert P., "The Association of American Geographers, 1903-1923," *Annals of the Association of American Geographers,* Vol. XIV, No. 3, September, 1924, pp. 109-116.

Brooks, Charles F., "The Society's First Quarter Century," *Weatherwise,* Vol. 12, No. 6, December, 1959, pp. 223-230.

Brouwer, Dirk, "One Hundred Years: 1849-1949," *The Astronomical Journal,* Vol. 55, No. 1, December, 1949, No. 1181, pp. 1-2.

Brown, Carleton, "A Survey of the First Half-Century," *Publications of the Modern Language Association of America,* Vol. XLVIII, Supplement, 1933, pp. 1409-1422.

Brown, Ralph H., "The Association of American Geographers," *AAAS Bulletin,* Vol. 2, No. 11, November, 1943, pp. 87-88.

Browne, Charles A., edit., "A Half-Century of Chemistry in America, 1876-1926", *Journal of the American Chemical Society,* Special Issue, Vol. 48, No. 8 A, Easton, Pennsylvania, 1926.

Browne, Charles A., and Mary Elvira Weeks, *A History of the American Chemical Society, Seventy-Five Eventful Years.* American Chemical Society, Washington, D. C., 1952.

Burgess, Charles F., "Early Days in our Society," *Transactions, American Electrochemical Society,* Vol. 82, 1942, pp. 16-27.

Burke, W. L. M., "Early Years of the College Art Association," *College Art Journal,* Vol. 1, No. 4, May, 1942, pp. 100-104.

Burkholder, Paul R., "The Botanical Society of America, Inc.," *AAAS Bulletin,* Vol. 2, No. 8, August, 1943, pp. 61-62.

Burns, R. M., "The First Decade; An Account of the Founding and Early Days of the Society," *Journal, American Electrochemical Society,* Vol. 99, No. 1, January, 1952, pp. 9c-16c.

Bush, Vannevar, *Science, the Endless Frontier.* Government Printing Office, Washington, D. C., 1945.

Cairns, W. D., "Herbert Ellsworth Slaught—Editor and Organizer," *The American Mathematical Monthly,* Vol. XLV, January, 1938, pp. 1-4.

Cairns, W. D., "Mathematics in Education," *AAAS Bulletin,* Vol. 3, No. 1, January, 1944, pp. 7-8.

Cannon, Paul R., "Editorials," *A. M. A. Archives of Pathology,* Vol. 62, No. 3, September, 1956, p. 173.

Chandler, Asa C., "The Making of a Parasitologist," *Journal of Parasitology,* Vol. 32, No. 3, June, 1946, pp. 213-221.

Cheever, Daniel S., and H. Field Haviland, Jr., *Organizing for Peace.* Houghton-Mifflin Company, Cambridge, Massachusetts, 1954.

Chittenden, Russell H., *The First Twenty-Five Years of the American Society of Biological Chemists.* New Haven, Connecticut, 1945. Printed by the Waverly Press, Baltimore, Maryland.

Clark, Eliot, *History of the National Academy of Design, 1825-1953.* Columbia University Press, New York, 1954.

Clarke, Hans T., "The Journal of Biological Chemistry," *Journal of Biological Chemistry,* Vol. 216, No. 2, October, 1955, pp. 449-454.

Cloud, Preston E., Jr., "Paleoecology—Retrospect and Prospect," *Journal of Paleontology,* Vol. 33, No. 5, September, 1959, pp. 926-962.

Coca, A. F., An unpublished historical summary of the *Journal of Immunology,* 1950. In the possession of Dr. Geoffrey Edsall.

Coffman, George R., "The Mediaeval Academy of America: Historical Background and Prospect," *Speculum,* Vol. I, January, 1926, pp. 5-18.

Cohen, Barnett, *Chronicles of the Society of American Bacteriologists, 1899-1950.* Williams and Wilkins Company, Baltimore, Maryland, 1950.

Colby, Charles C., "Changing Currents of Geographic Thought in America," *Annals of the Association of American Geographers,* Vol. XXVI, No. 1, March, 1936, pp. 1-37.

Colligan, Francis J., *Twenty Years After: Two Decades of Government-Sponsored Cultural Relations.* Department of State, Washington, D. C., 1958.

Colvard, Richard, "Foundations and Professions: The Organizational Defense of Autonomy," *Administrative Science Quarterly,* Vol. 6, No. 2, September, 1961, pp. 167-184.

"Congratulatory Messages on the 50th Anniversary of the American Society of Biological Chemists," *Federation Proceedings,* Vol. 15, No. 2, July, 1956, pp. 795-799.

Conklin, Edwin G. "Fifty Years of the American Society of Naturalists," *The American Naturalist,* Vol. LXVIII, No. 718, September-October, 1934, pp. 385-401.

Conklin, Edwin G., "A Brief History of the American Philosophical Society," *Year Book, American Philosophical Society,* January 1, 1947-December 31, 1947, pp. 7-26.

Consolidated Report Upon Activities of the National Research Council, 1919-1932. Mimeographed. National Academy of Sciences-National Research Council, Washington, D. C., 1932.

Cort, W. W., "Professor Henry Baldwin Ward and the Journal of Parasitology," *Journal of Parasitology,* Vol. XIX, No. 2, December, 1932, pp. 99-105.

Cowgill, George R., "John R. Murlin—Honor Volume," *Journal of Nutrition,* Vol. 31, No. 1, January, 1946, pp. 3-4.

Cox, Hiden T., "The AIBS After Ten Years," *AIBS Bulletin,* Vol. IX, No. 5, November, 1959, pp. 19-21.

Cram, Eloise B., "Stepping Stones in the History of the American Society of Parasitologists," *Journal of Parasitology,* Vol. 42, No. 5, October, 1956, pp. 461-473.

Crane, Robert I., "The First Ten Years of the Association for Asian Studies, 1948-58," *Journal of Asian Studies,* Vol. XVII, August, 1958, pp. 657-675.

Croneis, Carey, "Geology in War and Peace," *Bulletin, American Association of Petroleum Geologists,* Vol. 27, No. 7, 1942, pp. 1221-1249.

Culbertson, J. T., "American Society of Parasitologists," *AAAS Bulletin,* Vol. 3, No. 6, June, 1944, pp. 47-48.

Cummings, Thomas S., *Historic Annals of the National Academy of Design, 1825-1863.* Philadelphia, Pennsylvania, 1865.

Dark, Harris Jeremiah, *The Life and Works of Herbert Ellsworth Slaught.* George Peabody College for Teachers, Nashville, Tennessee, 1948.

Davis, Malcolm W., "The League of Minds," *Pioneers in World Order.* Edited by Harriett E. Davis. Columbia University Press, New York, 1944, pp. 240-249.

de Huszar, George, edit., *The Intellectuals.* Free Press, Glencoe, Illinois, 1960.

de Laguna, Frederica, edit., *Selected Papers From the American Anthropologist, 1888-1920.* Evanston, Illinois, 1960.

Dercum, Francis X., "The Origin and Activities of the American Philosophical Society and an Address on the Dynamic Factor in Evolution," *Proceedings, American Philosophical Society,* Vol. 66, 1927, pp. 19-46.

Deuel, Harry J., Jr., "Biography of Graham Lusk," *Journal of Nutrition,* Vol. 41, No. 1, May, 1950, pp. 3-12.

Dickson, James G., "American Institute of Biological Sciences, A Progress Report," *AIBS Bulletin,* Vol. IX, No. 1, January, 1959, pp. 15-16.

Divisia, Francois, "La Societe D'Econometrica A Atteint Sa Majorite," *Econometrica,* Vol. 21, No. 1, January, 1953, pp. 1-30.

Dreyer, William A., "The Ecological Society of America," *AAAS Bulletin,* Vol. 4, No. 2, February, 1945, pp. 15-16.

Dubois, Eugene F., "Prefatory Chapter, Fifty Years of Physiology in America," *Annual Review of Physiology,* Vol. XII, 1950, pp. 1-7.

Duff, A. Wilmer, "Arthur Gordon Webster—Physicist, Mathematician, Linguist and Orator," *The American Physics Teacher,* Vol. 6, No. 4, August, 1938, pp. 181-194.

Dunbar, Carl O., "A Half Century of Paleontology," *Journal of Paleontology,* Vol. 33, No. 5, September, 1959, pp. 909-914.

Dunn, Leslie C., edit., *Genetics in the 20th Century.* Macmillan Company, New York, 1951.

Dupree, A. Hunter, *Science in the Federal Government.* Harvard University Press, Cambridge, Massachusetts, 1957.

Dupree, A. Hunter, "Public Education for Science and Technology," *Science,* Vol. 134, No. 3481, September 15, 1961, pp. 716-718.

Eckhardt, E. A., "More About AGI History," *Geo Times,* Vol. III, No. 3, October, 1958, pp. 22-25.

Economic Theory and Measurement; a Twenty Year Research Report, 1932-1952. Published by Cowles Commission for Research in Economics, 1952.

Edsall, Geoffrey, "What is Immunology," *Journal of Immunology,* Vol. 67, No. 2, August, 1951, pp. 167-172.

Edwards, Agnes, "The Library of the American Antiquarian Society," *Massachusetts Magazine,* Vol. IX, No. 1, January, 1916, pp. 5-14.

Eggan, Fred, "The American Anthropological Association," *AAAS Bulletin,* Vol. 2, No. 5, May, 1943, p. 38.

Elmore, Jefferson, "The Philological Association of the Pacific Coast," *Transactions and Proceedings, American Philological Association,* Vol. L, 1919.

Ely, Richard T., "The Founding and Early History of the American Economic

Association," *American Economic Review,* Vol. XXVI, No. 1, Supplement, March, 1936, pp. 141-150.

Fairchild, Herman L., "The History of the American Association for the Advancement of Science," *Science,* Vol. LIX, No. 1530, April 25, 1924, pp. 365-369; No. 1531, May 2, 1924, pp. 385-390; and No. 1532, May 9, 1924, pp. 410-415.

Fairchild, Herman L., *The Geological Society of America, 1888-1930.* Published by the Society, New York, 1932.

Fernberger, Samuel W., "The American Psychological Association; A Historical Summary, 1892-1930," *Psychological Bulletin,* Vol. XXIX, 1932, pp. 1-89.

Fernberger, Samuel W., "American Psychological Association, 1892-1942," *Psychological Review,* Vol. 50, No. 1, January, 1943, pp. 33-60.

Fiske, Thomas S., "Mathematical Progress in America," *Bulletin, American Mathematical Society,* Vol. XI, February, 1905, pp. 238-246. This article also appears in *Science,* New Series, Vol. 21, February 10, 1905, pp. 209-215.

Fite, Emerson D., *Social and Industrial Conditions in the North During the Civil War.* Macmillan Company, New York, 1910.

Fitzpatrick, Paul J., "The Early Teaching of Statistics in American Colleges and Universities," *The American Statistician,* Vol. 9, No. 5, December, 1955.

Fitzpatrick, Paul J., "Statistical Works in Early American Statistics Courses," *The American Statistician,* Vol. 10, No. 5, December, 1956.

Fitzpatrick, Paul J., "Statistical Societies in the United States in the Nineteenth Century," *The American Statistician,* Vol. 11, No. 5, December, 1957.

Fleming, John A., "Origin and Development of the American Geophysical Union," *Transactions, American Geophysical Union,* Vol. 35, No. 1, February, 1954, pp. 5-46.

"The Formation of the American Society of Parasitologists," *Journal of Parasitology,* Vol. XI, No. 3, March, 1925, pp. 177-180.

Fosdick, Raymond B., *The Story of the Rockefeller Foundation.* Harper and Brothers, New York, 1952.

Franklin, Benjamin, *The Writings of Benjamin Franklin.* A. H. Smyth, edit., Macmillan Company, New York, 1907.

Franklin, Benjamin, *Autobiography.* Edited by Carl Van Doren. New York, Viking Press, 1945.

Frisch, Ragnar, "Editorial," *Econometrica,* Vol. 1, No. 1, January, 1933, pp. 1-4.

Gardiner, H. N., "The First Twenty-Five Years of the American Philosophical Association," *Philosophical Review,* Vol. XXXV, March, 1926, pp. 145-158.

Geiling, E. M. K., "Milestones in the Life of John J. Abel," Unpublished paper presented at a Seminar, Army Chemical Center, Edgewood, Maryland, November 13, 1959.

Gerard, R. W., "By-ways of Investigators: Thoughts on Becoming an Elder Statesman," *American Journal of Physiology,* Vol. 171, No. 3, December, 1952, pp. 695-703.

Gies, W. J., "American Society of Biological Chemists," *Science,* New Series, Vol. 25, No. 630, January 25, 1907, pp. 139-142.

Goode, G. Brown, "The Origin of the National Scientific and Educational Institutions of the United States," *Annual Report, American Historical Association, 1889,* Senate Miscellaneous Documents, 51st Congress, 1st Session, Vol. 4, 1889-1890, Government Printing Office, Washington, D. C., 1890.

Goode, G. Brown, "The First National Scientific Congress and its Connection with the Organization of the American Association," *Proceedings, American Association for the Advancement of Science,* Vol. XL, 1891, pp. 39-47.

Goodspeed, Stephen S., *The Nature and Function of International Organization.* Oxford University Press, New York, 1959.

Gray, George W., *Science at War.* Harper and Brothers, New York, 1943.

Greaves, H. R. C., *The League Committees and World Order.* Oxford University Press, London, 1931.

Hale, George E., "The International Organization of Scientific Research," *International Conciliation,* No. 154, September, 1920, pp. 431-441.

Hale, William H., "Early Years of the American Association," *Appleton's Popular Science Monthly,* Vol. XLIX, No. 4, August, 1896, pp. 501-507.

Harrison, George R., "Twenty Years of Age," *Physics Today,* Vol. 4, No. 10, October, 1951, pp. 12-13. This same issue contains brief histories of the American Institute of Physics and its five member societies, see pp. 14-27.

Hering, Carl, "The American Electrochemical Society," *Transactions, American Electrochemical Society,* Vol. XI, 1907, pp. 17-41.

Herring, Pendleton, "On Science and Polity," *Items,* Vol. 15, No. 1, Part 2, March, 1961, pp. 1-6.

Himstead, Ralph E., "Education and the Peace," *AAUP Bulletin,* Vol. 31, No. 3, Autumn, 1945, pp. 466-506.

Hiss, Priscilla, and Roberta Fansler, *Research in Fine Arts in the Colleges and Universities of the United States.* Carnegie Corporation of New York, New York, 1934.

"Historical Review," *Anatomical Record,* Vol. 11, No. 6, January, 1917, pp. 546-554.

Historical Scholarship in America. A Report of the Committee of the American Historical Association on the Planning of Research. Ray Long and Richard R. Smith, Inc., New York, 1932.

"History of the American Social Science Association in a Letter to Its Present Secretary, I. F. Russell, New York, by F. B. Sanborn of Concord, Massachusetts, a Founder," *The American Journal of Sociology,* Vol. XV, No. 5, March, 1910, pp. 592-595.

A History of the National Research Council, 1919-1933. Reprint and Circular Series of the National Research Council, No. 106, National Academy of Sciences-National Research Council, Washington, D. C., 1933.

Hitchcock, C. H., "Supplementary Note on the Organization of the Geological Society of America," *Bulletin, Geological Society of America,* Vol. 21, December 31, 1910, pp. 741-746.

Holton, Gerald, "Modern Science and the Intellectual Tradition," *The Intellectuals.* Edited by George de Huszar, Free Press, Glencoe, Illinois, pp. 180-191.

Howard, L. O., *A History of Applied Entomology.* Publication 3065. Smithsonian Institution, Washington, D. C., 1930.

Howe, Henry V., "Fifty Years of Micropaleontology," *Journal of Paleontology,* Vol. 33, No. 3, May, 1959, pp. 511-517.

Howell, William H., and Charles W. Greene, *History of the American Physiological Society, Semicentennial, 1887-1937.* Baltimore, Maryland, 1938.

Hull, L. W. H., *History and Philosophy of Science.* Longmans, Green, and Company, London, 1959.

Hunter, Ralph M., "The Electrochemical Society—Past and Future," *Journal, American Electrochemical Society,* Vol. 99, No. 7, July, 1952, pp. 155c-157c.

Hutchisson, Elmer, "AIP Annual Report, 1959," *Physics Today,* Vol. 13, No. 5, May, 1960, pp. 16-25.

Hylander, Clarence J., "The American Institute of Biological Sciences: A Historical Resume," *AIBS Bulletin,* Vol. 1, No. 1, January, 1951, pp. 6-8 and Vol. 1, No. 2, April, 1951, pp. 13-15.

"The Institute of Mathematical Statistics," *AAAS Bulletin,* Vol. 4, No. 3, March, 1945, pp. 23-24.

"The International Association of Academies," *Nature,* Vol. LXII, July 12, 1890, pp. 249-250.

The 1978 International Organizations Founded Since the Congress of Vienna. Document No. 7, Union of International Associations, Brussels, Belgium, 1957.

Jameson, J. Franklin, "The American Historical Association, 1884-1909," *The American Historical Review,* Vol. XV, No. 1, October, 1909, pp. 1-20.

Jameson, J. Franklin, "The American Historical Review, 1895-1920," *The American Historical Review,* Vol. XXVI, October, 1920, pp. 1-17.

Jewett, Frank B., "The Genesis of the National Research Council and Millikan's World War I Work," *Review of Modern Physics,* Vol. 20, No. 1, January, 1948, pp. 1-6.

Jones, H. Spencer, "The Early History of ICSU, 1919-1946," *ICSU Review,* Vol. 2, No. 4, October, 1960, pp. 169-187.

Jones, Howard Mumford, *One Great Society: Humane Learning in the United States.* Harcourt, Brace and Company, New York, 1959.

Just, Theodor, "Progress in Paleobotany," *Journal of Paleontology,* Vol. 33, No. 3, May, 1959, pp. 500-510.

H. T. K. [Howard T. Karsner], "Obituary—Richard Mills Pearce, Jr., M.D., 1874-1930," *Archives of Pathology,* Vol. 9, No. 3, March, 1930, pp. 714-716.

Kaufmann, B. P., "Genetics Society of America," *AAAS Bulletin,* Vol. 3, No. 7, July, 1944, pp. 55-56.

Kellogg, Vernon, "The National Research Council," *International Conciliation,* No. 154, September, 1920, pp. 423-430.

Kiger, Joseph C., *Operating Principles of the Larger Foundations.* Russell Sage Foundation, New York, 1954.

Kiger, Joseph C., "The Four Councils," *Educational Record,* Vol. XXXIX, October, 1958, pp. 367-373.

Kiger, Joseph C., "The American Society of Parasitologists: A Short History," *Journal of Parasitology,* Vol. 48, No. 5. October, 1962, pp. 641-650.

King, Willford I., "The Annals of Mathematical Statistics," *Annals of Mathematical Statistics,* Vol. 1, No. 1. February, 1930, pp. 1-2.

Kline, J. R., "American Mathematical Society," *AAAS Bulletin,* Vol. 2, No. 5, May, 1943, pp. 36-38.

Kopf, Edwin W., "American Statistical Association," *Proceedings of the Casualty Actuarial Society,* Vol. XI, Part 1, November 20, 1924, pp. 129-131.

Kraft, Charles F., "The Society of Biblical Literature and Exegesis, A Short Descriptive Article," Mimeographed, 2 pages, 1956.

Leach, MacEdward, "American Folklore Society," *Standard Dictionary of Folklore, Mythology, and Legend.* Edited by Maria Leach. Vol. I, Funk and Wagnalls Company, New York, 1949, pp. 48-49.

J. L. [Lear, John], "Engineer of the Intellect: John Erik Jonsson," *Saturday Review,* June 3, 1961, pp. 46-47.

Leavens, Dickson H., "The Econometric Society," *AAAS Bulletin,* Vol. 4, No. 7, July, 1945, p. 55.

Lecky, W. E. H., *History of the Rise and Influence of the Spirit of Rationalism in Europe.* Longman, Green, Longman, Roberts, and Green, 2 Volumes, London, 1865.

Leland, Waldo, G., "The International Union of Academies and the American Council of Learned Societies," *International Conciliation,* No. 154, September, 1920, pp. 442-457.

Leonard, L. Larry, *International Organization.* McGraw-Hill Book Company, Inc., New York, 1951.

Lessing, Lawrence, "MIT and the New Breed of Hairy Ears," *Fortune,* Vol. LXIII, No. 2, February, 1961, pp. 129-135; 172; 176; 178.

Linsley, E. G., "Consolidation of the Entomological Society of America and the American Association of Economic Entomologists," *Annals, Entomological Society of America,* Vol. 45, No. 2, June, 1952, p. 359.

Long, Esmond R., Manuscript history of American Pathology.

Long, Percy W., "The Association in Review," *Publications of the Modern Language Association of America,* 1948 Proceedings. Vol. LXIV, Supplement, Part 2, March, 1949, pp. 1-12.

Luck, J. Murray, "Introductory Remarks," *Federation Proceedings,* Vol. 15, No. 2, July, 1956, pp. 793-794.

Ludlum, David M., "The American Meteorological Society," *Weatherwise,* Vol. 12, No. 6, December, 1959, pp. 231-245.

Lumiansky, Robert M., "Toward a Broader Definition of Federal Responsibility in Education," *ACLS Newsletter,* Vol. XIII, No. 1, January, 1962, pp. 1-6.

Lyons, Henry, *The Royal Society, 1660-1940.* Cambridge University Press, Cambridge, England, 1944.

MacIver, Robert M., *The Nations and the United Nations.* Manhattan Publishing Company, New York, 1959.

McLaughlin, Dean B., "The American Astronomical Society," *AAAS Bulletin,* Vol. 2, No. 10, October, 1943, pp. 77-78.

Mangone, Gerard J., *A Short History of International Organization.* McGraw-Hill Book Company, Inc., New York, 1954.

Manly, John M., "New Bottles," *Publications of the Modern Language Association of America,* Vol. XXVI, 1921, pp. xlvi-lx.

Mather, Kirtley F., "Geology, Geologists, and the AAAS," *Science,* Vol. 129, No. 1108, April 24, 1959, pp. 1106-1111.

Meek, W. J., "The American Physiological Society," *AAAS Bulletin,* Vol. 4, No. 6, June, 1945, pp. 47-48.

"Meetings of Representatives of National Social Science Councils and Similar Bodies," *International Social Science Council Bulletin,* Vol. VII, No. 2, 1955, pp. 319-325.

Merritt, Ernest, "Early Days of the Physical Society," *The Review of Scientific Instruments,* Vol. 5, New Series, April, 1934, pp. 143-149.

Michels, Nicholas A., "The American Association of Anatomists, A Sketch of its Origin, Aims, and Meetings," *Anatomical Record,* Vol. 122, No. 4, August, 1955, pp. 679-714.

Mickel, Clarence E., "The Entomological Society of America," *AAAS Bulletin,* Vol. 2, No. 6, June, 1943, pp. 44-45.

Some Milestones in the History of Science to 1800. Linda Hall Library, Kansas City, Missouri, 1956.

Millikan, Robert A., *Autobiography.* Prentice-Hall, New York, 1950.

Miscellaneous Papers of the National Research Council. Series A. Volumes 1 and 2, 1916-1920; Series B. Volumes 1 and 2, 1916-1920, National Academy of Sciences-National Research Council, Washington, D. C.

Moe, Henry Allen, "Tercentenary of the Royal Society," *Science,* Vol. 132, No. 3442, December 16, 1960, pp. 1816-1822.

Moore, Barrington, "The Beginnings of Ecology," *Ecology,* Vol. 19, No. 4, October, 1938, p. 592.

Moore, Frank Gardner, "History of the American Philological Association," *Transactions and Proceedings, American Philological Association,* Vol. L, 1919, pp. 5-32.

Moulton, Forest R., "The American Association for the Advancement of Science —A Brief Historical Sketch," *Science,* Vol. 108, No. 2801, September 3, 1948, pp. 217-218.

Mueller, Justus F., "The Society Seal," *Journal of Parasitology,* Vol. 46, No. 1, February, 1960, pp. 112-115.

Mueller, Justus F., "The Henry Baldwin Ward Medal," *Journal of Parasitology,* Vol. 47, No. 2, April, 1961, pp. 206-208.

Mumford, Lewis, *The City in History.* Harcourt, Brace and World, Inc., New York, 1961.

Murlin, John R., "Editorial—Transfer of the Journal of Nutrition to the Wistar Institute," *Journal of Nutrition,* Vol. 7, No. 3, March, 1934, pp. 365-366.

Nasset, E. S., "John Raymond Murlin—Investigator, Teacher, Colleague," *Journal of Nutrition,* Vol. 31, No. 1, January, 1946, pp. 5-12.

"National Academy of Sciences to 1917," *AAAS Bulletin,* Vol. 2, No. 7, July, 1943, pp. 52-54.

Newell, Norman D., "Adequacy of the Fossil Record," *Journal of Paleontology,* Vol. 33, No. 3, May, 1959, pp. 488-499.

Nicholas, H. G., *The United Nations As a Political Institution.* Oxford University Press, London, 1959.

Nixon, Richard M., "The Scientific Revolution," Washington, D. C., September 8, 1960, Mimeographed.

Northrop, Filer S. C., *The Taming of the Nations; A Study of the Cultural Bases of International Policy.* Macmillan Company, New York, 1952.

"Notice of the Organization of the Institute of Mathematical Statistics," *Annals of Mathematical Statistics,* Vol. VI, No. 4, December, 1935, p. 227.

Oates, Whitney J., "An Evaluation of Graduate Work in the Humanities in the Land-Grant Institutions," address at the Centennial Convocation of the American Association of Land-Grant Colleges and State Universities, November 15, 1961, Kansas City, Missouri, Mimeographed, pp. 1-18.

Oehser, Paul H., *Sons of Science, The Story of the Smithsonian Institution and its Leaders.* Henry Schuman, New York, 1949.

Ornstein, Martha, *The Role of Scientific Societies in the Seventeenth Century.* University of Chicago Press, Chicago, Illinois, 1938.

Osborn, C. S., and Stellanova Osborn, "Schoolcraft and the American Ethnological Society," *Science,* New Series, Vol. XCVII, February 12, 1943, pp. 161-162.

Osborn, Herbert, *Fragments of Entomological History.* Published by the author, Columbus, Ohio, 1937.

Paine, Nathaniel, *An Account of the American Antiquarian Society.* Charles Hamilton, Worcester, Massachusetts, 1876.

Parker, William R., "The MLA, 1883-1953," *Publications of the Modern Language Association of America,* Vol. LXVIII, No. 4, Part 2, September, 1953, pp. 3-39.

Parr, Leland, W., "The Society of American Bacteriologists," *AAAS Bulletin,* Vol. 5, No. 4, April, 1946, pp. 30-31.

Parsons, Charles L., "The Activities of the American Chemical Society, A Half-Century of Chemistry in America, 1870-1926," *Journal of the American Chemical Society,* Edited by Charles A. Browne, Vol. 48, No. 8A, Easton, Pennsylvania, 1926, p. 48.

Parsons, Charles L., "The American Chemical Society," *AAAS Bulletin,* Vol. 2, No. 4, April, 1943, pp. 29-31.

Pound, Louise, "Then and Now," *Publications of the Modern Language Association of America,* Vol. LXXI, No. 1, March, 1956, pp. 3-13.

"Preface," *Annual Review of Entomology,* Vol. 4, 1959, pp. V-VI.

Price, Don K., *Government and Science.* New York University Press, New York, 1954.

Price, Don K., J. Stefan Dupre, and W. Eric Gustafson, "Current Trends in Science Policy in the United States," *Impact of science on society,* Vol. 10, No. 3, 1960, pp. 187-213.

Pritchard, Earl H., "The Association for Asian Studies, Inc., A Brief History," *Journal of Asian Studies,* Vol. XVI, August, 1957, pp. 679-680.

"Proceedings of the First Annual Meeting of the American Institute of Nutrition," *Journal of Nutrition,* Vol. 7, No. 5, Supplement, May, 1934, pp. 1-8.

"Proceedings of the preliminary and first annual meetings, first constitution and by-laws, and list of first officers and members of the Paleontological Society," *Bulletin of the Geological Society of America,* Vol. 21, March 31, 1910, pp. 69-86.

Rand, Edward K., "Editor's Preface," *Speculum,* Vol. I, January, 1926, pp. 3-4.

Reeves, Jesse S., "Perspectives in Political Science, 1903-1928," *The American Political Science Review,* Vol. XXIII, No. 1, February, 1929, pp. 1-16.

"The Relationship Between the Humanities and Social Sciences," *ACLS Newsletter,* Vol. XII, No. 3, March, 1961, pp. 3-18.

"Renaissance Society of America, an Account of the Executive Board," *Renaissance News,* Vol. VII, No. 1, Spring, 1954, pp. 7-11.

"Report and Recommendation of the Special Committee on the Scope of Research of the American Sociological Society," *Publication and Proceedings of the American Sociological Society,* Vol. XXVI, No. 2, June, 1932, pp. 1-39.

"Report of the Committee on Publications, American Society of Zoologists," *Anatomical Record,* Vol. 20, No. 2, January, 1921, pp. 166-169.

"Report of the Organization and Proceedings," *Papers of the American Historical Association,* Vol. I, No. 1, G. P. Putnam's Sons, New York, 1885.

Report of the Study for the Ford Foundation on Policy and Program. The Ford Foundation, Detroit, Michigan, 1949.

"A Report on the Organizational and Political Aspects of the XXVth International Congress of Orientalists," *ACLS Newsletter,* Vol. XI, No. 10, December, 1960, pp. 3-6.

Richards, A. N., Donald D. Van Slyke, and R. J. Anderson, *The Journal of Biological Chemistry, 1905-1953.* Privately published, 1953.

Richards, A. N., "Journal of Biological Chemistry: Recollections of its Early Years and of its Founders," *Federation Proceedings,* Vol. 15, No. 2, July, 1956, pp. 803-806.

Richardson, R. G. D., "American Mathematical Society," *Proceedings, Casualty Actuarial Society,* Vol. XI, Part 1, No. 20, 1924, pp. 131-133.

Romer, Alfred Sherwood, "Vertebrate paleontology, 1908-1958," *Journal of Paleontology,* Vol. 33, No. 5, September, 1959, pp. 915-925.

Roos, Charles F., "A Future Role For the Econometric Society in International Statistics," *Econometrica,* Vol. 16, No. 2, April, 1948, pp. 127-134.

Rosenberg Foundation, Report. The Foundation, San Francisco, California, 1946.

Schmeckebier, Laurence F., *International Organizations in Which the United States Participates.* Brookings Institution, Washington, D. C., 1935.

Science and Public Policy: A Report to the President. Report of the President's Scientific Research Board, Vol. I, Government Printing Office, Washington, D. C., 1947.

Shaffer, Philip A., "Origin and Development of the American Society of Biological Chemists," *Federation Proceedings,* Vol. 15, No. 2, July, 1956, pp. 800-802.

"Shall Geoscientists Unite," *Geo Times,* Vol. III, No. 3, October, 1959, pp. 6-8; 27-29.

Shelford, V. E., "The Organization of the Ecological Society of America, 1914-19," *Ecology,* Vol. 19, No. 1, January, 1938, pp. 164-166.

Shenton, Herbert N., *Cosmopolitan Conversation.* Columbia University Press, New York, 1933.

Shorey, Paul, "Fifty Years of Classical Study in America," *Transactions and Proceedings, American Philological Association,* Volume L, 1919.

Shryock, Richard H., "The Planning and Formal Opening of Library Hall," *Proceedings, American Philosophical Society,* Vol. 104, No. 4, August 15, 1960, pp. 349-356.

Shryock, Richard H., "The Library of the American Philosophical Society," *Proceedings, American Philosophical Society,* Vol. 104, No. 4, August 15, 1960, pp. 398-403.

Slaught, Herbert Ellsworth, "Retrospect and Prospect for Mathematics in America," *The American Mathematical Monthly,* Vol. XXVII, November, 1920, pp. 443-451.

Small, Albion W., "Fifty Years of Sociology in the United States," *The American Journal of Sociology,* Vol. XXI, No. 6, May, 1916, pp. 712-864.

Smith, Holmes, "Problems of the College Art Association," *Bulletin, College Art Association of America,* No. 1, 1913, pp. 6-10.

Snow, C. P., *The Two Cultures and the Scientific Revolution.* Cambridge University Press, New York, 1959.

The Social Sciences. Unesco and its Programme. Vol. XII, UNESCO, Paris, 1955.

Sponsored Research Policy of Colleges and Universities. American Council on Education, Washington, D. C., 1954.

Sprat, T., *The History of the Royal Society of London,* 2nd edit., London, 1702.

Stanerson, B. R., "Thanks a Million," *Chemical and Engineering News,* Vol. 37, No. 28, July 13, 1959, p. 114.

Stebbins, Joel, "The American Astronomical Society, 1897-1947," *Popular Astronomy,* Vol. LV, No. 8, October, 1947, pp. 404-413.

Steinbach, H. Burr, Excerpts from a Lecture given at an August 27, 1958 meeting of the American Society of Zoologists, held at Indiana University, Bloomington, Indiana. Unpublished.

Stevenson, J. J., "Our Society," *Bulletin, Geological Society of America,* Vol. 10, February 26, 1899, pp. 83-89.

Stewart, Irvin, *Organizing Scientific Research for War; the Administrative History of the Office of Scientific Research and Development.* Little, Brown and Company, Boston, Massachusetts, 1948.

Stimson, Dorothy, *Scientists and Amateurs; A History of the Royal Society.* Henry Schuman, New York, 1948.

Stocking, George W., Jr., "Franz Boas and the Founding of the American Anthropological Association," *American Anthropologist,* Vol. 62, No. 1, February, 1960, pp. 1-17.

Stone, George W., Jr., "The Beginning, Development, and Impact of the MLA as a Learned Society," *Publications of the Modern Language Association of America,* Vol. LXXIII, No. 5, Part 2, December, 1958, pp. 23-44. See other articles and papers of historical interest in this Seventy-Fifth Anniversary Issue, edited by George W. Stone, Jr.

Stout, D. B., "American Anthropological Association," *Dictionary of Folklore, Mythology and Legend.* Edited by Maria Leach. Vol. 1, Funk and Wagnalls Company, New York, 1949, p. 43.

Struve, Otto, "The Yerkes Observatory, 1897-1947," *Popular Astronomy,* Vol. LV, No. 8, October, 1947, pp. 413-417.

"Summary of the Actions of the Council of the American Association of Pathologists and Bacteriologists, 1900-1955," compiled by Drs. H. T. Karsner and E. A. Gall. Unpublished.

Tannehill, I. R., "The History and Status of the International Meteorological Organization (I.M.O.)," *Bulletin, American Meteorological Society,* Vol. 28, No. 5, May, 1947, pp. 207-219.

Taylor, Norman, "The Beginnings of Ecology," *Ecology,* Vol. 19, No. 2, April, 1938, p. 352.

"Ten Years of the American Geological Institute, 1948-1958," *Geo Times,* Vol. III, No. 3, October, 1958, pp. 12-17; 30-32.

Tippo, Oswald, "The Early History of hte Botanical Society of America," *American Journal of Botany,* Vol. 43, No. 10, December, 1956, pp. 852-858.

"Transactions and Memorabilia of the Fiftieth Anniversary Meeting of the Society," *Journal of Biblical Literature,* Vol. L, 1931, pp. i-lxxx.

True, F. W., edit., *A History of the First Half-Century of the National Academy of Sciences, 1863-1913.* National Academy of Sciences, Washington, D. C., 1913.

True, Webster P., *The First Hundred Years of the Smithsonian Institution, 1846-1946.* Published by the Smithsonian Institution, Washington, D. C., 1946.

True, Webster P., *The Smithsonian, America's Treasure House.* Sheridan House, New York, 1950.

Van Hoesen, Henry B., "The Bibliographical Society of America—Its Leaders and Activities, 1904-1939," *The Papers of the Bibliographical Society of America,* Vol. 35, No. 4, December, 1941, pp. 177-202.

Vokes, H. E., "The Paleontological Society," *AAAS Bulletin,* Vol. 4, No. 5, May, 1945, pp. 39-40.

Walker, Gordon L., "Publications of the American Mathematical Society," *Notices, American Mathematical Society,* Vol. 7, No. 2, Issue No. 45, April, 1960, pp. 169-178.

Walton, Ann D., and F. Emerson Andrews, edits., *The Foundation Directory,* Edition 1. Published for the Foundation Library Center by Russell Sage Foundation, New York, 1960.

Ward, Henry B., "The Founder of American Parasitology, Joseph Leidy," *Journal of Parasitology,* Vol. 10, No. 1, September, 1923, pp. 1-21.

Ware, Edith E., edit., *The Study of International Relations in the United States.* Columbia University Press, New York, 1934.

Wetmore, Ralph H., "Do We Need a National Center for Plant Sciences?" *Plant Science Bulletin,* Vol. 7, No. 2, May, 1961, pp. 1-3.

White, Lyman C., *International Non-Governmental Organizations.* Rutgers University Press, New Brunswick, New Jersey, 1951.

Whiting, P. W., "History and Organization," *Records, Genetics Society of America,* No. 2, 1933, pp. 5-8 and No. 3, 1934, pp. 5-7.

Winchell, Alexander, "Historical Sketch of the Organization," *Bulletin, Geological Society of America,* Vol. 1, February 15, 1890, pp. 1-6.

Wistar, Isaac Jones, *Autobiography of Isaac Jones Wistar, 1827-1905; Half a Century in War and Peace.* The Wistar Institute of Anatomy and Biology, Philadelphia, Pennsylvania, 1937.

Wolf, Abraham, *A History of Science, Technology, and Philosophy in the 16th and 17th Centuries.* Macmillan Company, New York, 1935.

Wolfle, Dael, "The Reorganized American Psychological Association," *The American Psychologist,* Vol. I, No. 1, January, 1946, pp. 3-6.

Wolfle, Dael, "The American Psychological Association," *AAAS Bulletin,* Vol. 5, No. 3, March, 1946, pp. 23-24.

Wolfle, Dael, *America's Resources of Specialized Talent: The Report of the Commission on Human Resources and Advanced Training.* Harper and Brothers, New York, 1954.

Zwemer, Raymund L., "The National Academy of Sciences and the National Research Council," *Science,* Vol. 108, No. 2801, September 3, 1948, pp. 234-238.

LEARNED SOCIETIES WHICH ARE MEMBERS OF COUNCILS AND SOCIETAL INSTITUTES

American Council on Education[1]:

American Historical Association
American Political Science Association
American Psychological Association

Mathematical Association of America
Modern Language Association
of America

National Academy of Sciences-National Research Council[2]:

American Anthropological Association
American Association of Anatomists
American Association of Immunologists
American Association of Pathologists and Bacteriologists
American Astronomical Society
American Chemical Society
American Geophysical Union
American Institute of Nutrition
American Mathematical Society
American Meteorological Society
American Physical Society
American Physiological Society
American Psychologcal Association
American Socety for Experimental Pathology
American Society for Microbiology

American Society for Pharmacology and Experimental Therapeutics, Inc.
American Society of Biological Chemists, Inc.
American Society of Parasitologists
American Society of Zoologists
Association for Symbolic Logic
Association of American Geographers
Botanical Society of America, Inc.
Ecological Society of America
Econometric Society
Electrochemical Society, Inc.
Entomological Society of America
Genetics Society of America
Geochemical Society
Geological Society of America, Inc.
Institute of Mathematical Statistics
Mathematical Association of America
Paleontological Society

American Council of Learned Societies:

American Academy of Arts and Sciences
American Antiquarian Society
American Anthropological Association
American Economic Association
American Folklore Society, Inc.
American Historical Association
American Musicological Society
American Numismatic Society
American Oriental Society
American Philological Association
American Philosophical Association
American Philosophical Society
American Political Science Association

American Psychological Association
American Society for Aesthetics
American Sociological Association
American Studies Association
Archaeological Institute of America
Association for Asian Studies, Inc.
Association of American Geographers
Bibliographical Society of America
College Art Association of America
History of Science Society
Linguistic Society of America
Mediaeval Academy of America
Metaphysical Society of America
Modern Language Association of America

American Council of Learned Societies: (Continued)

Renaissance Society of America
Society of Architectural Historians

Society of Biblical Literature and Exegesis

Social Science Research Council[3]:

American Anthropological Association

American Economic Association

American Historical Association

American Political Science Association

American Psychological Association

American Sociological Association

American Statistical Association

American Association for the Advancement of Science[4]:

American Anthropological Association
American Association of Anatomists
American Association of Immunologists
American Astronomical Society
American Chemical Society
American Economic Association
American Folklore Society, Inc.
American Geophysical Union
American Institute of Nutrition
American Mathematical Society
American Meteorological Society
American Philosophical Association
American Physical Society
American Physiological Society
American Political Science Association
American Psychological Association
American Society for Aesthetics
American Society for Experimental Pathology
American Society for Microbiology
American Society for Pharmacology and Experimental Therapeutics, Inc.

American Society of Biological Chemists, Inc.
American Society of Parasitologists
American Society of Zoologists
American Sociological Association
American Statistical Association
Archaeological Institute of America
Association for Symbolic Logic
Association of American Geographers
Bibliographical Society of America
Botanical Society of America, Inc.
Ecological Society of America
Econometric Society
Electrochemical Society, Inc.
Entomological Society of America
Genetics Society of America
Geochemical Society
Geological Society of America, Inc.
History of Science Society
Institute of Mathematical Statistics
Linguistic Society of America
Mathematical Association of America
Paleontological Society

American Geological Institute:

American Geophysical Union
Geochemical Society

Geological Society of America, Inc.
Paleontological Society

American Institute of Biological Sciences:

American Association of Anatomists[5]
American Physiological Society
American Society for Microbiology[5]
American Society of Parasitologists
American Society of Zoologists

Botanical Society of America, Inc.
Ecological Society of America
Entomological Society of America
Genetics Society of America

American Institute of Physics:

American Astronomical Society[6]   American Physical Society

Federation of American Societies for Experimental Biology:

American Association of Immunologists

American Institute of Nutrition

American Physiological Society

American Society for Experimental Pathology

American Society for Pharmacology and Experimental Therapeutics, Inc.

American Society of Biological Chemists, Inc.

[1] All of the named societies are called associate members.
[2] All of the named societies are called adhering societies.
[3] All of the named societies are called associated societies.
[4] All of the named societies are called affiliated societies.
[5] These societies are called affiliate member societies.
[6] This society is called an associate member society.

DATE OF FOUNDING OF 60 LEARNED SOCIETIES, 4 COUNCILS AND 5 SOCIETAL INSTITUTES.

American Philosophical Society, 1743

American Academy of Arts and Sciences, 1780

American Antiquarian Society, 1812

American Statistical Association, 1839

American Oriental Society, 1842

American Association for the Advancement of Science, 1848

American Numismatic Society, 1858

National Academy of Sciences-National Research Council, 1863

American Philological Association, 1869

American Chemical Society, 1876

Archaeological Institute of America, 1879

Society of Biblical Literature and Exegesis, 1880

Modern Language Association of America, 1883

American Historical Association, 1884

American Economic Association, 1885

American Physiological Society, 1887

American Association of Anatomists, 1888

American Mathematical Society, 1888

Geological Society of America, Inc., 1888

American Folklore Society, Inc., 1888

American Society of Zoologists, 1890

American Psychological Association, 1892

Botanical Society of America, Inc., 1893

American Astronomical Society, 1897

American Society for Microbiology, 1899

American Physical Society, 1899

American Association of Pathologists and Bacteriologists, 1901

American Philosophical Association, 1901

Electrochemical Society, Inc., 1902

American Anthropological Association, 1902

American Political Science Association, 1903

Bibliographical Society of America, 1904

Association of American Geographers, 1904

American Sociological Association, 1905

Entomological Society of America, 1906

American Society of Biological Chemists, Inc., 1906

American Society for Pharmacology and Experimental Therapeutics, Inc., 1908

Paleontological Society, 1908

College Art Association of America, 1912

Federation of American Societies for Experimental Biology, 1912

American Society for Experimental Pathology, 1913

American Association of Immunologists, 1913

Ecological Society of America, 1915

Mathematical Association of America, 1915

American Council on Education, 1918

American Geophysical Union, 1919

American Meteorological Society, 1919

American Council of Learned Societies, 1919

Social Science Research Council, 1924

History of Science Society, 1924

Linguistic Society of America, 1924

American Society of Parasitologists, 1924

Mediaeval Academy of America, 1925

American Institute of Nutrition, 1928

Econometric Society, 1930
Genetics Society of America, 1931
American Institute of Physics, 1931
American Musicological Society, 1934
Institute of Mathematical Statistics, 1935
Association for Symbolic Logic, 1935
Society of Architectural Historians, 1940

Association for Asian Studies, Inc., 1941
American Society for Aesthetics, 1942
American Institute of Biological Sciences, 1948
American Geological Institute, 1948
Metaphysical Society of America, 1950
American Studies Association, 1950
Renaissance Society of America, 1954
Geochemical Society, 1955

MEMBERS OF INTERNATIONAL COUNCILS

International Council of Scientific Unions:

International Astronomical Union
International Geographical Union
International Mathematical Union
International Scientific Radio Union
International Union of Biochemistry
International Union of Biological
Sciences
International Union of Crystallography
International Union of Geodesy and
Geophysics
International Union of
Geological Sciences
International Union of History and
Philosophy of Science
International Union of Physiological
Sciences
International Union of Pure and
Applied Chemistry
International Union of Pure and
Applied Physics
International Union of Theoretical
and Applied Mechanics

International Council For Philosophy and Humanistic Studies:

International Academic Union
International Association for the
History of Religions
International Commission for Folk
Arts and Culture
International Committee of Historical
Sciences
International Committee on the
History of Art
International Federation of Associations of Classical Studies
International Federation of Modern
Languages and Literature
International Federation of Societies
of Philosophy
International Musicological Society
International Permanent Committee of
Linguists
International Union of Anthropological and Ethnological Sciences
International Union of Orientalists
International Union of Prehistoric
and Protohistoric Sciences

International Social Science Council:

International Association of Legal
Science
International Economics Association
International Political Science
Association
International Sociological Association
International Union of Anthropological and Ethnological Sciences
International Union of Scientific
Psychology

INDEX

AAAS Bulletin, 135
Abbott, A. C., 82
Abel, John J., 88, 91-92
Abel Prize in Pharmacology, John J., 92
Abstracts of Bacteriology, 83
Academia dei Lincei, 7
Academia Naturae Curiosum, 7
Academia Secretorum Naturae, 7
Academie des Inscriptions et Belles Lettres, 196
Academie des Sciences, 175, 192; founding of, 7; influence on U.S. of, 12, 207, 220 ref. 11
Academy of Arts and Sciences in the United States of America, 220-221 ref. 11
ACE. *See* American Council on Education
ACLS. *See* American Council of Learned Societies
ACLS Newsletter, 161
Acoustical Society of America, 139, 140
Adams, Arthur S., 122
Adams, Charles Kendall, 37
Adams, Henry, 7
Adams, Herbert B., 37
Adams, John, 10
Adams, John A. S., 118
Adams, John Quincy, 10, 134
Aerospace Corporation, 217
Agassiz, Alexander, 11
Agassiz, Louis, 135
AGI. *See* American Geological Institute
Agricultural History Society, 38
AIBS. *See* American Institute for Biological Sciences
AIBS Bulletin, 143
AIP. *See* American Institute of Physics
Aircraft Nuclear Test Facility, 217
Alaskan Division, American Association for the Advancement of Science, 137

Alexandrine Museum, 7
Allegheny College, 30
Aluminum Corporation, 186
A. M. A. (American Medical Association) Archives of Pathology, 95
Amerada Petroleum Corporation, 188
American Academy of Arts and Letters, 218 ref. 5
American Academy of Arts and Sciences: grants to, 174, 237 ref. 4, 239 ref. 6, 239 ref. 8; history and activities of, 10-13; influence on U.S. of, 12, 128, 207
American Academy of Political and Social Science, 120, 232-233 ref. 2
American Anthropological Association: grants to, 153, 172, 173; history and activities of, 15, 46-48; other organizations and, 132, 136
American Anthropologist, 46-47
American Antiquarian Society: grants to, 153, 173; history and activities of, 14, 22-24, 27, 128
American Association for Applied Psychology, 43
American Association for the Advancement of Science: councils and, 121, 124; foundations and, 165-167; founding of, 134-135; government and, 183-184; grants to, 166-167, 184-185; history and activities of, 134-137, 175, 199, 233 ref. 2, 235 ref. 22; industry and, 184-185; institutes and, 142, 144, 235 ref. 24; sections of, 46, 135-136; societies and, 3, 47, 50, 54, 65, 73, 74, 76-81, 85, 90, 91, 97, 98, 103, 107, 115, 117, 120, 235 ref. 24; universities and, 185
American Association of Anatomists, 154; grants to, 171; history and activities of 69-71
American Association of Economic Entomologists, 90-91
American Association of Immunolo-

gists, 154, 172; history and activities of, 95-97; other organizations and, 85, 137, 229 ref. 90

American Association of Pathologists and Bacteriologists, 96-97; grants to, 151, 172; history and activities of, 84-86

American Association of Petroleum Geologists, 93-94, 143, 188, 236 ref. 35

American Association of Physics Teachers, 139, 140

American Astronomical Society, 140, 154; grants to, 170, 173; history and activities of, 78-80

American Botanical Club, 77

American Chemical Society: councils and, 126, 159; founding of, 15-16; grants from, 159; grants to, 154, 170, 239 ref. 7; history and activities of, 64-67; Research Fund of, 237 ref. 7; sections of, 66-67, 88, 141; universities and, 174

American Committee on Renaissance Studies (ACRS), 64

American Council of Learned Societies: councils and, 121, 232 ref. 1; foundations and, 160-162; founding of, 128-129; government and, 182-183; grants to, 160-162, 182-183; history and activities of, 128-131; industry and, 183; international relations and, 196, 203, 205; societies and, 3, 56, 59, 63, 120, 128-131, 133-134; universities and, 183

American Council on Education: councils and, 121, 128, 232 ref. 1; foundations and, 154-157; founding of, 121; government and, 180-182; grants to, 154-157, 180-182; history and activities of, 120-123; industry and, 181-182; international relations and, 199-200, 205; societies and, 120-123, 131, 134; universities and, 169, 179-180

American Crystallographic Association, 139, 140

American Economic Association: grants to, 150, 173; history and activities of, 14-15, 39-40; other

organizations and, 26, 48, 51, 52, 114, 128, 132, 238 ref. 2, 235 ref. 19

American Economic Review, 40

American Electrochemical Society, 86

American Ethnological Society of New York, 46-47

American Folklore Society, Inc., 14, 36, 47, 173; history and activities of, 40-42

American Geographical and Statistical Society, 223 ref. 33

American Geographical Society of New York, 50-51, 223 ref. 33

American Geological Institute: foundations and, 165; founding of, 143-145; government and, 188; grants to, 165, 188-189; history and activities of, 143-146; industry and, 188-189; societies and, 3, 74, 94, 143-146; universities and, 185

American Geological Society, 73

American Geophysical Society, 101

American Geophysical Union: grants to, 154, 170, 173; history and activities of, 100-103; other organizations and, 118, 236 ref. 35

American Historical Association: founding of, 1, 14-15, 37, 235 ref. 19; grants to, 148-153, 172, 214; history and activities of, 37-39; other organizations and, 48, 51, 54, 63, 123, 128, 132, 233 ref. 2

American Historical Review, 38, 39

American Institute of Architects, 57

American Institute of Biological Sciences: foundations and, 167-168; founding of, 141-142; government, 187-188, 212; grants to, 167-168, 187-188; history and activities of, 141-144, 226 ref. 66; industry and, 188; societies and, 3, 16, 76, 78, 83, 98, 107-108, 120, 141-143; universities and, 185

American Institute of Mining and Metallurgical Engineers, 236 ref. 35

American Institute of Nutrition, 137, 171, 173; history and activities of, 109-110

American Institute of Physics: councils and, 121, 159; foundations and, 159, 167; founding of, 138-139; government and, 186; grants from, 159; grants to, 139, 167, 186-187; history and activities of, 138-141; industry and, 186-187; societies and, 3, 81, 120, 141; universities and, 185, 187

American Journal of Anatomy, 70

American Journal of Archaeology, 32

American Journal of Archaeology and of the History of Fine Arts, 32

American Journal of Mathematics, 71

American Journal of Numismatics, 29

American Journal of Pathology, 84

American Journal of Physics, 140

American Journal of Physiology, 68, 138

American Journal of Sociology, 52

American Library Association, 49

American Mathematical Monthly, 98-99

American Mathematical Society: grants from, 159; grants to, 170; history and activities of, 71-73; other organizations and, 99-100, 115-116, 117, 159, 225 ref. 59

American Medical Association, 69

American Meteorological Society: grants to, 154, 170, 173; history and activities of, 103-105

American Morphological Society, 75

American Musicological Society: grants to, 153, 173; history and activities of, 15, 56-57

American Mycological Society, 77

American Naturalist, 114

American Numismatic and Archaeological Society, 28

American Numismatic Society: grants to, 153, 173; history and activities of, 14, 28-30, 223 ref. 33

American Oriental Society, 14, 153, 173; history and activities of, 27-28; other organizations and, 30, 34, 128

American Philological Association, 14, 173; history and activities of, 30-31; other organizations and, 32, 128

American Philosophical Association: grants to, 153, 172; history and activities of 15, 44-46; other organizations and, 117, 128

American Philosophical Society: European societies and, 12, 207; founding of, 1, 8-9; grants to, 237 ref. 4, 239 ref. 8; history and activities of, 8-10; 12-13; 219-220 ref. 5; other organizations and, 22, 128, 134

American Physical Society: grants to, 154, 170, 171, 173; history and activities of, 80-82; other organizations and, 103, 136, 138-140

American Physiological Society: grants to, 154, 170, 171, 173, 174; history and activities of, 67-69; other organizations and, 87-89, 137

American Political Science Association: grants to, 149, 151, 152, 172-173; history and activities of 15, 48-49; other organizations and, 149, 151, 152, 172-173

American Political Science Review, 49

American Psychological Association: grants from, 159; grants to, 151, 159, 172; history and activities of, 14, 42-44; other organizations and, 61, 132

American Psychological Society. *See* American Psychological Association

American Psychologist, 44

American Public Health Association, 235 ref. 19

American Quarterly (American Studies Association), 63

American Research Center, 32

American School of Classical Studies, 32

American School of Prehistoric Research, 32

American Social Science Association, 37, 39, 218 ref. 5, 234-235 ref. 19

American Society for Aesthetics: grants to, 153, 173, 174; history and activities of, 15, 61-62

American Society for Experimental Pathology: grants to, 154, 172, 173; history and activities of, 94-95; other organizations and, 137

American Society for Horticultural Science, 236 ref. 30

American Society for Microbiology: grants to, 154, 171, 173; history and activities of, 82-84

American Society for Pharmacology and Experimental Therapeutics, Inc.: grants to 154, 172, 173; history and activities of, 91-92; other organizations and, 67, 137

American Society for Professional Geographers (ASPG), 50-51

American Society for Promoting and Propagating Useful Knowledge, 8

American Society for Quality Control, 26

American Society of Architectural Historians, 58

American Society of Biological Chemists, Inc.: grants to, 154, 171; history and activities of, 87-89; other organizations and, 67, 109, 137

American Society of Geologists and Naturalists, 124

American Society of Naturalists, 75, 82, 226 ref. 66

American Society of Parasitologists: grants to, 154, 171; history and activities of, 105-109; other organizations and, 236 ref. 30

American Society of Plant Physiologists, 236 ref. 30

American Society of Tropical Medicine and Hygiene, 108

American Society of Zoologists: grants to, 154, 171; history and activities of, 75-76, 226 ref. 67, 227 ref. 68; other organizations and, 114, 236 ref. 30

American Sociological Association: grants to, 153, 173; history and activities of, 15, 51-52; other organizations and, 128, 132, 233 ref. 2

American Sociological Review, 52

American Sociological Society. *See* American Sociological Association

American Standard Version, 33

American Statistical Association: grants to, 172; history and activities of, 14, 24-27; other organizations and, 114, 115, 116, 132

American Statistical Society. *See* American Statistical Association

American Statistician, 26

American Studies (American Studies Association), 63

American Studies Association: grants to, 153, 173, 174; history and activities of, 15, 62-63, 120

American Telephone and Telegraph Company, 181

American Type Culture Collection, 83

American Universities and Colleges, 122

American Youth Commission, 155

American Zoologist, 76

Amory Fund, Francis, 11

Anatomical Journal Trust, 70

Anatomical Record, 70, 76, 114

Andrews, F. Emerson, 5

Angell, James R., 127

Annals of: Association of American Geographers, 51; Entomological Society of America, 90-91; American Academy of Political and Social Science, 232 ref. 2

Annals of Mathematical Statistics, 115

Annals of Mathematics, 71, 99

Ann Arbor (Mich.), 57, 61, 115

Annual Reports of: American Historical Association, 37-38; Archaeological Institute of America, 32

Annual Review of Entomology, 91

Annual Review of Physiology, 69

Anthropological Society of Washington, 46-47

APA. *See* American Psychological Association

Applied Microbiology, 83

Applied Psychology Monographs, 44

Arabian American Oil Company, 183, 188

Arabian Oil Company, 188

Archaeological Institute of America: grants to, 153, 173; history and activities of, 14, 31-33; other organizations and 30, 128

Archaeology, 32

Argentina, 182

Aristotle, 6

Armour Research Foundation, 237 ref. 1

Art and Archaeology, 32

Art Bulletin, 53, 58

The Art Journal, 53

Asia Foundation, 152, 153, 154, 167

Association for Asian Studies, Inc.: grants to, 150, 172-173; history and activities of, 15, 59-61

Association for Symbolic Logic: grants to, 154, 172, 174; history and activities of, 15, 116-118

Association for the Protection of the Insane and the Prevention of Insanity, 235 ref. 19

Association of American Anatomists, 69

Association of American Geographers: grants to, 153-154, 172, 173; history and activities of, 15, 50-51

Association of American Geologists, 73

Association of American Geologists and Naturalists, 73, 134-135

Association of American Physicians, 84

Association of Consulting Psychologists, 42

Association of Official Economic Entomologists, 90

Assos (Greece), 32

Astronomical and Astrophysical Society of America, 79

Astronomical Journal, 78-79, 140

Astrophysical Journal, 79

Athens, 32

Atlantic City (N. J.), 96

Atwood Research Fund, Wallace W., 51

Atwood, Wallace W., Jr., 5

Austin (Texas), 55, 78

Australia, 192

Austria, 194, 196, 241 ref. 8

Avalon Foundation, 153

B

Bache, Alexander Dallas, 124

Bacteriological News, 83

Bacteriological Reviews, 83

Bailey's Beads, solar phenomenon of, 11

Baltimore, 15, 31, 51, 76, 92, 93, 96

Barnes, C. R., 77

Barnes, Richard H., 109

Barton, Henry A., 5, 141

Batelle Memorial Institute, 237 ref. 1

Bauer, Louis A., 100

Bausch and Lomb Incorporated, 186

Baylis, C. A., 117, 232 ref. 115

Beard, Charles A., 150

The Beginnings of Christianity, 33

Belgium, 192, 196, 197

Bell Telephone Laboratories, 81, 173

Bell Telephone System, 177

Bendix Aviation Corporation, 173

Bennington College, 131

Bergson, Henri, 197

Berlin, 7

Bethesda (Md.), 110

Bibliographical and Special Series (American Folklore Society), 41

Bibliographical Society of America: grants to, 150, 153, 173; history and activities of, 15, 49-50

Bibliographical Society of Chicago, 49

Bibliography (Association for Asian Studies, Inc.), 60

Bibliography of American Literature (Bibliographical Society of America), 49, 153

Bibliotheca Americana (Bibliographical Society of America), 49

Binkley, Robert C., 1

Biological Abstracts, 83

Biometric Society, 26

Bloomfield, Leonard, 54

Boas, Franz, 46-47

Boas, George, 224 ref. 47
Bocher Memorial Prize in Analysis, 72
Bogert, Marston T., 66-67
Bollingen Foundation, 152, 153, 162
Bordeaux (France), 191
Borden Award, 110
Boston: learned organizations founded in, 10, 14, 24, 25, 27, 31, 128, 234 ref. 19; meetings of learned organizations in, 24, 26, 75, 84; members of learned organizations in, 12, 60; offices of learned organizations in, 11, 105
Botanical Society of America, Inc.: grants to, 151, 170; history and activities of, 76-78; other organizations and, 114, 136, 236 ref. 30
Boulder (Col.), 143
Bowditch, Henry P., 67
Bowdoin, James, 10
Bowie Medal, William, 102
Bowman, Isaiah, 150
Boyle, Robert, 7
Brandon Films, 181
Brazil, 192
Briggs, George M., 231 ref. 109
British Academy, 13
British and Foreign Anti-Slavery Society, 191
British Association for American Studies, 63
British Association for the Advancement of Science, 134-135
British Museum, Department of Medals and Coins of, 29
British Social Science Association, 235 ref. 19
Bronk, Detlev W., 126, 127, 144
Brookhaven National Laboratory, 217
Brookings Institution, 217
Brookline (Mass.), 11
Brooklyn Botanic Garden, 98
Brooks Award, Charles Franklin, 104
Brooks, Charles F., 103
Brown University, 232 ref. 115
Brussels, 7, 101, 191, 193, 196, 203
Bryn Mawr College, 226 ref. 67
Buckley Prize, Oliver E., 81

Bulgaria, 194, 241 ref. 8
Bulletin of: American Geographical Society of New York, 51; American Mathematical Society, 72; American Meteorological Society, 103; American Musicological Society, 57; American Physical Society, 81, 140; Archaeological Institute of America, 32; Ecological Society of America, 98; Entomological Society of America, 91; Geological Society of America, Inc., 74, 93
Bunsen Society (Germany), 86
Burkhardt, Frederick, 5, 131, 161-162

C

Cabinet des Medailles, 29
Cairns, W. D., 98-99
Calhoun, John C., 134
California, 42, 54, 100, 102, 105, 115
California Institute of Technology, 115
Cambridge (Mass.), 41, 56, 94
Canada: branches of learned organizations in, 33, 42, 91; International Research Council and, 192; meetings of learned organizations in, 51, 56, 79, 82, 85, 89, 100, 104
Canadian Department of Agriculture, 90
Canadian Institute of Mining and Metallurgy, 144
Canadian Section, Society of Biblical Literature and Exegesis, 33
Cantlon, John E., 229 ref. 92
Capen, Samuel P., 122
Carnegie, Andrew, 147
Carnegie Corporation of New York: councils and, 155-161, 164; grants from, 148-150, 152, 154-161, 164, 166; institutes and, 166; societies and, 148-149, 151-152, 154
Carnegie Endowment for International Peace, 156
Carnegie Foundation for the Advancement of Teaching, 156, 164
Carnegie Institution of Washington, 119

Carus Foundation, 154
Carus, Mary H., 99
Carus Mathematical Monographs, 99
Carver, H. C., 115
Catholic University of America, 61
Census of Medieval and Renaissance Manuscripts (Bibliographical Society of America), 49
Center for the Study of Democratic Institutions, 217
Central Group, Institute of Mathematical Statistics, 116
Central Powers, 106, 193, 196
Central States Branch, American Anthropological Association, 47
Chapel Hill (N.C.) 95, 116
Charles II, 8
Charleston (S.C.), 183, 184
Charlesworth, James C., 5, 233 ref. 2
Chemical Abstracts, 66
Chemical and Engineering News, 66
Chemical Foundation, 139, 158, 167
Chicago, 5, 60, 113, 122, 138, 144, 191
China, 59, 173, 184, 199
China Foundation, 162
Chittenden, Russell H., 89
Church, Alonzo, 117
Cincinnati, 53, 65, 184
Cincinnati Art Museum, 53
Clark University, 42, 80
Clay, Henry, 134
Cleland, R. E., 142
Cleveland Museum of Art, 62
Cleveland (Ohio), 62, 112, 125, 184
Coca, Arthur F., 96
Cole Prize in Algebra, Frank Nelson, 72
Cole Prize in the Theory of Numbers, Frank Nelson, 72
Collections of the American Statistical Association, 26
College Art Association of America: grants to, 149, 153, 173, 174; history and activities of, 15, 52-53; other organizations and, 57-58, 61
College Art Journal, 53
College of Physicians and Surgeons (Columbia University), 67
College Park (Md.), 91

Colombia, 182
Colorado, 112, 143
Colorado Springs (Col.), 112-113
Columbia University: College of Physicians and Surgeons of, 67; learned organizations founded at, 34, 80, 117; meetings of learned organizations at, 59, 139; members of learned organizations at, 71; offices of learned organizations at, 64, 82
Columbian Institute for the Promotion of Arts and Sciences, 134
Columbus (Ohio), 97, 99
Comfort, George F., 30
Commentaries of Averroes on the works of Aristotle, 56
Committee of Liaison of International Organizations (CLIO), 205
Commonwealth Fund, 153, 155, 158, 165, 166
Compendium of Meteorology, 103-104
Compton, Karl T., 139
Comstock, J. H., 90
Conant, Kenneth John, 57-58
Conference Board of Associated Research Councils, 232 ref. 1
Congress of American Physicians and Surgeons, 69
Congress of Vienna, 190
Conn, H. W., 82
Connecticut, 8, 28, 62, 77, 114
Constantine, 147
Cooley, Charles H., 51
Coolidge Foundation, 160, 162
Coonamessett (Mass.), 118
Cordilleran Section, Geological Society of America, 74
Cornell, S. D., 126
Cornell University, 37, 45, 46, 80, 81, 90, 109
Corning Glass Company, 177, 183
Corn Products Refining Company, 177
Cort, W. W., 106
Council for International Organizations of Medical Sciences, 242 ref. 23
Councilman, William T., 84

Council of Allied Ministers of Education (CAME), 200
Councils: administration of, 120-134; foundations and, 154-165, 180, 211-215; government and, 169, 174-177, 179-183, 211-215, 238-239 ref. 5; grants to, 154-165, 169, 174-183, 211-215; history and activities of, 120-134, 209, 232 ref. 1; increase in national responsibilities of, 215-216; industry and, 169, 173, 177-179, 181-182, 183, 211-215; international relations of, 194-196, 199-200, 203, 205, 209-210, 241 ref. 13; prospect for, 215-217; universities and, 169, 179-180, 183. *See also* individual councils and Appendices A and B
Cournot, Antione A., 111
Cowgill, George W., 109, 231 ref. 109
Cowles, Alfred III, 112-113
Cowles Commission for Research in Economics, 112-113
Cowles Foundation, 154
Cox, Hiden T., 5, 143
Cram, Eloise B., 106
Crane, Robert T., 133
Creole Foundation, 153
Creole Petroleum Corporation, 188
Croneis, Carey, 143-144
Cuba, 182
Curie, Marie, 197
Current Digest of the Soviet Press, 160, 165
Curry, H. B., 117, 232 ref. 115

D

Daedalus, 12, 174,
Danzig, 7
Darling, S. T., 106
Davis (Calif.), 100
Davis, Charles H., 124
Davis, Harold T., 112
Davis, William M., 50
Dead Sea scrolls, 33
de Beaurepaire, Quesnay, 220 ref. 11
Delo, David M., 145
Denmark, 196
Dessoir, Max, 61
Detroit, 83, 84

Dewey, John, 61
Dictionary of American Biography (DAB), 130, 160
A Dictionary of Books Relating to America (Bibliographical Society of America), 49
Directory (American Economic Association), 40
Divisia, Francois, 111
Doklady (Geology Series), 146
Doland Fund, 10
Dow Chemical Company, 186
Dublin, 7, 58
Ducasse, C. J., 117, 232 ref. 115
Dufay, Guillermus, 57
Duke University, 98, 232 ref. 115
Dumbarton Oaks Conference, 199, 200
Du Ponceau, Peter Stephen, 219 ref. 5
du Pont de Nemours and Company, E. I., 177, 181

E

Eastern Art Teacher's Association, 53
Eastern Branch, American Society of Zoologists, 75
Eastern Division, American Philosophical Association, 45, 46, 117
Eastern Group, Institute of Mathematical Statistics, 116
Eastern Manual Training Association, 53
East European Fund, 164
East Lansing (Mich.), 98
Eaton, John, 37
Ecole nationale des Ponts et Chaussees, 111
Ecological Monographs, 98
Ecological Society of America: grants to, 154, 171; history and activities of, 97-98
Ecologists Union, 97
Ecology, 98
Econometrica, 111-113
Econometric Society: grants to, 149, 154, 172; history and activities of, 16, 110-114; other organizations and, 218 ref. 6
Ecuador, 182

Edsall, Geoffrey, 229 ref. 91
Educational Facilities Laboratory, 167
Educational Record, 122
Egypt, 32, 147
Eighth Radar Weather Conference, 105
Einstein, Albert, 197
Electrochemical Society, Inc.: grants to, 154, 171; history and activities of, 86-87
Electronic Defense Laboratories, 217
Eleventh International Congress on Entomology, 171
Ellwood, Charles A., 51
Endowment Fund (American Society of Parasitologists), 107
Engineering Foundation, 126, 157, 158
England, 24, 134
Entoma (Entomological Society of America), 91
Entomological Club, 90
Entomological Society of America: grants to, 171; history and activities of, 90-91
Ernst, Harold C., 84, 85
Espinosa, Aurelio M., 41
European Association for American Studies, 63
Evanston (Illinois), 34, 40

F

Faber, Alex, 217
Falk Foundation, Maurice and Laura, 165
Fansler, Roberta, 53
Faraday Society (England), 86
Far Eastern Association, 59
The Far Eastern Quarterly, 59
Faulkner Farm, 11
Federation of American Societies for Experimental Biology: foundations and, 165; founding of, 137; government and, 185; grants to, 165, 185; history and activities of, 137-138, 199, 226 ref. 66; industry and, 185; societies and, 3, 16, 68, 76, 85, 89, 92, 94-97, 110, 141; universities and, 185
Federation of Plant Sciences, 78

Federation Proceedings, 138
Fellow Newsletter (American Anthropological Association), 48
Fife, Robert H., 123
Fifth International Congress of Anthropology and Ethnology, 172
Fifth International Congress on Nutrition, 110, 171
Finkel, B. F., 98
First International Congress of Trichinellosis, 172
Fisher, Irving, 111-113
Fisher, J. Francis, 219 ref. 5
Fiske, Thomas S., 71
Flexner, Abraham, 69
Florence, 7
Florida, 89
Ford Foundation: councils and, 156, 160-161, 164-165, 213; grants from, 149, 151-152, 156, 160-162, 164-165, 167-168, 213; institutes and, 167-168, 213; societies and, 149, 151-152, 154, 213
Ford, Guy S., 150
Ford, Henry, 147
Ford, Henry II, 151
Ford Motor Company, 182
Fort Worth (Texas), 144
Foundation Library Center, 5
Foundations, 147-149; councils and, 154-165, 211-214; grants from, 147-168, 211-213; institutes and, 165-168, 211-214; societies and, 149-154, 211-214. *See also* individual foundations.
Fourteenth International Congress of Psychologists, 172
Fox family, 9
Fragmentization of knowledge, 16, 210-212
France, 13, 24, 111, 192, 196, 199, 201
Franklin, Benjamin, 8, 9, 11, 147, 219 ref. 5
French Academy (Of Sciences). *See* Academie des Sciences
Frisch, Ragnar, 111-112
Fulbright, J. William, 200
Fuller Brush Company, 181

Fund for Adult Education, 156
Fund for the Advancement of Education, 149, 156, 167

G

Gainesville (Fla.), 89
Gaither, H. Rowan, Jr., 151
Galileo, 6, 213
Gardiner, Frederic, 33
Garrett Biblical Institute, 34
Gates, Frederick W., 150
Gatz, Felix M., 61
General Dynamics Corporation, 181
General Education Board: councils and, 155-156, 158-159, 163; grants from, 151-152, 155-159, 163, 166; institutes and, 166; societies and, 149, 151-152, 154
General Electric Company, 177, 186
General Electric Foundation, 165
General Mills Incorporated, 181
General Motors Corporation, 177, 181, 186
Genetics, 114-115
Genetics in the 20th Century, 115
Genetics Society of America: grants to, 150, 171, 173; history and activities of, 114-115; other organizations and, 75-76, 236 ref. 30
Geneva (Switzerland), 191, 202
Geochemica Acta, 118
Geochemical News, 118
Geochemical Society: grants to, 154, 170; history and activities of, 16, 118-119
Geological Society of America, Inc.: grants from, 94, 188; grants to, 154, 172; history and activities of, 73-75; other organizations and, 93-94, 118, 136, 144
Georgetown University, 69
George Washington University Medical School, 92
Geo Science Abstracts, 146
Geo Times, 146
German Society for American Studies, 63
Germany, 13, 24, 61, 105, 194 ,196, 241 ref. 8

Giddings, Franklin H., 51
Girard, Stephen, 147
Gold Headed Cane Award, 85
Goodrich Company, B. F., 181
Gordon Research Conferences, 166, 185
Göttingen, 30
Goucher College, 76, 227 ref. 70
Gould, Benjamin Apthorp, 78
Government, U.S. *See* U. S. Government
Graduate Research Center of the Southwest, 217
Grant Foundation, 156, 165
Grants. *See* individual organizations, grants to; foundations, industry, U.S. government, grants from
Graves, Mortimer, 131
Great Britain, 24, 40, 192, 196, 199
Greece, 147, 190, 192, 196
Greek Club, 30
Gresham, Sir Thomas, 8
Gresham's College, 8
Gribbin, John H., 19 ref. a, 21 ref. a
Griggs, Robert F., 142
Gross, Charles, 56
Guggenheim Foundation, Daniel and Florence, 154
Guggenheim Memorial Foundation, John Simon, 5, 153
Guide to the Study of Medieval History (Paetow), 56
Gulf Oil Corporation, 188

H

Hale, George E., 100, 125
Hall, G. Stanley, 42
Hall, Herbert F., 220 ref. 8
Hamilton, Alexander, 11
Handbook (American Economic Association), 40
Hanseatic League, 190
Harris, Joel Chandler, 41
Hart, Edward, 66
Harvard University, 5, 11, 225 ref. 59; learned organizations founded at, 57-58; Medical School of, 67, 68; members of learned organizations at, 70, 103, 111; Observatory

of, 78; offices of learned organizations at, 94
Haskins Medal, 56
Haverford College, 62
Hayes, Carleton J. H., 150
Hedrick, E. R., 98-100
Hedrick Lectures, Earle Raymond, 100
Hegner, R. W., 106-107
Helminthological Society of Washington, 105-106, 108
"Helmsoc." *See* Helminthological Society of Washington
Henry, Joseph, 124
Hering, Carl, 86
Herring, Pendleton, 5, 133
Herter, C. (Christian) A., 88
Herter Memorial Fund, Christian A., 88-89
Higher Education and National Affairs, 122, 155
Hiss, Priscilla, 53
History of Printing in America (Thomas), 23
History of Science Society: grants to, 172; history and activities of, 15, 53-54; other organizations and, 136
Hitchcock Medal, Alice Davis, 58
Hitchins, A. P., 96
Holland, 196
Hooke, Robert, 7
Hooker, D. R., 138
Hotelling, Harold, 113
Houghton Foundation, 162
House, E. M., 125
Howe, Calderon, 229 ref. 91
Howes, Raymond F., 5
Hughes Aircraft Company, 173
Humanities and social sciences: need for increased understanding and support of, 212-216
Humble Oil Company, 188
Hungary, 194, 241 ref. 8
Hunt, R., 92
Hunter College, 31
Hutchisson, Elmer, 141
Hylander, Clarence J., 142

I

ICPHS. *See* International Council for Philosophy and Humanistic Studies
ISCU. *See* International Council of Scientific Unions
Illinois, 5, 34, 40, 80, 108, 109, 132
Incunabula in American Libraries (Bibliographical Society of America), 49
Index of American Economic Entomology, 91
India, 41
Indiana University, 55, 112
Industry: councils and, 169, 177-179, 181-182, 183, 213; grants from, 169, 173, 177-179, 181-182, 184-189, 213; institutes and, 169, 184-189, 213; societies and, 169, 173, 213. *See also* individual industries
Ingerson, Earl, 118, 232 ref. 116
Insect Life, 90
Institute for Advanced Study, 217, 226 ref. 59
Institute for the Unification of Private International Law, 198
Institute of Intellectual Cooperation, 197-198
Institute of International Education, 155
Institute of Mathematical Statistics: grants to, 154, 170-171, 174; history and activities of, 16, 115-116; other organizations and, 26, 218 ref. 6
Institutes: administration of, 134-146; foundations and, 165-168, 211-215; government and, 169, 183-188, 211-215, 238-239 ref. 5; grants to, 165-168, 183-189; history and activities of, 134-146, 209; increase in national responsibilities of, 215-216; industry and, 169, 184-189, 211-215, 243 ref. 9; lack of in humanities-social sciences, 120; prospect for, 215-217; societies and, 218 ref. 7, 235 ref. 24, 236 ref. 30, 236 ref. 35; universities and, 169, 185. *See also* individual institutes and Appendices A and B

International Academic Union, 128, 130, 195-198, 202-205
International Arid Land Meeting, 184
International Association of Academies, 192, 240-241 ref. 4
International Association of Legal Science, 204
International Association of Universities, 205
International Astronomical Union, 193, 194. *See also* Appendix C
"International Bibliography" (*Publications of the Modern Language Association of America*), 35
International Botany and Horticulture Conference, 191
International Business Machines Corporation, 181
International Chemistry Conference, 191
International Commission on Zoological Nomenclature, 94
International Committee of Historic Sciences, 203
International Committee on Folk Arts and Folklore, 203
International Committee on Intellectual Cooperation, 197, 200
International Congress of Anatomists, 171
International Congress of Orientalists, 242-243 ref. 4
International Council for Philosophy and Humanistic Studies (ICPHS), 203-206. *See also* Appendix C
International Council of Scientific Unions (ICSU): founding and early history of, 192-195; League of Nations and, 198; other organizations and, 159, 175, 205; United Nations and, 202-203. *See also* Appendix C
International Economics Association, 204. *See also* Appendix C
International Educational Cinematographic Institute, 198
International Education Board, 158
International Federation of Philo-

sophic Societies, 203. *See also* Appendix C
International Geodetic and Geophysical Union, 101-102, 193. *See also* Appendix C
International Geographical Union, 193. *See also* Appendix C
International Geological Congress, 118
International Geological Review, 146
International Geophysical Year (IGY), 102, 202
International History Conference, 191
International Mathematical Union, 193. *See also* Appendix C
International Mathematics Conference, 191
International Oceanographic Congress, 184
International Organization for Intellectual Cooperation, 198
International organizations. *See* International relations, international unions, individual international organizations.
International Political Science Association, 204. *See also* Appendix C
International relations: development of, 1-2, 190-191; United States of America and, 192, 195-196, 198-200, 203, 205. *See also* individual international organizations; Appendix C
International Religious Science Conference, 191
International Research Council. *See* International Council of Scientific Unions (ICSU)
International Scientific Radio Union, 193. *See also* Appendix C
International Social and Economic Sciences Conference, 191
International Social Science Bulletin, 205
International Social Science Council (ISSC), 203-206. *See also* Appendix C
International Sociological Association, 204. *See also* Appendix C

International Statistical Conference, **191**

International Studies Conference, 198

International Union of Academies. *See* International Academic Union

International Union of Anthropological and Ethnological Sciences, 204. *See also* Appendix C

International Union of Biochemistry, 193. *See also* Appendix C

International Union of Biological Sciences, 193. *See also* Appendix C

International Union of Crystallography, 193. *See also* Appendix C

International Union of Geodesy and Geophysics, 193. *See also* Appendix C

International Union of Geological Sciences, 193. *See also* Appendix C

International Union of History and Philosophy of Science, 117-118, 193. *See also* Appendix C

International Union of Nutritional Sciences, 110.

International Union of Physiological Sciences, 193. *See also* Appendix C

International Union of Pure and Applied Chemistry, 193. *See also* Appendix C

International Union of Pure and Applied Physics, 193. *See also* Appendix C

International Union of Scientific Psychology, 204. *See also* Appendix C

International Union of Theoretical and Applied Mechanics, 193, 195. *See also* Appendix C

International Unions, pp. 191-198, 201-216, 240 ref. 1. *See also* Ap-**pendix C**

International Zoological Congress, 75

The Interpreter's Bible, 33

IRC. *See* International Council of Scientific Unions (ICSU)

Ireland, 58

Isis (History of Science Society), 54

ISSC. *See* International Social Science Council

Isvestiya (Geology Series), 146

Italy, 7, 24, 58, 192, 196, 213

J

James, Edmund J., 232-233 ref. 2

Jameson, J. Franklin, 1, 38

Japan, 59, 192, 196

Japanese Society for American Studies, 63

Jefferson Medical College, 67

Jefferson, Thomas, 9, 11, 73

Jerusalem, 32, 33

John Carter Brown Library, 23

Johns Hopkins University, 71, 125, 225 ref. 59; founders of learned organizations at, 37, 67, 80, 92; members of learned organizations at, 70; School of Hygiene and Public Health of, 105

Johnson Research Fund, 10

Joint Commission on Educational Television (JCET), 156

Joint Genetics Section, 114

Jordan, E. O., 82

Journal of: American Chemical Society, 66; American Musicological Society, 57; American Oriental Society, 27-28; American Statistical Association, 26; Electrochemical Society, Inc., 86; Society of Architectural Historians, 58

Journal of Abnormal and Social Psychology, 43

Journal of Aesthetics, 61

Journal of Aesthetics and Art Criticism, 61

Journal of American Folklore, 41

Journal of Analytical and Applied Chemistry, 66

Journal of Applied Meteorology, 230 ref. 96

Journal of Applied Physics, 140

Journal of Applied Physiology, 69

Journal of Applied Psychology, 44

Journal of Asian Studies, 60

Journal of Bacteriology, 83, 151

Journal of Biblical Literature, 33

Journal of Biological Chemistry, 88-89

Journal of Chemical Physics, 140

Journal of Comparative and Physiological Psychology, 44
Journal of Consulting Psychology, 44
Journal of Economic Entomology, 90-91
Journal of Experimental Psychology, 43
Journal of Geophysical Research, 102
Journal of Immunology, 96
Journal of Immunology, Virus-Research, and Experimental Chemotherapy, 96
Journal of Mathematical Physics, 140
Journal of Medical Research, 84
Journal of Meteorology, 103
Journal of Morphology, 76
Journal of Nutrition, 109
Journal of Paleontology, 93-94
Journal of Parasitology, 105-107, 171
Journal of Pharmacology and Experimental Therapeutics, 92
Journal of Philosophy, 46
Journal of Philosophy, Psychology, and Scientific Methods, 46
Journal of Social Science Abstracts, 163
Journal of Symbolic Logic, 117
Journal of the Acoustical Society of America, 140
Journal of the Boston Society of Medical Sciences, 84
Journal of the Optical Society of America, 140
Junto, 8, 219 ref. 5

K

Kansas City (Mo.), 143, 220 ref. 8
Keele, Harold M., 5
Kellogg Foundation, 156
Keynes, John Maynard, 113
Kiger, Jean M., 5
Kleene, S. C., 232 ref. 115
Kofoid, C. A., 105
Kress Foundation, Samuel H., 153
Kruse, Cornelius, 131

L

Lafontaine, Henry, 197
Langford, C. H., 117

Language (Linguistic Society of America), 55
La Rue, George R., 107, 231 ref. 107
League of Nations, 197-199
Learned organizations, lack of history of, 1-2
Learned Societies: adminstration of, 16-17, 209; basic information regarding, 18-22; branches of, 243 ref. 5; cities and, 14, 208, 216; criticism of, 207, 210-212, 243 ref. 6, 244 ref. 14; definition of, 2, 218 **ref. 4; early, 8-13,** 16, 207, 219-220 **ref. 5,** 220-221 refs. 6-11; European, 6-8, 219 refs. 1-4; foundations and, 148-154, 159, 212-215; government and, 169-173, 212-215, 238-239 ref. 5, 243-244 ref. 11; grants to, 148-154, 169-174; humanistic and social science, 16, 22-64; increase in national responsibilities of, 215-216; industry and, 169, 173, 212-215, 243 ref. 9; modern, 22-113; natural science, 16, 64-119; origins of 6-7, 14-17, 207; over-specialization of, 15-16, 208, 211, 215; prospect for, 215-217; universities and, 169, 174, 244 ref. 14. *See also* individual learned societies; Tables 1, 2, and 3; and Appendices A and B
Lee, Milton O., 5, 138
Leibnitz, Gottfried W., 117
Leidy, Joseph, 70, 105
Leipzig, 7
Leland, Waldo G., 131
Lenox Library, 23
Lewis and Clark Expedition, 9
Lewis Prize, John M., 10
Libbey-Owens-Ford Glass Company, 186
Lilly Award in Bacteriology (Eli Lilly and Company), 83
Lilly, Eli and Company, 92
Lilly Endowment, 152, 156
Lilly Research Laboratories, Eli, 126
Limnological Society of America, 236 ref. 30
Lincoln Laboratory, 219
Linda Hall Library, 220 ref. 8

Linguistic Atlas of New England, 130, 160
Linguistic Atlas of the United States and Canada, 130
Linguistic Institute, 55
Linguistic Society of America, 173; history and activities of, 15, 54-55, other organizations and, 30, 36
Lisbon, 7
Littauer Foundation, 153
Lodge, Henry Cabot, 199
London, 8, 85, 95, 191, 192, 200
London Conference, 201
London Statistical Society, 24
Lord and Taylor Company, 183
Los Angeles, 54, 102

M

Macelwane Award, Father James B., 104
Maclure, William, 73
Macy Company, R. H., 181
Madison, James, 11
Maine, 11
Mall, Franklin P., 70, 82
Manly, John M., 55
Mann, Charles R., 122
Markle Foundation, John and Mary R., 158, 162, 165
Martin, Henry N., 67
Maryland, 51, 76, 91, 92, 110, 143, 185
Massachusetts: learned organizations founded in, 10, 15, 22, 25, 41, 42; meetings of learned organizations in, 75, 118; offices of learned organizations in, 11, 12, 56, 94, 105
Matchette Foundation, 153
Mathematical Association of America: grants from, 159; grants to, 151, 170; history and activities of, 98-100; other organizations and, 72, 115, 122
Mathematical Reviews, 72
McGee, W. J., 46-47
McGraw-Hill Book Company, 116
Mediaeval Academy of America: grants to, 153, 173, 174; history and activities of, 15, 55-56
Meisinger Award, 104

Mellon Institute, 237 ref. 1
Meltzer, S. J., 94
Memoirs of: American Academy of Arts and Sciences, 11; American Anthropological Association, 47; American Folklore Society, 41; American Philosophical Society, 10
Mercer Award, George, 97
Merck and Company, 126
Merrell-Soule Company, 177
Merriam, Charles, 150
Merrill Trust, Charles E., 162
Merritt, Ernest, 80
Metaphysical Society of America: grants to, 154, 173, 174; history and activities of, 15, 62, 120
Meteorological Abstracts and Bibliography, 103
Meteorological Monographs, 103
Metropolitan Society, 134
Mexico, 42, 82, 91, 118, 182, 203
Mexico City, 217
Meyer Foundation, 160
Michigan, 57, 61, 83, 84, 98, 115
Michigan State University, 98, 229 ref. 92
Mid-West Branch, Modern Language Association of America, 36
Mid-West MLA, 36
Mid-West Section, Society of Biblical Literature and Exegesis, 33
Midwestern Conference of Parasitologists, 108
Milbank Memorial Fund, 155, 160
Millikan, Robert A., 157, 197
Mineralogical Society of America, 74, 236 ref. 35
Minneapolis (Minn.), 96
Minot, Charles S., 70
Miscellaneous Publications (Entomological Society of America), 91
Missouri, 42, 46, 143, 220 ref. 8
Mitchell, Maria, 12
Mitchell, S. Weir, 67
Mitchell, Wesley C., 111, 113
Mitchell, William J., 224 ref. 44
MLA. *See* Modern Language Association of America
MLA Style Sheet, 35

Modern Language Association of America: grants to, 151, 153, 172, 214; history and activities of, 14, 34-36; other organizations and, 31, 41, 55, 61, 63, 123, 128

Modern Spanish, 36

Moment, Gairdner B., 227 ref. 70

Monograph Series (Association of American Geographers), 51

Monthly Weather Review, 103

Mont St. Michel and Chartres (Adams), 7

Moore, A. B., 5

Moore, Arthur L., 111

Moore, Barrington, 98

Moore, Raymond C., 94

Morse, Samuel F. B., 233 ref. 3

Mount Wilson Observatory, 125

Mueller, Justus F., 231 ref. 107

Munro, Dana C., 150

Murlin, John R., 109

Mycological Society of America, 236 ref. 30

N

Naples, 7

NAS-NRC. *See* National Academy of Sciences-National Research Council

National Academy of Design, 120, 233 ref. 3

National Academy of Sciences-National Research Council: councils and, 121, 232 ref. 1; divisions of, 75, 126, 127, 142, 159, 195; foundations and, 157-160; founding of, 123-126; government and, 169, 174-177, 182, 241 ref. 13; grants to, 157-160, 169, 174-179; history and activities of, 123-128, 175; industry and, 169, 177-179, 182; institutes and, 142, 144, 187; international relations and, 194-195, 203, 205; societies and, 3, 75, 78, 100-102, 103, 107, 110, 116, 117, 120, 131, 134, 232 ref. 1; universities and, 179

National Astronomical Laboratory, 217

National Committee on Mathematical Requirements, 100

National Conference of Charities, 235 ref. 19

National Education Association, 34, 121

National Geographic Magazine, 223 ref. 33

National Geographic Society, 50, 223 ref. 33

National Institute of Arts and Letters, 218 ref. 5, 235 ref. 19

National Institution for the Promotion of Science, 124, 134, 135

National Prison Association, 235 ref. 19

Natural Resources Council, 97

National Science Foundation, 215

Natural science societies: 64-119

The Nature Conservancy, 97

The Netherlands, 117

New England Branch, Modern Language Association of America, 36

New England Section, Society of Biblical Literature and Exegesis, 33

New Haven (Conn.), 28, 62, 114

New Jersey, 33, 217

New Mexico, 32, 184

New Orleans, 15, 48, 114, 118

News Bulletin (American Anthropological Association), 47

Newsletter of: American Society for Microbiology, 83; American Society of Zoologists, 76; Association for Asian Studies, 60

Newton, Isaac, 7

New York (City): chapter of learned organizations in, 25; learned organizations founded in, 14, 28, 34, 45, 65, 77, 88, 233 ref. 3; meetings of learned organizations in, 38, 84, 96, 144; members of learned organizations in, 33, 60; offices of learned organizations in, 29, 30, 31, 33, 36, 50, 52, 64, 75, 82, 87, 97, 131, 134, 139, 141, 223 ref. 33, 233 ref. 3

New York Mathematical Society, 71

New York Public Library, 5
New York Society of Serology and Hematology, 96
New York (State), 73, 89, 139; learned organizations founded in, 15, 28, 37, 39, 88; members of learned organizations in, 87; offices of learned organizations in, 30, 31, 33, 36, 50, 52, 64, 75, 82, 97, 134, 141
New York Statistical Society, 24
New York University, 52, 174
New Zealand, 192
Nichols, Edward L., 80-81
Nobel Prize, 217
Noise Control, 140
North Carolina, 42, 95, 116
North Dakota, 42
Northumberland (Penn.), 65
Northwestern University, 34, 40, 233 ref. 2
Norton, Charles Eliot, 31
Norway, 105
Numismatic Literature, 29
Numismatic Notes and Monographs, 29
Nuttall, George H. F., 105

O

Oak Ridge National Laboratory, 217
Oates, Whitney J., 215
"Observations on the geology of the United States, explanatory of a geologic map," (Maclure), 73
Ockeghem, Jean De, 57
Odegaard, Charles E., 131, 224 ref. 44, 224-225 ref. 47
Office of International Relations. *See* National Academy of Sciences-National Research Council, divisions of
Office of Scientific Personnel. *See* National Academy of Sciences-National Research Council, divisions of
Ohio, 62, 97, 99, 112, 125
Ohio State University, 115
Old Dominion Foundation, 153
Oppenheimer, Robert, 217
Optical Society of America, 139, 140

Osborne-Mendel Award, 110
OSRD. *See* U. S. Office of Scientific Research and Development
Otto, G. F., 231 ref. 107
Overbrook Foundation, 153
Owsley, Harriet C., 5
Oxford University, 8

P

Pacific Coast Branch: American Historical Association, 39; American Philological Association, 31
Pacific Coast Section, Society of Biblical Literature and Exegesis, 33
Pacific Division: American Association for the Advancement of Science, 137; American Philosophical Association, 45, 46
Paetow, Louis J., 56
Palais des Academies, 196
Paleontographical Society of London, 94
Paleontological Society, 152, 174; history and activities of, 92-94; other organizations and, 74, 236 ref. 30
Palladio, Andrea, 58
Papers and Memoirs (American Geological Society), 74
Papers and Proceedings (American Economic Association), 40
Papers of the American Musicological Society, 57
Papers of the Bibliographical Society of America, 49
Parasitology, 105
Paris, 7, 29, 111, 114, 192, 196, 202, 204
Parke, Davis and Company, 108, 173
Parker, Francis H., 225 ref. 48
Parliament of Science, 167
Pasadena, (Calif.), 115
"Path and Bac" (American Association of Pathologists and Bacteriologists), 85
Patten, Simon N., 233 ref. 2
Peabody Fund, 147
Pearce, Richard M., 94-95
Pegram, George B., 139

Pennsylvania, 10, 42, **59, 62, 63, 65,** 71

Pennsylvania State University, 232 ref. 115

Penrose: Bequest, 74; Medal, 74; Research Fund, 10

Penrose, R. A. F., 74

Pergamon Press, 118

Permanent International Committee of Linguists, 203

Permanent Science Fund (American Academy of Arts and Sciences), 11

Petroleum Research Fund, 237 ref. 7

Pharmacological Reviews, 92

Philadelphia: chapter of learned organizations in, 25; learned organizations founded in, 8, 10, 50, 70, 86, 135, 232 ref. 2; meetings of learned organizations in, 41, 97; members of learned organizations in, 67; offices of learned organizations in, 10, 42, 63, 71

Philadelphia Anthropological Society, 47

Phillips Prize, Henry M., 10

Phillips Petroleum Company, 188

Philological Association of the Pacific Coast, American Philological Association, 31, 36

Philosophical Hall, 9

Philosophical Review, 46

Physical Review, 81, 140

Physical Review Letters, 81

Physics Abstracts, 140

The Physics of Fluids, 140, 186

Physics Today, 140

Physiological Reviews, 69

Physiologist, 69

Pickering, John, 27

Pittsburgh, 53, 59

Plant World, 98

Plato, 7, 147

PMLA. See *Publications of the Modern Language Association of America*

Polain, Jules, 240 ref. 2

Poland, 192, 196

Polar Front Theory Conference, 105

Popular Astronomy, 79

Porter, Vernon C., 5

Porter, W. T., 68

Portugal, 41, 192

Poughkeepsie (New York), 30

Poultry Science Association, 236 ref. 30

Prague, 7

Presser Foundation, 153

Price, Don K., 5

Price, W. E., 107

Priestley Centennial Celebration, 65

Prince, Morton, 44

Princeton (N.J.), 217

Princeton University, 111, 225-226 ref. 59

Proceedings and Addresses (American Philosophical Association), 46

Proceedings of: American Academy of Arts and Sciences, 11, 12; American Antiquarian Society, 24; American Association for the Advancement of Science, 135, 183; American Chemical Society, 66; American Geological Society, 74; American Historical Association, 39; American Mathematical Society, 72; American Numismatic Society, 29; American Philosophical Society, 10; American Political Science Association, 49; Federation of **American** Societies for Experimental Biology, 95; Helminthological Society of Washington, 106

The Professional Geographer, 51

Providence (R.I.), 73, 118

Psychological Abstracts, 44, 151

Psychological Bulletin, 43

Psychological Index, 43

Psychological Monographs, 43

Psychological Review, 43

Publication Fund (American Academy of Arts and Sciences), 11

Publication and Proceedings of the American Sociological Society, 52

Publications of: American Astronomical Society, 79; American Statistical Association, 26

Publications of the Modern Language Association of America (PMLA), 36

Q

Quarterly Publication of the A. S. A. (American Statistical Association), 26

R

Radio Corporation of America, 126
RAND Corporation, 217
Ransom, B. H., 106
Records (Genetics Society of America), 114
Reed, C. J., 86
Renaissance News, 63-64
Renaissance Society of America, 154, 173; history and activities of, 15, 63-64
"Research in Progress" (Modern Language Association of America), 35
Resources for the Future, 164, 165
Review of Metaphysics, 62
Review of Modern Physics, 81, 140
Review of Scientific Instruments, 140
Revised Standard Version, 33
Rhode Island, 65, 73, 118
Richards, Joseph W., 86
Richmond (Va.), 220 ref. 11
Rietz, H. L., 115
Rietz Lecture, 116
Rockefeller Brothers Fund, 156, 164
Rockefeller Foundation: councils and. 156-160, 163-164; grants, 5, 150-152, 156-160, 163-164, 166-167, 184; institutes and, 166-167, 184; societies and, 105, 115, 125, 149-154
Rockefeller Institute, 88, 126, 157, 217, 244-245 ref. 15
Rockefeller, John D., Sr., 147, 150, 151
Rockefeller Memorial, Laura Spelman: councils and, 155-156, 158, 162-163; societies and, 44, 111, 149-152, 154
Rocky Mountain Division, American Association for the Advancement of Science, 137
Rocky Mountain MLA, 36
Rocky Mountain Section, Geological Society of America, 74

Roman Catholic Church, 6
Rome, 7, 32, 114, 190
Roos, Charles F., 111-112
Roosevelt, Franklin D., 198
Root, Francis M., 107
Rosenwald Fund, Julius, 165
Ross, Edward A., 51
Rossby Award, Carl-Gustaf, 104
Rowland, Henry A., 80
Royal College of Physicians, 85
Royal Society of London: establishment of, 7; history of, 8, 12-13, 175, 192, 207, 219 ref. 4
Royal Statistical Society, 24
Rubey, W. W., 144
Rumania, 192, 196
Rumford, Count, 11
Rumford Fund, 11
Russia, 130, 146, 150, 196, 199, 210, 214, 242 ref. 4

S

Sage Foundation, Russell, 153, 158, 165
Sammlung der Deutschen Philologen und Schulmänner, 30
San Francisco, 105
San Francisco Conference, 199-200
Santa Fe (New Mexico), 32
Santayana, George, 61
Saratoga (New York), 37, 39
Sarton, George, 54
Say Foundation Monographs, Thomas, 91
Scholasticism, 6
School of American Research, 32
School of Oriental Research, 32, 33
Schuchert, Charles, 92
Schumpeter, Joseph A., 113
Science, 79, 106, 135
Science, changing attitude toward, 212-213
Scientific and Technical Societies of the United States and Canada (Gribbin *et al*), 19 ref. a, 21 ref. a
Scientific Monthly, 135
Scripps Foundation for Research in Population Problems, 165
Sedgwick, William T., 82

Seismological Society of America, 236 ref. 35

Seitz, Frederick, 126

Selected Papers in Statistics and Probability by Abraham Wald, 116

Serbia, 192

Shattuck, Lemuel, 25

Shelford, V. E., 97, 229 ref. 92

Shell Development Company, 187

Shell Oil Company, 188

Shryock, Richard H., 131, 220

Silliman, Benjamin, 73

Slater Fund, 147

Slaught, H. E., 98-99

Slaught Memorial Papers, 99

Sloan Foundation, Alfred P., 154, 160, 167

Small, Albion W., 51

Smithsonian Institution, 37, 124, 172, 214

Smithson, James, 147

Social Science Research Council: councils and, 232 ref. 1; foundations and, 162-165; founding of, 131-132; government and, 182-183; grants to, 162-165, 182-183; history and activities of, 131-134, 234-235 ref. 19; industry and, 183; international relations and, 205; societies and, 3, 120, 131-132; universities and, 183

Societal Institutes. *See* Institutes

Societies. *See* Learned Societies

Society for Industrial and Applied Mathematics (SIAM), 72

Society for Philosophy on the Pacific Coast, 45

Society for Plant Morphology and Physiology, 76-77

Society for the Psychological Study of Social Issues, 43

Society for the Study of Development and Growth, 236 ref. 30

Society of American Bacteriologists, 82, 236 ref. 30

Society of American Vertebrate Paleontologists, 93

Society of American Zoologists, 75, 227 ref. 68

Society of Architectural Historians, 154, 173; history and activities of, 15, 57-59

Society of Biblical Literature and Exegesis: grants to, 153, 173; history and activities of, 14, 33-34

Society of Economic Geologists, 74, 118, 236 ref. 35

Society of Economic Paleontologists and Mineralogists, 93-94, 236

Society of Exploration Geophysicists, 236 ref. 35

Society of Rheology, 139, 140

Society of Vaccine Therapists, 95

Society of Vertebrate Paleontology, 93, 236 ref. 35

Sociometry (American Sociological Association), 52

Socony — Vacuum Oil Company, 181

Sollmann Award in Pharmacology, Torald, 92

Sources and Literature of English History from the Earliest Times to about 1485 (Gross), 56

South Atlantic MLA, 36

South Carolina, 42, 183

South Central MLA, 36

Southeastern Section, Geological Society of America, 74

Southern California Parasitologists, 108

Southern Historical Association, 38

Southern Philosophical Association, 45

Southern Research Institute, 237

Southern Section, Society of Biblical Literature and Exegesis, 33

Southwestern Division, American Association for the Advancement of Science, 137

Southwestern Section, Society of Biblical Literature and Exegesis, 33

Soviet Union. *See* Russia

Spain, 41

Speculum (Mediaeval Academy of America), 55

Speekaert, G. P., 240 ref. 2

Spelman Fund of New York, 163

Springfield (Ill.), 109
SSRC. *See* Social Science Research Council
Standard Oil Corporation, 188
Stanerson, B. R., 174
State University of Iowa, 115
Statistical Research Monographs, 115
Stephenson, Robert C., 5, 145
Sterling Memorial Library, 28
Stiles, C. W., 105, 107
St. Louis, (Mo.), 15, 46, 49, 50, 103
St. Mary's Hospital (London), 95
Stockholm, 191
Stoll, Norman R., 231 ref. 107
St. Petersburg (Russia), 7
Stratton, S. P., 80
Strong, Richard P., 107
Studies in the Renaissance, 64
Stunkard, Horace W., 231 ref. 107
Sumner, William G., 51
Swasey, Ambrose, 125
Sylvester, J. J., 71
Synnott, Gordon J., 95

T

Tasdon Foundation, 160
Taylor, Norman, 98
Technometrics, 26
Teheran Declaration, 199
Tennessee State Department of Archives and History, 5
Tenth International Congress of Genetics, 171
Tenth International Congress for the History of Science, 172
Texas, 55, 78
Texas Gulf Sulphur Company, 177
Thomas, Charles C., 109
Thomas, Isaiah, 22, 23
Thompson, Benjamin, 11
Thoms, William John, 40
Thorndike, Lynn, 54
Transactions and Proceedings (American Philological Association), 31
Transactions of: American Antiquarian Society, 24; American Geophysical Union, 102; American Mathematical Society, 72; American Philological Association, 31; American Philosophical Society, 9, 73; Electrochemical Society, Inc., 87
Treatise on Invertebrate Paleontology (Moore), 94
Trytten, M. H., 5, 126
Tukey, H. R., 142
Twentieth Century Fund, 165
Tyler, Moses Coit, 37
Tyzzer, E. E., 107

U

Uncle Remus tales, 41
UNESCO. *See* United Nations: Educational, Scientific, and Cultural Organization of
UNESCO House, 203
Union Académique Internationale. *See* International Academic Union
Union of International Associations, 197, 240 ref. 2
Union of South Africa, 192
United Air Lines, 173
United Nations: Declaration, 199; Economic and Social Council of, 201; Educational, Scientific, and Cultural Organization of, 117, 184, 200-206, 210; intellectual organizations and, 198-206, 209; Library of, 5
United States Military Philosophical Society, 134
Universities: councils and, 169, 179-180, 183; institutes and, 169, 185; over departmentalization of, 211, 215, 216, 244 ref. 14; societies and, 169, 174. *See also* individual universities
University of Alabama, 5
University of California, 54, 100, 102, 105
University of Chicago, 52, 79, 97, 113, 226 ref. 67
University of Florida, 89
University of Illinois, 80, 105, 109, 126, 179, 229 ref. 92, 232-233 ref. 2
University of Kansas Medical School, 86

University of Michigan, 37, 55, 57, 61, 91, 115
University of Mississippi, 5
University of Nebraska, 97, 105
University of New Hampshire, 122
University of North Carolina, 55, 95, 116
University of Oslo, 111
University of Pennsylvania, 42, 63, 70, 71, 174
University of Pittsburgh, 59
University of Rochester, 109
University of Scranton, 61
University of Texas, 55, 78, 122
University of Virginia, 225 ref. 59
University of Wisconsin, 232 ref. 115
U Nu Lectures, 60
Urbana (Ill.), 80, 109
U. S. Air Force: Materiel Command, 187; Office of Scientific Research, 171, 185, 186
U.S. Armed Forces Institute, 180
U.S. Armed Forces Institute of Pathology, 85, 216
U.S. Army: Chemical Warfare Service, 66, 187; Institute of Pathology, 85; Medical Museum and Library, 85; Quartermaster Corps, 176, 185; Signal Corps, 157
U.S. Atomic Energy Commission, 177, 186, 187
U.S. Bureau of the Budget, 25
U.S. Bureau of the Census, 25, 183
U.S. Bureau of Weights and Measures, 80
U.S. Civil Aeronautics Authority, 176, 180
U.S. Coast Survey, 124
U.S. Congress, 65, 134, 175
U.S. Council of National Defense, 175, 182
U.S. Department of Agriculture, 90, 105, 171, 175, 176
U.S. Department of Commerce, 183
U.S. Department of Defense, 180, 181
U.S. Department of Health, Education, and Welfare, 172, 181, 182, 187

U.S. Department of State, 175, 180, 181, 182, 184, 199
U.S. Department of the Interior, 175
U.S. Department of the Navy, 175, 181, 182
U.S. Department of the Treasury, 175
U.S. Department of War, 175, 176, 180, 182
U.S. Economic Cooperation Administration, 181
U.S. Central Statistical Board, 25
U.S. Government: Federal control question in support by, 211-215; councils and, 169, 174-177, 179-183, 211-216; grants and contracts of, 169-173, 175-177, 180-189, 212-215, 238-239 ref. 5; institutes and, 169, 183-188, 211-216; societies and, 169-173, 211-216. *See also* individual governmental agencies
U.S. Information Agency, 53, 181
U.S. Library of Congress, 5, 23
U.S. National Archives, 38
U.S. National Bureau of Standards, 80, 118, 175, 176
U.S. National Defense Education Act, 182, 214
U.S. National Defense Research Committee (NDRC), 176
U.S. National Institutes of Health, 76, 110, 171, 183, 185, 187, 212, 217
U.S. National Science Foundation, 214, 238 ref. 4; councils and, 126, 169, 177, 182, 183; grants of, 118, 140, 143, 167, 169-172, 177, 182-188, 214, 217, 238; institutes and, 140, 143, 167, 169, 184-188; societies and, 76, 78, 118, 169-173
U.S. Navy: Bureau of Navigation, 124; Office of Naval Research, 76, 171, 186, 187
U.S. Office of Armed Forces Information and Education (OAFIE), 180
U.S. Office of Civil and Defense Mobilization, 181
U.S. Office of Coordinator of Inter-American Affairs, 180

U.S. Office of Education, 155, 157, 172, 180
U.S. Office of Scientific Research and Development, 176, 177
U.S. Office of Statistical Standards, 25
U.S. Public Health Service, 95, 105, 171, 187
U.S.S.R. *See* Russia
U.S. Tennessee Valley Authority, 181
U.S. Yellowstone National Park, 97

V

Veditz, C.W.A., 51
Venezuela, 182
Venus, transit of, 9
Vicenza (Italy), 58
Vienna, 191
Vincent, George, 157
Virginia, 220 ref. 11
Voegtlein, C., 92

W

Wald, Abraham, 116
Wald Lectures, 116
Walras, Leon, 111
Ward, Henry Baldwin, 105-106
Ward, Lester H., 51
Ward Medal, Henry Baldwin, 107-108
Ward, Robert De Courcy, 103
Warren Fund, Cyrus M., 11
Washington, D. C., 65, 118; learned organizations founded in, 50, 61, 69, 106, 139, 142, 145; meetings of learned organizations in, 38, 81, 84, 96, 102, 122, 182, 199, 200; members of learned organizations in, 60; offices of learned organizations in, 27, 37, 39, 44, 48, 49, 51, 67, 68, 69, 92, 103, 119, 123, 128, 131, 137, 138, 143, 146, 185
Washington, George, 11
Washington University (St. Louis), 46
Weatherwise, 103
Webster, Arthur Gordon, 80

Webster, Daniel, 134
Weiss, Paul, 62
Welch, William H., 125
Welles, Gideon, 124
Wenner—Gren Foundation for Anthropological Research, 153, 166
Wesleyan University Press, 174
Western Branch, American Society of Zoologists, 75
Western Division, American Philosophical Association, 45, 46
Western Drawing and Manual Training Association, 53
Western Group, Institute of Mathematical Statistics, 116
Western Philosophical Association, 45
Westinghouse Educational Foundation, 166
Whipple, George H., 85
White, Lyman C., 2
Whitman, C. O., 226 ref. 67
Willcox, Walter F., 51
Williams and Wilkins Company, 96
Wilson, E. B., 226 ref. 67
Wilson, Edwin B., 111, 133
Wilson, Logan, 122
Wilson, Woodrow, 125, 157, 198, 199
Winthrop, John, 8
Wistar, Caspar, 70
Wistar Institute of Anatomy and Biology, 70, 76, 109, 114, 217
Wistar, Isaac Jones, 70
Wolcott, Robert H., 97
Wolfle, Dael, 5, 137
Woodward, R. S., 101
Woodworth, R. S., 133
Worcester (Mass.), 24, 42
Wren, Christopher, 7
Wright, Almroth E., 95
"Writings on American History" (American Historical Association), 39
Wyeth Laboratories, 92

Y

Yale University, 28, 62, 82, 111, 113, 114
Yalta Conference, 199

Year Book (American Philosophical Society), 10
Yerkes Observatory, 78
Yerkes, Robert M., 43
York (England), 134
Young, Donald R., 133

Z

Zeitschrift für Immunitätsforschung, 96
Zook, George F., 122, 199
Zoological Society of America, 75, 227 ref. 68

About the Author

Joseph C. Kiger holds degrees from Birmingham-Southern College (A.B.), University of Alabama (M.A.), and Vanderbilt University (Ph. D.)

He has taught history at Vanderbilt University, the University of Alabama, and Washington University (St. Louis) and is presently a Professor of History at the University of Mississippi. He directed research for the 1952 Select (Cox) Committee to Investigate Foundations and has served as an official of the American Council on Education and the Southern Fellowships Fund. He has held a Guggenheim Fellowship and has acted as consultant to various philanthropic and governmental agencies. He is a member of the American Historical Association, Southern Historical Association, and American Studies Association.

Dr. Kiger is the author of several articles in intellectual and social history and has previously published two books—*Operating Principles of the Larger Foundations,* Russell Sage Foundation, New York, 1954 and *Sponsored Research Policy of Colleges and Universities* (with others), American Council on Education, Washington, D. C., 1954.